Selling the Dream

Selling the Dream

The Gulf American Corporation and the Building of Cape Coral, Florida

David E. Dodrill

The University of Alabama Press

Tuscaloosa and London

Copyright © 1993
The University of Alabama Press
Tuscaloosa, Alabama 35487–0380
All rights reserved
Manufactured in the United States of America
designed by Paula C. Dennis

∞

The paper on which this book is printed meets the minimum requirements of American National Standard for Information Science–Permanence of Paper for Printed Library Materials, ANSI Z39.48-1984.

Library of Congress Cataloging-in-Publication Data

Dodrill, David E., 1953–
    Selling the dream : the Gulf American Corporation and the building of Cape Coral, Florida / David E. Dodrill.
        p.   cm.
    Includes bibliographical references and index.
    ISBN 0-8173-0597-1 (alk. paper)
    1. Real estate development—Florida—Cape Coral—History.   2. Gulf American Corporation—History.
I. Title.
HD266.F62C363   1993
333.33'06'075948—dc20   92-39732
                                             CIP

British Library Cataloguing-in-Publication Data available

0-8173-1189-0 (pbk: alk. paper)

Contents

	Acknowledgments	vii
1	Grand Dreams in Southwest Florida	1
2	Leonard and Jack Rosen	15
3	The First Five Years	29
4	Purchasing a Land Empire	50
5	Selling Florida Land	67
6	Financing the Gulf American Corporation	90
7	Promoting Florida Living	105
8	Growing Pains: 1964 to 1967	135
9	Regulating the Land Giants	161
10	The Takeover of Gulf American	207
11	GAC's Demise	222
12	After Gulf American	249
	Notes	263
	Bibliography	295
	Index	303

Acknowledgments

During the 1950s and early 1960s in Florida, several large land development firms began marketing Florida real estate on a national level. Four of the largest firms, in terms of money spent on advertising and promotion, were Lehigh Acres Development Corporation, General Development Corporation, Gulf Guaranty Land and Title Company (later Gulf American Corporation), and Deltona Corporation. The most aggressive in its marketing strategies was Gulf American Corporation. The vast size of its land holdings (589,738 acres) and large volume of sales ($143,862,000) gave it the distinction of being the largest land sales company in the United States.

Without question, the story of Gulf American was inseparably connected with the lives of Leonard and Julius J. Rosen. The brothers rose from selling household appliances on the installment plan in Baltimore to heading one of the largest corporations in Florida. The Rosens had little formal marketing training, but used their practical sales experiences to develop innovative strategies that were copied throughout the land industry. Besides their creativity, the brothers' dynamic personalities helped them assemble an aggressive and highly-effective sales force for Gulf American.

This book originated in my curiosity about the city in which I was living at the time I began my research—Cape Coral, Florida. As a history teacher at Cape Coral High School, I discovered that much of the story of the Rosen brothers and

Gulf American had never been written down and was still locked away in the memories of aging residents of Cape Coral and former employees of Gulf American. Since the corporation had such a visible impact on Lee County, the state of Florida, and the entire country, I felt that the events surrounding Gulf American's history needed to be recorded. As I began to talk with people, I learned of a wealth of experiences and knowledge about the company and the Rosens that few others, including other employees of Gulf American, knew about. Therefore, the core of my research, in addition to news articles, was thirty-one taped oral history interviews with former Gulf American employees and executives, close observers of Gulf American, and residents of Cape Coral. My only regret was that I was unable to get an interview with Leonard Rosen, who died about the time I began my research.

As I continued to do interviews, I was impressed with a sense of urgency because of the advanced age of many of those interviewed. Many of them were seventy years of age or older. Because much of what they knew was recorded nowhere else, the interviews often became the only link with some parts of the past. In addition, most of the documents from the corporation itself are still held in the archives of Gulf American's ultimate successor, Avatar Holding Inc. Legal counsel for Avatar refused to allow any access to their documents or interviews with any of their employees who had worked for Gulf American. Despite this obstacle, the story of the Rosens and the building of Gulf American and the city of Cape Coral emerges clearly.

In doing my research and writing, I was greatly assisted by several professors: Dr. Daniel Schafer, Dr. Joseph M. Perry, and Dr. Samuel Proctor. Their insights made this a much more thorough project. I especially want to thank Dr. Proctor for his invaluable comments and his sense of humor during this lengthy project. More than that, in many ways, he was a friend and an encouragement in the process. The most valuable aspect of this project to me was gaining his friendship.

I also want to express my appreciation to the research staffs of the following libraries for their assistance in the long hours of research: the University of Florida, the P. K. Yonge Library of Florida History, the University of North Florida, Florida State University, the Miami Public Library, the Fort Myers Public Library, and the Cape Coral Public Library. In addition, my thanks go to the staffs at the Florida State Division of Archives and Records Management and the Florida State Library.

I would also like to thank Eileen Bernard, author of *Lies That Came True* and former Gulf American employee, for her encouragement and helpful suggestions on how to contact former employees. Betsy Zeiss Lewis, author of *The Other Side of the River: Historical Cape Coral,* also gave me several helpful comments for which I am grateful. Rob Loaf-man's artistry turned two maps in the book into something far more understandable than I was able to do. Many thanks go to Meg Lassiat, Shelly Epple, and Colette Ladbrook, who transcribed, typed, and re-typed the many interviews.

Finally, I want to express my love and appreciation to my wife, Cathron, and my parents, who continued to encourage me through the years of part-time research and writing. To my mother and father, I can say that I have come full circle, from a small child who learned to read books to one who writes books. To Cathron, whom I met, dated, mar-ried, and with whom I had two children while working on this project, I want to say that I love her and that I never could have finished the book without her. To Cathron, I dedicate this work.

Selling the Dream

1

Grand Dreams in Southwest Florida

On a warm southwest Florida day in early autumn 1957, several men gathered on Redfish Point near Fort Myers to examine a 1,724-acre tract of land that Leonard and Jack Rosen had recently purchased. The Rosens had parlayed their marketing talents into a small fortune in Baltimore, Maryland, and Leonard eagerly wanted to apply their skills to the selling of homesites. After cautiously driving nine miles along the unpaved and nearly impassable Harney Point Road, Kenneth J. Schwartz and Harry Dempsey arrived at the proposed site. Dempsey was a free-lance writer who had known Leonard when they both had worked in carnivals together; he later would write radio advertisements for Rosen's Gulf American Land Corporation. Schwartz was interviewing for the job of general manager of the new development. The pair was greeted by an exuberant Leonard Rosen, along with advertising man Charles K. Hepner, developer Milton M. Mendelsohn, and the recently hired resident engineer, Thomas W. Weber.[1]

For the rest of the day, Rosen described in great detail the dreams and design he had for the new community. Although the assembled men were surrounded by Florida prairie and mosquitoes, they visualized the new community with its streets, houses, and country clubs. When discussing any promising new product with his associates, Leonard frequently launched into a sales pitch that captured the attention of all those within hearing distance. Never content to let his words alone be sufficient, he scrambled to the top of a nearby earth-mover, looked around himself, and proclaimed, "We're going to build a city here!" Although Hepner told him to get down before he broke his neck, the men watching were caught up in the excitement of the dream. Rosen's confidence in the success of the project was contagious. He understood the effect of his enthusiasm clearly when he stated years later: "No matter what mistakes we made, we knew it was going to work. A lot of people caught this spirit."[2]

The Rosen brothers sold their dream of living in Florida to hundreds of thousands of people throughout North America and Europe. Their enthusiasm and persuasiveness convinced many that a new city was going to be built near Fort Myers and that they should be a part of it. Using promotional campaigns that vividly presented the allure of living in tropical Florida, the Rosens provided an almost irresistible sales feature: installment purchases of land. While several firms pioneered the method, the Rosens marketed the concept more successfully than the others. Training a talented sales force, the brothers rapidly built the largest land sales company in the United States during the late 1950s and the 1960s, naming it the Gulf American Land Corporation. Cape Coral, located on the west bank of the Caloosahatchee River near Fort Myers, became the brothers' first and most complete project.

Gulf American was not alone, however, in promoting large-scale subdivisions in south Florida during the 1950s and 1960s. General Development Corporation and Lee County Land and Title Company launched massive land sales projects in southwest Florida while Arvida Corporation and Coral Ridge Properties Corporation, along with General Development, inaugurated developments on Florida's southeast coast. While land sales were generally booming in the region, Gulf American faced more public scrutiny and eventual governmental opposition than its competitors, due in large part to its aggressive sales philosophy and huge size. Newspapers and magazines across the United States during the 1960s carried articles accusing Gulf American, as well as some other developers, of fraud and abusive sales practices. A bitter personal feud between the Rosens and the governor of Florida contributed to the company's difficulties. Despite these problems, the Rosens built Gulf American into the land sales leader of southwest Florida and eventually the nation.

Before the mid-1900s, other promoters had dreamed of building cities on undeveloped Florida land. The settlement of many parts of Florida was due to large-scale development schemes. With the close of the Civil War, wealthy northerners considered the South, including Florida, as prime for investment in agricultural projects. The warm climate, cheap land, and the prospect of huge profits in citrus cultivation inspired innumerable investors, including Henry S. Sanford. In 1870 Sanford purchased 12,547 acres of raw land on Lake Monroe in Orange County for $18,000.[3] Convinced that his town of Sanford would become an agricultural and shipping center at the head of the St. Johns River, Sanford actively promoted the region and began to sell plots to settlers. He invested heavily in the project, including $120,000 in his Belair citrus grove by 1888.[4] Despite being considered the founder of the modern Florida citrus industry, Sanford consistently lost money on his projects because of his absenteeism, inept managers, and labor problems.[5] Land sales at Sanford declined during the late 1870s, and as the decade ended, only 1,943 acres of the original 12,547 had been sold.[6]

Sanford shared his concept of investing in Florida land with others, including his wealthy Philadelphia friend, Hamilton Disston. Having first come to Florida in 1877 on a fishing trip, Disston became intrigued with the possibility of building a huge agricultural development by draining swamplands and overflowed lands held by the state of Florida. By January 31, 1881, Disston had negotiated a contract with the trustees of the Internal Improvement Trust Fund to drain overflowed lands in the Kissimmee River valley and adjacent to Lake Okeechobee in return for half of those lands. Later that year, Governor William D. Bloxham persuaded Disston to purchase 4 million acres of overflowed lands for $1 million in order to remove the trust fund's indebtedness and enable it to grant clear title to those lands.[7]

Reclamation proceeded rapidly and by August 1884 more than 2 million acres had been permanently drained. Several of the resulting canals enabled steamships to travel from Kissimmee to the Gulf of Mexico via Lake Okeechobee and the Caloosahatchee River by 1883.[8] Hoping to subdivide his lands for sale to settlers, Disston established a sugar cane plantation at St. Cloud in order to advertise the amazing possibilities of Florida agriculture. By 1895, however, poor management and various crop failures resulted in heavy mortgaging of his entire project.[9] When Disston died suddenly in April 1896, his family abandoned his dream of an agricultural empire in Florida and sold his remaining acreage.

Developers during the last part of the nineteenth century began to see more profits through the promotion of winter tourist traffic than from the sale of farmlands. In order for these well-heeled guests to get to the wintering spots and to be pampered once they arrived, effective railroad transportation and luxury hotels were needed. Henry M. Flagler and Henry B. Plant provided those new railroads along with extravagant resort hotels along the lines. By January 1888 Flagler had completed the massive Ponce de Leon Hotel in St. Augustine. In response, Plant finished the equally flamboyant Tampa Bay Hotel by 1891. Encouraged southward by state land grants of 8,000 acres for every mile completed,

Flagler extended his railroad to Miami by 1896.[10] While Flagler's East Coast Railway bordered the Atlantic coast, Plant expanded rail service throughout central Florida and down the Gulf coast. Plant's southernmost resort hotel was the Fort Myers Hotel, which offered "about a hundred cozy rooms" in 1898 and was serviced by a Plant steamer because the rail line ended in Punta Gorda, twenty-four miles to the north.[11]

With Flagler's East Coast Railway reaching Miami in 1896, south Florida was on the verge of a significantly different development scheme. In order to build a larger clientele for his railroad, Flagler began to encourage permanent settlement along the rail lines. Throughout the 1890s and the early 1900s, Flagler heavily advertised and promoted Florida living and his Model Land Company in northern cities. He founded experimental farms along Florida's east coast in order to encourage settlement. A person coming to Florida as a home seeker was offered a 50 percent discount on a railroad ticket as an inducement. Flagler's promotions resulted in the increased settlement of Florida's east coast and a growing awareness in the northern cities of Florida's benefits.[12]

As World War I ended, national interest in Florida increased dramatically. The popularity of the automobile added to this interest by making Florida more accessible to the heavily populated northern cities. Dade County attracted thousands of tourists and prospective purchasers of real estate due to intense national advertising of Miami Beach by Carl G. Fisher and of Coral Gables by George E. Merrick.[13] Other developments along the southeast Florida coast included Hollywood, Hialeah, Opalocka, and Boca Raton.

By 1925 easy credit and the binder system had encouraged speculation in south Florida land, and prices skyrocketed. A binder was an option to purchase a parcel of land, and it usually cost 10 percent or less of the purchase price. The binder was valid until the papers had been processed and the first substantial payment made. The holder received a document indicating ownership. The property then could be resold for a profit. A parcel may have been sold several times in the thirty days prior to the first substantial payment, and the down payment increased dramatically with each resale because the holder would require not only the amount of the binder but a profit as well. Therefore, a parcel that had been sold several times might require a down payment of one-half or three-fourths of the purchase price in cash.[14]

As demand for new property increased, waterfront lots were at a premium. Normally, dredging created canals and the spoils were used to build up low-lying areas. Responding to the demand in 1923 for waterfront property, Charles G. Rodes of Fort Lauderdale began digging canals in such a way so that nearly all of the lots in his Venice subdivision fronted on waterways. Finger-islanding, as it was called, became an efficient method of developing high-quality waterfront lots and was copied throughout the state.[15]

The Miami area received the majority of the attention during the 1920s boom, but Florida's southwest coast experienced a land boom of its own. David P. Davis found great public enthusiasm for his project at Tampa and was able to sell all of his residential lots on Davis Island within one year of its opening in 1924.[16] Other large subdivisions along the coast included the developments of John and Charles Ringling near Sarasota and the 30,000-acre settlement at Venice sponsored by the Brotherhood of Locomotive Engineers.[17] The boom reached as far south as Fort Myers with the completion of the Tamiami Trail from Tampa to Fort Myers in 1924. Before the opening of this highway, Fort Myers, along with southwest Florida generally, lagged behind other Florida cities in the boom prosperity.[18]

Despite its slow start, Fort Myers grew in visible ways during the 1920s boom. Between 1922 and 1925, building permits soared from $246,310 to $2,794,075. Numerous bond issues, totaling $3.5 million, were passed for street paving, water systems, and sewers.[19] The city received another boost to its optimism when Connie Mack decided in 1924 to bring his Philadelphia Athletics baseball team to Fort Myers for spring training.[20] By 1925, various subdivisions were promoted throughout the city and surrounding areas. These included, among others, the 60-acre Stadler Central Heights, Seminole Park, Riverside, Edison Park, Palmwood, Russell Park, and San Carlos. Enthusiasm ran high for the rest of the year as plans were announced for a million-dollar, ten-story, 250-room hotel in downtown Fort Myers. Subdividers, wishing to have access to city utilities, convinced the Fort Myers government to increase the city boundaries in 1925 from 1,900 to 15,000 acres.[21] As in the rest of Florida, however, speculators bid land prices above the market, and when confidence in the boom dwindled, real estate prices fell.

With the collapse of the boom in 1925 and 1926, Fort Myers was left with heavy bond debts, and new construction began to slow down. With the stock market crash in 1929 and the ensuing depression, banks began to fail and business activity ground to a halt. By 1932, most of the banks in Fort Myers had closed their doors. The city found itself able to collect only 35 percent of the total taxes due in 1935. Within one year, nearly two-thirds of the households in Lee County were on some form of relief.[22] Public construction projects, such as the Edison Bridge across the Caloosahatchee River, the new post office, and the city yacht basin, helped with the unemployment problem.[23] Promotions for new subdivisions were virtually nonexistent because of the glut of unused lots, most of which could be purchased by paying off their back taxes.

During World War II, thousands of members of the armed forces crowded Fort Myers. The Army Air Corps had established a flexible gunnery school in 1942 at Buckingham in eastern Lee County. Later in that year, the army took over Page Field on the south side of Fort Myers and expanded the facilities for advanced fighter training. At one point during the war, approximately 20,000 army personnel were stationed at the two airfields. Despite being deactivated shortly after the war, these two military installations exposed many people to life in lightly populated southwest Florida.[24]

After the war the entire state began to experience a building boom. Lee County, where the Rosen brothers would later start Cape Coral, was no exception. Housing shortages appeared because little civilian construction had occurred during the war. In addition, many veterans who had seen southwest Florida during the war wanted to return. With the advent of air conditioning, people from northern cities began to find year-round Florida living more attractive. Retired workers, who were eligible for Social Security benefits, wanted to spend their remaining years in a warm climate. As existing platted lots were sold and developed, demand increased for more residential sites during the early 1950s.[25]

As demand soared, several large land developers began projects in southwest Florida that dwarfed anything that had preceded them. Demand was already high for new residential lots, and developers further encouraged the demand with heavy advertising and promotion. Beginning in 1954, the Lee County Land and Title Company (later called the Lehigh Development Corporation) began a planned community in eastern Lee County called Lehigh Acres. Financed by millionaire Lee Ratner, the company owned 60,000 acres of ranch land and sold lots through installment contracts. In 1955 the first family moved into the new community.[26] Forty miles northwest of Lehigh Acres, General Development Corporation purchased 90,000 acres of land in 1954 for development into the city of Port Charlotte. Construction began in 1956 and lots could be purchased with ten dollars down and payments of ten dollars a month.[27] Encouraged by the initial success of these two projects, the Rosens purchased a much smaller tract of land in western Lee County and in 1957 started work on their future city, Cape Coral.

Large tracts of inexpensive land remained in southwest Florida in the 1950s. Farming and ranching still occupied most of the residents in the sparsely populated area. While Fort Myers had emerged as a leading city in the region, an impartial observer would have classified it as little more than a small town when compared to other urban centers of the state. Several factors contributed to the lack of development and settlement in the region until the mid-1950s.

The vast size of the region provided the most obvious obstacle to

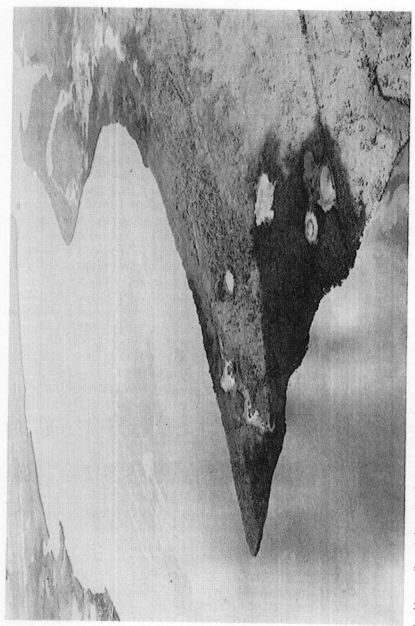

Looking southwest down the Caloosahatchee River, this aerial view of Redfish Point was taken in 1957, just prior to any development. Redfish Point is today the site of the Cape Coral Yacht Club.

settlement in southwest Florida. Situated more than 250 miles from the Georgia border, southwest Florida encompassed an area generally considered to begin at Charlotte Harbor and ranging south to the Ten Thousand Islands and Cape Sable. Bounded in the west by the Gulf of Mexico, it extended east into the Everglades midway across the peninsula to the vicinity of Lake Okeechobee. For purposes of description, southwest Florida was roughly equal to the 5,766 square miles found within the 1880 borders of Monroe County. The area included what later became the modern counties of Lee, Hendry, Collier, and Monroe.[28] While several rivers crossed the region, the Caloosahatchee flowed westward, providing the largest navigable inland waterway.

Geographically, southwest Florida possessed little that would have promoted white settlement during the early nineteenth century. Numerous factors discouraged commercial farming. Large portions of the region were dry grassy flatlands, but the greatest part of the interior consisted of uninhabitable marshy areas known as the Big Cypress Swamp and the Everglades. The warm, wet, subtropical climate contrasted dramatically with the more temperate zone in northern Florida. While the raising of vegetables was promoted for the region as early as 1833, transporting the produce to a market proved difficult.[29]

Although the region remained generally isolated during the Territorial Period (1821–45), some economic activity was beginning along its Gulf coast. From the late 1700s, Spanish fishermen seasonally visited Charlotte Harbor, drying their catch there and sending it to the markets of Havana and the West Indies. As early as 1772, 300 to 400 fishermen could be counted working the waters of the harbor.[30] Benjamin Strobel's 1833 account noted another Spanish fishery of ten to twelve houses at Punta Rassa near the mouth of the Caloosahatchee River.[31] While these fisheries were not permanent settlements, they flourished until 1836 when attacks by bands of Indians forced their relocation to the Tampa Bay area.[32]

Also in the early nineteenth century, a New York company attempted to establish an agricultural settlement on Sanibel Island near the mouth of the Caloosahatchee River. The remoteness of its location and the fear of Indian attacks hurt the project's chances from the beginning.[33] John Lee Williams observed the project's failure when he found the settlement nearly deserted on a visit in 1837.[34]

A major reason for the region's lack of settlement during the first half of the nineteenth century focused on the Indian policies of the Florida and United States governments. During the 1700s and extending into the early 1800s, various groups of Creek Indians migrated south across the Georgia and Alabama borders into northern Florida. Known as Seminoles, these Indians were forced to move south into the peninsula because of white raids on their villages. Many of these Florida Indian groups welcomed runaway slaves from Georgia and Alabama. Because they gave refuge to slaves and because they made periodic raids across the border into the United States, Gen. Andrew Jackson and his forces invaded Spanish Florida in 1818 to punish the Indians.[35]

Prior to 1800, no Seminole villages appear to have existed south of Tampa Bay. By 1823, however, Capt. Horatio S. Dexter noted that scattered bands of Seminoles had moved southward to Tampa Bay and that the Seminole hunting area extended to the tip of the Florida peninsula.[36] Government attempts to remove the Seminoles from Florida after 1836 resulted in armed resistance by a large number of the Indians. The conflict lasted until 1842 at a cost of more than $40 million and the lives of more than 1,400 regular army troops.[37]

Even though much of the fighting was in central Florida, settlement in southwest Florida was affected by these Indian wars. Fishermen had abandoned Charlotte Harbor as a result of Indian attacks in 1836. Few settlers felt free to return to the area, particularly after a massacre that occurred on the Caloosahatchee on July 23, 1839. A large force of Indians, feeling that they had been betrayed by the conditions of a truce, attacked the new trading post under the command of Col. William S. Harney and killed sixteen of his men.[38] As a result of this attack and previous Indian activity in the area, the United States established several military forts along the Caloosahatchee. By 1837 Fort Dulany was founded at the mouth of the river and Fort Denaud was constructed further upstream. Because of increased determination by the U.S. government to patrol the region, Fort Harvie (later renamed Fort Myers) and Fort Simmons were built in 1841.[39]

At the close of hostilities in 1842, most of these military installations were abandoned. Even the reactivation of many of the forts in 1849 and 1850 did not result in an increase in the sparse civilian population.[40] Efforts increased in the early 1850s to induce the remaining Seminoles to leave their reservation in the Big Cypress Swamp. Sporadic fighting broke out between 1855 and 1858. With the removal of the Indian leader, Billy Bowlegs, and 164 other Seminoles in May 1858, the Indian wars in Florida came to a close.[41] With fewer than 100 Seminoles left in the state, a major obstacle to settlement in southwest Florida was eliminated. An additional result of the wars was that much of the interior of south Florida was explored and mapped for the first time.[42]

Following the removal of the majority of the Seminoles from the lower part of the peninsula, open-range cattle ranching flourished in southwest Florida because white settlers had uninhibited access to the old Seminole reservation lands. While the Preemption Act of 1841 and the Military Bounty Act of 1855 allowed settlers to claim or cheaply purchase 160 acres each of public land, most ranchers grazed their cattle on the unclaimed public domain.[43] During the 1850s, herds were grazed over a wide area from the Myakka River south to the Caloosahatchee and shipped from Tampa to Cuba.[44] During the Civil War, however, southwest Florida beef was destined for the railhead at Baldwin in northern Florida. The cattle were then shipped north to supply Confederate armies. With the close of the war, the best market for Florida cattle was again Cuba with Punta Rassa and Punta Gorda as the largest shipping points.[45]

During the Civil War, southwest Florida produced a considerable share of the Confederate army's beef supply.[46] Each week from April to August, Jacob Summerlin, who was the largest rancher in the region, drove more than 600 head of cattle from the Caloosahatchee basin north to Baldwin. By 1863 it was estimated that he had sold more than 25,000 steers to the Confederacy.[47] In order to break up these cattle drives and provide a refuge for Union loyalists, federal troops landed and occupied the abandoned Fort Myers in January 1864. These Union forces raided the countryside for cattle, capturing an estimated 4,500 head.[48] The success of these raids prompted the troops to build a wharf and a large barracks at Punta Rassa.[49] Despite a Confederate attempt to recapture Fort Myers in February 1865, Union forces operated freely along the southwest Florida coast until the end of the war.

At the close of the war, cattle ranching resumed as the most profitable venture in the region. With the coming of revolution in Cuba in 1868, buyers from Havana were eager to pay high prices for the scrawny Florida cattle.[50] During this period, other cattlemen such as Francis A. Hendry and Ziba King began large operations in the area. Between 1870 and 1880, 165,669 head of cattle were shipped from Jacob Summerlin's pens and wharf at Punta Rassa.[51] Summerlin's son, Samuel, continued this operation at Punta Rassa, shipping an additional 160,000 cattle to Cuba from 1879 to 1926.[52]

The boom in the cattle industry following the Civil War was dramatic, but it failed to bring prosperity to southwest Florida as a whole. The major obstacle to a stable economy in the region was the lack of good transportation. With few roads of any kind in the area, small riverboats carried most of the cargo and passengers.[53] In July 1886 Henry Plant's Florida Southern Railway completed the first rail line into the region with an extension being built to the small village of Punta Gorda, located some twenty-four miles north of Fort Myers. Although Plant appeared committed to making that area into a major commercial center, many Charlotte Harbor produce shippers complained of excessive freight charges from the railroad. A severe blow to the development of the region occurred when Plant decided to invest nearly $3 million in improvements at Port Tampa. Virtually nothing was spent on further development of Punta Gorda. Plant apparently abandoned plans for development in southwest Florida, and it was not until after his death that the rail line was extended to Fort Myers in 1904.[54]

Even before Monroe County and the Fort Myers area were connected by railroad to the rest of the state, the population slowly began to grow. Capt. Manuel A. Gonzalez and his family were the first to settle after the Civil War at the site of the abandoned Fort Myers.[55] Another early settler in the area, John Powell, arrived in 1867. According to his granddaughter, Powell and his wife came shortly after Gonzalez and were the first white settlers to homestead the north bank of the Caloosahatchee River in 1872.[56] By 1880, however, Monroe County, excluding Key West, remained sparsely populated with only 1,050 people in the 5,000 square miles from Charlotte Harbor to the Keys.[57]

Wanting more control over their own affairs, the 600 residents of Fort Myers petitioned the state legislature in 1887 to create a new county out of a portion of Monroe County. Named after Robert E. Lee, Lee County was formed on May 13, 1887, from the northern 80 percent of Monroe County.[58] The *Fort Myers Press* bragged to prospective settlers of the benefits of living in Lee County, including a healthy climate, good farmland, 40,000 head of cattle, and the thriving town of Fort Myers with its six public schools.[59] Despite the population growth and the favorable newspaper stories, three visitors to Fort Myers in December 1891 described the town as "very dead and uninteresting. One main street parallel with the water and one or two side streets comprise the whole settlement . . . the whole town seemed in need of paint and repairs."[60]

Within the next twenty years, Fort Myers and Lee County grew rapidly with Fort Myers recording more than 2,400 residents in 1910.[61] Two main factors explained much of the increase. By 1904 the Atlantic Coast Line extended the railroad from Punta Gorda to Fort Myers, opening the region to the commerce and markets of the rest of the nation.[62] While this improvement aided agricultural development, a cold wave in 1894–95 helped even more because it gained for southwest Florida a reputation as a frost-free region of the state. Several south Florida counties, including Lee, escaped serious damage, while the freeze did $75 million in damage to citrus groves in central and northern Florida.[63] As a result of these events, immigration of new residents to Lee County increased during the early 1900s.

Along with an additional 1,200 new residents by 1920, Fort Myers had attracted some nationally known people. Forced to leave his medical laboratories in Indiana because of chronic bronchitis, Dr. Franklin L. Miles moved to Fort Myers in 1909 with his family and began a second career in horticulture. Miles soon was recognized as an expert on such matters and he contributed many innovations to Florida truck gardening such as using crushed shells as fertilizer. Until he died in 1929, Miles continued to purchase large tracts of land, including an extensive section on the west bank of the Caloosahatchee in the area south of what later became Cape Coral Parkway.[64]

During his residence in Fort Myers, Miles frequently visited the winter home of Thomas A. Edison. Edison had built a house on the river in the mid-1880s in order to provide a base for laboratories for experiments during the winter season. On a later visit in 1887, the inventor was intrigued by a sixty-foot-tall stand of bamboo that he hoped might serve some purpose in his development of the incandescent lamp.[65] His most significant work at the Fort Myers laboratories, however, revolved around the development of a cheap domestic source of rubber. After 1927 this project dominated Edison's time in Fort Myers and eventually yielded success with a hybrid goldenrod plant.[66] Because Edison's close friends, Henry Ford and Harvey S. Firestone, were vitally interested in Edison's rubber experiments, they were often in Fort Myers. The three men had grown close on seven camping trips throughout the United States, and eventually Ford built a home next to Edison's in Fort Myers.[67]

Fort Myers grew steadily during the early 1900s with the population increasing from 2,463 in 1910 to 13,195 in 1950. The west side of the river, however, remained the domain of a few small homesteaders and ranchers. From the Caloosahatchee River to Pine Island Sound, the flat grassland was dotted with scattered groves of virgin yellow pine. During the early 1920s, J. W. McWilliams began buying up nearly 125,000 acres of pine land in Lee and Charlotte counties, much of it in the area that would later become Cape Coral. By 1925 McWilliams had established a sawmill and company town at Slater in the northern part of Lee County. Rail spurs were laid down throughout the western part of the county for the logging trains. In 1929 William H. Dowling of Dowling and Camp Lumber Company bought out McWilliams and increased the sawmill's capacity to more than 100,000 board feet per day.[68]

At its height, the Slater mill was one of the largest in southwest Florida with ten locomotives used in its logging operations.[69] The company town of Slater boasted a post office and commissary for its several hundred employees. As the land was deforested, the lumber company sold it for as little as one dollar per acre.[70] By the time the mill shut down in January 1944, the land was being used primarily for agricultural purposes again.

During the 1940s and 1950s little was done to develop the vast area north and west of the Caloosahatchee River, although ranching was a preferred use for the land. The largest cattle operation was the Matlacha Cattle Company, a cooperative that owned 25,000 acres of land that would become western Cape Coral. In 1955 wealthy sportsman Ogden M. Phipps purchased 15,109 acres from the cooperative.

A longtime resident of Palm Beach, Ogden Phipps had been an avid fisherman and hunter since childhood. He hoped to develop his new Lee County land into a private game preserve similar to others that he owned in the state. According to F. F. "Fingers" O'Bannon, general manager of Phipps's Matlacha Plantation, Phipps invested about a quarter of a million dollars for pasture improvements, 139 miles of fences, barns, kennels for bird dogs, a lodge, and five homes for staff. Although the plantation was considered one of the finest quail-hunting areas in the world, Phipps preferred to live on his yacht, the *Virgemere,* at the Fort Myers yacht basin and seldom lodged at the preserve.[71]

Phipps's land, along with vast areas of southwest Florida, remained virtually undeveloped into the 1950s. At that time, however, several promoters saw the sales potential of Florida homesites in northern markets. One factor that separated these promoters from previous ones in Florida history was the vast size of their operations. Instead of concentrating on several thousand acres, they envisioned subdivisions made up of tens of thousands of acres. While the aggressiveness of their sales staffs was nothing new in Florida land promotions, few regions of the United States went untouched by their marketing ploys.

Thus the Rosen brothers saw an opportunity to use their creative salesmanship to make a profit. Leonard Rosen once remarked about his motives, "I had no intention of doing anything else except coming in here and buying this land for a dollar and selling it for ten."[72] As they progressed with actual construction, however, the brothers also wanted to see a viable city emerge, at least at their first development, Cape Coral. Perhaps as Gulf American grew and diversified, the brothers became more interested again in profit and less in city building.

Evaluation of the personal motives of the Rosens may result in conflicting conclusions. However, Gulf American's impact on Florida during the 1960s cannot be underestimated. Criticized heavily in later years because of its destruction of the natural environment at its developments, the company used construction methods, primarily dredge and fill, that were commonly practiced throughout the industry at that time in Florida. As Gulf American and other large developers brushed aside any environmental concerns in the rush to subdivide more land, they provided many environmentalists with a focus for their efforts in the late 1960s and 1970s.

Gulf American changed Florida in two other ways. The company's aggressive sales approach resulted in more stringent state laws governing land sales. Because of its size and its far-reaching sales organization, Gulf American drew the consistent attention of state regulators. While the company became the focus of regulators, it also provided working class and middle class families throughout the United States with an affordable way to buy Florida real estate. With Gulf American's installment contracts, tens of thousands of Americans purchased homesites in Florida who would not otherwise have been able to afford to do so.

In any analysis of Gulf American, observers consistently return to Leonard and Jack Rosen. Without their vision and personal drive, the company would not have accomplished what it did. Their personalities infused the firm with a direction and dynamic that other companies found difficult to duplicate. Because of changes in the law and the public's environmental priorities, no company will be able to duplicate Gulf American's record in sales or land development. While several large subdividers benefited from the general boom in Florida land following World War II, the Rosen brothers and their Gulf American Land Corporation carved out a unique place in a colorful and unrepeatable era.

2

Leonard and Jack Rosen

The story of the Gulf American Corporation is inescapably intertwined in the lives of Leonard (1915–87) and Julius "Jack" (1921–69) Rosen. They were the driving force that created the venture and kept it moving forward for nearly twelve years. From a minimal initial investment in 1957, the Rosens built a company that was the largest land sales business in the United States during the mid- to late-1960s.[1] Their family relationships and business backgrounds were important ingredients in the formation of Gulf American and need to be examined.

The Rosen family was headed by Abraham and Fannie Rosen, Russian Jewish émigrés who had settled in Baltimore, Maryland. Through hard work, Abraham Rosen had purchased several movie theaters in town and was constantly looking for new enterprises. Numerous times he acquired considerable wealth only to lose it a short time later. Leonard maintained that his father at one time had owned the rights to the motion picture, *Birth of a Nation*. He was in Chicago, trying to raise money for a new venture, when he was run over by a streetcar and killed at age thirty-two. The tragedy left the responsibility of raising the Rosen children—Edith, Leonard, Jack, and Sylvia—to their mother during the depression of the 1930s.[2]

Fannie Rosen operated a small grocery store for income, and the entire family worked in the store. Despite being poor, Fannie kept her family close and still found time to become involved actively in charitable work in Baltimore. Besides giving her own money, she spent considerable time raising funds for these efforts. She cared greatly about other people, even to the extent of raising an orphan cousin, Paul Venze, in her home.[3]

The Rosen family was basically self-educated. While all the children received some formal education and Jack attended a few classes at the Johns Hopkins University, Leonard dropped out of school in the sixth grade in order to work. Despite this limited formal education, the brothers continued to read extensively, often completing twenty to forty books each year. Their practical education was expanded when they hired themselves out as pitchmen, selling various products on the boardwalks of Atlantic City, at county fairs and carnivals, and in the streets of Baltimore. Leonard, in particular, had a captivating quality about himself when he gave his sales pitch that made it difficult for the buyer to resist his offer.[4]

In addition to developing a unique style of salesmanship, the Rosens learned early in their business careers about the value of "the book" or the receivables account. Even though initially they were only selling pots, pans, and other household items, many of the sales were made on an installment basis. For numerous customers short of cash, this was the only way to purchase needed items. The brothers understood that installment sales were just as important as cash transactions. Many years later at a funeral wake for a business associate, Leonard emphasized this concept when asked if new laws would adversely affect land developers. He was heard to say: "The only thing that's important is the book. If you keep the book healthy, let the damn fools [politicians] do anything they want. They're not going to hurt you. But if you let the book get sick, you're in serious trouble."[5]

In 1940 the Rosen brothers established their own furniture and appliance business, called the Rosen Home Equipment Company. Based in Baltimore, the operation sold appliances directly to households primarily on installment accounts. Sales grew as the company expanded its range into Virginia and North Carolina. Once the business was firmly established, Jack Rosen and Leonard's wife, Dorothy, were left to manage the company while Leonard went on the road to train salespeople and to look for new opportunities.[6]

With salespeople traveling as far as the Carolinas, Leonard and Jack Rosen developed various sales techniques that would be perfected later in Florida. The brothers discovered that installment selling was a powerful inducement for customers to buy. In their appliance business, anything could be purchased over time with several weekly or monthly payments. In addition, they would have their salespeople knock on doors, offering a hurricane lamp for sale at an inexpensive price. Once a customer had purchased the lamp, the salespeople found it relatively easy to offer and sell a much higher priced product such as a stove or refrigerator.[7]

The experience of pitching various products on midways at fairs and carnivals helped the Rosens develop a style of selling that would prove helpful in their later operations. They became experts at building excitement in the audiences as they spoke. Once, Leonard was trying to sell coat hangers to a small crowd. In order to build the pitch excitement, Leonard's partner, Charles Finkelstein, would ask from the crowd, "Can I have two?" Leonard would reply, "I'm sorry. Only one to a customer." Finkelstein would say, "But I really need two. One for my brother-in-law." Leonard would then angrily reply, "You better get out of here, I'm going to call the police. Only one to a customer!" Believing they were getting a great bargain, people would demand two, three, or even four of the hangers.[8]

As they were looking for new products to sell, the brothers discovered the popular appeal of hair-care products containing lanolin. Lanolin was not a new ingredient in hair preparations, but it had never been promoted to any great extent. By the late 1940s, Leonard and his associates could be seen selling lanolin products in front of a small store on Forty-ninth Street in Manhattan. People were enticed off the sidewalk to hear Leonard's half-hour presentation.[9] Successful sales demonstrated that the Rosen brothers had discovered an audience that was open to their style of marketing and to this "new" product.

By 1950 Jack Rosen was convinced that the brothers could sell products on television. Because they had been selling lanolin hair creme successfully on a local basis in New York, they decided to start a new nationwide mail-order marketing scheme for hair products with the majority of the advertising to be placed on television. The brothers needed capital in order to get their operation started and therefore formed a partnership with Charles D. Kasher, who had been a pitchman with Leonard and had a strong background in advertising. Using Kasher's first name and his mother's maiden name of Antell, Kasher and the Rosens incorporated their company as Charles Antell in 1950.[10]

Kasher had been involved in advertising and sales for most of his life. Quitting school at age sixteen in 1928, he joined a team of tonic pitchmen in Ohio. Within three years he was earning $100 a night selling his products on the boardwalk at Asbury Park, New Jersey. In 1950 he joined with the Rosen brothers, founding Charles Antell. Although the company recorded gross revenues of $12 million by 1953, Kasher was attracted to the field of theatrical production. In order to raise funds, he sold his interests in Charles Antell in 1955 to the Rosens. Eventually he produced two plays (*The Crystal Heart*, 1960, and *Staircase*, 1968) that

Leonard Rosen, 1915–87. Co-founder of the Gulf American Corporation.

were reviewed favorably in the *New York Times*. Kasher also opened his own off-Broadway theater in the New York City area in 1961. The theater was located on the ground-floor level of the old Huron Club in Greenwich Village, a favorite location in the past for Tammany Hall politicians.[11]

Beginning with a lanolin-based hair creme called Formula No. 9, Charles Antell expanded its line to include shampoo, hairspray, and liquified makeup. The products were originally sold only through mail order, but demand increased to the point where a wholesale distribution system was set up to supply drug and department stores nationwide. While few of the cosmetic products were actually innovations, the advertising methods were both creative and aggressive. Company president Kasher was convinced that Charles Antell television commercials

Julius J. "Jack" Rosen, 1921–69. Co-founder of the Gulf American Corporation.

that featured real salespeople were the most effective because, he argued, "no one can sell like a salesman."[12]

Television during the early 1950s was a new phenomenon and was limited primarily to evening programs that ended at 10 P.M. The Rosen brothers began to purchase cheap air-time when stations were normally off the air. As the need for more advertising air-time increased, the Rosens began to barter with local television stations, trading old movies for blocks of broadcast time. Large numbers of these movies had been purchased from film distribution companies at low cost.[13] This system enabled Charles Antell to acquire cheaper air-time than would have been otherwise possible.

The Charles Antell television commercials were effective and demonstrated the creativity of Leonard and Jack Rosen. Unlike most modern video advertising, these commercials lasted from five to thirty minutes. A typical Formula No. 9 hair creme advertisement began with Leonard Rosen, the narrator, saying, "Pull up a chair because I'm going to tell you a hair-raising tale." The audience would begin to listen because they thought it was going to be an exciting story. The announcer then asked if anyone had ever seen a bald-headed sheep. He then explained that sheep produce lanolin, which helps their hair to grow. After extolling the benefits of lanolin on human hair, the announcer told the television audience where to send money for the product. The sales pitch was extremely successful and sales mounted rapidly.[14]

As the company grew, ideas about advertising and new products came to the Rosens from numerous sources. In 1953 a new Charles Antell product known as liquified makeup was introduced, and more than a million bottles were manufactured. Nearly all women at the time used powder or pancake makeup. The new concept was not selling, and the liquid in the bottles was drying up. Leonard Rosen gave this small marketing account to an advertising agency known as Product Services, which was under the direction of Charles K. Hepner, who had experience in television production. Hepner created a commercial for the liquified makeup. With clever use of stage lighting and basic makeup techniques, a homely, plain-looking woman was transformed in one minute into someone who looked gorgeous, all by the supposed use of liquified makeup. The advertisement was a success and Hepner was hired later that year by Leonard to plan more advertising for the company.[15]

With Hepner as director of advertising for Charles Antell, the Rosens set up their own advertising agency in New York called the Paul Venze Agency. Venze, the Rosens' cousin, later located the agency at Fifty-seventh Street and Madison Avenue in New York City. He handled much of the Charles Antell marketing and, subsequently, many of the later Rosen promotions.

In addition to the hair products, the Rosens experimented with mail-order sales of a variety of retail items. Under Hepner's direction, television commercials were produced that featured celebrities such as sports announcer William "Bill" Stern and baseball star Mickey Mantle. Children's vitamins were presented on commercials by then seven-year-old actress Patty Duke. The company found that even a child's bicycle could be successfully mass-marketed. Another product was a diet pill that expanded in the stomach, causing the user to eat less. Often an idea for a product was marketed before it was even known if the merchandise could be delivered. For the Rosen brothers, it was more important to know if the product could be successfully sold.[16]

A key individual in the purchasing of air-time for Charles Antell was Bernice Freiberg, who was originally Leonard Rosen's secretary and a longtime family friend. Believing that she needed a larger role in the company, Leonard asked her what she wanted to do. Freiberg replied that she wanted to purchase air-time from local stations. Rosen, who at the time was purchasing the blocks of television air-time, agreed, and she began working with general managers of television stations across the country. As each new television market was added, careful accounting of mail-order sales from that area was kept in order to see if that advertising was paying for itself. Eventually, Charles Antell commercials were seen on more than two hundred stations in the United States, including at least two stations in each of the top television markets.[17]

The success of the Charles Antell operation can be traced in large part to the relationship between Leonard and Jack Rosen. The brothers were different in many ways, but their strengths complemented each other so that they formed a powerful business combination. While Leonard was traveling extensively and representing the company to the public, Jack remained more behind the scenes, managing the operation and concentrating on new marketing and advertising ideas. In many ways, Leonard was the extrovert and Jack the introvert. Although Leonard was constantly initiating new business deals, he would never do anything without consulting Jack. After Jack died in 1969, Leonard seemed to lose much of his initiative. While he still functioned well in business, he needed certain playback from Jack to feel completely secure.[18]

Another characteristic that dominated the brothers' relationship was a competitive tension that remained throughout their lives. Jack was essentially a shy, gentle man who possessed great creative talent. Most of the major innovative marketing and publicity ideas came from his efforts. Jack had a difficult time, however, accommodating Leonard's aggressiveness and public success. He ascribed most of the problems he had in life to Leonard. While Leonard adored his brother, he often lost patience with Jack, and their arguments forced employees to take sides. The tension may even have had roots in their childhood. For example, someone talking with Fannie Rosen, even on Jack's birthday, frequently heard about how wonderful Leonard was.[19]

Jack's finest hours were those moments when major business difficulties produced a desperate situation. When most of the staff was in a state of panic, Jack was cool, encouraging, and supportive. Rallying people during tough times was one of his greatest strengths. He was usually calm in other intense situations also, while Leonard found it difficult to contain his boundless energy and enthusiasm. Jack was able quietly to discuss a new million-dollar marketing proposal with his executives without getting excited, knowing intuitively that it would be a successful campaign.[20]

Several other aspects of Leonard's life disturbed the younger Rosen. A major point of contention was Leonard's womanizing. While Leonard loved his wife and children, he often had outside female interests. Jack, on the other hand, was a devoted family man, hence Leonard's actions were particularly unpleasant to him. Jack also strongly disliked tennis clothes because they represented to him the casual attire and life-style of his brother. Leonard, who had become an avid tennis player in Florida, often came to business meetings in dirty tennis shorts and dusty sneakers. Jack's anger at his brother was sometimes directed at anyone who reminded him of Leonard. On one occasion at Cape Coral, Jack sent Kenneth Schwartz, the general manager of the Cape Coral development, home from a sales meeting to change his clothes because he had arrived in tennis shorts. "Don't emulate Leonard with me!" the younger Rosen angrily stated.[21]

In many ways, Jack saw Schwartz as more loyal to Leonard than to himself. While it was not impossible, most employees found it difficult to stay on good terms with both brothers. The brothers eventually operated in separate camps with Jack in Baltimore and Leonard in Miami, and employees increasingly found themselves as either a "Leonard man" or a "Jack man." While this situation did not stop communication within the organization, it strained some staff relationships. Despite the tension between the two brothers, most workers and executives remarked about feeling a sense of family closeness and loyalty in the Rosen companies. If the employees did their jobs, they could expect the loyalty and support of the brothers. Likewise, most workers labored for lower salaries than they could have received elsewhere because they were attracted to what the Rosens were doing. There was an excitement about the whole operation that could be directly traced to the two brothers.[22]

Leonard Rosen differed from his brother in several other significant ways. He exhibited a confidence that bordered on arrogance. In order to make sure that no one misunderstood him, Leonard once bragged, "I can outsell any competitor at four o'clock in the morning or any other time."[23] His crude, vulgar language and actions shocked many associates, and they simply had to get used to it. On one occasion, Leonard was meeting with some of the top company executives in a hotel room and was naked from the waist down because he was going to take a shower. Thinking nothing of it, he continued his conversation outside the room on a balcony in full view of passersby.[24] His short-lived career in amateur boxing during his teenage years carried over into his business life, giving him a tough fighter's image to outsiders. Leonard

Rosen was a hard-driving individual who would not back down from anyone.

More than anything else, Leonard respected competent individuals who took initiative and completed their tasks. He worked hard and he expected others to do the same. He once complimented Bernice Freiberg on her excellent job of getting seemingly impossible amounts of typing finished. She never told him that she had commandeered a secretary from another department to help her.[25]

Leonard despised indecision in his subordinates. When Kenneth Schwartz was offered the job of managing the new Cape Coral development in 1957, he said that he wanted to discuss it with his wife. Schwartz later recalled that from that moment Leonard "dismissed me as if I had never lived." Shortly thereafter, Schwartz decided that he wanted the job, but Leonard refused to take his calls. A meeting was finally set up two weeks later by Jack for Schwartz and the elder Rosen. Schwartz eventually was hired but had to settle for $10,000 a year, instead of $12,000 as originally discussed, because of his indecisiveness.[26]

Schwartz was able to redeem himself somewhat in Leonard's eyes several weeks later. After only two weeks of training in Baltimore in late 1957, Schwartz was instructed by Rosen to leave the next Monday for Florida. With a blizzard descending on the city and closing many airports in the region, Rosen recommended that he cancel the trip until the weather cleared. Waiting until Leonard had left the room, Schwartz proceeded to the airport and eventually arrived in Fort Myers. The next morning, he was riding through the property with Thomas Weber, the company's chief engineer, when the car phone rang. (While car phones were not common, they had been in commercial use in the United States since 1946 and Leonard enjoyed such technological innovations.) Leonard told Weber to be expecting Schwartz as soon as the planes could get through. When Weber replied that he was there already, Leonard spoke to Schwartz: "Kenny, I'm proud of you. Give me back to Weber." For Leonard Rosen, persistence in pursuing a goal was a highly admired quality.[27]

Although he appeared rough and aggressive on the surface, Leonard was able to empathize with people on occasion. An important writer for the Charles Antell television commercials had argued heatedly with Charles Hepner and had quit. Unable to get him to return, Hepner talked to Leonard about it. Rosen did not preach to Hepner or blame him for the loss of a valued employee, although Hepner admitted that Leonard might have had some justification. Instead of criticizing, Leonard demonstrated some compassion for his dejected associate by saying, "Hepner, no matter how dark something may look today, if you have faith and hang in there, something better is going to happen." Years later, Hepner remarked that Leonard was an interesting combination of aggressiveness and compassion.[28]

Leonard Rosen would not allow a relationship to end on a bad note. During most of his life, he was careful to repair a damaged relationship when he hurt someone's feelings. On one occasion, he angrily blasted Kenneth Schwartz for hiring a doctor for Cape Coral without consulting him. On the following day, Leonard called Schwartz and apologized for what he had said. These types of actions bred a deep sense of loyalty in many of the staff. Leonard had a magnetism to his personality that encouraged friends and former employees to maintain contact with him throughout his life.[29]

A common thread that united Leonard and Jack Rosen, despite their many differences, was their Jewish faith. Both brothers had attended the Hebrew Day School in Baltimore, and Jack later started an alumni association that raised considerable funds for the school. They also belonged to Beth Jacob, an orthodox synagogue in Baltimore, and helped financially with its building program. Every morning, whether at home or on the road, they would excuse themselves, go to a quiet corner of the room, and recite their prayers. The Rosens were extremely serious about their Jewish faith and culture. While some critics claimed that they, particularly Leonard, did things that good Jews would not have done, the brothers expressed their faith by keeping their personal word and through charitable fund raising.[30]

During the mid-1950s Charles Antell began to experience greatly increased competition in the cosmetics business from Revlon and other companies. The Rosens needed new sources of financing if they were to compete successfully. They considered going public with their corporation but instead decided to see if there were any buyers. While negotiating the sale of Charles Antell to the B. T. Babbitt Company, Leonard took a vacation to Miami, Florida, in hopes that the warmer climate would help an arthritic condition he had developed. Hearing that promoters were actively subdividing land and selling homesites in the state, he became curious and decided to investigate the business possibilities.[31]

Shortly afterward, Leonard sent Bernice Freiberg to Florida to survey a sales operation in southeast Florida. Posing as a customer, she discovered that little in the way of promotion was being done by any subdivider. Most prospective customers had learned of the project when they saw the entrance signs. Receiving a call from an Antell salesman in Chicago, Solomon S. Sandler found out that a company was advertising southwest Florida land by using television broadcasts in the Chicago area. Sandler was on staff with Charles Antell and he advised the brothers. The Rosens were able to get a copy of the commercial, which showed Lee Ratner's Lehigh Acres development near Fort Myers. After viewing the film on a makeshift screen in the shipping room of Charles Antell in Baltimore, Leonard and Jack wondered if Florida property could be successfully marketed on television. Sending Sandler to Florida, Leonard instructed him to buy a small parcel of land with which to test the market. Sandler purchased eight acres about a half mile from a lake near Deland. Leonard presented the property in a televised sales pitch in Baltimore and the response was overwhelming. Responding to all the inquiries that the property had been oversold, the Rosens attempted to refine what they had learned and began to look for a large piece of land in Florida.[32]

Leonard Rosen went to Florida to look for land for a subdivision, but he was also motivated by the advice of his doctor. Diagnosed as having crippling arthritis, Rosen spent several weeks recuperating in late 1956 and early 1957 in Miami and in Punta Gorda at the Charlotte Harbor Spa.[33] Convinced at age forty-one that he would have to move south permanently for the warmer weather, Rosen began to look for a place to retire. He had found Fort Myers to be an "unusually attractive and beautiful city," and he "thought of buying a small farm to use as a retirement place."[34] In the warmer climate, his arthritis subsided, and in later years that condition seldom bothered him. While in Florida, Leonard took up tennis and played nearly every day before work. As his health returned, Rosen put aside thoughts of retirement and started a determined search for a tract of land suitable for development.

Land development was a totally new field for the Rosen brothers. Leonard later admitted, "I knew about as much about development as a six-month-old baby." Relying on his marketing background, he realized that "if we could get enough land sold, we could afford to do all we wanted" in the way of development. He needed to determine if Florida land could be marketed successfully. Investigating further, he became more intrigued with the concept: "I was a salesman sold on his own goodies."[35]

With many questions about land development still unanswered for the brothers, Leonard met Milton M. Mendelsohn in Punta Gorda in early 1957, probably at the Charlotte Harbor Spa. Mendelsohn contributed as much as anyone to the emerging concept of the proposed development of Cape Coral. The colorful and immodest Mendelsohn was a developer associated with Harbour Heights, a subdivision north of Punta Gorda in Charlotte County. Starting in the recreational land business in Chicago with L. B. Harris, Mendelsohn met Lee Ratner and helped Ratner and Gerald H. Gould launch the Lehigh Acres development. Despite his brilliant promotional innovations, he was never fully trusted by the Rosens even though he was to remain associated with them for much of the rest of his life as a consultant to Leonard. While Leonard respected Mendelsohn's creativity, he openly distrusted many of Mendelsohn's ideas because some of them bordered on being illegal. Leonard made this reservation clear in his first instructions to Kenneth Schwartz. Rosen told Schwartz to listen and learn from Mendelsohn but under no circumstances ever allow him to sign for the company. Although he was mistrusted, Mendelsohn served as a mentor for many individuals in the Rosens' operation.[36]

A humorous incident at Gulf American's Miami headquarters provides some insight into Mendelsohn's role in the company. Leonard and several other executives deliberated over some recurring problems at Golden Gate Estates, the company's second major development. After lengthy discussion, they could not agree on any suitable solutions. Several of the people present were architects and finance people who were not part of the regular Gulf American organization. Suddenly Leonard, with a straight face, took his keys out of his pocket and turned to one of his associates, saying, "Here. Take this and go into my office and open up the closet and let Milt out and bring him down here. Now, hang onto his belt so that he doesn't get away." After the subordinate left, Leonard looked at the startled faces in the room and said without smiling, "I suppose I should explain this to you. Milt Mendelsohn is a genius. Whenever you have a problem, all you have to do is ask Milt and he'll give you the answer. The only thing is, you have to keep him locked in a closet. Because if you didn't, he'd own the company and you'd be out of a job." While the assembled executives were not sure if Leonard was serious or only joking with them, Leonard revealed not only some of his personality but also his mixture of respect and distrust for Mendelsohn's creative talents. Striking out on his own in the early 1960s, Mendelsohn was later convicted of fraud in connection with his failed development near Orlando called Rocket City.[37]

After several conversations with Mendelsohn, Leonard became convinced that southwest Florida land could be marketed like any other product. With this conviction in mind, he returned to Baltimore to confer with Jack. He commented several years later that they "recognized that there must be a tremendous vacuum in the land sales market. Only one company, General Development, was doing any volume business."[38]

General Development Corporation had its origins in the early 1900s as the Mackle family building business. In 1908, Francis E. Mackle (1883–1941) launched the Mackle Construction Company in Jacksonville, Florida, a firm that specialized in steel frames for commercial structures. By 1913 he had expanded his operations to include general contracting and soon was building offices, apartments, and hotels throughout Florida, Georgia, Alabama, and Tennessee. While vacationing one winter in Delray Beach, Florida, Mackle built twenty low-cost residences and was surprised at how rapidly they sold. As a result, he abandoned commercial construction in favor of residential construction and in 1939 moved to West Palm Beach.[39]

Following Mackle's death in 1941 and the end of World War II, Mackle's three sons, Elliott J., Robert F., and Frank, Jr., took over the business, building houses in Miami, Coral Gables, West Palm Beach, and Bradenton. The brothers also purchased an old coconut plantation on a slender island just off the coast from Miami. Naming the new subdivision Key Biscayne, they erected 1,000 houses, a shopping center, and a hotel on the island. In the mid-1950s, the Mackles purchased Lewis Island at St. Petersburg for development as a residential community called Coquina Key. As the largest residential contractors in Florida, they built 300 houses in the project before a business opportunity of vastly greater proportions was presented to them.[40]

Selling Coquina Key, the Mackles joined in a partnership in 1954 with Toronto financier Louis A. Chesler to develop properties on both coasts of Florida. Within two years, the partnership was formalized into a single company, General Development Corporation, with Chesler emerging as the dominant stockholder. In December 1956 sales began on their largest project, the 108,000-acre development north of Punta Gorda, Florida, known as Port Charlotte. Aside from the opening of Port Charlotte, General Development launched Port St. John, Sebastian Highlands, Vero Beach Highlands, and Vero Shores on the east coast of Florida in the same year. Massive national advertising campaigns accompanied the opening of each project. While Frank Mackle, Jr., admitted that the Mackles did not invent grandiose national sales techniques, he claimed that "we were the first in Florida."[41]

During the same period, another large development had started in southwest Florida. In 1951 millionaire Lee Ratner sold his Chicago-based company that manufactured D-Con rat poison and began to purchase land in eastern Lee County for the Lucky Lee Cattle Ranch. Convinced by Miami advertiser Gerald Gould and by Milton Mendelsohn that subdividing the land would be more profitable than ranching, Ratner founded Lehigh Acres three years later on his 60,000-acre holdings. Experimental advertising on radio and television and in northern newspapers produced steady sales.[42]

The success of other land sales operations encouraged the Rosens. They, like many others in Florida at the time, were motivated in their new venture by the hope of generating a quick profit. Leonard's plan was simple. He hoped to keep a large tract of land for himself by subdividing part of it and quickly selling the lots. As it later became apparent that sales would remain high, the brothers grew more enamored with the idea of building a city. Although he rarely visited the project, Jack Rosen talked readily to his associates about his vision of their great future city.[43] In the early stages of development, however, profit was the key motivating factor for the brothers.

Returning to Lee County in early 1957, Leonard Rosen set out to find an appropriate tract of land. Accompanied by Mendelsohn, Rosen was flown over various tracts of land by Edward F. Wilson, a local pilot. After several flights, Rosen began to favor some acreage at Fort Myers Beach because of its proximity to the Gulf of Mexico.[44] After discovering the low elevation of that land, he was introduced to another piece of property with higher elevation by William H. Reynolds, Jr., a Fort Myers realtor. Totaling nearly 1,724 acres, the tract was a peninsula that extended into the Caloosahatchee River and was called Redfish Point. Except for the coastal portions, the property was well drained and covered with scattered stands of pines and palmettos. While negotiations were in progress, Rosen set up his first headquarters at Reynolds's office.[45]

By mid-1957 Leonard and Jack had decided to purchase the Redfish Point property. The tract was part of the estate of Franklin Miles of Miles Laboratories and was owned by Granville W. and Cathryn C. Keller, Donald and Louise Miles Bass, and eight other heirs. In order to raise money for the purchase and additional acquisitions, the Rosens sold Charles Antell to B. T. Babbitt Company for $2 million in 1958. With several Baltimore friends, the brothers formed an investment group called the Sandy Investment Company and purchased the land for $678,000 in late July 1957.[46]

Although they initially invested only an estimated $125,000 of their own funds, the brothers were firmly committed to developing a small residential community on the property.[47] Later that year, they formed the Gulf Guaranty Land and Title Company, which was later renamed the Gulf American Land Corporation. With their corporate structure in place, the Rosens began assembling a construction force that was soon to transform the tract of Florida pine land into homesites.

3

The First Five Years

A visitor to Cape Coral in late 1961 would have been staggered by the swarm of activity that had engulfed the first Rosen brothers development. With an average of 125 couples visiting the project every day, an observer would have noticed dozens of salespeople deftly guiding prospects on tours. The company boat provided river cruises to 60 visitors a day while Gulf American planes flew 1,200 prospects over the project in a typical weekend. During a seven-month period in 1961, more than 100,000 cars passed through the fledgling development. By the end of the year, the Rosen brothers had sold almost 28,000 homesites to people throughout the country. Although the company had achieved such a high level of sales by the early 1960s, the success of the Cape Coral project was far from certain in early 1957.[1]

Confident in his own mind of the development's ultimate success, Leonard Rosen also realized how precarious his situation was in 1957.[2] Earlier in that year, after tentatively selecting a suitable piece of land, Rosen had begun to study the entire land development business in southwest Florida. He discovered that most projects had not been planned adequately with regard to sales and promotion.[3] After consulting with his brother, who was still in Baltimore managing Charles Antell, Leonard decided that their new development would need to have features that no other project had. Therefore, many of the design features of Cape Coral were planned so that company advertising could boast that it had bigger and better features than any of the other competing developments. "The first thing we did," Leonard said, "was decide to build the largest harbor and the longest pier. We thought it would be quite an attraction."[4] For the Rosens, if the amenities of their new project were attractive to prospective buyers and larger than those of their competitors, then the promotion and sales of the property would be relatively simple tasks.

Leonard decided that his first piece of research was to determine the legal requirements for subdividing the property he was considering. While the five county commissioners had the final consideration in all such matters, Rosen discovered several interesting aspects about local government in Lee County. With a population in 1957 of fewer than 50,000 people, Fort Myers was a quiet, slowly growing Florida town where the office of county commissioner was only a part-time job. No master building plan existed for the county, and zoning was determined by the general direction of development. Virtually any project that would add to the tax assessor's rolls was approved.[5]

Feeling assured, Rosen entered the Lee County courthouse in early spring 1957 to question the commissioners directly. Unfortunately, the entire commission had gone to a convention in Tampa. Impatiently inquiring of the commissioners' secretary, Lavon Pigot Wisher, Rosen learned that she had been left in charge. After discovering that one of her responsibilities was issuing building permits, Rosen began questioning her concerning the county's construction laws. Although Wisher observed that he had a disorganized look about him because of his rumpled suit, she noticed that he had an air of confidence and a sense of excitement as he squatted and unrolled on the courthouse floor a large aerial photograph of Redfish and Harney points, both located on the west bank of the Caloosahatchee River. Rosen soon learned that the county requirements included filing a plat plan, submitting drainage plans to the commission for approval, and having an engineer direct the construction. The county also required that he put up bonds guaranteeing that all roads would be built according to the plan and that they would meet county specifications. With Rosen making such detailed preparations for development, Wisher did not realize until later that he had not yet completed his purchase of the land.[6]

As planning continued, the Rosens required the technical expertise of engineers. The Miami firm of Rader and Associates, headed by Earle M. Rader, was hired in April 1957 to begin engineering and design work on the new project. Rader was a client of Milton Mendelsohn's at the Harris and Whitebrook Advertising Agency in Miami Beach, and Mendelsohn put the Rosens in contact with Rader. Rader was the largest engineering firm in the southeastern United States and had numerous branch offices, including several international offices. It also had done extensive engineering work at Lehigh Acres in Lee County.[7]

Because much of the Rosens' land was too low in elevation to build on, it was concluded that dredging would be needed to provide fill material. The result was not only a higher elevation for the land but the creation of a vast series of canals and waterways. Leonard recalled, "We decided to build a community with lots of water."[8] Later nicknamed the "Waterfront Wonderland," the presence of so many canals in the community proved to be a major positive factor in sales.

The Rosens soon settled on the name Cape Coral for the new community. The exact origin of that name was unclear, and even Leonard Rosen had difficulty remembering its source. "I think we just kept kicking names around and that's what we liked," he admitted.[9] Charles Hepner and Milton Mendelsohn frequently argued about names for the company's projects. Mendelsohn ended one of these arguments by saying to Hepner that "the only thing you know about the land business is the dirt that you have under your fingernails." Mendelsohn was superstitious and believed that the project needed to have two identical initials in the name. His influence was obvious in the names of the Rosens' developments: Cape Coral, Golden Gate, River Ranch Acres, Remuda Ranch Grants, Barefoot Bay, and Rio Rico.[10]

In June 1957 Rader and Associates produced the first working design of Cape Coral, including streets, canals, and lot divisions.[11] The engineering firm laid out the community on a grid pattern, primarily because it produced the largest number of homesites on a piece of real estate. The design was common for the time period, as evidenced by the grid pattern of Port Charlotte and Lehigh Acres. With plan in hand, Leonard Rosen actively pursued the purchase of the initial 1,724-acre tract. By late July the property belonged to his company, Gulf Guaranty Land and Title Company, which had just been incorporated in Florida on July 18. Because the Rosens started with a personal investment of less than $125,000 and with mostly borrowed money, it was necessary to begin homesite sales as quickly as possible.[12] Under the Rosens' plan, Cape Coral would have such amenities as a yacht club, golf course, and country club that would dramatically aid sales. Construction thus would have to be immediate and swift. After moving his wife Dorothy and three children to Miami in September, Leonard began looking for several key people for his Cape Coral project.

One of the earliest members of the development team, Thomas Weber, was hired on November 4, 1957, by Leonard to oversee all on-site engineering and construction. Weber had studied civil engineering at the University of Cincinnati and at the University of Dayton and had eventually gravitated toward heavy construction projects. At age forty-eight, Weber had already directed numerous large building projects around the world. Working for the U.S. Army Corps of Engineers in Brazil, he directed the building of roads, water systems, and bridges in

View of Redfish Point in May 1958 after six months of excavation and dredging. The first four single-family houses are visible.

that country. In Iceland, Weber was the resident engineer for the construction of radar installations near the Arctic Circle. By the mid-1950s he had been transferred to the Azores Islands and was supervising the building of the international airport at Santa Maria Island. Other projects in Italy and Greenland added to his ability to work in virtually all kinds of terrain and climates.[13]

Leonard Rosen had met Weber in the autumn of 1957 at the Bradford Hotel in Fort Myers. Although Weber was on his way out of the country on another assignment at the time, Leonard persuaded him to take a look at the land he had purchased on Redfish Point. Rosen had been impressed with the ability of this soft-spoken engineer to get projects finished rapidly and competently. Weber also greatly admired ability in people, and he recognized in Leonard Rosen a high level of competence and motivation. Weber noted, however, that upon first seeing the property he thought Rosen "had rocks in his head" because Weber did not think it would sell after they had finished developing it. He even suggested that Leonard abandon the project. Leonard was able to convince him that they were going to build a city on the site, although Weber later admitted that he "kept his traveling bags packed for three weeks, deciding whether to stay." Leonard's drive and ability convinced Weber to give up his alternate plans and remain in Cape Coral.[14]

Weber's first task was building a road into the development that would be passable year round. The only existing road was Harney Point Road, a narrow bumpy lane that flooded to nearly a foot deep during heavy rain. Renamed Del Prado Expressway in 1957 and later Del Prado Boulevard, it extended nearly nine miles south of Pondella Road and abruptly ended a quarter of a mile before reaching Gulf Guaranty's northern property line (present-day Cape Coral Parkway). Weber immediately ordered an initial shipment of earth-moving equipment that cost approximately $250,000. He also hired, in late 1957, a construction crew that averaged 150 workers. Although work began immediately on the reconstruction of the road, it was October 1958 before the worst six miles had been rebuilt though not yet paved.[15]

Prior to the beginning of the land sales operation in January 1958, another significant individual, Kenneth Schwartz, was hired by the Rosen brothers to act as general manager for the Cape Coral development. Schwartz had served in the marines in the Pacific in World War II and upon his discharge had attended the Wharton School at the University of Pennsylvania. During the 1950s he had managed a large ice cream company in Baltimore, supervising more than 100 trucks as they sold ice cream in the neighborhoods of the city. Schwartz was approached in 1957 by Sylvan Abrams, a friend of Jack Rosen, about applying to work for Charles Antell. Thinking that he would like to

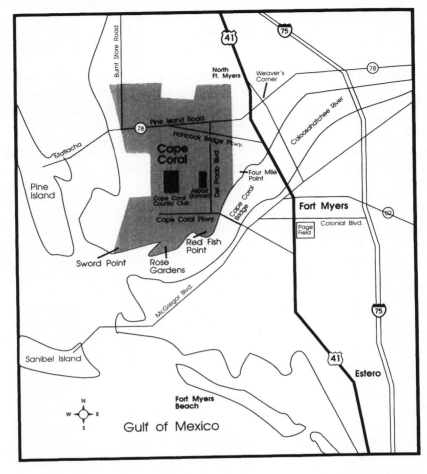

learn the cosmetics business, Schwartz interviewed first with Jack and then with Leonard. He soon discovered that although he was only thirty-one years old, he was being considered for general manager of the Rosens' new land development project in Florida. After readily admitting to Leonard that he knew nothing about construction, engineering, or the land business, Leonard asked, "What do you consider your qualifications for this job?" Schwartz replied, "In anything I'm involved with, there will be no complacency."[16] Leonard admired that kind of aggressive attitude, and Schwartz was hired in late 1957.

Known as "Kenny" by most company personnel and residents of Cape

Coral, Schwartz is a tall, handsome man who was captivated by the energy and dream of the Rosens. He later commented, "I wasn't a multi-millionaire. I didn't have a lot to lose and it seemed like an exciting opportunity."[17] Everything that he did was done in a rapid fashion and he had little patience for those who were slow or unable to get a job finished quickly. Although his personality is warm and engaging, Schwartz aggressively pursued the task of building a community at Cape Coral, often trampling on people's feelings in the process. Despite this aspect, he was popular with the majority of the people, and his enthusiasm for the project motivated other company personnel at the site to take pride in their jobs.[18]

Within three weeks of the hiring of Schwartz, Leonard brought Connie Mack, Jr., into the organization. Rosen was interested in hiring a local personality with name recognition over a large part of the United States, and Mack was suggested by realtor William H. Reynolds, Jr.[19] Mack is the son of Connie Mack, Sr., the longtime owner of the Philadelphia Athletics baseball team. The elder Mack had used Fort Myers as the spring training center for his team during the 1920s and 1930s. His son had settled permanently in the area and was actively involved in real estate when Rosen approached him.

The importance of Connie Mack's association with Gulf Guaranty cannot be overstated. The elder Mack was widely known and respected in all levels of American society, and his son was heir to much of those warm feelings. Rosen understood the promotional potential of celebrities, but even he at first probably underestimated Mack's appeal. Early in the company's history, an experimental land sales banquet was held in Washington, D.C. Connie Mack, Jr., made the sales pitch to the prospective customers by pointing out that he would not lend his name to the Cape Coral project unless he thought it was a worthwhile venture. Most of the guests were so enthralled with the chance to meet a celebrity like Mack that virtually no land was sold that night. They were more interested in shaking hands with Mack than with listening to the salespeople seated at their tables. After that experience, company officials used Mack's endorsement more in printed advertisements and less in public sales presentations. Despite the change in sales strategy, the tremendous appeal of Connie Mack to the American public was a fact not unnoticed by the Rosen brothers.[20]

Throughout the early months of the corporation's existence, Leonard Rosen was virtually unknown in Lee County, and most influential people doubted whether anything would come of his new development. Because the Rosens needed financial backing and few individuals or financial institutions would lend on such a speculative venture, the brothers needed to reduce costs wherever possible. To address this prob-

Kenneth Schwartz, general manager at Cape Coral, and Robert Parmalee, excavation superintendent, stand near one of the large draglines used to build canals in Cape Coral. (The third man in the distance is unidentified.)

lem, Rosen approached key community business leaders, such as Homer T. Welch, Jr., with his dream in late 1957. Welch, general manager of the Lee County Electric Cooperative, was impressed with Rosen's intense determination and vivid description of the city he wanted to build on the west side of the Caloosahatchee River. The development needed electrical power but the cost of bringing it to Cape Coral was going to be high because of the project's distant location from main power lines. Having serious reservations about the project, Welch told him that he could not afford to gamble the cooperative's funds on Rosen's well-intentioned dreams.[21]

Learning from Welch that the cost of extending the power lines from Pine Island Road to the construction site would be approximately $10,000, Rosen immediately wrote out a check for the full amount to guarantee that the cooperative would not lose any money and to prevent any delays in the raising of funds by the cooperative. Satisfied that Rosen was able to complete the project, the amazed Welch quickly countered by promising to refund the company's money if Rosen completed even half of the promised houses. A little over a year later, Welch made a special trip to Kenneth Schwartz's office in Cape Coral and returned the deposit to the company. Knowing nothing of the handshake agreement between Welch and Leonard, Schwartz discovered that his boss had written the check on his own personal account. The incident convinced Welch that Rosen was "quite a promoter, a man who accomplished what he set out to do."[22]

Leonard and Jack Rosen did not need to have a product in hand in order to begin marketing it. As with most land developments of the era, the brothers had been undercapitalized when they began Cape Coral. In order to raise the needed construction funds, lot sales began almost immediately, in January 1958. Leonard was convinced, however, that the construction of streets, canals, and completed recreational facilities was necessary to a strong sales program. He later admitted, "I didn't know what comes first, the development or the people [buyers]."[23] Finding it impossible to balance the two, the Rosens pursued both directions as rapidly as they could.

Construction of roads and canals surged forward in early 1958 because of the need to get buyers to the site. As Thomas Weber's road crews rebuilt Del Prado Expressway, other workers began construction of the first two-mile section of Cape Coral Parkway. Running four lanes wide west from the end of Del Prado, Cape Coral Parkway formed the northern boundary of the original tract of land. By February, paving and landscaping were completed, and the workers were proceeding south on Coronado Boulevard to the yacht basin area.[24]

As the road building continued, construction of the yacht basin and the first canals began. Before any dredging could occur, the area needed to be cleared of any trees and then surveyed. Dense mangroves covered the Caloosahatchee shoreline for up to one hundred yards inland, and the daily tides left much of that area under water. Despite the swampy areas near the river, the remainder of the property was high, dry grassland that was full of palmettos and young pines. Only the stumps of the original virgin-growth pines remained when the bulldozers arrived because of lumbering that occurred from the 1920s to the 1940s. Using bulldozers with huge rakes on the front, live vegetation and dead stumps alike were cleared to ease surveying and later construction. While Weber maintained that his crews tried to save as many trees as possible, any trees that might have interfered with road, canal, or housing construction were automatically removed. As a result, few trees remained after the clearing process. Instead of clearing and burning the mangroves, tractors were "walked" over them and they were left to rot. Salespeople with customers carefully avoided the area because of the intense stench.[25]

In early 1958, visitors to Cape Coral traveled down rough Harney Point Road (present-day Del Prado Boulevard) until they reached this intersection at Cape Coral Parkway.

While the bulldozers scraped the property clear of vegetation, Weber's survey crews were already at work staking out the boundaries of canals and road rights-of-way. Living in tents on Redfish Point, they determined that even the higher land would need to receive fill dirt to reach the county-mandated minimum elevation of five and one-half feet above sea level. As more material was required to build up low-lying areas, Weber calculated the volume of fill needed and made the canals wider and deeper in those vicinities. For this reason, many of the canals in the yacht club area ended up nearly two hundred feet wide. Underestimating how much material he would require in that area, Weber was forced to dredge the yacht basin to a depth of thirty-two feet. In contrast, canals throughout the higher lands were often widened to only eighty feet at a depth of six to fifteen feet.[26]

While Weber organized the field operations, the sales and administration for Gulf Guaranty Land and Title Company were housed after January 1, 1958, in a recently vacated fruit and orange juice store in North Fort Myers. Located at Weaver's Corner at the intersection of Business 41 and Pine Island Road, it held the offices of Kenneth Schwartz, Connie Mack, Jr., Thomas Weber, Gwen McGinn, and various others. Before the

Cape Coral venture, McGinn had worked as the head of the mailing department for Charles Antell in Baltimore. With seven years of experience running the direct-mailing operation and keeping statistics for the large cosmetics firm, she was invited by Leonard Rosen to come temporarily to Fort Myers to start a mailing department. Humorously, she asked him if they were going to mail out samples of land to people. Her new mailing department turned out to be a small outbuilding with orange crates for furniture. By the end of the year, however, McGinn was still in Florida and was overseeing ten women who handled a 200,000-name mailing list.[27]

Hundreds of letters from prospective buyers were flooding into the crowded office. All of the inquiries needed specific answers, ranging from the tax rate to the pollen count in the area. In early 1958, Eileen Bernard, among others, was hired to type replies to all the questions. Bernard had worked as the editor of the house magazine at American Cyanamid Corporation in New York. After moving to Fort Myers because of her husband's health, Bernard went to work for Leonard Rosen at the North Fort Myers office, although at a substantially reduced salary from her former pay of $15,000 per year. Beginning in February 1958, she and one other person attempted to answer each of the hundreds of letters individually with little guidance from the Rosens. Bernard remembered that she phrased her responses in such a way that they did not discourage the buyers from coming to Cape Coral but at the same time did not misrepresent the property. Admitting that the salespeople's descriptions of the property sometimes overstepped reality, she said, "My biggest job was to keep it factual."[28]

After finding the procedure too slow, Bernard persuaded Kenneth Schwartz to order an autotype machine. Hiring a woman to use the machine, Bernard composed various paragraphs that could be used interchangeably in a variety of response letters. By numbering these paragraphs, she could write the appropriate numbers at the top of the customers' letters, and the autotypist would do the rest. This successful innovation was important because many of the early lot sales in Cape Coral were by mail.[29]

Even with the autotypist, the process of answering thousands of letters each week was time consuming, and many letters asked the same questions. In another effort to economize, Bernard chronicled a sampling of the most common letters plus short stories about Cape Coral in the first edition of a promotional newspaper in June 1959. Written by Bernard and named the *Cape Coral Sun,* the paper told of new residents to the community, described the great fishing in the area, and provided pictures of pretty women in swimsuits. Although it was primarily a promotional effort by Gulf Guaranty, the *Sun* also provided a major source of local news to the community and an efficient way of communicating between the company and residents. The paper became entirely promotional when the local Cape Coral newspaper, the *Gulf Breeze* (later renamed the *Cape Coral Breeze*) was started in May 1961.[30]

The small company office at Weaver's Corner also served as the primary sales office for customers who came to look at the new subdivision. The salespeople in the early months of 1958 had a difficult task because Cape Coral had little to inspect except for a multitude of bulldozers and nine unpaved washboard miles of Del Prado Expressway. With Mary Anderson Harborn, Edward V. Pacelli, and John M. Warren as some of the earliest salespeople, the customers were told about what Cape Coral was envisioned to be in the future. The sales force tried earnestly to ignite a customer's imagination concerning Cape Coral's great potential. Thus, salespeople routinely did not refer to "lots" and "canals" but to "homesites" and "waterways."[31]

The majority of the early salespeople strongly believed in the Cape Coral project and were convinced that it would be everything the Rosens claimed it would be. They believed that customers would benefit because they were receiving a quality product. Working in land sales for most of his adult life, salesman John Warren was convinced that any Cape Coral lot would increase in value. Kenneth Schwartz felt the same way: "Every customer we persuaded through our energetic sales methods, I felt we were enhancing his life, bettering the lives of everyone we got to buy and move to Cape Coral." For many of the sales staff, their confidence was directly focused on Leonard and Jack Rosen. Edward Pacelli expressed this focus when he remembered that the brothers "had a magical air about them."[32]

In March 1958 the sales operation moved into the first modern building in Cape Coral, a quadriplex on the southwest corner of Coronado Boulevard and Cape Coral Parkway. By this time four miles of waterways had been dredged and the yacht basin and marina were nearing completion. To assist the salespeople, small airplanes were used to give customers an aerial view of the property. With Cape Coral Parkway divided by a median, the planes landed on the southernmost lane to avoid cars. As traffic increased, security guards at each end of the parkway stopped cars as planes took off and landed on the street.[33]

With advertising for the new development spreading, hundreds of visitors stopped at the quadriplex in Cape Coral. Busloads of prospective buyers were also brought in from Miami to hear the sales pitch. Served orange juice and lunches by a hostess, the couples were taken to the salesroom, which had a large full-color map of the development hanging on the wall. Upon hearing the benefits of owning property in Cape Coral, they were given the choice of homesites that ranged in price from $990 to $3,390.[34] Although most of the lots were still inaccessible by automobile, company pilots flew the customers over the subdivision, dropping a bag of flour from the window of the plane to mark a designated site.[35] The accuracy of these methods was often suspect because in most areas neither roads nor canals provided the pilots with sufficient landmarks. Despite this problem, sales totals soared past $9 million by the end of 1958.[36]

The impressive sales totals of the first year removed any doubts that the Rosens had harbored about Cape Coral. Leonard later commented that he "always knew it was going to be successful after the first fifteen months." For Leonard, however, initial successes were overshadowed by something greater. "When you are a dreamer," he said, "you dream of more dreams, and the dream is more fun than the actuality." His intense motivation came from the skeptics who doubted his ability to accomplish his dreams: "My drive came from when people would say 'You can't.' Then there is nothing else to do but what they are questioning."[37] With a strong conviction that they could not fail, the brothers expanded their operations.

Construction, which had never operated at anything less than full capacity, was accelerated by the purchase of more and better heavy equipment. The earliest shipments of machinery included largely second- and third-hand dozers and draglines that had been purchased on credit and were frequently breaking down. Maintenance superintendent Robert Parmalee explained the problems: "How the earliest construction work got done, I do not really know . . . no Caterpillar equipment for the first two years, and not much else of worth. . . . We got by because of some terrific workers, and their respect for Tom [Weber]."[38] As sales revenues increased, however, equipment purchases rose to a total of $3.2 million by early 1963.[39]

During the first five years, all construction in Cape Coral depended on the speed of the canal dredging. Because the excavated dirt was needed to build up the homesites, dredging continued throughout the nights with huge spotlights illuminating the scene. By mid-1962 the three dredges were accompanied by ten draglines in the project. The hydraulic dredges were floating barges that pumped out dirt in liquid solution. The draglines were cranes that dragged huge buckets across the ground, picking up dirt from canal sites and dumping it on higher ground. Although pressed to work all night, Thomas Weber discovered that some dragline operators were jumping off the machines, allowing them to rotate aimlessly in place, in order to sleep and to keep the time clocks running. Inspections in the middle of the night by Weber kept the work moving forward.[40]

As Gulf American increased its rate of development at Cape Coral, the size of the excavating machines used in the project also grew. In 1962, six Euclid scraper/earth-movers were purchased by the company and placed at Cape Coral by Weber to work on the construction of the golf course. Costing $400,000, the mammoth scrapers were capable of moving earth at the rate of 2,000 cubic yards per hour. In June 1962 Weber took delivery of a Lima 1250 dragline, which was the largest piece of equipment the company had purchased up to that time. The huge dragline boasted a 120-foot boom that guided an 8-cubic-yard bucket. The $200,000 machine was so large that it required special transportation for delivery to the site at Cape Coral. "It took five days to bring the dragline in by barge from the Florida Keys," said Weber. "The carrier ran aground twice, but finally made it through Lake Okeechobee and the [Caloosahatchee] river canal." By late 1963, Gulf American had added six more draglines, including an even larger Lima 2400 that could move 8,000 cubic yards a day.[41]

By early 1963 Weber reported that approximately 50 million cubic yards of dirt had been removed at Cape Coral. This amounted to about 100,000 cubic yards a week since 1958, or a weekly amount of material equivalent to an area the size of a football field piled over fifty feet high. In some areas, a heavy layer of coral rock had to be blasted with explosives. Nearly forty tons of dynamite had been used to break up the rock over the five-year period. With so much excavated material, the company did not have to buy and haul in any more fill dirt. The result of five years of dredging and grading was 168 miles of canals, three basins—Bimini, Bikini, and the yacht basin—and fourteen artificial lakes. Eighty miles of paved roads also crisscrossed the growing development.[42]

Beginning in March 1958, housing construction became an important part of the Rosens' building plan. The brothers knew that promotional efforts would be effective only if customers actually saw a city with houses being built. The first four homes, located on Riverside and Flamingo drives, were completed in May 1958, and the Kenneth Schwartz family moved in one month later as Cape Coral's first resident family. Building some of the first houses in the community was Connie Raymond Construction Company of Punta Gorda. The second housing contractor was Clarence Duffala of Duffala Construction Company.[43]

With several builders operating in Cape Coral from the beginning, Leonard became increasingly frustrated by the wide range of quality in the houses being built in the development. He felt that he needed more control over the quality of residential construction. In discussing the situation with close associates, Leonard voiced his discontent to developer Julius Wetstone of Clearwater, Florida. Wetstone owned property in Lee County and had sold Rosen one of the earliest tracts of land for

Cape Coral. He told Leonard about a qualified young builder in the St. Petersburg area named Arthur Rutenberg. After Leonard asked to meet him, Rutenberg flew to Fort Myers and then was shuttled to Cape Coral aboard a company Cessna aircraft. Landing on one of the streets in the new community, Rutenberg met Leonard at the lunch tent, a temporary structure used to feed company employees before any restaurants were built in Cape Coral.[44]

Leonard soon learned that Rutenberg had been building homes in Florida since 1954 and had earned a reputation for quality construction. The two men worked out an agreement and Rutenberg began building homes in Cape Coral in 1959. Rutenberg later remarked that he normally would not have been interested in building homes for Rosen. However, he had just purchased a new airplane and he wanted a business excuse to fly it on a regular basis. Originally Rutenberg operated under a typical contractor's agreement whereby he would buy the lots from Gulf American, build the homes, and then sell them. Within a short time, the agreement was expanded so that Gulf American salespeople would sell the homes. Eventually Leonard decided that he wanted Gulf American itself to build homes, and he formed a new subsidiary called Cape Coral Construction Company. In reality, however, Leonard had contracted with Rutenberg to operate Cape Coral Construction for 40 percent of the profit. Between 1959 and the mid-1960s, Rutenberg continued his relationship with Gulf American, building more than 500 homes in Cape Coral.[45]

Rutenberg believed that Leonard wanted to get into housing construction in Cape Coral because it produced a positive cash flow. Because most home buyers secured mortgages on their houses, Cape Coral Construction would receive its entire cost and profit immediately. With the sale of vacant lots, however, Gulf American was required to invest all of the cost of developing the homesites at the beginning. Therefore, the entire land sales program operated on a negative cash flow. Gulf American received its costs back only when a lot payment was complete. Because most homesites were purchased on an installment basis, the company needed subsidiaries that produced immediate positive cash flows.[46]

Throughout the early 1960s, Rutenberg built the largest share of homes in Cape Coral through Cape Coral Construction. Although other contractors continued to build some houses, the majority were erected by Cape Coral Construction because Gulf American shuttled customers directly from its land salespeople to housing salespeople. Other builders simply had difficulty intercepting customers before they had signed a contract for a Gulf American house.[47]

By the mid-1960s Rutenberg became interested in other aspects of residential construction and ended his association with Gulf American. In 1968 he was approached by Robert Winnerman of New Jersey about a joint operation. On February 22, 1969, several companies owned by Arthur Rutenberg and his brother, Charles, including Imperial Homes, were merged into U.S. Homes and Development Corporation. While on the surface it appeared that the Rutenbergs' companies had been absorbed by U.S. Homes, it was actually the Rutenbergs who controlled the company. Within months Arthur became frustrated with the way decisions were made, explaining, "We were three co-equals and I don't work well in groups." Although he had served as president of the corporation, he left U.S. Homes on August 31, 1970. After an aborted attempt to found another national public construction company in 1973, Rutenberg formed Arthur Rutenberg Corporation in 1975 to supervise his real estate investments and to pursue a concept of franchising regional building firms.[48]

Besides their need for a positive cash flow in their businesses, the Rosens stressed residential housing construction for a second important reason. Large funding institutions and investors had been enticed by other development schemes that had failed, and they were wary of operations that did not show visible growth. As a demonstration of legitimacy, funding institutions wanted to see people moving into the project. Wanting to encourage housing sales, Gulf American began a program in the early 1960s that flew homesite customers to Cape Coral to look at model houses. The $300 fee could be used as a down payment if a house was purchased or was refunded if one was not. The program was extremely successful, accumulating nearly $9 million in sales. While the cost of airline tickets sometimes soared to more than $60,000 per month, the Rosens' goal of selling houses was becoming a reality.[49]

Housing growth increased steadily throughout the first year of the development so that more than fifty houses had been completed by February 1959. With the coming of autumn, an additional fifty residences were finished, and the first model home village opened on York Court in October. Two additional model home villages opened over the next five years, bringing the total of showplace houses to twenty-seven. As housing sales soared, Cape Coral increased to 3,825 residents by October 1964, including 3,008 adults and 817 children.[50]

In order to promote further land sales, the Rosens had from the beginning promised customers a wide variety of recreational amenities. With the opening of the Surfside Restaurant in August 1959 and the Nautilus Inn the following January, the brothers added several resort features to Cape Coral. In July 1960 the fishing pier near the yacht basin was completed, extending 600 feet into the Caloosahatchee River with a 200-foot T at the end. By the next summer, the first round of golf on the initial nine holes at the Cape Coral country club was played by the foursome of H. D. "Andy" Anderson, Clarence "Butch" Duffala, Browning Wharton, and Monte Hodo, all early residents of the community. Needing additional facilities, the Rosens expanded the Nautilus Inn to ninety-three units in 1962 and the Surfside Restaurant to 300-seat capacity. The most important recreational addition of that year, however, was the opening of the $1 million Cape Coral yacht and racquet club in June 1962. The complex included a 200-boat capacity yacht basin, an Olympic-size swimming pool, tennis and shuffleboard courts, a bathing beach on the river, a performance stage, meeting rooms, and a $50,000 youth club building. All of the facilities were open to residents of the community.[51]

Many investors failed to see the benefits of recreational facilities that probably would never make a profit, and they were sharply critical of the Rosens. At the opening of the Cape Coral country club in July 1961, three of the major stockholders privately berated Leonard Rosen for his extravagant waste of funds in building the facility. Taking the criticism for a short time, Rosen finally lashed back: "You know what you guys' problem is? You think this is a country club. You're looking at it as a capital investment. That's not what it is. It's the biggest goddamn bulletin board in the United States. It's to sell land."[52] For the Rosens, the primary purpose of the resort facilities at Cape Coral was to attract customers for their land sales operation. They soon recovered the funds they had invested in the country club because it was shortly sold to the Woodmen of the World Life Insurance Company with a future buy-back option for the Rosens.[53]

Because Leonard and Jack Rosen wanted to attract working-age customers as well as retirees, they needed to convince light industry to relocate in Cape Coral to provide jobs. Establishing a 160-acre industrial park near Del Prado Boulevard and Viscaya Parkway, the Rosens pursued small businesses throughout the country. After talking with company representatives Charles Hepner and Edward Pacelli in New York, sportswear manufacturer Sam Nahama was not convinced that southwest Florida had the fifty to one hundred skilled workers he needed. An advertisement in a local newspaper produced many responses. Still hesitant, Nahama insisted on interviewing several applicants and testing them on his machinery. Set up by Pacelli at the Bradford Hotel in Fort Myers, the interviews were to Nahama's satisfaction, and in May 1960 construction began on Nahama Sportswear in the Cape Coral Industrial Park.[54] A short time later, Fullerton-Kearney Plastics, a manufacturer of flags and plastic products, became the second industrial plant in Cape Coral.

During the first five years of Gulf Guaranty Land and Title Company's existence, the administrative structure developed into two, possibly three, separate but related organizations. During the Charles Antell period (pre-1958), Leonard had directed advertising and packaging for the various cosmetic lines, although Jack greatly influenced the advertising with his creative ideas. Jack, on the other hand, was primarily responsible for the national sales force, marketing, and promotion. Inasmuch as both brothers worked out of the same offices in Baltimore, they constantly talked over matters with each other. Changes in structure began to take place, however, when they entered the land sales business.[55]

In September 1957 Leonard moved to Miami, establishing the head office of the land business in a small strip shopping center at 5420 Biscayne Boulevard. In order to get off to a solid start, Rosen brought accountants and attorneys with him from Charles Antell in Baltimore. Two of the first to arrive were accountant George London and attorney Bernard H. Herzfeld. The latter functioned as chief counsel for the corporation. Rosen trusted Herzfeld's legal opinion completely and rarely agreed to anything without his confirmation.[56] The Miami office handled most of the corporate administration, finances, development, and Florida land sales.

Several corporate functions were initially carried on in Lee County instead of Miami. Thomas Weber, the head of development construction, was located on the Cape Coral site and not in Miami. The mailing of promotional brochures and the building of the mailing list were directed by Gwen McGinn at the North Fort Myers office. The answering of customer inquiries was also handled in North Fort Myers, although it and the mailing services were moved to Miami in early 1959.[57] At the beginning, the sales force was also prominent at the Cape Coral office.

Jack Rosen remained in Baltimore until many years later, and several key functions remained with him. All marketing, advertising, and promotion were under his supervision. Charles Hepner assisted the younger Rosen and produced many of the advertising films and television commercials for the company. In addition, the developing national sales program was headquartered in the Baltimore office at 2 West Twenty-fifth Street. Rosen had remained in Baltimore to oversee the sale of Charles Antell in 1958. Keeping in constant communication with his brother, Jack was already working on marketing strategies for Cape Coral before the Antell sale was complete.[58]

As the corporation grew, the division of various functions into a Baltimore camp and a Miami camp became more apparent, splitting personal loyalties, and leaving most employees identified as either a "Leonard man" or a "Jack man." This division of personnel was perceived by many employees to be more of Jack's doing than Leonard's.

Some doubt that Leonard even noticed such a distinction.[59] A major cause of the split may have been Jack's jealousy of his brother. A simpler explanation was that two extremely intelligent and aggressive entrepreneurs needed a certain amount of space from each other. As two dynamic leaders, they attracted the loyalties of different men and women within the organization. In any case, the result left key individuals unaware of many events in the other camp.[60]

Some individuals discounted the seriousness of the split, claiming that people outside the organization saw greater problems than really existed. Solomon Sandler, administrator of the Miami office, noted that individuals in the corporation could discuss an idea or problem with anyone else in the company. The organizational lines were simply not very strict. While Edward Pacelli admitted that difficulties sometimes occurred between Jack and Leonard, he attributed them to differing personal strengths that sometimes meshed and sometimes clashed. Convinced that they cared deeply about each other, Pacelli summed them up this way: "If you didn't know them, you'd say there was friction, but God help the man who tried to come between them."[61]

As the need for more administrative office space grew, the Miami office moved into a much larger building at Northeast Eighty-first Street and Biscayne Boulevard. As the Rosens added computers to handle the burgeoning mailing list, the second story of the building was taken over, along with other storefronts in the city. Eventually the Rosens purchased a Howard Johnson's Motor Lodge at Northeast Seventy-ninth Street and Biscayne Boulevard, demolished it, and erected an eleven-story office building. Expecting to use only the first three floors, the company occupied all eleven stories when it moved in during early 1964.[62]

Besides housing the headquarters, the new office building stood as the Rosens' symbol to onlookers of the legitimacy and stability of their operation. The impressive-looking structure with a heliport on the roof had cost the corporation $1,979,550. The Rosen brothers, however, were not content to waste funds recklessly on promotion if any other possibility presented itself. The building was, therefore, sold in March 1964 for $2.7 million to the Woodmen of the World Life Insurance Company and leased back by the corporation for twenty years. The Rosens had needed to "get more operating capital into the business," according to company sources, and the building served its purpose whether owned or leased.[63]

As sales volume increased, the Rosens began to acquire a variety of subsidiary companies to aid their sales organization. In order to reflect these differences, they decided to change the name of the corporation from Gulf Guaranty Land and Title Company to Gulf American Land

Corporation on May 8, 1961. To complement this new image, Gulf American common stock was listed on the American Stock Exchange for the first time.[64]

As knowledgeable businessmen, the Rosens avoided many financial disasters in the early years of Gulf American and Cape Coral. Cape Coral and the corporation, however, narrowly escaped a major natural crisis in September 1960. Packing winds in excess of 120 miles per hour, Hurricane Donna swept in from the Gulf of Mexico directly across Cape Coral on September 10. The storm had been traveling in a westerly direction when it approached the Florida Keys early that day but unexpectedly turned northward toward Cape Coral. Hurricane winds of 74 miles per hour were first recorded at 12:32 P.M. at Page Field in Fort Myers. Highest sustained winds in the area were 92 miles per hour with gusts reaching 121 miles per hour. The eye of the storm passed over Fort Myers and Cape Coral from 2:20 P.M. until 3:31 P.M. with hurricane-force winds resuming at 5:00 P.M.[65]

While Caribbean hurricanes typically have affected only the Gulf coast and the southeastern coast of the United States, Donna swept up the northeastern coast of the country. Coming fully ashore again in the New England area, winds of 140 miles per hour were recorded in Boston. The storm eventually lost strength and died out as it moved across eastern Canada. Besides widespread property damage, Donna resulted in 143 deaths, 25 of them in the United States.[66]

In the Fort Myers/Cape Coral area, wind damage from Donna was extensive. Three days after the storm, electrical power had been restored to only 65 percent of Lee County. As a result, 60,000 pounds of dry ice were rushed to Fort Myers for refrigeration purposes. One hundred fifty homes in Lehigh Acres were unroofed in the storm. Three local deaths (none in Cape Coral) were attributed to the storm, and by September 13 Lee County, along with several other areas of the state, was declared a disaster area by President Dwight D. Eisenhower.[67]

Cape Coral residents witnessed similar destruction from the wind. Everywhere trees were blown over, carports ripped away from houses, boats sunk in their canals, and roofs damaged. The roof of one house on El Dorado Parkway had blown off and sat intact in the middle of the street. Several homes in Cape Coral were completely wrecked and fewer than 15 percent of the residences in the city escaped damage.[68]

Fear of flooding was great, but Donna was a relatively dry hurricane, resulting in only 4.66 inches of rain. Flooding had been the worst on the barrier islands of Sanibel and Captiva because of tides four to six feet above normal. On some of the islands' roads, a foot of sand was left by the tidal surge. The majority of water damage in Cape Coral resulted from wind-damaged roofs. Company officials had ordered all files placed on top of tables and desks in the office in expectation of flooding.

When Gwen McGinn returned to the office after the storm, the roof had been blown away and the exposed records were soaked.[69]

Assuming the worst, company officials, such as community relations director Richard G. Crawford, assisted residents during the storm by opening the Surfside Restaurant and Nautilus Inn as emergency shelters. Nearly eighty people gathered to wait out the storm. After Donna had passed, many people whose homes had been severely damaged were housed and fed for days at the Nautilus and Surfside at company expense.[70] While Gulf Guaranty officials had humanitarian motives, the happiness of the residents was also critical to the promotion of future land sales.

Publicity about the storm shook the confidence of many potential customers. In order to show that things were back to normal in Cape Coral, a public relations representative from the Miami office visited in the hurricane's aftermath. Taking photographs of a house on Nautilus Drive, he had postcards made and had them sent out to thousands of people across the country with the caption, "Donna has visited Cape Coral and left it unscathed." The printing on the photograph covered the part of the home where the carport and a damaged automobile and boat had once stood.[71]

Hurricane Donna frightened many northerners with the dangers of living in Florida. Immediately after the storm, therefore, Kenneth Schwartz knew that it was psychologically important to sell a house or lot to show that Cape Coral had been only slightly affected. Spotting a couple huddled by the fireplace at the Nautilus, Schwartz convinced them to buy. "I don't remember how many television sets or meals it cost us, but we used every ounce of our persuasiveness," Schwartz recalled. "It was important to us that they buy, to demonstrate to the whole world that Cape Coral was still alive."[72]

During the first five years of Gulf American's existence, everything occurred at a furious pace. Rarely was anything planned long in advance. A project that would have taken a month to accomplish elsewhere was pushed to completion in a week. The excitement of something new always happening attracted many of the early employees.[73] As the company grew, the sense of being driven forward increased. Raymond Meyer, a designer for the company, witnessed something that demonstrated this feature. He had seen a sales manager in his office in Cape Coral talking on four different phones at the same time. When the fifth phone rang, the manager introduced the new caller to another man on one of the other phones. Laying the two phones side by side on his desk so that they could talk to each other, he introduced the one caller from Baltimore to another caller from California and placed a towel over the phones so they could hear. He then continued with the other three calls. At Gulf American, the pace never slackened.[74]

4

Purchasing a Land Empire

Leonard and Jack Rosen characterized themselves as dreamers who had a passion for challenges. They viewed success in any project as an opportunity for new ventures. Describing himself and his brother, Leonard commented, "People who are creative and doers are more interested in what they're doing tomorrow than what they did the day before yesterday."[1] During the first full year in operation in Florida in 1958, the brothers' new company, Gulf Guaranty Land and Title Company, recorded more than $9 million in lot sales in Cape Coral.[2] These homesites had primarily been subdivided from an original 1,724-acre tract that had cost the Rosens $678,000.[3] Although these statistics represent a remarkable achievement, the brothers hoped to accelerate their sales operation.

As the number of homesite purchases increased, the Rosens were faced with a dilemma. The growing sales staff under Jack was depleting rapidly the company's inventory of land. Describing the pressure on himself and others within the sales management, Edward Pacelli explained: "You were either pushing for sales or you were pushing for [land] inventory."[4] Because sales were exceeding the number of homesites they could produce, the Rosens constantly were trying to acquire adjacent properties. Eventually, they even had to look beyond the Lee County area for land.

In order to promote their land sales operation, the Rosens chose the corporate name Gulf Guaranty Land and Title Company in 1957. Their advertising of Cape Coral through the mail brought objections from several state governments to the word *Guaranty* in the title. They were concerned that the word *Guaranty* persuaded customers that the company was more financially stable and reliable than it actually was. The name of the company was changed, therefore, on May 8, 1961, to the Gulf American Land Corporation. As the firm diversified, the brothers deleted *Land* from its name in December 1966 to reflect its varied operations that included an airline named Modern Air Transport, restaurants at their various developments, the Congress Inn motel chain, and the Guild Life Insurance Company. The title remained unchanged until the corporation's sale to GAC Corporation of Allentown, Pennsylvania, in 1969.[5]

The purchase of land by Gulf American followed several recognizable patterns. Throughout the company's twelve-year existence, Leonard Rosen handled the majority of property acquisitions. Although Jack was rarely involved directly in the transactions, Leonard always conferred with his brother to see if the tract could be marketed. If Jack did not think the proposed site had sales potential, Leonard dropped it from consideration.[6]

When looking for new project sites, Leonard often took several advisers with him. On the initial property search in Lee County in early 1957, Milton Mendelsohn and Charles Hepner accompanied Rosen on several small-plane flights. Rosen needed Mendelsohn's experience and knowledge of the Florida land development business. Hepner was brought along because of his ability to promote new products. He assisted Rosen on many subsequent purchasing trips, as did banking expert Joseph S. Maddlone and sales manager Edward Pacelli.[7]

While Leonard cleared every land purchase with Jack, he soon discovered the necessity of having his resident engineer, Thomas Weber, with him to analyze new sites. Venturing outside the Cape Coral area, the Rosens bought a 26,000-acre tract in Collier County in 1960.[8] Although the property was low swampland, Leonard assumed that it could be drained by canals as easily as Cape Coral's few marshy areas had been remedied. After examining the land, Weber found a heavy layer of rock under the surface that would likely hamper any dredging operations. He advised Rosen to abandon his plans for the property and try to sell it. Development proceeded regardless. The dredging eventually required up to $1,500 per day just for dynamite to break up the underground rock formations. Subsequently, Rosen included Weber on inspections of any new properties he was considering.[9]

The Rosen brothers devised a definite plan for acquiring land. They looked for property in areas that had warm climates but were yet undeveloped. Florida, for Leonard Rosen, had unlimited potential because he noted that "people wanted to come to the sun." He explained his reasoning further: "The demand is here. With the climate, the casual way of living, the general pioneering spirit, we have a natural market going for us. Everybody wants to come to Florida."[10] Always looking toward future growth, the brothers selected tracts of land that had additional vacant parcels nearby. On his earliest visits in 1957 to the Fort Myers office of realtor William H. Reynolds, Jr., Leonard made clear his instructions. He was interested in purchasing land that was near much larger tracts of property so that he could expand at a later time.[11]

After buying a particular tract, the Rosens ensured the availability of adjacent land by taking options on nearby tracts. This procedure enabled their company to control large areas with a relatively small outlay of cash. Leonard outlined that the optioned parcels in theory would be purchased as needed, a development plan for the land would be drawn up by an engineering firm, and construction would follow shortly. The sale of homesites within that parcel would begin sometime after the purchase of the property.[12]

In reality, the sequence of events for development in Cape Coral was often reversed. As the primary negotiator for the company, Leonard frequently had only a handshake agreement to purchase a parcel of land. The Miami engineering firm of Rader and Associates prepared the development map of the tract, complete with canals, streets, and lot and block numbers. The homesites were placed on sale to the public, and a large number were sold before a written option was taken on the parcel. After several payments on the lots were received by the company, Leonard proceeded with the purchase of the property. The procedure enabled them to buy land with a minimum of bank financing.[13]

Gulf American, as well as other land developers, was able to follow this procedure for several reasons. Customers bought homesites at Cape Coral by signing a contract-for-deed. Essentially, this was an installment agreement that allowed the company to refrain from issuing a warranty deed until payment for the homesite was complete. Without any compulsion to issue deeds, the company was under no pressure to obtain a deed to the property it purchased. This problem was compounded by the lack of stringent state and county regulations on land development. The procedure obviously appealed to Gulf American officials because it required little cash outlay.[14]

The purchase of the first 1,724-acre tract in Lee County by Gulf Guaranty in 1957 demonstrated the complex nature of land acquisition. The property was owned by Granville W. and Cathryn C. Keller of Fort Myers and nine other descendants of Franklin Miles of Miles Laboratories. The Kellers were approached in 1955 by realtor James S. Fortiner about selling their property. Nearly a year later, all of the heirs, including the Kellers, finally agreed to sell. Fortiner in the meantime had opened (in August 1956) the Fortiner-Miller Realty and Development Company in Fort Myers with Naples developer Addison B. Miller. The Kellers, representing their relatives, listed the tract with Fortiner in early autumn 1956.[15]

During the year it took for the Miles heirs to agree to sell, Fortiner had notified E. G. Green of the possible future listing. Green, a land syndicator from Palm Beach, Florida, operated a private organization of Palm Beach millionaires called the Ninety-Nine Club. While frequently gathering to have lunch and play cards, these men were also interested in speculating in Florida land and were willing to base their decisions on Green's recommendations. Fortiner described the Lee County property with its nearly three miles of river frontage to Green and found him enthusiastic about the parcel. By November 1956, a deposit of $42,000 had been delivered to Fortiner from Green, based on a final selling price of $250 per acre. It was unclear whether Green was purchasing the land or if he represented other investors.[16]

The sale was Fortiner's first large acreage transaction, and he wanted to close the contract as soon as possible. In order to expedite the deal, Keller, himself a real estate broker, proceeded with a quiet title suit to clear up any conflicting ownership claims to the land. E. G. Green and his attorneys, however, objected to several aspects of the title, and the closing was delayed for many months. Fortiner suspected that Green was looking for a "flip," a quick profitable resale of the property to a third party before the closing. Later, Green approached Fortiner about cooperating in a resale but was refused because Fortiner needed the commission fee immediately to get his realty business established.[17]

As Green continued to stall the closing, Leonard Rosen began looking in early 1957 for a suitable piece of property in Lee County and initially contacted realtor William H. Reynolds, Jr., for assistance. Rosen had been operating from Harbour Heights, Milton Mendelsohn's development near Punta Gorda. Although he had flown over the area, examining several sites, he was not satisfied with any of them. Meanwhile, Reynolds became aware that Green had contracted with Fortiner to buy the Miles property on Redfish Point. Reynolds had sold land to Green previously and knew that he would be open to a resale offer.[18]

Driving to Harbour Heights with maps and aerial photographs of the tract, Reynolds presented Rosen with the information. He learned that Rosen wanted to locate near Fort Myers because it had much better name recognition than Punta Gorda. He also was looking for land that was well drained and contained few swampy areas. After further discussions and an inspection of the site, Rosen decided to purchase the land. Because the property was already under contract, Reynolds negotiated a second agreement with Green for $375 per acre or 50 percent more than the $250 per acre price of the original contract. The Rosens paid a total of $678,000 for the property, which included a $300,000 mortgage to the Miles heirs and a $165,000 mortgage to Jupiter Properties of West Palm Beach.[19]

The simultaneous closing of both contracts demonstrated the complexity of some of the Rosens' land transactions. Granville Keller set up the meeting on July 23, 1957, in Palm Beach, hiring the law firm of Cook and Cook to oversee the transfer. Besides Keller, Green, Fortiner, Reynolds, and various lawyers, Leonard Rosen was present with his representative, Fort Myers attorney William H. Carmine, Jr. The property was sold from the Miles heirs to Green's Jupiter Properties in the first contract and from Jupiter Properties to Baltimore Investment Associates and the Sandy Investment Company in the second agreement. The Baltimore Investment Associates was a partnership of seventeen Baltimore friends and business acquaintances of the Rosens who supplied the venture capital for the initial purchase of Florida land.[20]

The purchase of the tract was announced in the *Fort Myers News-Press* on July 28, 1957, but the reported size of the parcel has been disputed. The article noted that 2,100 acres were acquired in the deal, but realtor James Fortiner recalled the acreage to be 1,721. Leonard Rosen, in an interview several years later, remembered the initial piece of land covering 1,781 acres. An examination of the deeds for the land, however, showed that the total size of the parcel was 1,724 acres. Another tract of 320 acres adjacent to the original site was purchased later by Leonard and Jack Rosen, on November 19, 1957, from Ogden and Lillian B. Phipps.[21] As construction began on Cape Coral in late 1957, the engineers were working with an initial site that covered 2,044 acres.

One of the primary reasons for Leonard's selection of the Miles property was its proximity to a vast amount of land directly to the west owned by Ogden Phipps.[22] Phipps was one of several grandchildren of Henry Phipps, a childhood friend and business partner of Andrew Carnegie. Henry Phipps helped Carnegie develop Carnegie Steel Corporation and, in the process, accumulated a personal estate worth $75 million. He formed Bessemer Investment Company with his fortune, leaving total control of the wealth to his five children in 1911. As his children and grandchildren received their inheritance, they began several corporations of their own. Grandson Ogden pursued land investments in Florida with a company named Bessemer Properties, using Palm Beach as his winter residence. In addition to his business interests, Ogden Phipps was an avid hunter and sportfisherman who frequently traveled throughout the world on big-game hunting trips.[23]

During April 1955 Phipps purchased 15,109 acres of land in western Lee County from the Matlacha Cattle Company, a cooperative ranching venture headed by Elmore Daniels. Intended by Phipps to be a private hunting preserve, it was the largest of his several land acquisitions in the area. Managed by his resident guide, F. F. "Fingers" O'Bannon, the property extended west from present-day Santa Barbara Boulevard to Matlacha Pass and north to Pine Island Road. In order to have large supplies of quail on the preserve for the hunting pleasure of visitors and guests, Phipps spent approximately $25,000 each year on feed for the wild game birds.[24] Although Phipps had several guest houses constructed on the tract, the land remained undeveloped by the late 1950s.

After the first full year of land sales in 1958, the Rosens were convinced that their corporation would be so successful that additional land was needed. While the brothers began to purchase various tracts immediately north of Cape Coral Parkway, they wanted to acquire the Phipps acreage on their western boundary. As Leonard was trying to work out an agreement with Phipps, two other parties were negotiating on the Rosens' behalf for the same goal.

Understanding the company's need for additional land, Milton Mendelsohn introduced Leonard Rosen to a real estate broker named Robert Henshaw. Rosen hired Henshaw for the specific purpose of acquiring adjacent lands for the Cape Coral development. Later, he was to purchase tracts in other parts of the state for new Gulf American projects. Looking for a way to approach Ogden Phipps about selling his Lee County land, Henshaw became acquainted with Palm Beach resident Lilly Pulitzer, wife of Herbert "Peter" Pulitzer, Jr., and daughter of Ogden Phipps's wife. Although she was married to the grandson of Pulitzer Prize founder Joseph Pulitzer, Lilly had established herself as an entrepreneur by the early 1960s by starting a resort clothing and sportswear company called Lilly Pulitzer. Gaining access to Phipps by means of his daughter, Henshaw was told that Phipps would be receptive to a purchase offer. Notifying Leonard of the prospect, Henshaw believed that the sale would be his.[25]

By mid-1959, however, Henshaw had been eliminated from all discussions about the property by an agreement negotiated directly with Phipps by Leonard Rosen and the William H. Reynolds Company. On September 28, 1959, Gulf Guaranty Land and Title Company signed an option agreement with Phipps for 16,181 acres in western Lee County. The contract called for an initial $50,000 option payment, with the total purchase price of $8.4 million payable over seven years. The price averaged $520 per acre, which William H. Reynolds, Jr., considered substantially higher than the market value for such land. Later, at a party at his hunting lodge located on the Lee County land he had just sold,

Phipps joked with his guests about the Rosens buying the property at such an inflated price.[26]

The exact roles of Rosen and the Reynolds company in the negotiations were unclear, and the contract noted that no broker had negotiated the agreement. Apparently, however, realtors from Reynolds's office had made contact with Phipps through his hunting guide F. F. O'Bannon, who had invited them to one of Phipps's hunting parties. Phipps and Rosen acknowledged the participation of William H. Reynolds, William H. Reynolds, Jr., and Thomas H. Baker and paid them a small commission. Henshaw subsequently resigned because he felt entitled to a commission on the sale also. By 1961, however, he had returned to work for the Rosens and continued with them through the late 1960s.[27]

Several years later, Leonard Rosen and company secretary Joseph Maddlone had a chance meeting with Ogden Phipps on a commercial airline flight. Rosen related to Phipps that Gulf American sales at Cape Coral were above projections and that construction was ahead of schedule. Phipps commented that he never would have sold them the property if he had suspected how successful they would become. Doubting the viability of the Cape Coral development, he had expected to foreclose on the property when the Rosens' project failed.[28]

Besides the Phipps's land, the Rosens attempted to purchase all the tracts adjoining their Cape Coral holdings. With the July 1960 acquisition of 1,150 acres for $561,000 near Pine Island Road and Del Prado Expressway, Gulf Guaranty had expanded Cape Coral's boundaries to include most of the area south of Pine Island Road and between the Caloosahatchee River and Matlacha Pass.[29]

One of the few exceptions was the Four Mile Ranch, owned by Granville Keller. Consisting of approximately 800 acres, the property was located on the Caloosahatchee River north of present-day Everest Parkway at Four Mile Cove. Although the land had been advertised for sale when Leonard Rosen was looking for his first piece of property in the area, a large portion of the ranch was coastal marshland and would be unusable for development without considerable dredging. The property was passed over in favor of the Miles tract at Redfish Point and was subsequently never purchased by the Rosens.[30]

Motivated by the success of Cape Coral, Gulf Guaranty began expanding in 1960 to new development sites outside Lee County. In November 1960 the company purchased 26,000 acres northeast of Naples in Collier County for $128 per acre. Within one month, the property was offered for sale to the public as Golden Gate Estates. By March 1962 Leonard Rosen added 7,447 acres of cutover cypress lands to the project at a cost of $1,368,640 or $184 per acre. The new development nearly doubled in size in August 1962 with the acquisition of 28,101 acres purchased from the J. C. Turner Lumber Company of Perry, Florida, for $189 per acre. Another adjacent 44,600-acre tract was bought in January 1963 from the holdings of Barron G. Collier, Jr., for $7,444,000 or $167 per acre. With these purchases and several other smaller land purchases, Leonard Rosen had increased the area within the expansive boundaries of Golden Gate Estates to 112,000 acres, or 175 square miles.[31]

The concept behind Golden Gate Estates was considerably different from the idea the Rosens had used in their first community. Cape Coral had been designed as a city, complete with residential, industrial, commercial, and recreational areas. Gulf American prepared all property sold from that development so that it was ready to be built on by the customer. The raising of the elevation of all homesites, along with the construction of roads, canals, and recreational facilities, was the responsibility of the company and the cost was included in the sale price of the lots.[32]

The plan behind Golden Gate Estates, on the other hand, promoted the sale of raw acreage in five-acre parcels. The tracts were provided with graded but unpaved access roads and were capable of being subdivided into sixteen quarter-acre homesites by the buyer at some later date. In the future, Gulf American planned two cities within the development, one on the southwest corner of the vast property near Naples called Golden Gate and the other immediately south of the Lee County line near Immokalee called North Golden Gate. As the twin cities grew, the company anticipated a steady increase in the value of all five-acre tracts located between them. The cost of subdividing and preparing each parcel for building was left to the buyer. Customers were shown the investment potential of purchasing such raw acreage. The sales slogan, "Buy by the acre, sell by the lot," expressed the concept.[33]

Market research had indicated to the Rosen brothers that a large unsatisfied demand existed for undeveloped Florida acreage for investment purposes. By limiting Gulf American's capital improvements of the land, the property could be sold at lower prices. Charles Hepner concurred, noting that Golden Gate Estates and later projects helped Gulf American to diversify its product line. This diversification enabled the company's sales operations to reach new, untouched markets and provided Gulf American with a vast inventory of salable land.[34]

The Rosens undoubtedly had other motivations for selling undeveloped acreage at Golden Gate Estates. Edward Pacelli, the head of sales at Golden Gate during the early 1960s, observed that construction costs in Cape Coral had far exceeded Leonard's expectations. In addition, many of the areas of Cape Coral had been sold before streets and canals were started. As construction costs rose, Pacelli believed that Gulf American had not charged enough for the thousands of homesites it had already sold. Although the company continually raised prices on the remaining lots, the increased revenue was still inadequate to offset the higher cost of development.[35]

According to Pacelli, the concept behind Golden Gate Estates was to sell land without promising to develop a completed city. With the substantial investment in construction thus greatly reduced, the project would yield a higher rate of profit. The lucrative return on Golden Gate Estates sales was to counterbalance the unexpected high building costs at Cape Coral.[36]

The accuracy of Pacelli's observation was strengthened by the admission of Gulf American officials that sales at Golden Gate Estates began with raw acreage and not with homesites in the cities of Golden Gate and North Golden Gate. Describing the concept as "revolutionary," the company's management acknowledged that this was a reversal of the conventional sequence of events in development. Reinforcing this idea, stockholders were told that Gulf American planned to begin the sale and construction of individual homesites in Golden Gate "only after acreage sales were well under way."[37]

The Rosen brothers had planned a limited number of canals and unpaved roads in the acreage section of Golden Gate Estates, but serious construction problems soon arose. Although the land had a relatively high elevation above sea level, much of it was under water at various times of the year and needed to be drained. Unlike the easily dredged waterways in Cape Coral, the canals in Golden Gate had to be blasted through a thick layer of rock. Resident engineer Thomas Weber estimated that workers were detonating up to $1,500 of dynamite a day to break up the rock. The frequent explosions caused considerable anxiety for many residents of nearby Naples during 1962 and 1963. With the increasing tensions between the United States and Cuba, some people, according to one observer, found it difficult to ignore the similarity between the blasts and military explosions.[38]

Sales of acreage tracts at Golden Gate Estates were dramatic, with more than 20,000 purchases recorded by the end of 1964. Spanning the huge development by December of that year were twenty-four miles of canals and fifty-three miles of unpaved roads. With the success of the sales program, Gulf American officially dedicated the city of Golden Gate on July 15, 1964, and the first family moved to the community on March 1, 1965. By the end of 1966, Golden Gate boasted 305 residents, along with paved streets, a country club, a golf course, a Congress Inn motel, and an airport with two 4,000-foot runways. Construction crews also had completed more than ninety-five miles of paved and unpaved roads, four bridges, and more than seventy-two miles of canals. The extensive dredging had a noticeable effect because the water table was lowered on the property by approximately 14 feet.[39] Sales of Golden Gate Estates parcels continued strong for the company with 89,000 of the then total 114,406 acres sold to investors by 1966.

As the Collier County development progressed, the Rosens looked for additional sites for new projects. In October 1962, Gulf American took title to the 42,000-acre Kicco Ranch in Polk County for about $100 per acre. The $4.2 million central Florida tract was located directly south of State Road 60 and nineteen miles east of Lake Wales. Before firm plans for the land were made, company officials entertained business guests on the property on hunting trips. In June 1965 Leonard Rosen announced the opening of a third project on the first 7,600 acres of land, calling it River Ranch Acres. He anticipated that the tract would generate sales of approximately $25 million annually and $100 million eventually.[40]

River Ranch Acres continued the Rosens' trend away from endeavors that required the building of a completed community like Cape Coral. According to Leonard, the full cost of development at Cape Coral averaged $1,700 per acre, excluding administrative, overhead, advertising, and promotional expenses. Even at the second project, Golden Gate Estates, engineering and construction expenses had reached $400 per acre. The brothers planned to market River Ranch Acres as raw acreage without any hint of future development by Gulf American. "We're promising nothing, absolutely nothing," said Leonard Rosen. "We're offering what we believe to be an excellent investment at low cost and with the company's good name behind it."[41]

While Rosen portrayed the property as an attractive investment, the major inducement to buyers was the free membership until 1971 in the various clubs and recreational facilities at the site. Located in a grove of large oak trees, the main lodge and motel contained 130 rooms and featured a forty-foot fireplace in the lobby. In addition, Gulf American built a marina that led to the Kissimmee River, horse stables, tennis and shuffleboard courts, archery and shooting ranges, a heated swimming pool, a campground, and a 20,000-acre hunting area. The company operated a barbeque restaurant and a trading post–style store while providing equipment rentals for virtually all outdoor activities. Designed like a western dude ranch, the recreational complex cost Gulf American in excess of $1 million.[42]

Because the company had owned but had not marketed the land for nearly three years, rumors circulated that the Rosens were short of cash and were selling off the 42,000 acres to recoup their $4.2 million investment. Leonard denied that assessment, explaining that River

Ranch Acres gave the company "a third strata of development to work with. Just as a stock broker, we will have several types of land to sell to the customer." Describing it from a buyer's point of view, Rosen called it "a place where the unsophisticated investor can come for an inexpensive vacation and take pleasure in his property." Sales volume grew rapidly and an additional 45,238 acres in Polk County and southwestern Osceola County were purchased in 1966.[43]

The marketing success of River Ranch Acres inspired the Rosens to pursue a second Florida land recreational complex. Locating a large tract adjacent to Golden Gate Estates in Collier County, the brothers purchased the 68,267 acres in February 1966.[44] The property, intersected by the Tamiami Trail (U.S. Highway 41), was twenty-three miles east of Naples and eighty miles west of Miami. The project was named Remuda Ranch Grants, and sales to the public of totally undeveloped land began in May 1966. By the end of August 1967, more than 7,800 parcels had been sold although the recreational facilities were not opened until six months later.[45]

As with River Ranch Acres, Gulf American planned no development of Remuda Ranch Grants into homesites.[46] Instead, the company constructed an expansive recreational complex and gave property owners free privileges at all clubs and facilities at the site until 1976. Located north of the Tamiami Trail, the 100-room Remuda Ranch Grants lodge included a swimming pool, horse stables, kennels for hunting dogs, shooting ranges, a campground, an airstrip, and various equipment rental shops. On the south side of the highway, a marina was dredged that could accommodate 190 outboard boats and 30 large cruisers. A 150-foot-wide canal more than four miles long provided boaters and sportfishermen with direct access to the Ten Thousand Islands area in the Gulf of Mexico. A companion clubhouse at the marina contained 61 rooms for guests and various service shops.[47] The concept of buying a minimum 1.25-acre tract for investment purposes and receiving a free vacation club membership was appealing to many customers.

Remuda Ranch Grants property consisted primarily of flooded swampland with hundreds of scattered hammocks or higher mounds of earth. The only major portion of the tract that was dry for most of the year was a large section of the Fahkahatchee Strand. Prospective buyers were notified in a property report that the land was not suitable for building purposes because it was unsurveyed and without roads, drainage, or other improvements. The company maintained that it had no further plans for development besides the recreational facilities. Salespeople countered this negative information by pointing out that Miami Beach had been nothing but mangrove swamps a century ago.

GULF AMERICAN'S
MAJOR FLORIDA DEVELOPMENTS

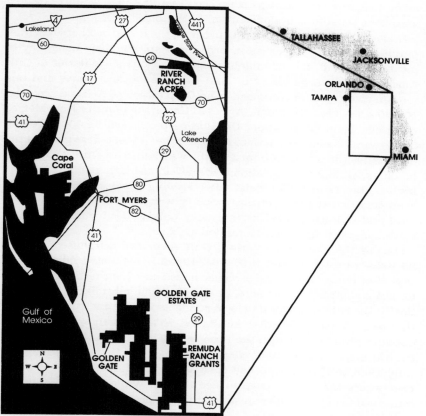

Persuaded by the talk of a profitable investment in such land, buyers contracted for thousands of 1.25-acre parcels at $1,250 each.[48]

Despite Gulf American's claim that it intended no further development of the Remuda Ranch tract, there were indications that Jack Rosen wanted to pursue drainage of the area in order to make the land usable. According to Charles Hepner, who worked closely with Jack Rosen, the company was planning drainage until blocked by the Collier County government. Leonard Rich, a marketing executive with the company, received a personal pledge from Jack Rosen that the swampland at Remuda Ranch would be drained. Rich had refused to participate in any further sales at the property because of its unusable condition. A financial reserve of $7 million was set up within Gulf American for the purpose of draining Remuda. Jack Rosen, along with other company officials, was convinced that drainage would provide a long-term benefit to development in the region.[49]

Besides their four main Florida projects, the Rosen brothers had been purchasing other properties in order to maintain their inventory of inexpensive land. By the middle of 1961, various subsidiaries of Gulf American held large tracts of land in three western states and one foreign country. Gulf American Land Corporation of Arizona acquired 10,680 acres near Kingman, Arizona. Under the name of New Mexico American Land Corporation, the Rosens purchased 51,000 acres located twenty-five miles south of Albuquerque. A 5,680-acre tract on the Green River in Emery County, Utah, was added to Gulf American's holdings, although its isolation made development there doubtful. One high-ranking company official, after viewing the desolate Utah land, suspected that the inexpensive property was never going to be developed and was being held as inventory only to assure investors and stockholders of the Rosens' intention to expand.[50]

During the same time period, Gulf American purchased a huge 95,102-acre tract of land in British Honduras. Located north of the capital of Belize, the acreage was acquired as a long-term investment for about eight dollars per acre. Held under their subsidiary of Colgerry Realty, the land was leased to local residents who extracted chicle from the trees. Chicle, a latexlike substance, is used in the production of chewing gum.[51] Although the Rosens anticipated growth in the area, the property remained undeveloped.

By 1965 Gulf American had once again begun acquiring property near where they had started in Lee County. While the company had continued to buy various parcels near Cape Coral in the western part of the county, attention now was focused on the vast undeveloped ranch land in eastern Lee County. During early October 1965, Gulf American purchased a 5,000-acre tract and a 2,560-acre tract for a total of $991,000. Both parcels were located just south of Immokalee Road and within a few miles of Lehigh Acres. By January 1, 1967, Gulf American had purchased more than 16,000 acres in the area and was holding it in the name of its subsidiary, Lee Investment Company. Although Lee Investment president William Carmine said that Gulf American had no immediate plans for the property, most observers believed that a new development was likely because of the company's past record in Florida.[52]

One observer was George Sanders, a Fort Myers investor and owner of Edison Mall, the largest shopping center in Lee County. In mid-January 1967 Sanders announced that he had purchased 9,422 acres on Immokalee Road, across from the western extremity of Lehigh Acres. The $1,839,000 property also adjoined acreage on the east that belonged to Gulf American. Strategically located, much of the Sanders tract lay between Gulf American's property and the city of Fort Myers. Sanders's only comments were: "It was purchased only as an investment and there are no plans. The land is strategically located for possible major highways in development of the county."[53]

During 1965 the Rosens began to study the feasibility of a land sales project in another state. Influenced by the rapid economic growth and heavy tourist traffic in Arizona, the brothers entered into a $3.4 million contract in early 1966 to purchase the picturesque Baca Float Ranch, which was located approximately five miles north of Nogales. The sale was not completed, however, until July 1967. Comprising 55,000 acres of grazing land and citrus groves, the property was watered by the Santa Cruz River. Gulf American planners took particular note of the river, naming the new project Rio Rico, which means "rich river."[54]

The overall concept for the Rosens' fifth major development was significantly different from that for the previous two projects. While River Ranch Acres and Remuda Ranch Grants were essentially raw acreage sales operations, the master plan for Rio Rico called for four fully developed communities with an eventual total population of 30,000. These urban centers were designed to have paved streets, parks, churches, community centers, and a golf course. Gulf American also budgeted $2 million for the construction of a recreational complex to include a 100-room motel, recreational halls, a swimming pool, four tennis courts, shooting ranges, stables, a rodeo arena, and campgrounds.[55]

While the Rosens planned for the four communities to become fully developed cities like Cape Coral, they incorporated several aspects of their successful acreage sales at River Ranch Acres into the project. In addition to offering finished urban homesites, Gulf American subdivided more distant areas into ranchettes of five acres and provided only unpaved roads for access. The company also sold totally undeveloped land to buyers without any promise of future improvements by the corporation. In summary, the concepts of selling completely developed homesites and of selling raw acreage were combined in this project. In the succeeding decade, the Rosen brothers anticipated spending a total of $30 million to finish Rio Rico.[56]

Problems arose quickly, however, with the new project. Leonard Rosen had originally sent Milton Mendelsohn to Arizona to oversee the completion of a land survey on the Baca Float Ranch. As a consultant to the Rosens, Mendelsohn had made many visits to the site in the first half of 1967, granting news interviews on Rio Rico and setting up meetings between Gulf American officials, the Santa Cruz County Board of Supervisors, and Arizona state officials. Apparently Mendelsohn had presented himself to Arizona officials as the chief representative for Gulf American and the Rio Rico project without the knowledge or consent of Leonard Rosen. When a series of articles in the *Arizona Republic* highlighted Mendelsohn's record of business troubles and bankruptcies, Rosen officially removed him from the project by stating: "He had no authority on the project. . . . He is a consultant. . . . He is no longer connected with Rio Rico."[57]

Rosen also discovered that the Sam R. Kaufman Real Estate, Investment, and Mortgage Company of Tucson had issued a seven-page press release about Rio Rico in early 1967, describing itself as the "exclusive franchise broker" for the project. At the time, the Kaufman firm exhibited blueprints of the first stage and discussed present and future plans for the development. Rosen reprimanded the firm strongly by phone and mail and stated that "Kaufman is not our broker at this moment, nor do I anticipate that he will be our broker in the future."[58] Inasmuch as Gulf American had always handled its own sales, and the Kaufman firm had been led to believe otherwise, indications pointed to Mendelsohn as the source of the confusion.

With Mendelsohn's ouster, Leonard Rosen appointed Ronald S. Sandler, an assistant secretary for Gulf American, to oversee Rio Rico's development. Sandler, a Baltimore attorney and brother of Solomon Sandler, administered the overall operation with Thomas Weber directing construction through the Fort Myers Construction Company.[59] By spring 1968 Weber had completed the main administrative and sales building and had finished a bridge over the Santa Cruz River. Land sales commenced in mid-1968 with optimistic local support.[60] The entire project, however, was stunted by allegations of sales irregularities by Gulf American in Florida and by the sale of the company to GAC Corporation in early 1969.

Two smaller projects started by Gulf American were both located in central Florida. Barefoot Bay, a 5,200-unit mobile home park, was situated on 1,100 acres of land sixteen miles south of Melbourne. The company purchased the property from John D. MacArthur of Bankers Life and Casualty Company in late 1967, in an even trade for Gulf American's Congress Inn motel chain. The fourteen motels, including one in Cape Coral and one in Golden Gate, were scattered throughout the United States. In the $2.8 million deal, Gulf American acquired a bankrupt and partially developed retirement village formerly owned by Allstate Development Corporation. Allstate went bankrupt as it promoted Rocket City, a project located between Cocoa Beach and Orlando, and the property reverted to MacArthur. Leonard Rosen purchased the property for future development but in 1967 had no immediate plans to build on it.[61]

Although buildings on the property were dilapidated and largely deserted, Rosen promised that future development would take place: "I'll guarantee you it won't be a ghost town after we get through with it. We intend to make it a model community with swimming pools, tennis courts, and a golf course."[62] Gulf American began planning Barefoot Bay, but development and sales were not initiated until September 1969, several months after Gulf American's sale to GAC Corporation. According to Thomas Weber, the project engineer, initial sales were slow, but eventually all of the several thousand spaces were sold.[63]

The second community, Poinciana Park, comprised 47,300 acres of ranch land in Osceola and Polk counties. The Rosens had envisioned rapid growth for the property during the 1970s because of its proximity to Walt Disney World and Orlando. Located ten miles south of Kissimmee, Poinciana Park was designed with radiating streets from a central core city. The original plan called for 25,900 acres to be developed, while 21,400 were to be left in their natural state. The Rosens' difficulties with the Florida Land Sales Board hampered their efforts with the proposed community, and by early 1969 the project was still in the planning stages. GAC Corporation, after its purchase of Gulf American, actively pursued the development of Poinciana Park, with construction and sales beginning in November 1971.[64]

By the end of 1967, Gulf American properties covered a total of 589,738 acres in four states and one Central American country. Included in this sum were 182,872 acres in the various tracts that had already been sold as homesites and acreage. Of the total holdings, 372,276 acres were located in Florida, 65,680 acres in Arizona, 51,000 acres in New Mexico, 5,680 acres in Utah, and 95,102 acres in British Honduras. Based on their purchase prices, the lands represented an investment of $68 million by Gulf American. In order to develop the active properties, the company's construction force under Thomas Weber had risen to a peak of approximately 1,200 workers by the mid-1960s.[65]

The land acquisitions of Gulf American demonstrated two conclusions about the company. Primarily, the Rosen brothers intended to enlarge the corporation's sales operations and they needed vast amounts of inexpensive land with which to do it. After their agents had located large tracts of property, the brothers used their combative style of negotiating in order to buy the land at bargain prices. Secondly, the sales operation of Gulf American was consuming enormous volumes of land, and new projects had to be opened to supply the marketing program the Rosens had constructed. With these two forces working together, Gulf American Land Corporation emerged during the 1960s as one of the largest property owners of any development company in the country.[66]

5

Selling Florida Land

From the beginning of the Gulf American Corporation, land sales were the central focus of nearly every operation within the company. The Rosen brothers believed that land and home ownership were basic drives common to all levels of society. Leonard emphasized this belief by stating, "There is only one thing to which we can attach ourselves with security of mind and that is our home on our own tract of land."[1] As interest in Florida increased throughout the United States, the brothers designed their sales efforts to meet the rising demand for Florida real estate.

The emphasis on sales dominated corporate life at Gulf American from its first day until its last in 1969. Sales managers and salespeople felt constant pressure to increase their volume. Whenever a question of direction arose within the company, the marketing of land was given top priority. Leonard Rosen noted the brothers' singleness of purpose in 1964: "We are one of the most sales-minded firms in this business—everything we do is directed toward the establishment of a solid volume of sales which will hold over the long term."[2]

Total revenues for Gulf American increased dramatically from a mid-1958 volume of $5,213,659 to a peak of $143,862,440 in mid-1966 (table 1). Over 90 percent of the total revenue came from land sales, with houses and other sources accounting for the remainder. The steady rise in sales was temporarily halted by public apprehension during the Cuban missile crisis of October/November 1962. As cancellations of the old and new con-

Table 1 Sales Volume and Earnings for Gulf American Corporation

Year Ending	Sales Volume	Total Earnings	Earnings/Share
8/31/58	$5,213,659	$400,053	$.06
8/31/59	12,830,949	1,380,736	.18
8/31/60	25,948,614	3,358,511	.42
8/31/61	39,294,721	6,154,319	.72
8/31/62	73,683,758	10,838,259	1.18
8/31/63	69,676,278	6,565,961	.71
8/31/64	94,363,985	10,595,577	1.14
8/31/65	111,201,743	13,442,257	1.43
8/31/66	143,862,440	22,076,933	2.31
8/31/67	131,381,196	16,808,240	1.75
8/31/68	95,700,000	(1,600,000)	—

Sources: Gulf American Land Corporation, Annual Report, 1963, 1; *Wall Street Journal,* November 14, 1963, October 12, 1965, October 18, 1966, October 17, 1967, October 23, 1968.

tracts rose sharply, Leonard Rosen assessed the situation: "This affected us more than moderately."[3]

Gulf American's prominence in the Florida land sales market was more apparent when compared with its competitors. General Development Corporation was already well established by the time the Rosens began operations in Cape Coral in January 1958, having a total of $28.1 million in sales in the previous two years. By the end of 1961, General Development had increased its annual revenue to $68.4 million while Gulf American recorded $39.3 million for the same period. Although both firms received income from lot sales, a larger part of General Development's revenue (28 percent) came from housing sales, while less than 10 percent of Gulf American's income came from that source. This difference can be explained by viewing the marketing background of the Rosen brothers as contrasted to the construction experience of General Development's Frank, Elliott, and Robert Mackle.[4]

The relative positions of both of these corporate giants had switched dramatically by the end of 1965, with Gulf American reporting sales of $111,201,743 and General Development recording $29.4 million. Aggressive sales strategies by the Rosens accounted for much of Gulf American's gain. General Development's weakened position was partially the result of the departure of the Mackle brothers from the company in 1962. They set up a new operation called Deltona Corporation, which recorded annual sales of $15,604,000 by the end of 1965. Regardless of the competition, Gulf American had become the largest land sales development company in Florida and one of the most profitable in the United States.[5]

The reasons for Gulf American's success were varied but could be traced to two important factors. While the Rosen brothers had extensive experience in marketing, they were novices in the field of land development. In order to sell land, they concluded that experimentation was going to be essential. Jack Rosen described the sales operation as a laboratory, and he realized that the cost of good research was often expensive. He was willing to hear any new idea from anyone and willing to try it in the field. Once a new concept proved successful, however, Jack concentrated on making it cost effective.[6]

While the Rosens were creative, they were constantly reviewing any sales innovations of their competitors. Pride did not prevent them from taking an idea that worked for General Development Corporation, improving on it, and bringing it into their operation. According to Kenneth Schwartz, the brothers' insatiable appetite to learn and try out new ideas was an important factor in their success. Their strong desire to be the largest company in their industry required constant research and fine-tuning of the sales methods.[7]

Another factor in the success of the Gulf American sales program was the marketing genius of Jack Rosen. While both brothers were effective salesmen, Jack dominated the sales division, which included marketing and advertising. Leonard's expertise lay in his ability to arrange financing for the company's developments such as Cape Coral and Golden Gate Estates. He also concentrated on the acquisition of tracts of land for the new projects. Jack, on the other hand, was constantly focusing on new ways to improve the efficiency of the sales staff. Leonard summed up most employees' view of Jack by describing him as "a great, great thinker and motivator."[8]

Personal conflict between Jack and Leonard had an important impact on the sales operation as well as the company's entire structure. The result of this conflict was that Jack directed the sales and marketing from Baltimore throughout most of the corporation's history while Leonard ran the remainder of the operations from his Miami office. Jack was assisted in Baltimore by Charles Hepner.[9]

Jack's unilateral rivalry with Leonard left the corporation split into two spheres of authority until it was sold to GAC Corporation in 1969. While Hepner handled the creative side of sales, the administrative operations were directed by Robert P. Carroll. Leonard oversaw the other corporate divisions in Miami, including administration, development, and financing. Although there was considerable mixing of responsibilities and much communication between the two spheres, most employees felt an allegiance to one brother over the other, depending on the division in which they worked. The separation into different spheres was further evidenced by Leonard's rule that any high-level employee hired to work in Florida, including sales executives, had to be first interviewed by him.[10]

The differing abilities of the two brothers contributed further to the split. Leonard was the initiator in most of the Rosens' ventures, conceptualizing and building the new schemes from the beginning. Before Gulf American, Leonard had lost interest in Charles Antell, once it was operating smoothly, and he turned over its management to Jack. The older Rosen saw himself as a builder of new ventures, and he had little desire for administrative duties. With any project, Leonard acknowledged that "the anticipation is greater than the actual fulfillment."[11] For this reason, rapid expansion was more important to Leonard than to Jack.

Jack, on the other hand, focused on the people within Gulf American, particularly the salespeople. He believed that it was more important to find the right person for a task than to originate a new sales idea. Although a particular plan had failed several times previously, Jack would encourage sales managers to pursue it again if the right person for the job had been found. To emphasize the point, he prepared motivational signs for the offices of sales managers that read, "It's The Man."[12] As he emphasized the employee over the ideas, he prided himself on bringing out the best in his employees.

Jack also took great satisfaction in his ability to make assets of people whom few other executives would consider using. When Gulf Guaranty Land and Title Company was formed, he brought with him from Charles Antell a number of former carnival pitchmen such as Lester Morris and Harry Dempsey. While some of these men even had criminal records, Jack prided himself on his ability to control them. Instinctively, he seemed to know when to reprimand and when to encourage in order to bring out their talents. Jack saw himself as a benefactor who used his wealth to help others improve themselves. His efforts inspired intense loyalty from his associates.[13]

The original plan for selling homesites at Cape Coral in January 1958 focused heavily on mail-order sales. The Rosens had perfected this method with cosmetics at Charles Antell and had passed $12 million in annual sales by the mid-1950s.[14] Researching Florida land development companies, the brothers discovered that mail-order sales of homesites were already successful for Lehigh Acres and General Development Corporation. The Mackle brothers of General Development had placed a test offer in several national publications in 1955. Advertising a house-and-lot package for $4,950 in its Pompano Beach Highlands project, the company received 18,000 replies, 80 percent indicating interest in buying lots for use in the future.[15] Realizing the potential, the Rosens believed that they could improve even further on the technique.

The first mail-order department was set up in January 1959, in several back rooms of the Gulf Guaranty offices in North Fort Myers, directed by Gwen McGinn. The list of prospects grew within one year to more than 200,000 names. The huge number of responses to the mailings and advertisements overwhelmed the small staff. Many of the early employees were surprised at the success. Bea Cleaves, a former Fort Myers realtor who worked as secretary for Connie Mack, Jr., was astounded that hundreds of the inquiries were turning into definite orders. Having sold Florida real estate for many years, she found it difficult to believe that people were willing to buy land without first seeing it.[16]

The Rosens also hired a sales staff to handle visitors who came to Cape Coral. Under the direction of Kenneth Schwartz, salespeople, such as John Warren and Mary Anderson Harborn, guided prospects in their own automobiles down Del Prado Expressway to Cape Coral. Schwartz enlarged the sales staff in Cape Coral in the early years to an average of thirty to fifty people.[17] Within a short time, however, the sales headquarters was transferred to Baltimore under the direction of Jack Rosen and the mail-order operations were moved to Miami. Before the sale of Charles Antell, Jack had been occupied primarily with the cosmetics business while Leonard began the Cape Coral project. With Jack's full-time involvement in land sales, the corporation's sales structure rapidly evolved and grew.

Operating from his larger offices now at 25 West Charles Street in Baltimore, Jack developed three major off-site sales divisions and was a strong influence in a fourth area. The first three branches of the company's marketing effort included the national independent brokers, the Gulf American "owned-and-operated" sales offices, and the international sales offices. Combined volume from these divisions accounted for an estimated 70 to 80 percent of all sales. At Gulf American's peak in 1966, the independent brokers and the "owned-and-operated" offices numbered 218 nationwide and required the efforts of a majority of Gulf American's 4,160 employees.[18]

Sales at offices within Florida and at the properties themselves made up the balance of sales. These operations were considered a separate division because they were directed by Leonard, although Jack wielded considerable influence. The exact boundaries of the two brothers' authority in Florida was unclear, but the state was generally considered by employees to be Leonard's domain.[19]

The effort to recruit independent brokers throughout the United

States was begun shortly after the opening of Cape Coral. Originally, Edward Pacelli was sent from Cape Coral to enlist independent real estate brokers in major and mid-sized cities to sell Cape Coral property. Pacelli had been a real estate agent with the William H. Reynolds Company in Fort Myers but was hired by Leonard to bolster the sales force in Cape Coral. On his three- to four-week trips throughout the United States, Pacelli placed advertisements in newspapers describing the experimental sales plan to brokers. Although large numbers of offices were eager to speak with him and to get a franchise from Gulf American, the attrition rate was high because many brokers lacked the effort or knowledge to make the sales. To ensure a better success rate, Pacelli and others developed a plan whereby real estate agencies provided a Florida theme in their offices complete with palm trees and beach murals. The brokers were also required to visit Cape Coral and other later properties in order to be franchised. Because the recruitment of a chain of national brokers was a relatively new concept, Pacelli, and later recruiters such as Daniel L. Coel, experimented with various formats.[20]

During the late 1950s, the system of independent brokers began in New York, expanding next into the New England states and then into the midwestern states. Pacelli concentrated on large metropolitan areas, interviewing the directors of several real estate firms before selecting one to represent Gulf American. Some cities, however, had more than one office. Detroit, for example, had three independent brokers with distinct geographical areas in addition to a company-owned office. A broker franchised by Gulf American was paid by commissions of approximately 1 percent of the selling price of the lots. In addition, Gulf American provided some funds for advertising and promotions. Describing Pacelli's successful efforts during those early years, Kenneth Schwartz commented that wherever Pacelli went recruiting brokers, volume sales soon followed.[21]

The most successful brokerage firm for Gulf American was Comet-Marks in Ohio. Headed by a businessman named Louis S. Rosen, the company turned in sales estimated between $20 million and $30 million in peak years. In Chicago a broker named Herman Harris built a huge volume of Gulf American land sales because of his aggressive and talented sales force. His firm recorded an estimated $20 million in annual sales at its zenith.[22] Although agencies were constantly leaving the program and others were joining, the national chain of independent brokers contributed substantially to Gulf American's total volume.

With the success of the independent brokerage program, the Rosens wanted to expand sales operations even faster. In order to accomplish this expansion, new sales ideas needed to be tested on a nationwide scale. Jack Rosen discovered that few independent brokers were enthusiastic about funding and testing new marketing ideas. Because constant experimentation with sales innovations was critical to the Rosens, they began opening sales offices that were wholly owned and operated by the corporation.[23]

These company-owned real estate agencies, nicknamed "O-and-Os" by employees, often operated in the same city as franchised independent brokers. Gulf American assigned separate areas within a metropolitan region to individual offices in order to avoid conflicts. In a typical O-and-O setting, Gulf American hired a sales manager who recruited a sales staff. The offices were completely funded by the company and administered directly from Baltimore by Charles Hepner and Ronald D. Nitzberg. Located throughout the country, these Gulf American offices were assisted by traveling groups of salespeople during special promotions.[24]

The third major sales division in Gulf American began when the company opened its first European office in Frankfurt, West Germany, in 1963. The sales effort was directed at vacationing American tourists and U.S. military personnel stationed in Western Europe. International sales were directed by Seymour Reis, who formerly had helped to direct sales in Florida for the company. Reis's responsibilities had previously focused on opening sales offices throughout Florida from which prospective buyers were brought to Cape Coral and Golden Gate Estates. Because of Reis's competence and energy, the European offices expanded rapidly. He was succeeded in international sales by Peter Luss.[25]

Jack Rosen had insisted on pursuing the European market, and the offices the company had in London, Rome, Frankfurt, and other major cities were a source of great pride for him. In order to get the program started quickly, he sent Bernice Freiberg from the Baltimore office to West Germany to select a public relations firm and an advertising agency for the company. She brought the current sales literature with her for translation because Jack hoped that sales would be expanded to Europeans as well as Americans.[26]

Gulf American sales methods in Rome appeared typical of most of its European offices. Hiring good-looking young women to attract customers, the company invited American tourists to take advantage of a free tour of the city. The prospects were bused to sights not usually seen on standard tours and then were treated to a substantial meal at the Hilton Hotel in a beautifully decorated private hall, where a sales presentation was made with the showing of films on Cape Coral and Florida. Although many of the salespeople could hardly speak English, closings of sales averaged between 30 and 40 percent of those present. The company wanted to show the prospective buyers a good time in luxurious surroundings and many salespeople attributed their success to that special emphasis.[27]

The fourth major division in the Gulf American sales program represented more of a geographical difference than a contrast in methods. All sales at the Florida properties and at the O-and-O offices within the state were considered generally separate from national marketing and were administered by Leonard Rosen. Advertising and promotions were handled locally unless a manager asked the Baltimore office for assistance. Jack Rosen and Charles Hepner, however, traveled weekly to the Miami office to settle sales matters, demonstrating that Leonard's control was far from complete in the state. Jack felt little influence from Leonard in his management of national sales, but he had to deal with his brother on sales issues within Florida.[28]

Under the direction at various times of Kenneth Schwartz, Edward Pacelli, and Seymour Reis, the Florida sales division was heavily influenced by the refund policy of Gulf American. Because many of the early sales appeals occurred away from the properties or through the mail, the company allowed customers who signed a contract up to six months to travel to Cape Coral to inspect their homesite. If they found the lot unsuitable, they were given the choice of exchanging the value invested in their lot for the same amount in another homesite or of receiving a refund of their money. A buyer who wanted a refund after the six-month period was refused unless a particular personal hardship was demonstrated. A customer who stopped payments on a homesite forfeited the land and the amount already paid. Gulf American subsequently resold those homesites.[29]

The problem with this policy was that the customer cancellation rate exceeded Gulf American's expectations. The company improved the situation by taking prospects from the popular vacation centers in Florida directly to the properties. In the late 1950s, salespeople used their own vehicles and typically brought two couples from Florida's east coast to Cape Coral. Other sales representatives, who owned small Cessna aircraft, flew potential customers to the property.[30] People who signed contracts at Cape Coral who had seen the development were less likely to cancel.

Gulf American expanded the program by enlisting hundreds of workers who invited tourists to take a free trip to Cape Coral or Golden Gate. These canvassers were called outside public consultants, or "OPCs," by the company. Headed in Florida by Joseph Klein, the OPCs were placed at various attractions throughout the state such as Cypress Gardens at Winter Haven and Parrot Jungle and Monkey Jungle in Miami. They boldly approached tourists, offering premiums or gifts to the prospects if they would visit one of the sites. In a typical solicitation in Miami, tourists were offered a free boat tour of Miami if they would listen to a presentation about the "City of Tomorrow," Cape Coral. At the end of the tour, the boat docked at the office of World Wide Realty Corporation, which was Gulf American's agent in Miami. Some OPCs attempted to get contracts signed at that time, while others concentrated on lining up customers for a bus or plane trip to the properties. The program experimented constantly with new gimmicks, growing rapidly until full-size buses and DC-3 aircraft were needed. The aggressiveness of the program was readily admitted by the company and, in the opinion of some company officials, may have contributed to later difficulties with state regulators. Company secretary Joseph Maddlone noted that Gulf American differed from most real estate operations because it did not sit back behind a sales counter but went in search of customers.[31]

With the goal of ever-increasing sales volume, Jack Rosen understood the need for communication throughout all levels of the organization. He believed that a leader could not force people to do various tasks but could only persuade them. Therefore, Jack required weekly sessions with all department heads, and attendance averaged forty-five people. With Leonard Rich, the director of sales promotion, in charge, the meetings served to improve communication within the corporation and to promote the brainstorming of new sales ideas.[32]

Jack rarely decided the benefit of any idea without exploring the concept with several other people. He often began by discussing it at length with the department head who had the most expertise on the subject. If the idea held promise in Jack's mind, he met in a large conference room on the second floor of the Baltimore office with small groups of people, including Charles Hepner, to discuss it further. By the time Jack presented the new concept to a large meeting of department heads, he was convinced that it was worth developing.[33]

Although Jack encouraged anyone in the corporation to submit new ideas, he made the final decision concerning a proposed scheme. In 1961 the concept of time sharing was discussed at length for Gulf American's Congress Inn motels. Under the plan, the company would presell ten years of vacations that the buyer could use in any one of the Congress Inn's nationwide locations. Despite the novelty of time sharing, Jack did not like the idea and it was shortly abandoned.[34]

Both Jack and Leonard worked to make themselves personally accessible to feedback from their employees. Many workers stressed that the organizational lines of Gulf American were not as rigid as most large corporations and that the Rosens were willing to listen to employees' ideas and complaints. As much as Jack Rosen liked people, a one-on-one meeting with him in his Baltimore office was an intimidating experience. Jack was a handsome man whose dazzling white teeth enhanced his powerful personality. He reinforced this dominating perception of himself by having the legs of all chairs in his office shortened while his chair and desk were elevated so that visitors had to look up to maintain eye contact.[35]

New sales concepts approved by Jack were tested in the field as rapidly as possible. Usually the promotions were incorporated immediately at the various property sites or were used in telephone sales in order to get the fastest consumer reaction. Although the innovations were only being tested, Gulf American management presented them to the salespeople as definite new programs to be fully implemented. The plans were later evaluated on the basis of actual results from field operations.[36]

When new programs were initiated, Jack often presented a subordinate with a budget and authorization to start it. He and Leonard were not interested in the details but rather in formulating the overall concepts. Jack preferred to delegate the administration of various new promotions to employees, who kept him informed as to their progress. Because he emphasized finding the right person for the task, he spent much of his time recruiting new employees for the firm.[37]

In addition to policy decisions, the Baltimore office coordinated the majority of advertising for the company. Gulf American used a variety of media to publicize its sales efforts, including television, radio, newspapers, magazines, fairs, and trade shows. The primary purpose of the advertising was to present to the public an image of stability for the company. The Rosens also wanted people to write or telephone so that Gulf American could get leads for later follow-up by salespeople.[38]

The Rosens wanted much of the advertising to promote the benefits of living in Florida. Many of the television commercials presented the pleasures and allure of Florida instead of trying just to sell a homesite. This theme was seen in many of the Gulf American promotions of its properties. One-minute spots on the "Today Show" with Dave Garroway and the "Tonight Show" presented viewers with the tropical beauty of Florida and encouraged them to write to the network for a free copy of the *Florida Opportunity Digest.* The thirty-one-page booklet listed significant facts about the growth potential of Florida in general and the Gulf Coast of Florida in particular. In addition, the benefits of living in Cape Coral were clearly noted in print and in color pictures in the publication.[39]

The overall advertising program for the corporation was supervised by Charles Hepner. He had originally been hired by the Rosens to produce television commercials for Charles Antell products. With his extensive film and advertising background, Hepner also completed several sales and training films for Gulf American. When Hepner moved into sales supervision in the early 1960s, he hired William Baron to oversee film production out of his New York City office.[40]

Hepner was considered a key individual in the sales organization for several reasons. First, his creativity and advertising expertise were well known throughout the corporation. In addition, he helped to organize various programs and give them solid foundations. For example, he and Leonard Rich developed the commissions structure for all sales-people. This program was critical because the commissions provided a primary regulation of the actions and motivations of the sales staff. Hepner was also important because he was one of a small number of people who were able to work closely with Jack Rosen for extended periods of time without losing patience. Jack's tendency to talk about an issue for hours left many associates exasperated.[41]

In order to produce the mass of brochures and other promotional materials, the Rosens enlarged their house advertising firm, the Paul Venze Agency, which was located in New York City. Under the direction of the Rosens' cousin Paul Venze and agency vice-president Bernice Freiberg, the operation employed between thirty and forty writers and artists. In addition, Jack constantly kept various Madison Avenue agencies under contract to do things that he felt required more expertise than the Paul Venze Agency had. A primary task of these companies was the promotion of Gulf American's image among the public and the business community, particularly after bad publicity concerning sales irregularities began to surface in the mid-1960s. Many of these public relations firms refused to take the job, however, because they claimed that Gulf American's reputation was already so poor in Florida.[42]

Billboard signs were used in Florida until the early 1960s to direct tourists to Gulf American properties, particularly Cape Coral. At the time, most visitors to the state vacationed along the east coast and knew little of Florida's Gulf coast. Jack decided that he wanted billboards placed on every major road in the state. Bernice Freiberg, representing Gulf American, traveled from Jacksonville throughout Florida, negotiating sign contracts in every major city. Her trip took more than a week, and hundreds of billboards were rented. Most of the advertisements pictured an aerial view of Cape Coral, describing it as the "Waterfront Wonderland" because of the multitude of canals. The signs also provided the readers with directions and mileage to the site.[43]

Some advertising was generated in Florida instead of Baltimore because Florida sales were considered more under Leonard's control than Jack's. For example, St. Petersburg admen Charles Roberts and Arthur Jacobson were hired to design billboard signs for the opening of sales at Golden Gate Estates in late 1960. In order to get travelers to venture to the Naples area on Florida's Gulf coast, they needed a clever new idea.

They came up with a sign that showed the back side of a gorgeous woman with a magnificent body reclining in the sun in her bathing suit. The caption teasingly proclaimed, "See the other side of Florida!" Dozens of the successful billboards were placed over the entire state.[44]

One of the most effective advertising schemes for Gulf American involved participation in the 1964 New York World's Fair. While company representatives previously had been setting up booths at state fairs and trade shows across the country, the Rosens decided to saturate the New York World's Fair by placing five separate exhibits in different buildings throughout the fairgrounds. Presentations included films about Gulf American and Cape Coral, descriptions of Gulf American housing, and a complimentary travel center.[45]

To bolster these efforts, the company placed sales exhibits in the lobbies of New York–area hotels, shuttling guests to Gulf American hospitality parties. Free trips to Florida, along with other prizes, were given away to visitors. Most of these promotions were designed to gather names and addresses of future sales prospects. Teams, consisting typically of several men with a pretty young woman, signed up visitors for a free copy of the *Florida Opportunity Digest*. The sales leads garnered by this and other promotions totaled in the millions.[46]

Gulf American developed several techniques for the selling of its Florida homesites away from Cape Coral and the other property locations. The various off-site sales programs accounted for 65 to 75 percent of all sales by the company.[47] Compilation of the massive lists of prospective buyers was followed up by home visits from salespeople associated with the company's nationwide chain of owned-and-operated offices. Called "home-sits" by company personnel, these presentations involved a single salesperson making an appointment to explain the benefits of owning Cape Coral property and attempting to close a sale. Using Philadelphia as a test site in the late 1950s, Jack Rosen sent a team consisting of Bernard Musket, a dynamic Florida land salesman, Bernice Freiberg, and others to experiment with home-sits. Although the program was expanded to other cities, the best salespeople closed deals in only one out of five situations and as many as half of those who signed agreements eventually cancelled.[48]

Looking for a more efficient sales method, the Baltimore staff began experimenting with free cocktail parties. After evaluating the high cost of such gatherings, home-sit supervisor Lester Morris suggested that a chicken dinner could be provided for about the same price. The resulting dinner party technique proved much more effective than the home-sit and was believed by Gulf American officials to be the first of its kind in the industry. Morris, an excellent speaker who had been a carnival pitchman before working for the Rosens, was selected to head the program.[49]

The dinner party became the primary sales tool for Gulf American. Through trial and error, the optimum size for the dinner was determined to be twenty to thirty couples, with one salesperson assigned to each pair. A husband and wife were considered a prospective buying unit, and most salespeople avoided talking seriously with a person whose spouse was not present. Often the company brought in a local sports star or celebrity to draw more public interest. Held in posh restaurants, the free meals cost the company about four dollars per person as compared to three dollars for a cocktail party. Monroe J. Klein, assistant director of Gulf American's New York office, was convinced of the program's value by the mid-1960s: "It's the best vehicle to display our product to the greatest number of people in the fastest possible time at the lowest practical cost."[50]

The staffing for a dinner party came from two sources. Most of the salespeople present were connected with the branch sponsoring the presentation, whether it was an owned-and-operated office or an independent broker. Five company-paid teams of salespeople and professional pitchmen traveled through the United States, assisting local offices with this program. One roving team, for example, had Charles Cavanagh leading a group that was on the road between thirty and forty-five days at a time, driving from Baltimore to Seattle and back again on a typical trip. Cavanagh had come from a general sales background and was hired by Jack Rosen so that Rosen could teach him all aspects of Gulf American sales. His roving team consisted of ten to fifteen young men who carried in their vehicles maps, contracts, displays, films, and even liquor in case a presentation was held in a dry state or county. Making a presentation every night, Cavanagh's team returned with more than $1 million in sales from a single trip.[51]

Gulf American used its vast lists of prospective buyers, categorized by geographical area and zip code, to select couples for a dinner party. Charles Hepner wanted an invitation sent out that would give the company a greater appearance of legitimacy. Because the 400th anniversary of Florida's settlement (September 1565) was approaching, Leonard Rich, director of sales promotion, designed an invitation that closely resembled the commemorative anniversary seal released by the state of Florida. Included in the mailing was a letter from Connie Mack, Jr., stating that a friend had recommended the recipient for a free dinner. The invitation, called the "Conquistador," tripled responses and was broadly imitated in the land development industry.[52]

The success of the Gulf American dinner program motivated other land sales companies to develop their own dinner or cocktail party formats. General Development Corporation officials claimed that they sold a home or homesite to one of every ten couples they served. Although

Deltona Corporation officials stated that no one got drunk at their cocktail parties, their ratio of sales to attendance was one to five. In 1965 that company spent $72,000 on cocktail sales presentations and magazine advertisements in New York alone and generated more than $1 million in sales from them.[53] Despite increasing public skepticism during the 1960s, the dinner party technique continued as the most effective sales method for Gulf American as well as for other companies.

The dinner party program was dependent on the company's ability to generate lists of prospective buyers. Originally, responses to printed advertisements and mailings provided Gulf American with the names of thousands of interested people. As more names were needed, the sales management staff purchased mailing lists and used telephone books, consciously avoiding addresses in poorer neighborhoods. Throughout the history of the corporation, Bernice Freiberg directed the lead procurement effort. She had considerable influence on the advertising budget and was expected by Jack to keep much of that budget focused on the generation of leads. In addition, she was responsible for evaluating the quality of the prospect lists and the effectiveness of the various advertising media used by the company.[54]

With thousands of new leads coming in each month, the Rosens purchased several IBM computers in early 1959 to manage the information. Constantly improving their computer system with state-of-the-art equipment, the brothers hired a data processor named David Isaacs to direct the operation. While Isaacs was unable to write the complex programs, he was familiar with the IBM equipment and he understood Gulf American's marketing approach. Whenever someone was brought in to write a new program or to update the system, Isaacs insisted on additions that would enable the company to extract various combinations of information in the future. His constant looking to future information needs of the marketing staff greatly improved the company's ability to use the leads it had received.[55]

With continual upgrading of the equipment, Gulf American's computer system emerged as one of the most powerful information processors in Miami. During every election, the Rosens gave government officials and television stations the free use of the computers for tabulating final vote totals. The election results were usually broadcast from the same location. In addition, the system was used without charge during various charitable fund-raising efforts. While these actions were motivated by altruistic interests, the Rosens also were aware of the public relations benefits to their corporation.[56]

Use of telephone rooms was another successful off-site sales technique. Leonard appointed James R. Layden to oversee the operation. In addition to the phone rooms, Layden administered much of the day-to-day business at the Miami office, and he worked closely with Leonard. From the Miami office, the primary targets of the company's telemarketing efforts were people who already owned a lot in a Gulf American development. As prices for homesites were increased by the company, salespeople called lot owners and informed them that their investment had already appreciated. Many buyers purchased additional property after repeated calls. The salespeople also phoned prospects who had never been approached by the company.[57]

The telephone rooms expanded because of their success and began to take on other functions, including pursuit of delinquent accounts, and testing of new sales ideas. Telemarketing provided the sales management staff with the fastest and most economical way to try out an innovation. In Baltimore, the phone room operation was used to contact prospects in a particular geographical area for a sales promotion. For example, if a dinner party was being planned in Zanesville, Ohio, the phone room staff of more than 100 people would call everyone they could from the telephone book or from a list of leads. If a prospect was interested in coming to the chicken dinner and hearing a presentation on Cape Coral, an invitation was sent. The Baltimore office received the returns from the invitations and set up the dinner party. The roving team of salespeople and the speaker were notified then of the party date. The telephone rooms became even more important to the dinner party program as the cost of mailing increased faster than the cost of the telephone WATS lines.[58]

The telephone sales division, however, was a source of problems for the company. The program had the highest cancellation rate of any Gulf American marketing ploy. Despite this problem, it was nevertheless profitable. Telemarketing was also prone to abuse by unscrupulous salespeople because it was difficult to supervise. According to Leonard Rich, "If you think that a direct salesman would tell lies, he doesn't have the imagination of a phone man." It was discovered that some salespeople were introducing themselves to customers on the phone as Connie Mack, Jr. Visibly upset, Mack protested loudly to Leonard when he learned about the deception, and the practice was halted, although no one admitted how long it had been going on.[59]

The marketing staff of Gulf American also concentrated a large part of its efforts on sales at the property sites. At Cape Coral three separate divisions or product lines were established to cater to the differing needs of the customers. These divisions included cold prospect sales, homesite owners (HSO) sales, and housing sales. The sales force for each of these groups of customers acted independently of the others, but they were all originally under the direction of Kenneth Schwartz at Cape Coral.[60]

The cold prospect line was developed in January 1958 to handle people who visited Cape Coral but had never been approached about purchasing a homesite. Many of these visitors had been attracted to the project by billboards and promotional brochures. Others were brought to the site by the outside public consultants (OPCs). These salespeople convinced tourists visiting on Florida's east coast to visit Cape Coral at the salespeople's expense. They were driven to the site, given a free lunch, and taken on a tour of the property. Some OPCs transported prospects in their own small airplanes, landing on one of the unused streets in Cape Coral.[61]

As the general manager of the Cape Coral project, Kenneth Schwartz supervised all of the sales personnel at the site. He maintained that the Rosens' aggressive sales philosophy had two unbreakable rules. First, salespeople were never to misrepresent the property to a client. According to Schwartz, the Rosens did not encourage any of their representatives to lie or exaggerate. The second rule was that the salespeople were not to abuse their customers. They were to be treated always with courtesy and respect.[62]

These restrictions were counterbalanced, however, by the Rosens' training philosophy for salespeople that stressed persistence. The entire sales staff was constantly pushed to exceed the previous month's sales quotas. While sales managers were responsible for maintaining order, salespeople were encouraged to "try as hard as you can, keep coming back, keep persisting . . . don't accept the first, second, or fourth 'no.' Keep talking and trying to sell." While Schwartz was certain that the Rosens were not encouraging misrepresentation and exaggeration, the aggressive style of marketing at Gulf American drew salespeople in conflicting directions.[63]

In the early years of on-site sales at Cape Coral, salespeople vividly described to clients development that was to take place in the future. They spoke of Cape Coral as a community where a person did not have to be a millionaire in order to live like one. Customers heard not only of the company's plans for the development but also of Gulf American's ability to complete the task. Because buyers often were unable to drive to a prospective homesite, salespeople had to utilize their own persuasive ability to convince clients to buy. Many of the salespeople believed that a homesite purchase was a great investment and that they were working in the best interests of the customers.[64]

Some buyers, however, resented the "hard sell" tactics of the marketing staff. John Warren drove one unenthusiastic couple to Cape Coral in 1958, before any buildings had been constructed. As he described the future development, the man became so angry at what he felt was a deception that he hit Warren in the mouth and knocked him down.

Although unsure that Cape Coral was going to be finished, the man later apologized to Warren and purchased the highest-priced piece of property (for $3,390) that was for sale.[65]

A vivid description of the aggressive Gulf American sales methods was noted by Al Hirshberg in *Life* on November 13, 1964. While vacationing on the Gulf coast at Indian Rocks Beach, Florida, Hirshberg and his wife accepted an invitation to visit Cape Coral for the day and hear a presentation about buying a homesite. Describing it as "high velocity land speculation salesmanship," Hirshberg said he and his wife were encouraged and later pressured to sign a contract for a homesite. Objections were routinely deflected by three separate salespeople whose only salary consisted of sales commissions. After realizing that Hirshberg was not going to buy, one salesman commented, "Anyone who doesn't buy land at Cape Coral is either poor or stupid." "Maybe I'm both, but I'm not buying," replied Hirshberg. Later, as the Hirshbergs were driven back to their vacation hotel, their salesman admitted: "This is a tough business. Sometimes you make a dollar. And sometimes you kill a whole day."[66]

The second on-site sales effort developed by the Rosens was a homesite owners (HSO) division that catered to people who already owned a piece of Gulf American property. During Cape Coral's early years, salespeople were prone to view homesite owners as nuisances because they had been sold a lot by someone else. The HSO operation was an important public relations tool to keep the homesite owners satisfied, but sales manager John Warren, among others, saw the owners as high-quality prospects for additional sales because they were already convinced of the value of Cape Coral property. When Warren suggested the HSO division to Leonard Rosen, he placed Warren in charge of it.[67]

This new division had several functions. Because people who purchased a lot away from the development were given a six-month inspection privilege, a sale was not considered solid until the customer visited the homesite. Travel allowances were provided to encourage people to make the trip. Any complaints about misrepresentation were directed to the HSO division. The primary function of HSO salespeople, however, was to prevent the cancellations of contracts.[68]

Disgruntled customers were often referred to the office of Connie Mack, Jr. Mack had been hired by the Rosens because of his celebrity name recognition and his family's reputation for honesty. His task in this situation was to intimidate disgruntled lot owners into keeping their homesites. Sometimes these buyers had suffered a hardship due to the loss of a job or a severe illness. Convinced that many of the people also had been misled into buying Gulf American property, Mack contacted William Carmine in Miami. (Carmine had been county attorney in

Lee County before going to work as counsel for Gulf American.) When Mack's requests for refunds were sent to him, Carmine routinely granted them. Mack estimated that nearly $2 million was refunded in the last several years of the company's existence. Once Leonard Rosen discovered what was going on, however, he relieved Carmine of that responsibility and the refunds were dramatically reduced.[69]

Another important task of the HSO division was to upgrade a sale. In other words, salespeople tried to get customers to exchange their lots for other more expensive homesites. Upgrading became easier after homesite owners were shown that large blocks of lots were not going to be ready for construction for many years. When customers were ready to build a house, they often exchanged their homesites for lots south of Cape Coral Parkway, because most construction was already finished there.[70]

A third purpose of the HSO division was to encourage buyers to purchase an additional piece of property. After customers were shown the development that had occurred at Cape Coral in the previous year and the plans for the future, salespeople recommended that they buy another homesite for investment purposes. Gulf American placed its best salespeople in this line, and they were so successful that the program was enlarged with additional sales representatives.[71]

To ensure a better customer response, the various sales offices at the properties were specifically built to promote a positive attitude in the buyers. Raymond Meyer, who had been originally hired by Gulf American because of his background in design, planned the sales facilities so that most psychological advantages were given to the salespeople, such as preventing different buyers from talking to each other during the sales process. The Rosens did not overlook even the visual environment for customers in their efforts to increase the effectiveness of their sales operation.[72]

The sales managers at Cape Coral were pleased with the growth of their sales volume, but they noticed a potential problem. Many customers wanted to purchase lots in the finished area south of Cape Coral Parkway for investment purposes only. The customers reasoned that people who wanted to build homes were most likely to construct them on lots in that section. Therefore, their investment lots would appreciate more rapidly. The foreseeable result was a development with isolated houses that never would become a true community. Sales managers argued that ultimately sales would be adversely affected if prospects did not see a community emerging. Therefore, homesite sales in the area south of Cape Coral Parkway were restricted to those buyers who planned to build a house within six months. Gulf American even bought back homesites owned by speculators so that they could be resold and immediately developed. John Warren, director of the HSO division during the early 1960s, recommended that warranty deeds not be issued to purchasers until house construction began on the lots. The new policy resulted in the early population concentration of Cape Coral in the southeast portion of the development.[73]

The third on-site sales effort by Gulf American was the sale of finished houses to property owners. Housing sales were located at various model villages in Cape Coral. While several small contractors built some of the first homes, Leonard Rosen wanted to hire a builder of good reputation who would be able to handle a larger volume. Arthur Rutenberg from the St. Petersburg area was selected, and he built houses for the company from 1959 through the mid-1960s. Eventually Gulf American formed its own housing company called Cape Coral Construction Company. By 1962 more than 500 homes had been built with an average of 30 new houses started each month.[74]

At each sales location on the property, several salespeople were given a specialized task. Cash was always in short supply because of the small down payments, so these representatives were responsible for encouraging customers to make a full cash payment for their house or lot. Nicknamed "Mr. Cash," these salespeople offered discounts or reduced interest rates to the customers. This operation also served to solidify sales because the management realized that buyers were less likely to cancel a deal if they had paid a large down payment.[75]

In order to prevent further cancellations, the sales officers in Baltimore began to develop a profile for a high-quality prospect. According to Charles Hepner, the company targeted married couples in which the husband was between the ages of twenty-five and fifty-nine and was employed. The primary focus was on the moderately well-educated blue-collar worker who was looking to build an investment for the future. The installment purchase of homesites through small monthly payments was designed with the "average American" in mind.[76]

While some groups of potential customers were avoided because of their low incomes, blacks were discouraged generally from purchasing Gulf American homesites. Originally, blacks were excluded completely from Cape Coral by a "Caucasian only" clause printed in the sales contract and in the brochures. (While this policy was promoted by a high-level adviser to the Rosens, the brothers strongly opposed it.) Cape Coral was to have a large percentage of retirees, and it was argued that they would be reluctant to settle in a community with blacks. The "Caucasian only" clause remained for a short time, until the late 1950s when the National Broadcasting Corporation refused to accept Gulf American commercials until the restriction was dropped. The Rosens were reportedly delighted with the result, although thousands of brochures had to be destroyed.[77]

Although the Rosens were seen by close associates as liberal thinking and opposed to racial prejudice, sales to blacks rarely occurred. By 1966 *Wall Street Journal* reporter Richard E. Rustin noted that very few blacks attended the Gulf American dinner parties and that company spokespersons acknowledged the absence of blacks at their developments. While discrimination generally was opposed at the top of the company, Charles Hepner commented that controlling the actions of thousands of salespeople at the sites and throughout the country was difficult. Referred to as "double-Xs" within the sales staff, blacks were discouraged from buying. Some salespeople at the properties showed them to swampy parts of the development to dissuade purchases.[78]

With the dramatic growth in Gulf American's sales volume, the training of new salespeople was a constant task. Gulf American recruiters often hired people with no real estate experience and placed them in company-owned training schools so that they could secure a real estate license. After gaining additional knowledge of the various types of land and housing the company offered, the trainees were placed in management positions, owned-and-operated sales offices, or on the property sites.[79]

Recruiters sought aggressive young people when looking for new salespeople. In addition, the Rosens required all salespeople to purchase property in the development they were marketing. They believed that lot ownership made the sales staff more convincing to customers, and it increased the employees' commitment to the project. They also encouraged salespeople from their chain of independent brokers, as well as from their own real estate offices, to visit the Gulf American properties. Some salespeople were surprised at what they saw. After touring Cape Coral, one salesman from St. Louis remarked, "Gee! I wasn't lying after all. It's all here."[80]

The majority of the company's marketing staff members were men. Although independent brokers hired some women for their operations and some party programs used women to make the sales pitch, female salespeople at the properties were rare. Besides the chauvinistic attitudes of many salesmen, the saleswomen at the sites were the targets of numerous tricks and jokes by the salesmen.[81]

The attrition rate for Gulf American salespeople was high, with turnover rates ranging up to 90 percent in some programs. Many recruits were hired from diverse backgrounds and were unable to master sales techniques. In addition, marketing people at the properties had to make sales quickly because they were paid only by commissions, which ranged from 1.0 to 1.5 percent of the homesite price. The main reason, however, for the great loss of salespeople was the recruitment of Gulf American personnel by other land sales companies. These corporations valued Gulf American salespeople because of their quality training and their experience with the company's successful marketing techniques. Charles Hepner estimated that by the late 1960s a majority of the sales staff in the entire industry originally had been trained by Gulf American.[82]

Leonard Rosen understood the importance also of such employees as waitresses, busboys, gardeners, and others in the selling of Cape Coral and his other communities. Many of these employees, particularly waitresses, were instructed when they were hired to tell prospective customers that they lived in Cape Coral and that they liked the community. Few, in fact, lived in Cape Coral and many did not like it. In an effort to encourage them to be positive about the community, Leonard held an awards banquet every year for these people to recognize with gifts any outstanding achievements. As a result, it was difficult to find anyone working for the corporation at the properties who had anything negative to say in public. Although they were receiving only minimum wage, many employees at Cape Coral were outspoken about the benefits of the community. Rosen considered a customer's chance conversation with a maid or a busboy to be part of the sales pitch.[83]

Customers who wished to resell their lots were left with few opportunities. Because nearly all of the prospective new buyers coming into Cape Coral were handled by Gulf American salespeople, people who wanted to market their own homesites discovered that they were forced to list them with the company-owned Cape Coral Realty. This real estate agency handled all lot resales in Cape Coral.[84]

A major conflict arose in Cape Coral when a competing real estate office was opened in 1960 by Granville "Pete" Petrie. Petrie had been a Cessna pilot and salesman for the company and was the community's second permanent resident. He left Gulf American in an attempt to make more from sales commissions than from his pilot's salary of $7,200. Petrie's release from the company was also attributed to his repeated promises to customers of a new bridge over the Caloosahatchee River.[85]

In either case, Petrie's real estate office was opposed actively by the management of Gulf American. "Leonard Rosen didn't believe in the free enterprise system," Petrie noted. "His crews would park trucks in front of my office to keep people from getting in. When my salesmen would walk by the Nautilus, they'd be sprayed with water hoses."[86] Also, large trees were planted in front of his office to block it from the customers' view.[87] Despite the conflict, Petrie's office remained and others were eventually opened by other residents.

Gulf American officials faced another serious problem as they attempted to control the company's salespeople. Many members of the sales staff were prone to exaggerate or misrepresent information to the customer in order to secure a sale. A typical example was a Cape Coral sales representative who showed customers a homesite near the yacht basin while actually selling them a lot several miles away. The most common lie, according to Leonard Rich, was the promise by a salesperson that Gulf American would buy back the homesite if it did not appreciate in value. The truth was that it was against company policy to repurchase a lot from a customer.[88]

As customer complaints started to surface, newspapers and magazines began investigating Gulf American's sales practices. Kenneth Schwartz noted that two articles in particular had a damaging effect on the public's confidence in the company. The first was an article in the *Miami Herald* in 1962 entitled, "Free Trip Is Spoiled by Land Sales Pitch." The author, James Buchanan, described in detail the presentation at Golden Gate Estates, pointing out six major discrepancies between the sales pitch and known facts.[89] The second article appeared in 1963 in the *Saturday Evening Post* under the title, "Land Frauds." While the majority of the story concerned unscrupulous land promoters throughout the country, a large section focused on Gulf American's high-pressure sales tactics.[90]

The Rosens responded to gross misrepresentations by salespeople in various ways. While higher sales volume remained the company's primary goal, some salespeople were fired for lying to customers. In one instance, Mrs. Anthony Pelleriti sued Gulf American in late 1962 for falsely promising that Golden Gate Estates canals would have boat access to the Gulf of Mexico. Leonard Rosen's response to the suit was to settle out of court and to hire a detective agency to help him control the statements of company salespeople. In answering other accusations, Rosen said: "Perhaps we haven't done as much in the past as we should. . . . We don't need the type of selling the reporter experienced."[91]

Early in Gulf American's history, a potentially powerful technique was instituted to monitor the sales staff. According to Edward Pacelli, sales management was convinced that it wanted the best-trained marketing staff in the industry. Improving training for a floundering salesperson was difficult because managers did not know what the customer was actually being told. The solution adopted by company management was to install electronic listening devices in all sales rooms at the property sites. Frequently a salesperson admitted their existence to buyers.[92] As a salesperson attempted to close a deal, therefore, a manager monitored the conversation in another room and reviewed it later with the salesperson.

While the acknowledged purpose of eavesdropping was to keep track of the salespeople, the technique also became an effective way of determining the true reasons why customers refused to buy. A salesman typically excused himself from the room, leaving the couple to talk over the proposed purchase. After listening to their conversation in another room, he was better able to counter their objections. In other situations, a sales manager entered the closing room after hearing the entire conversation, and took over the sales pitch. Referred to as the "T-O man," the manager had more sales experience and was able to overcome a customer's excuses. The use of monitoring devices, according to Leonard Rich, was a common practice among automobile dealers when it was adopted by Gulf American.[93]

During Gulf American's twelve-year history from 1957 to 1969, company salespeople recorded total sales of more than $800 million. Much of the reason for the rapid increase in volume was due to the aggressive marketing style of Jack and Leonard Rosen. Many employees were captivated by the brothers' single-minded focus on building the largest land development company in the country.[94] There was never a sense that the operation would fail. Leonard summed up the feeling: "No matter what mistakes we made, we knew it was going to work. A lot of people caught this spirit."[95]

Throughout the 1960s, the Rosens pressed their organization for greatly increased sales. Some individuals within the company felt that the brothers' goals were impossible without a general loss of control over the sales staff in the field. Although increasing sales volume was a focus, the brothers made sure that the first community of Cape Coral was built with the highest standards. As the project developed into reality, it became a primary tool for selling customers on later developments such as Golden Gate Estates and other less complete Gulf American properties.[96]

The sales operation at Gulf American dominated all other aspects of the company. Despite huge construction efforts, the marketing of land overshadowed every major decision. To many observers, the momentum of the sales organization became self-sustaining and it carried many people along with it. Leonard Rosen described the feeling: "Something is happening, a swell builds up and at first you're pushing it, then it's pushing you."[97]

6

Financing the Gulf American Corporation

Ralph and Geraldine Cramer of Illinois first visited Cape Coral in 1959 when relatives purchased a homesite in the community. Typical of many early customers, the Cramers had serious doubts that the project would ever be completed. After hearing the sales pitch and being satisfied that the company was trustworthy, they bought a waterfront building site in Block 98, several streets south of Cape Coral Parkway. After the contract was signed, the two were taken on an airplane ride to see their new property.[1]

The building site that the Cramers chose was advertised by Gulf American for $5,200. While some buyers paid the entire purchase price at once, most customers preferred to make a down payment and regular payments each month for anywhere from thirty-three to sixty-six months. The Cramers' homesite required an initial payment of $120 and payments of $120 per month thereafter. Other early lot purchasers took advantage of payment schedules that varied from $20 per month on a $1,320 lot to monthly payments of $200 on a $7,200 riverfront homesite. All installment sales contracts included a 5 percent interest charge in each monthly payment.[2] The company increased the price of all remaining lots as new areas were added.

While the installment sales of homesites were attractive to buyers, the plan left Gulf American short of funding for construction, land purchases, and salaries. At Cape Coral, much of the lots' cost was expended before the buyers had finished paying for their homesites. Gulf American officials estimated that the company's investment in the lots was a minimum of 20 percent of the sale price but often ranged much higher. By 1969 that figure had risen to 47 percent.[3] Installment sales left the company, as well as other land developers, with a negative cash flow in the early years. These shortfalls were partly disguised from the public by Gulf American's accounting procedures, which recorded the full price of a homesite when a down payment was made.[4] Despite the glowing financial reports, the Rosens needed other sources of funding to make up the difference.

The primary source of funding throughout the company's history was the monthly payments from the thousands of installment contracts. From 1958 through the mid-1960s, Leonard Rosen found that cash collections from customers averaged 2 percent per month of the total outstanding contracts receivable. Based on the length of the sales agreements at Cape Coral and Golden Gate Estates, Gulf American was scheduled to begin having a positive cash flow within three to six years. In other words, as contracts were paid off, the company was able to pay for the heavy initial development costs of roads, canals, and facilities. Leonard noted in May 1964, however, that the company had not yet achieved a positive cash flow but expected to do so by the end of the year.[5]

Constant expansion into new projects resulted in additional debts for the company before the installment payments could provide the necessary operating funds. The Rosens, particularly Leonard, believed in corporate growth. He was not content for the company simply to generate surpluses.[6] By 1961 Gulf American had begun construction at Golden Gate Estates, a development projected to be twice the size of Cape Coral. The result was that the company was in need of long-term financing.

The company initially had a serious problem in attracting loans from financiers or banks because it had few tangible assets to use as collateral. The land, which had been purchased cheaply, was mortgaged, and construction equipment had been bought on credit. As sales continued, however, Gulf American built a huge accounts-receivable fund because of its aggressive sales operation. "The book," as Leonard called the receivables, was critical in Rosen's plan because it provided the collateral for any loans to the company.[7]

Of the two brothers, Leonard handled the majority of the financing arrangements for the corporation.[8] In order to persuade bankers to lend him money, he had to convince them of the secure nature of "the book." A speech made by Rosen before a group of security analysts in Cleveland, Ohio, in May 1964 summarized his position. As of February of that year, he stated, the contracts receivable for Cape Coral and

Golden Gate totaled $149,749,126, although he noted that the age of the contracts was critical for an accurate assessment of the company's cash situation. Because Gulf American had a six-month inspection and refund privilege, most cancellations occurred within the first half-year of the sale. Rosen pointed out that 61 percent of Cape Coral's receivables and 40 percent of the newer Golden Gate's receivables were over one year old. Of all contracts receivable, 96 percent were current and being paid on time.[9] Bank officials agreed with Rosen's positive outlook, and numerous loans were made to the company during the 1960s.

The difficult task for Leonard was to secure financing during the late 1950s and early 1960s. One of the earliest financial supporters of the Rosens in Florida was Harry Fagan, president of First National Bank of Fort Myers.[10] Fagan not only loaned the company money when few other financial institutions were willing to do so but also supported the new Cape Coral development by publicly vouching for Gulf American's stability. Numerous early sales brochures listed First National Bank as the company's main financial reference.[11] Fagan's assistance and counseling were seen as critical to the company's early success. Leonard Rosen recalled an incident that demonstrated Fagan's unwavering support: "I needed a check for $140,000. Fagan certified the check, and later found out we didn't have the funds to cover it."[12]

The reason for Fagan's support of Leonard and for Gulf American was not entirely obvious at the time. Apparently, however, he was impressed with Leonard personally and he believed that the Rosens were going to do something good for the area. In addition, Fagan was convinced that Leonard was an extremely wealthy man. When Connie Mack, Jr., contacted Fagan in late 1957 regarding some lingering doubts about Rosen's plans and his own possible involvement with him, Fagan portrayed Leonard in such a positive way that Mack eventually went to work for the company. Another possible reason for Fagan's support of the new development was the potential for hundreds of home loans his bank would be able to make in the future. Whatever the reason, Fagan regularly met with Leonard and other company officials to discuss business at the coffee shop at the Surfside Restaurant in Cape Coral.[13]

Finding banks cautious about lending to land development companies, the Rosens offered $750,000 of 7 percent convertible bonds to the public on March 8, 1961. Underwritten by Street and Company and by Lieberbaum and Company of New York, the debentures were redeemable in 1968 and partially convertible to common stock. The proceeds were used to reduce various loans at higher interest rates and to finance the construction of the golf course and interim sewage disposal plant at Cape Coral.[14]

During the early 1960s Leonard hired a young man named Robert J.

Granger to assist with Gulf American's borrowing difficulties. Granger had worked previously for General Electric in its marketing and finance departments. His knowledge of numerous financial institutions made him an invaluable asset to the Rosens. Referred to by company associates as "Leonard's bagman," he knew where thirty- to ninety-day loans of a million dollars or more could be located. Usually these short-term loans were at high rates of interest, and it was necessary to repay them as quickly as possible.[15]

Needing a major refinancing of several bank loans, the Rosens took advantage of the general public optimism for the company in January 1962 and authorized a major bond issue of $12 million. The proceeds from the sale of the debentures were to be used primarily to repay $5.7 million in bank loans secured by accounts receivable and as a $1 million down payment on land subject to expiring options. Although the bonds were originally intended to be purchased by stockholders, the underwriting firms of Morris Cohen and Company and Street and Company suggested that they be sold to the public because of then-current market conditions. Eventually, $10 million of the debentures were issued in July 1962 at 6.5 percent interest.[16]

The marketing of these bonds demonstrated Leonard's ability to surround himself with talented individuals. Joseph Maddlone had been brought into the firm in 1959 because of his strong background in banking, and he eventually became company secretary. A graduate of the Rutgers Graduate School of Banking, Maddlone had worked in various aspects of bank operations and tax accounting in New York. In addition, he became proficient at guiding corporations through the legal and financial intricacies of offering their stocks and bonds to the public. After moving to Miami, Maddlone had assisted investors in the early 1950s in the founding of the North American Milk Company, an early manufacturer of canned milk. Familiar with governmental processes, Maddlone helped Miami businessmen Dexter Saunders and Peter Luss work out an agreement with the Dade County government for the building of a privately owned pier on the oceanfront. (Luss later went to work for Gulf American as its director of international sales.) When store owners in Miami Springs needed banking services in their area, Maddlone assisted them in establishing one of the first banks there.[17]

With Gulf American selling such a large amount of bonds for the first time, Maddlone and the underwriters, Morris Cohen and Company, were concerned that investors were unfamiliar with the company and southwest Florida in general. Maddlone suggested to Leonard Rosen that potential investors be brought to Florida to see the property. The company chartered a plane and brought twenty to thirty financiers to

Cape Coral. They toured the development and Maddlone answered questions about the operation. They were particularly interested in proposed purchases of land by Gulf American. The enthusiastic investors placed orders for debentures worth $12 million, effectively oversubscribing the issue by $2 million. The underwriters were so pleased that they wrote in a bonus of $25,000 for Maddlone, but Leonard disallowed it, stating: "No, I'm not going to give him a bonus. It's his job."[18]

As Gulf American demonstrated its ability to sell real estate, lending institutions became more willing to offer the company working capital. Before 1963, loans were available but only at high rates of interest. In October 1963, Gulf American obtained a $7.5 million loan from John D. MacArthur of Bankers Life and Casualty Company of Chicago at 6.5 percent interest. At the same time, the company borrowed $1.5 million at 6.0 percent from a group of Florida and New York banks led by Boca Raton National Bank. As part of the second loan, Milton Weir and his son, John, former Arvida Corporation officials, became directors of Gulf American. Leonard stated that some of the money was going to be used to retire high-interest loans. He described the agreements as "a vote of confidence" from the financial community, commenting that "borrowings at favorable market rates have increased the capability of the company to expand at a much greater rate than heretofore possible."[19]

During 1964 Gulf American sought additional loans because many previous agreements had been for only two years. In July 1964 Leonard announced that the company would borrow an additional $2.5 million at 5 percent interest from Boca Raton National Bank and six other banks, including Delray National Bank and the National Bank of Westchester (Florida).[20] Gulf American had floated another loan from the Boca Raton National Bank by December of that year. With First National Bank of Boston and Chemical Bank of New York cooperating, the banks loaned $8 million to the company at 6 percent, using $24 million in sales contracts as collateral. An additional $1 million from Prudential Insurance Company of America was borrowed by Gulf American at the same time. A large portion of these funds was used to repay a two-year-old $8 million note from AIC Financing Corporation of Chicago at 12 percent interest. The remainder was used to repay other short-term debts and for general operations.[21]

By the middle of 1964, Gulf American's loans had risen to $56,498,308, not including the various bonds it had sold.[22] This figure made many observers uneasy about the company's long-term stability. Collier County financial adviser Walter Rogers had noted that the giant land development concern was extremely short of cash, paying as high as 15 percent interest on loans and having pledged much of its accounts receivable as collateral for those loans. Company secretary Joseph Maddlone responded by explaining that the cash level fluctuated daily and that "we're got $30,000,000 to pay our debts and we'll pay them." He added that less than 2 percent of the company's loans involved rates of 15 percent. He later commented that 1964 appeared to be "our best year ever" financially and that the company was going to experience basically a positive cash flow throughout the year. Leonard agreed, describing 1964 as "the turning point" in the cash flow performance of the company.[23]

While Gulf American officials presented an image of stability, Leonard had been exploring new sources of funding for over a year. In July 1963 Gulf American purchased a substantial block of common stock of Fenestra, a Detroit-based manufacturer of auto springs, steel and aluminum doors, and other building products. The stock, owned by several Fenestra directors, amounted to 46 percent of all outstanding shares and resulted in Gulf American's becoming the major stockholder in the firm. According to Fenestra officials, the four directors had been acquiring the stock for about a year. The agreement called for Gulf American to pay $6,167,322 for the shares.[24]

Within three weeks of the purchase, Fenestra filed suit in the Circuit Court of Wayne County (Michigan) against Gulf American, charging the company and the four Fenestra directors with conspiracy to take over Fenestra for "unlawful" purposes and asking for $1 million in damages. The suit maintained that Gulf American planned to gain control of the smaller company in order to use the firm's $10,926,463 in liquid assets, plus other assets, to pay for Gulf American's "huge, pressing, and fast-maturing obligations." Fenestra president Orren S. Leslie argued that the four directors knew that Gulf American did not have the funds for such a purchase and that it planned to use Fenestra's assets to pay off the directors.[25]

The suit also complained that Gulf American had not even used its own funds for the $1.75 million down payment on the stock. Instead, the money was borrowed from the Atkinson Corporation, a Wisconsin company owned or controlled by Abraham, Jay, Robert, and Jack Pritzker. The Pritzker group, the suit alleged, "knew or had reason to know" that Gulf American planned to repay the loan with Fenestra assets. They were to receive a $245,000 bonus for granting the loan. An additional $600,000 bonus allegedly was paid to an unnamed individual for arranging the financing.[26]

The Pritzkers of Chicago were well acquainted with large acquisition deals but usually avoided publicity. Abraham N. Pritzker, the son of a Russian immigrant, was an attorney who founded one of the largest privately held fortunes in the United States, estimated at his death in

1986 to be worth $1.5 billion. Beginning with a small family law firm, Pritzker, along with his sons Jay, Robert, and Donald and a brother, Jack, began acquiring businesses in a wide variety of manufacturing industries. Under the corporate name of the Marmon Group, the family specialized in making traditionally marginal enterprises profitable. By the early 1970s the Marmon Group had expanded into a half-billion-dollar conglomerate that included the Hyatt Hotel chain, vast tracts of timberland, farm machinery manufacturing, banking, mining interests, and real estate interests in Chicago. In addition to business, the family was known for its philanthropy, such as the June 13, 1968, gift of $12 million to the University of Chicago medical school.[27]

Although Gulf American officially denied all conspiracy charges in the lawsuit, Judge Edward S. Piggins of the Circuit Court of Wayne County ruled in January 1964 that Gulf American's moves were a "contrived scheme" to cloak its intention to use Fenestra's resources for its own interests. He noted that Gulf American's need was for cash and not for investments as diverse as Fenestra. In addition to the Detroit firm's cash assets, Gulf American was interested in the possible use of Fenestra's New York Stock Exchange listing and its favorable tax loss situation. The court, therefore, ordered Gulf American to sell its 46 percent interest in the company.[28]

Gulf American appealed the decision to the Michigan Supreme Court. Two years later, in April 1966, that court reversed the decision, granting the Florida land development company full use of its 46 percent of Fenestra stock. Immediately, Gulf American replaced five Fenestra directors and four of the top officers. Jack Rosen was named the new president and Bernard Herzfeld, general counsel for Gulf American, took over as chairman. By November 1966, however, Leonard Rosen announced that his company's interest in Fenestra had been sold for an undisclosed amount of cash to the Marmon Group. By December 1967 the Pritzker family had acquired additional Fenestra stock, bringing their control to 84 percent of the outstanding shares. The resulting combination enabled the Marmon Group to substantially increase its sales revenues to nearly $100 million for 1967.[29]

While the Rosens' initial intentions appear to have been to strip Fenestra of its cash assets, whether that actually took place is unknown and unlikely. During the two-year appeal, the court held all disputed stocks and dividends in trust, removing them from Gulf American's use.[30] By the time Gulf American regained control of Fenestra, the Rosens were able to borrow all the money they needed from banks.

The Rosens also raised funds by selling non-income-producing properties for cash. Soon after it was completed in 1964, Gulf American sold its new eleven-story headquarters building at Northeast Seventy-ninth

Street and Biscayne Boulevard in Miami. The sale was to the Woodmen of the World Life Insurance Company for $2.7 million. Gulf American continued to use the property, leasing it back with a twenty-year buy-back option. The country club complex at Cape Coral's main golf course was sold to the same insurance company.[31] The result of these transfers left Gulf American with the benefits of ownership without the heavy investment.

A final major source of liquid assets for the corporation involved the acceleration of payments on the outstanding balances of sales contracts. Cash collections on Gulf American's $250 million in contracts receivable were estimated by Leonard Rosen to amount to $64 million in 1966. Because of a generally tight national money situation during the latter part of that year, the company offered discounts of up to 5 percent for any customers who made additional payments during the month of November. The firm also issued S&H green stamps on the amount paid in advance. The program generated an additional $8.5 million in cash during the month over anticipated receipts, but it resulted in reduced earnings for the quarter. The increased funds allowed Leonard to repay company short-term debts amounting to $22 million without resorting to refinancing.[32]

As the size of its contracts receivable grew in the mid-1960s, Gulf American appeared to achieve some financial stability. By 1967 the company had $280 million in receivables, with $78,045,954 in bonds, mortgages, notes, and other debts.[33] As a result of a thirty-day suspension of the company's sales program in late 1967 and early 1968 by the Florida Land Sales Board, sales were lower for the year, but still a profit was recorded for 1967. The figures prompted Leonard to announce at the corporation's annual stockholders' meeting in Cape Coral in late 1967 that the corporation was in the "best financial condition ever." Even less enthusiastic officials such as Joseph Maddlone noted that the huge land sales operation was "modestly but adequately financed."[34]

The listing of Gulf American's stock on a major exchange greatly assisted in gaining the confidence of the financial community. While it provided little direct benefit for the firm's profitability, the listing attracted the attention of potentially large investors. It also gave the impression of stability for a corporation involved in a speculative industry. Therefore, the Rosens received permission to list Gulf American Land Corporation stock on the American Stock Exchange on June 26, 1961. By the end of the year the stock had achieved so much customer interest that it had risen from 12⅝ per share to 56⅞. As a result of the stock's volatile record, the American Stock Exchange and the Securities and Exchange Commission began investigating to determine if the Rosens were manipulating the price. Leonard Rosen denied any interference in the trading, stating, "I don't even know what it [the stock price] is." Rosen's only accounting for the rapid increase in the stock's price was the substantial rise in the company's earnings for that year. After a one-day suspension of trading in November 1961, activity resumed on the shares with the price dropping more than sixteen points in two days.[35] The investigation ended soon afterward without any evidence of wrong-doing.

A major reason for the rapid rise in the price of Gulf American's stock was undoubtedly the increased public interest in the company and the relatively small number of shares available for trade. At the time of the investigation, the Rosen brothers owned about 70 percent of the 2,286,766 shares of common stock outstanding. In addition, during 1961, company official Solomon Sandler held 24,150 shares, George London, a longtime business associate of the Rosens from Baltimore, owned 15,300 shares, and chief counsel Bernard Herzfeld owned 12,500 shares. The Rosens were probably more concerned about maintaining control of all corporate decisions than with manipulating their own stock's price. Although they eventually sold varying amounts of their securities, they still owned a total of 56 percent of all voting stock by the late 1960s. Much of the stock that they did relinquish was given to their children.[36]

While control of the corporation's major decisions was vital to the brothers, they also realized how rapidly their company was accumulating assets. The Rosens' desire in the late 1950s to repurchase a large number of Gulf American shares resulted in an incident in 1959 involving their purchase of 1,000 shares of stock from Milton J. Baumel and Earl L. Weiner, two early investors in the company. The two men purchased the securities in 1957 when the company was in its infancy and the Rosens owned only 52 percent of the voting shares. On August 24, 1959, Leonard told Baumel that Gulf American needed his stock if the company was going to get a badly needed loan. Baumel sold his stock to Rosen for $21,000, which was $10,000 more than he had paid for it. Weiner also sold his shares to the Rosens. Discovering that the brothers did not need the stock for loan collateral, the men brought charges against the Rosens for misrepresentation. In May 1968 Harrison L. Winter, judge of the federal district court, found the brothers guilty of misrepresentation and deception and ordered them to return to the two men stock valued then at $1.7 million. The judge noted that the Rosens' true intention was plain by the record of their steady acquisition of Gulf American stock from a 52 percent interest in 1957 to a 79 percent share in March 1961.[37]

Another method of presenting the appearance of financial stability was diversification. Besides Fenestra, the Rosens began purchasing or creating various companies in the early 1960s that would directly or indirectly help the land sales program. Cape Coral Realty was established to handle resales of Cape Coral homesites. Cape Coral Construction Company became the primary builder of homes at Cape Coral and subsequent Gulf American properties. Under Thomas Weber's direction, the Fort Myers Construction Company supervised all heavy construction on company developments. Congress International was purchased by the Rosens because it operated a nationwide motel chain and franchise operation. Many of these motels eventually housed customers while at Gulf American properties. At Cape Coral, Gulf Communicators was formed in 1964 to provide television programming via cable to the city's residents. The diversification became so extensive that stockholders approved deleting the word *Land* from the company's name in 1966, retaining Gulf American Corporation.[38]

Besides various other operational subsidiaries, Gulf American controlled a number of corporations whose sole function was to hold title to property and land. Colgerry Realty owned the vast company lands in British Honduras while Gulf American Land Corporation of Arizona had reduced its holdings to 10,588 acres near Kingman, Arizona. New Mexico American Land Corporation and Utah American Land Corporation were land-acquisition subsidiaries that purchased Gulf American properties in their respective states. GALC was organized as a holding company in Illinois to control the common stock of Fenestra.[39]

In the early 1960s, Gulf American officials realized that the financial community wanted to see more tangible evidence that the company was stable and growing. An obvious sign of legitimate growth was the building of houses on the thousands of homesites, particularly at the first development at Cape Coral. In order to foster housing construction, Gulf American established Parkway Mortgage Company to offer inexpensive loans to home builders. Gulf American officials knew that bankers perceived that a development with mortgaged homes was more stable than one with completely paid-for homes.[40]

The newly formed mortgage company experienced several problems. To get it started, Robert Granger called Raymond Meyer in Cape Coral, sending him to a savings and loan company in Sarasota to get a one-day crash course in running a mortgage company. Granger directly assisted Leonard Rosen on financial matters because of his expertise and contacts in the field. Although Meyer was an interior designer for the company and had no background in finance or banking, he went to Sarasota and returned to start Parkway Mortgage Company. Besides the lack of experience, the new company initially was illegally operating from the mortgage broker's license of a Gulf American employee at Golden Gate Estates.[41]

Raymond Meyer discovered two other problems with the operation. Funding was scarce because few savings and loan companies in southwest Florida were willing or geographically able to cooperate on the loans. Robert Granger's contacts in the financial community, however, secured commitments for millions of dollars from Prudential Insurance Company and Metropolitan Life Insurance Company. Meyer also learned that many of the housing customers had large sums of cash because they had sold their northern homes and they did not want mortgages. After convincing buyers that it was in their best interest to take out mortgages on their new houses and keep their cash as a reserve, Parkway Mortgage was able to write numerous housing loans.[42] The plan resulted in an increasingly stable appearance for Gulf American's operations.

During the mid-1960s Gulf American brought thousands of potential buyers to its Florida developments through its numerous promotions. As a result, the company purchased Modern Air Transport in June 1966. The small charter airline cost $807,500, and its offices were immediately transferred from New Jersey to Miami. One of twelve permanently certified supplemental air carriers in the country, the airline catered to the charter tour market and the movement of government military personnel. Its primary function, however, was to transport customers to Gulf American properties. Leonard Rosen reported that although it lost $2.5 million in its first year of operation, he planned to continue the conversion of the airline to a fan-jet fleet featuring Convair 990 aircraft. The subsidiary flew an average of 20,000 northerners a month into Florida, most of them ending up in Gulf American sales offices.[43]

After flying customers to Cape Coral or Golden Gate and concluding homesite transactions, sales managers found that some buyers were concerned about the fate of their sales contract or mortgage if they died prematurely. Seeing an opportunity for a different type of sale, the Rosens began searching for a life insurance company to purchase so they could offer credit insurance to their customers. On October 12, 1963, Leonard announced that he and his brother planned to acquire 10 percent of the stock of Reinsurance Investment Corporation for approximately $1 million. Reinsurance was a holding company that controlled four life insurance firms. The proposed purchase was never carried through because there was apparently no interest on the part of any other major stockholders to sell to the Rosens.[44]

Still interested in acquiring an insurance company, the brothers bought the underdeveloped Guild Life Insurance Company in May 1964 for $1.65 million. Based in Austin, Texas, the concern became a subsidiary of the Rosen Investment Corporation, a firm owned completely by Leonard and Jack Rosen. Originally intended to sell life insurance to Gulf American property and housing customers, the company expanded into health and accident coverage. In February 1966 the Rosens sold Guild Life to Gulf American in a cash deal, having added more than $83 million in life insurance to the company since May 1964. By August 1967 Guild Life had grown to include more than $132 million of life insurance in force with about 32,000 policyholders. The success of Guild Life was largely the result of the complementary nature of the Rosens' contract land sales business and their customers' need for credit insurance.[45]

The Rosens embarked on an interesting investment at Golden Gate Estates, although it did not involve the creation of a subsidiary corporation. Believing that oil might be located beneath the property, the brothers authorized the drilling of two exploratory wells on the vast acreage. Monitored by Joseph Maddlone, the wells were abandoned after reaching 11,700 feet without finding oil. The project cost Gulf American $127,000.[46]

The motivation in all of the Rosens' diverse operations was ultimately to make a profit. Many close associates noted that it was probably the challenge of acquiring the wealth rather than the profit itself that spurred the brothers forward. In their personal life-styles, neither man flaunted his wealth with any dramatic spending, though both contributed liberally to various Jewish charities, the United Way, and the Parkinson's Disease Association. Of the two, Jack was the more generous to his employees in terms of salaries, while Leonard was content to settle for verbal recognition of associates' fine work. Jack came up with the idea of sharing some of the wealth with company officers through stock options.[47]

Leonard in particular had a somewhat curious attitude toward money. When a former company attorney commented that Leonard had changed and become more generous in the mid-1960s, Kenneth Schwartz disagreed. He observed that Leonard constantly pressed employees and business associates to get the absolute best bargain for himself. Some associates, as a result, viewed Leonard as miserly. Even though Schwartz noted that Leonard kept his word in business dealings, Leonard personally had a difficult time letting the money be paid out. Schwartz characterized Leonard's attitude toward money as a "stomach problem": "Leonard Rosen may understand with his mind that he has to pay the money. He might even understand with his heart that he should pay the money. But the thing that would preclude him from paying the money would be his stomach."[48]

Leonard also rarely carried any money with him. Typically he would see people he knew in a store or office and ask them to lend him some money, instructing them to call his secretary at his office for a refund. Many associates thought it was for effect, although it was uncertain whether he wanted to downplay his wealth or subtly emphasize his importance.[49]

Raymond Meyer's first encounter with Leonard involved a similar experience at the Surfside Restaurant in Cape Coral in the summer of 1960. Leonard walked in the entrance and stood there, dressed in a dirty T-shirt and tennis shorts. Approaching Meyer, he asked, "You work for the company?" Meyer replied, "Yes." After asking his name, Leonard announced, "I'm Leonard Rosen. I need a pack of cigarettes. Have you got seventy-five cents?" Meyer remembered thinking, "Now, he could have just asked the bartender, 'Give me the cigarette machine!' It was his cigarette machine." Amazed, Meyer gave him the money.[50]

The value of the money involved in any deal was not the primary issue for Leonard. He focused his attention on working the most favorable financial arrangement for himself because he saw it as a personal challenge for his ability as a salesman. An incident in the late 1960s that illustrated that tendency in Leonard's personality involved Barry Horenbein, a Tallahassee lobbyist who worked for Gulf American. In an attempt to help Leonard in building political relationships in the state capital, Horenbein suggested, "Leonard, you need to establish some foothold in Tallahassee." Explaining further, he told Leonard about a 500-acre tract of land about five miles from Tallahassee that could be purchased for $750 per acre. Horenbein proposed that a hunting lodge could be built there by Gulf American to entertain and lobby political officials. After flying over the property in a helicopter and walking it on foot, Leonard was interested in the idea. Although Horenbein remembered that the property was a remarkable bargain at $750 per acre, Leonard surprisingly offered $300 per acre. While he eventually offered somewhat more for the land, the owners refused to sell for anything less than $750. The purchase was never made. Horenbein asked Leonard about not taking advantage of such a bargain. "I wanted to see if I could buy it at that, Barry," he said. "It's the challenge of outsmarting them to buy it at that."[51]

Although Leonard passionately wanted Gulf American to succeed, he was sometimes indifferent to the company's financial situation at important times. Personal matters were often more important to him. At a security analysts meeting in the late 1960s, Joseph Maddlone had used his Wall Street contacts to set up an opportunity for Leonard to present Gulf American's attributes to the brokers. The luncheon was scheduled to begin at eleven o'clock, but Rosen did not arrive until shortly before the analysts had to return to their offices. Maddlone discovered that Rosen had spent the time on the phone in the hotel, arranging a date with a stewardess who had been on his flight. The luncheon, designed to promote Gulf American's image in the financial community, was a failure, and Maddlone told Bernard Herzfeld on the flight home that he would not set up any more such meetings for Leonard.[52]

Throughout the history of Gulf American, the company's ability to secure adequate financing dramatically improved. During the late 1950s working capital was in short supply because most banks viewed land development firms as speculative ventures. Even in later years, no cash dividends were ever declared because excess funds were used for development expenses or for expansion.[53] As Leonard told stockholders at the annual meeting in Cape Coral in 1962: "Let us be frank. There is a lack of confidence generally in land companies all over the United States."[54] With the growth of the firm's contracts receivable, funding from banks became easier.

The corporation reached solid financial footing in 1964 when collections and income began to increase faster than expenses. The positive cash flow prompted Leonard to describe 1964 as "the turning point" in the company's financial situation.[55] From that time, Gulf American's receivables were so large that a positive cash flow was virtually guaranteed. Some observers in the company speculated that the positive cash situation would have occurred earlier than 1964 if the brothers had not continued to push new projects with extensive outlays of capital.[56] The company's cash flow was so good that Leonard had difficulty understanding how GAC Corporation was able to bankrupt the operation by the mid-1970s. Baffled by GAC's demise, he stated in 1977: "I never dreamed in my wildest dreams the company could have so much trouble."[57]

The entire Gulf American family of companies was interrelated and interdependent. For Jack and Leonard Rosen, land sales were still the central core of the corporation's profit-making potential. In order to promote sales, outside sources of financing were necessary. Banks and other lending institutions were reluctant to loan money to Gulf American because most of the land development industry was unstable and undercapitalized. The Rosens presented a picture of stability by acquiring subsidiaries that assisted the sales operation and showed steady growth through land acquisition. As the contracts receivable swelled in the mid-1960s, Gulf American was able to borrow sufficient funds.

In the critical years prior to 1964, Leonard Rosen was responsible for supervising the multitude of financing schemes that kept the firm operating. Much of what he accomplished required the expertise and administrative assistance of associates such as Joseph Maddlone, Robert Granger, and James Layden. Rosen's powerful personality was also an invaluable asset in promoting the company. Without the financing he helped to put together, Gulf American would not have grown as rapidly as it did.[58]

7

Promoting Florida Living

Land sales at Cape Coral were greatly boosted by various promotional and publicity efforts of Gulf American. During the late 1950s and early 1960s, more Americans were becoming attracted to Fort Myers and southwest Florida as vacation destinations. While tourist numbers in the region were increasing, most visitors to the state still stayed in hotels on the Atlantic coast. Gulf American officials immediately began developing schemes that would introduce the corporation and particularly Cape Coral to the American public. As company officials developed strategies, thousands of people were attracted to Cape Coral and other Gulf American properties by offers of free gas, free accommodations, reduced airfares, and other inducements.

The most important ingredient in the company's promotional efforts was the creativity of Jack Rosen and his staff. While Leonard was instrumental in the early promotions, Jack regularly met in Baltimore with advisers to develop national strategies for attracting customers to Gulf American properties.[1] Jack also insisted that the company use major Madison Avenue advertising and public relations firms to present Gulf American's image to the buying public. A major thrust of these efforts was to get a third party talking positively about Cape Coral and Gulf American. Many of these agencies were hired specifically because the corporation had received negative publicity from critical newspaper and magazine articles in the mid-1960s.

While the company's own firm, the Paul Venze Agency, developed many new promotional strategies, Jack felt that other firms were better able to build an image of legitimacy and stability for the giant land company.[2]

An example of the positive national publicity that company officials wanted was the proposed feature article on Jack Rosen and his family in *Fortune* magazine in the late 1960s. Several reporters and photographers virtually lived with his family for several weeks, compiling a "rags to riches" story of the younger Rosen. Jack was unhappy with the direction of the article because he did not want to be associated anymore with his carnival pitchman's background. The entire feature was canceled, however, because of the December 17, 1968, kidnapping and ransom of Barbara Jane Mackle, the twenty-year-old daughter of Robert Mackle. (Mackle, along with his two brothers, headed the $65 million Florida land development firm called Deltona Corporation.) Held by two captors for $500,000 ransom, the young woman was buried in a coffinlike box in a wooded area north of Atlanta, Georgia, for more than three days. While FBI agents ultimately rescued her unharmed, Jack Rosen refused to allow the article and photographs of his family to be published for fear of similar kidnapping attempts on his family.[3] Although the *Fortune* piece was not used, Jack and his staff aggressively pursued other third-party publicity.

A major publicity venture for the Rosens was the Gulf American Galleries, an art collection housed on the 10,000-square-foot third floor of their Miami headquarters building at Seventy-ninth Street and Biscayne Boulevard. Assembled by Leonard, the collection specialized in Latin American paintings and sculpture, particularly Mexican art and some pre-Columbian pieces. Entire sections of the gallery were devoted to surrealist, cubist, and expressionist works. Significant Israeli and African collections were also included. Visitors were able to view paintings by Picasso, Cezanne, Chagall, Dali, Degas, Dufy, Renoir, Rivera, and Utrillo. Sculptures by Arp, Epstein, Giacometti, Moore, and Rodin were also on display. Selected exhibits from the gallery toured schools, charitable organizations, and other galleries. The collection was included with Gulf American's assets in the 1969 sale to GAC Corporation but with a buy-back provision, and most of it remained the property of Leonard Rosen. While several pieces were eventually sold to close Rosen associates, most of the collection remained in Leonard's possession until his death in 1987.[4]

The gallery was created for several reasons. Leonard and his wife Dorothy enjoyed collecting artwork, and by 1967, at its peak, the 1,500-piece exhibit was valued at more than $2.5 million.[5] Leonard's interest in art, however, was not entirely aesthetic. When he began assembling the collection in Europe in 1963, he admitted: "I didn't know a Picasso from a Degas." Open to the public at no charge, the display attracted visitors and greatly publicized Gulf American's eleven-story headquarters building. Leonard also considered the artwork a great investment because its value increased at better than 6 percent a year. In addition, company officials regularly took important corporate visitors through the gallery. Such dignitaries as the mother and sister of Ferdinand Marcos were shown the exhibits, but the collection was more important in presenting an image of stability to the financial community.[6]

Another opportunity to expand Gulf American's national image rose in 1964 when the American Football League announced that it would soon be awarding a football franchise in Miami. Leonard, along with company vice-presidents Robert H. Finkernagel, Jr., and Connie Mack, Jr., met with AFL owners at the Waldorf Astoria Hotel in New York City to discuss purchasing the franchise. Among those present were Joseph F. "Sonny" Werblin, new owner of the New York Jets, Lamar Hunt, owner of the Kansas City Chiefs, and Joseph F. Foss, commissioner of the American Football League. Later in 1965, Foss gained recognition because he was able to negotiate a $36 million television contract with NBC for the AFL that assured the struggling league's ultimate success. After interviewing several potential franchisees, the new team was awarded to Gulf American and a $250,000 deposit was paid by the company.[7]

As news of the purchase reached the financial community, Leonard began receiving negative reactions from bankers as well as sales brokers in the field. They complained that the company needed to speed up the development schedule at the Gulf American properties instead of diversifying into such a speculative venture as professional football. As a result, Rosen asked Mack and Finkernagel to fly to Dallas, Texas, to meet with the owners and get the down payment refunded. Leonard, however, had not communicated his desire to cancel the agreement to the AFL owners, and they thought Mack and Finkernagel were coming with the balance of $1.75 million for the franchise. While under no obligation to do so, Foss authorized the refund on the condition that no public announcement was made until other candidates were interviewed. Eventually, the Miami Dolphins franchise was awarded to Joseph Robbie on August 15, 1965, and the team played its inaugural season in the autumn of 1966.[8]

Additional nationwide publicity was achieved through the company's use of advertising on highly rated television shows such as "Today," "Concentration," "Queen for a Day," and "The Price Is Right." On "The Price Is Right" program, Gulf American had by 1964 given away nineteen houses in Cape Coral valued at an average of $18,000 each. The promotion displayed the company's homes to a large nationwide audience and resulted in public awareness of the Cape Coral development in Florida. Because this advertising was aimed at a national audience, it was directed by Jack and his staff in Baltimore.[9]

In order to gain the widest appeal, the Rosens sought spokespersons for the company who already had widespread recognition. The first and primary representative for Gulf American was Connie Mack, Jr. Mack, whose real name was Cornelius McGillicuddy, was hired in January 1958 by Leonard because he already lived in the Fort Myers area and he had name recognition throughout the country. Mack's father had owned the Philadelphia Athletics baseball team and was noted for his honesty and integrity. Mack's appeal was readily apparent by the large number of customers who wanted to meet him. Richard Crawford, community relations director for Cape Coral during the early 1960s, remarked that his decision to buy a Cape Coral lot sight unseen was because of Connie Mack's association with the company.[10]

Gulf American also hired William "Bill" Stern to represent the company in advertisements and commercials. The widely known Stern, nicknamed the "Dean of American Sportscasters," had a strong radio following and he enthusiastically endorsed Cape Coral. While Mack and Stern were the company's most prominent spokesmen, other celebrities who worked for Gulf American included Canadian sportscaster William "Bill" Hewitt, trick pro golfer Paul Hahn, baseball personality Yogi Berra, and star football quarterback Y. A. Tittle. Although they were not celebrities, the local support of Homer Welch of the Lee County Electric Cooperative and Harry Fagan of First National Bank of Fort Myers gave Gulf American credibility during its early years. During the late 1960s, Will Rogers, Jr., son of the famous humorist, became the main spokesman for the Rio Rico development in Arizona. Gulf American wanted to hire golfer Arnold Palmer and "Tonight" show host Johnny Carson, but the company was unable to negotiate agreements with their agents.[11]

At the community of Cape Coral, several individuals were significant in promoting and publicizing the project. Connie Mack, Jr., assisted the company because of his visibility at the property and his accessibility to people who had complaints. The waiting room to his second-floor office in the Gulf American building at Cape Coral was often crowded by the time he came to work each morning. Of all the personalities who worked for Gulf American, customers most frequently recognized Mack's name and his family's reputation of integrity. Standing six feet, seven inches tall, Mack's stature combined with his kind personality to add an atmosphere of dignity in the midst of the high-pressure sales operation. Although he lived in Fort Myers, Mack served as the most prominent representative of the company in the community, officiating at grand openings, ground breakings, and other ceremonial functions. As other people became needed for promotions, Mack's association with the company helped establish initial contact with those celebrities.[12]

Another important official at Cape Coral was the managing director of the community, Robert H. Finkernagel, Jr. Before coming to Cape Coral in December 1961, Finkernagel had been the director of the Gainesville, Florida, Chamber of Commerce. From Cape Coral's beginning in 1958, Kenneth Schwartz was placed in charge of all operations at the property including sales, construction, and community relations. However, Connie Mack and Richard Crawford actually handled most of the company's relationships with the residents. As the permanent population of Cape Coral approached 2,000 people in 1961, Leonard employed Finkernagel to act as a city manager, relieving Mack of many of those duties. The two men worked closely together, sharing office space in the Gulf American building at the corner of Del Prado Boulevard and Cape Coral Parkway.[13]

As the city expanded, Finkernagel hired Paul W. Sanborn in May 1962 to assist him with community relations and other city manager–related duties. Sanborn had previously directed the Kissimmee Chamber of Commerce and the Kissimmee Boat-A-Cade, a promotional boat tour through the inland waterways of central Florida. After coming to Cape Coral, Sanborn arranged for the next boat-a-cade to end its journey from Kissimmee in Cape Coral. As a result, 350 boats arrived at the yacht basin in Cape Coral on October 27, 1962.[14]

Finkernagel's chief function involved "cutting the umbilical cord between the developer, Gulf American, and the residents."[15] At the time of his arrival, Cape Coral operated like a company town with Gulf American providing the majority of community services. Finkernagel was responsible for assisting the residents in developing a city independent of the corporation. As various promotions at Cape Coral began to take up more of Finkernagel's time, Paul Sanborn carried many of the community relations duties. Sanborn had replaced Richard Crawford, a retired United States Army officer who oversaw the position from October 1959 to May 1962.[16] The community relations job was significant to Gulf American not only because it helped reduce company costs but because a vibrant, satisfied, independent community was critical in the Rosens' land sales effort.

Because Cape Coral had no city government, Gulf American provided basic municipal functions. For police protection, Crawford, and later Sanborn, directed a security force of six Lee County sheriff's deputies and one patrol car. By 1963 a full-time deputy was supplied for Cape Coral, eventually relieving Gulf American from this reponsibility. Concern over the lack of fire protection resulted in Finkernagel's founding of a volunteer fire department for Cape Coral in the early 1960s. Much of the groundwork had been done by Crawford and one of his employees, Peggy Tanfield. A tax district was formed in 1963, and approximately $22,000 was raised to purchase a firetruck and equipment for the department. The first truck was delivered in 1964, but it was not yet outfitted on its first night in Cape Coral to fight a fire in the Surfside Restaurant.[17]

As Cape Coral grew, the residents needed the services of a permanent post office. Originally, mail was brought from Fort Myers in the company Volkswagen bus to the guard shack at the corner of Coronado Boulevard and Cape Coral Parkway. Residents had to go there to receive their mail. In 1959 the post office, under the direction of Joseph Bradford, was moved to a room in the Surfside Restaurant. In October of that year, the mailboat *Santiva* began delivering mail to the community. The *Santiva* also serviced St. James City on Pine Island, along with Sanibel and Captiva islands. One of Finkernagel's first tasks at Cape Coral was to end Gulf American's financing of the postal service in the community. A branch office of the Fort Myers post office and a full-time postal employee were assigned to Cape Coral in 1963, with the operations housed in a facility in the Cape Coral shopping plaza on Cape Coral Parkway.[18]

Most early buyers of Gulf American homesites had voiced concern over the lack of any medical facilities for Cape Coral. In September 1960 Kenneth Schwartz negotiated with Dr. Theodore David, a Fort Myers surgeon, to come to the community one to three days a week. Gulf American furnished a complete medical clinic in the Cape Coral shopping plaza for him with equipment worth $7,000. Initially Leonard was furious that Schwartz had overstepped his authority in hiring David, but later he endorsed the idea. With more than 2,000 residents in Cape Coral by 1962, Finkernagel concluded that a full-time doctor was necessary if the community was to grow. He located Dr. Robert R. Tate, a young physician who was looking for a place to set up his medical practice. Already a homesite owner, Tate opened his office in Cape Coral on August 27, 1962, with the promise that Gulf American would guarantee his income for the first year. As the only doctor in the city for several years, Tate had no problem supporting himself, but the arduous schedule damaged his health. Eventually, he brought in a partner, Dr. Wallace L. Dawson. The third doctor in the community was Dr. Thomas G. Hinkle.[19]

In the early 1960s, Gulf American officials realized that a newsletter was necessary to keep residents informed of the community's increasing number of activities and events. The image of a growing community also required the founding of a small newspaper. According to Richard Crawford, the paper started almost by accident. Crawford's wife, Sally, had been writing a regular column about Cape Coral for the *Fort Myers News-Press*. Among other things, the column contained Gulf American and private announcements, names of visitors, and news supplied by residents. When the *News-Press* cancelled the column because it was taking up too much space, Richard Crawford was also printing two to four bulletins of news a week from the community relations office for the 320 families in the city. Combining company announcements with the news of the city's residents, Crawford and his wife put out their first weekly issue of the *Gulf Breeze* on May 22, 1961.[20]

Within a few months, the *Gulf Breeze* had increased to twenty mimeographed pages and included advertisements. Advertising by individuals was free because the paper was owned by Gulf American. Throughout 1961 Crawford was encouraged by several businessmen, particularly H. D. "Andy" Anderson, an early Cape Coral resident, to start a regularly printed newspaper. Deciding to launch the enterprise in late 1961, Crawford resigned from Gulf American and issued the first printing of the *Cape Coral Breeze* on December 14, 1961. The initial staff included Crawford, his wife Sally, and his former secretary, Joyce Parish.[21]

Wholly owned by Crawford, the paper's circulation quickly increased from its initial five subscriptions, due largely to Gulf American publicity. Anxious to show that the Cape Coral community was growing, an article about the independent newspaper was included in the company promotional newspaper, the *Cape Coral Sun,* in mid-February 1962. Within weeks the paid circulation jumped to more than 2,000 customers, many of whom were homesite owners who lived throughout the United States. The paper was successful, but the Crawfords wanted to spend more time at their favorite pastime, fishing. In October 1962 they sold the *Breeze* to Thompson K. Cassel of Gainesville for $32,000. Cassel, who owned several radio stations throughout Florida, hired a number of editors, beginning with Winsor W. Brown of Gainesville, until he was able to convince Crawford to return in 1966.[22]

With Cassel's death in 1967, ownership of the paper changed again. Cassel had been close friends with Robert Finkernagel, and they had an unwritten agreement that Finkernagel could buy 50 percent of the newspaper at any time for one dollar. Cassel's will transferred half ownership to Finkernagel outright and allowed him to purchase the remainder for what Cassel had paid, $32,000. Crawford continued to publish the paper, and eventually he bought a minor percentage of the business from Finkernagel. During Crawford's tenure the editorials were noted for clearly and fairly addressing community issues. The size of the paper increased from fourteen pages in 1967 to fifty-two in early

1970. At that time, the staff had risen to fourteen employees who published the paper for 7,000 subscribing customers. More than half of the readers lived outside Cape Coral. Finkernagel and Crawford eventually sold the *Breeze* in 1974 to Ogden Newspapers of Wheeling, West Virginia, for $1.2 million. Headed by G. Ogden Nutting, the publishing syndicate owned newspapers in smaller cities in the eastern and midwestern United States.[23]

Finkernagel had been brought originally to Cape Coral to develop community services for the growing city. The Rosens reasoned that the success of future sales depended on customers seeing an expanding community offering a multitude of municipal services. During the mid-1960s the responsibilities of community relations fell more to Paul Sanborn, and Finkernagel increasingly was given control of Cape Coral–based promotions. Finkernagel had gained a reputation for a sharp mind and an ability to complete projects for the company rapidly and competently. On one occasion, when Kenneth Schwartz needed to contact movie star Loretta Young about a promotion, he called Finkernagel, who was able to locate her private phone number within a couple of hours.[24]

One of the primary goals of the Cape Coral–based promotions was to project an image of youth for the new city. Throughout the country developments such as Cape Coral were perceived as retirement communities. In reality the population was actually much more balanced, with 817 children among the 3,825 residents in 1964. In order to fight the geriatric image, Finkernagel worked closely with Bernice Freiberg in Baltimore and Paul Venze of the Paul Venze Agency in New York to create promotions that accented young adults. As Finkernagel noted, it would have been easy for the company to pay a promotional fee for the national professional golf tour to hold a tournament in Cape Coral. The image, however, did not portray youth and thus other promotions were developed.[25]

In keeping with the youthful image, the public relations personnel at Gulf American, with the help of University of Miami golf coach William Henson, invited ten colleges from across the country to send four-man teams to Cape Coral. The result was the first Florida Intercollegiate Golf Championship in 1963, with Gulf American paying all costs. Eventually growing into a field of forty teams, the tournament remained at Cape Coral even after the company's sale to GAC in 1969. Gulf American also began sponsoring in 1963 the Florida Intercollegiate Tennis Tournament, a competition that eventually grew to a field of twelve major university teams by the late 1960s. Another event that resulted in major national publicity for Cape Coral was the Miss Florida World contest, first held in Cape Coral in 1963. Using the recently completed Cape

Coral yacht and racquet club, the beauty pageant remained in the city for several years with Miami radio personality Larry King as master of ceremonies.[26]

The promotional events were often originated in Miami at Woody Kepner and Associates, a public realtions firm hired by Leonard Rosen. The firm was able to convince the franchise holder to have the Miss Florida World contest transferred from Coral Gables to Cape Coral. Fond of using the descriptive adjectives "first annual," the public relations agency arranged for the First Annual National Inboard Hydroplane Championships to be held at Cape Coral in August 1960. An estimated 30,000 spectators lined Dolphin Drive near the yacht basin to watch seven world records set. The race, however, was never repeated at Cape Coral, and as Finkernagel joked, the "first annual" became "the first and only."[27]

Another means of publicity for the Cape Coral community was the filming of television commercials and movies. The Rosens were well acquainted with the effectiveness of broadcast media from the merchandising of Charles Antell cosmetics. As American audiences became more sophisticated, Gulf American public relations staff found it more credible to try to get indirect advertising by having a third party talk or write about Cape Coral or use the community as a background location for commercials. Therefore, Finkernagel, Bernice Freiberg, and others often had detailed negotiations over the size of Cape Coral street signs in the background of a commercial or over the number of times Cape Coral was mentioned in a script. A large number of companies made television commercials in the city, including Chevrolet, Ford, Oldsmobile, Listerine, Johnson Motors, U.S. Rubber, and Maidenform bathing suits.[28]

U.S. Rubber was also convinced by Gulf American to name one of its styles of bathing caps the "Cape Coral." The promotion allowed the name "Cape Coral" to be printed inside the cap. A coupon was included that offered the cap purchaser a vacation at the Cape Coral development for a reduced rate. The program proved successful for about one year.[29]

Several complete television programs were also filmed at Cape Coral. Three episodes of the popular television series, "Route 66," starring Martin Milner, Glenn Corbett, Albert Salmi, Rip Torn, Jack Warden, Miriam Hopkins, and Sussue Hayakawa, were completed in spring 1963. In return for references to Cape Coral in the filming, Gulf American provided, among other considerations, housing and food for the seventy-five cast and crew members. When the script called for a swamp and nothing in the vicinity was suitable, Gulf American provided dredging equipment to build one for the filming on some unused property. In addition to "Route 66," a television special called "Sun Country" was filmed in Cape Coral, featuring Hank Williams, Jr., and Merle Kilgore. The program was never aired, however, because of legal problems.[30]

The filming of a full-length motion picture at Cape Coral was another attempt to gain national publicity. In the spring of 1965, *The Fat Spy* was shot in the community. The comedy, about a cosmetics manufacturer who wanted to find, bottle, and sell the waters of the fountain of youth, starred Jayne Mansfield, Phyllis Diller, Jack E. Leonard, and Brian Donlevy. Besides supplying housing for the entire production company, Gulf American assigned Richard G. Sayers and Joseph Miller, among others, to attend to the needs of the stars. Sayers had been hired in 1964 to direct the Cape Coral news bureau, and Miller had been hired in 1961 to manage a variety of projects for which a need might exist. One of Miller's chief tasks was to keep Jack E. Leonard from talking to reporters because he was extremely vocal about the mosquitoes and the heat. The film premiered in Fort Myers, but the theater stopped showing it after three days because almost no one was purchasing tickets. *The Fat Spy* was also a failure at box offices across the country.[31]

One of the most successful promotions of Cape Coral in the company's history was the Cape Coral Rose Gardens. The concept for the project originated with Jack Rosen, who had been trying to solve a particular difficulty in the company's Florida sales efforts. In the early 1960s, Gulf American canvassers (or OPCs) were being threatened with arrest because they were soliciting customers at Florida's tourist attractions such as Cypress Gardens. As it became increasingly difficult to generate prospects in this way, company officials attempted to get Cape Coral literature approved by the Florida Public Attractions Association so that it could be displayed throughout the Florida tourist industry. The approval was refused because Cape Coral had no public attractions.[32]

As a result of the refusal, Gulf American purchased and tried to develop two tourist-oriented businesses in Miami. One was the defunct Musa Isle, an Indian village located near the Orange Bowl that featured alligator wrestling. As that program was being revived, Gulf American set up an attraction on Miami Beach called Pearl Lagoon. Posing as a tourist in early 1966, *Miami Herald* reporter Matthew Taylor described Pearl Lagoon as "a cheap reed fence around a lot with a couple of thatched-roof shelters in it. There's a dusty little case of ordinary sea shells. A tank full of tropical fish. It's dark, murky, incomplete." At the only exit, a woman tried to get him to sign up for a free flight to see Golden Gate Estates. Pearl Lagoon was, in the opinion of company employee Joseph Miller, nothing more than a thinly disguised ploy to generate more prospects, "just an obvious trap." The Florida Public Attractions Association refused approval of both attractions, citing that they had not been in business for the required two years. As a consequence, Jack Rosen began investigating other alternatives.[33]

In nearly every way, Jack was the creator and driving force behind the rose gardens. In the early 1960s he had been speculating with two friends, Milt Kessler and Sylvan Abrams, about how to get more people to the southwest coast of Florida. Kessler and Abrams were close friends and employees of Jack who shared interests in the arts and cultural matters. Jack often spent time with these two men, concentrating on new marketing and promotional ventures. They proposed that a major tourist attraction at Cape Coral would suit their needs. Bernice Freiberg was immediately sent to Florida by Jack to drive the length of the state, surveying the types and sizes of attractions available to the public. Jack wanted to know what was being done so that his new tourist venture would be bigger and more dramatic. He reasoned that as more people came to see the promotion, more would take the sales tour of Cape Coral and buy homesites.[34]

By the time Freiberg returned, Jack had seen a unique water fountain display at the German-French Flower Show in Saarbrucken, West Germany. Intrigued by the device, he sent Freiberg to Germany in 1963 to meet the inventor, Otto Przystawik, and negotiate a purchase. The ensuing agreement called for the construction of the largest fountain of its kind in the United States and stipulated that it was to be completely set up and demonstrated to the Rosen brothers before being shipped to Cape Coral. Freiberg was sent to various locations to ensure that the Cape Coral version was going to be the largest. Originally, the display was to be placed in the median of Cape Coral Parkway, immediately east of Del Prado Boulevard. As plans for a Gulf American tourist attraction developed, the fountain's location was switched to the newly proposed rose gardens. Installation began in February 1964 and took nearly four months.[35]

Otto Przystawik, an electrician by trade, began developing his fountains in Germany in the 1930s. With the close of World War II in 1945, he reopened a restaurant in West Berlin called the Residence Casino or "Resi." Boasting a large dance floor and a twenty-five-piece orchestra, the night club featured many of Przystawik's technical special effects from his unique use of colored lights, water fountains, and music. As Przystawik perfected his "Dancing Waters" and made them portable, he was able to build a large-scale version and to present it at the Industrial Exhibition in West Berlin in the summer of 1952. The beauty of the fountains so impressed New York showman Harold Steinman that he arranged to bring the display to the United States.[36]

The Dancing Waters show made its American debut at Radio City Music Hall in New York City on January 15, 1953, to an enthusiastic audience. During its initial eight weeks in New York, the attraction was seen by more than 1.5 million theatergoers. In 1954 Gunter Przystawik, the inventor's son, took the show on tour throughout the United States, sometimes putting on ten performances a day. In addition, the company performed constantly throughout central Europe with more than three hundred engagements annually. By the early 1960s more than one hundred of the musical fountains had been built with no two exactly alike. Jack Rosen probably became acquainted initially with the "Dancing Waters" by seeing or hearing about one of the many American performances; he then traveled to Germany to view it on a larger scale.[37]

The fountains, renamed the Waltzing Waters, were brought to Cape Coral in early 1964 and assembled in a desolate stretch of filled land that would become the rose gardens. Under the supervision of Gunter Przystawik, the 170-foot-long apparatus took shape, using 3,500 feet of two- and three-inch piping. The fountain eventually lifted water more than 60 feet in the air. The display was capable of moving 7,000 gallons of water per minute through 800 jets that varied in diameter from one-fifth inch to one and one-half inches. The uniqueness of Waltzing Waters came from the swaying of the water spouts and the changing of colored lights in rhythm to the background music. The entire performance originally was choreographed by hand from a control booth but later was adapted to computerization. Numerous patents were held by Przystawik on the apparatus. In addition to the piping, the Waltzing Waters required 5,200 feet of electrical cable, sixteen pumps of seven and one-half horsepower, and fifty-five 250-watt colored lights.[38]

Many features of the gardens were the result of Jack Rosen's promotional schemes. With the largest fountain in the United States being constructed for them, Jack also wanted the new attraction to have the largest rose collection. He sent Freiberg and Finkernagel in 1963 to Newark, New York, to negotiate with the Jackson and Perkins Rose Company. Discovering that a shipment of 35,000 rosebushes was being sold to an Ohio group, Freiberg and Finkernagel agreed to purchase 40,000 bushes, assured by the growers that Cape Coral then would have the largest rose display in the country. To gain additional publicity, a new coral-colored rose was developed by Jackson and Perkins in the same year and named the "Cape Coral." In a related promotion, rosebushes were given to the governors of various states. After naming Mrs. Lyndon B. Johnson as the honorary chairperson of the rose distribution program, Jack was invited to the White House where he presented the First Lady with hundreds of Cape Coral rosebushes for beautification of the White House grounds.[39]

Opened in late 1964, although not yet completed, the rose gardens

Construction of the Rose Gardens in early 1964. The Waltzing Waters piping is visible in the man-made lagoon.

were located on a forty-five-acre tract in the southernmost tip of Cape Coral, near a bay called Glover Bight. Because the ground was extremely low, Gulf American used dredges to obtain fill material from the bottom of the Caloosahatchee River. In addition to the Waltzing Waters and the rose displays, the complex contained a porpoise show, a carillon, an exhibit called the Garden of Patriots that featured sculptures of famous Americans, a tropical rainforest called the Aloha Lagoon, a hibiscus showcase, a bird aviary, and a gift shop. During its peak years of 1965 and 1966, the rose gardens hosted more than 300,000 visitors annually. Although guests were charged a nominal entrance fee, most entered free as part of the Gulf American sales tour.[40]

The Garden of Patriots drew more national attention than any other aspect of the park. Sculptures on the grounds included busts of Washington, Truman, Eisenhower, and Kennedy. A replica of the Mount Rushmore carvings, created by sculptor Lincoln Borglum, was placed in the garden. Borglum was the son of Gutzon Borglum, sculptor of the original monument in South Dakota. A huge copy of the famous *Flag Raising on Iwo Jima* was made for Gulf American by Felix de Weldon, the sculptor of the original. A high point in media coverage occurred on February 12, 1966, when Bob Hope was given a special award as "Patriot of the Year." The award was a bust of Hope done by Robert Berks, and a copy was placed on display in the Garden of Patriots. Other monuments on the grounds included the $25,000 AMVETS carillon, a copy of Michelangelo's *Pietà*, and a six-foot-tall, 2,700-pound shell casing from the battleship *Massachusetts* presented by Governor John A. Volpe.[41]

An important addition to the rose gardens was a house designed entirely by women as part of a promotion with *McCall's* magazine. Inasmuch as most houses were designed by men, Gulf American promoters reasoned that a house designed totally by women would create a great deal of media attention. A symposium was held at the Cape Coral yacht and racquet club with numerous women's club leaders invited. The innovations proposed at the symposium were incorporated by architect Harold B. Davis into the McCall's Certified House, which was built on the grounds of the rose gardens and completed in April 1965. The house was displayed in an article in the July 1965 issue of *McCall's*. Duplicates of the house were built at Cape Coral and given away as prizes from a drawing at the New York World's Fair and on "The Price Is Right" television show. A similar promotional scheme was used at Golden Gate with *Parent's* magazine.[42]

Despite the beauty and appeal of the gardens, the attraction suffered from the beginning from numerous economic problems. The trained porpoises periodically died, and new ones had to be caught and trained. The difficult task was estimated to cost $3,000 for each porpoise. A much larger cost was the estimated $50,000 annual expense of maintaining the 40,000 rosebushes. Gulf American officials soon discovered that roses did not flourish in southwest Florida and had to be replaced constantly. The attrition rate for the rose displays was so great that by the late 1960s the Cape Coral Rose Gardens were renamed the Cape Coral Gardens. By 1970 the roses that had lined the three-mile-long drive into the gardens were gone and only the bushes in select formal rose beds remained.[43]

Some observers felt that the gardens needed more daytime activities if the needed crowds of paying tourists were to be attracted. The Waltzing Waters and many of the other displays were designed to have their greatest effectiveness at night. Except on rare occasions, the Waltzing

Leonard and Jack Rosen present Bob Hope with the "Patriot of the Year" award at the Rose Gardens on February 12, 1966.

Waters display was shown only at night because daylight shows could not use the colored lights. Gunter Przystawik explained the reasoning: "It's like seeing fireworks in the daytime." The problem was that the majority of tourists visited Cape Coral and the gardens during the day as guests of the company and few wanted to return again at night. Przystawik suggested that Gulf American invest in a large building so that the Waltzing Waters could be seen in full color during daylight hours. Commenting on the cool reception that his suggestion received from company management, he noted: "I couldn't sell the idea. I didn't do a good enough sales pitch."[44]

Another problem with the Cape Coral Gardens was that the attraction was not designed to be a profit-making venture. It was simply a $2 million promotion, similar to the Cape Coral country club, whose goal was to attract customers to Cape Coral to take the sales tour. In addition, the property was managed by Larry Rosen, an employee whose primary interest was the gift shop at the gardens and not the profitability of the whole attraction. Losses ranging as high as $250,000 annually during the late 1960s prompted several top-level staff meetings in Baltimore, presided over by Jack Rosen.[45] As Gulf American sold the majority of its Cape Coral lots in the mid-1960s and began concentrating on its other properties, the need for a major attraction at its first community was eliminated.

The gardens had outlived their usefulness to the land sales operation, so Gulf American offered in December 1966 to deed them to the state of Florida as a park. Although state officials initially estimated operational costs at $100,000 per year, they apparently were impressed by the growing popularity of the gardens with large numbers of tourists. Florida Park Board director N. E. "Bill" Miller declared: "I personally would like to have it. If we get a favorable report from our board, we will go back to the governor and ask for funds until we can get an appropriation." Negotiations continued, with Governor Haydon Burns promising to investigate the proposal. Gulf American was preparing to use the gift as a $2 million tax deduction. Although state officials visited the attraction for an on-site inspection, no action was ever taken.[46]

The Cape Coral Gardens were again offered to the state of Florida in May 1969 by the successor to Gulf American, GAC Corporation. The proposition, however, was part of a complex deal. Between 1957 and 1963, Gulf American had been authorized by the trustees of the Internal Improvement Trust Fund to dredge approximately 600,000 cubic yards of material to create a boating channel in the Caloosahatchee River near Cape Coral. The company later admitted to overdredging an estimated total of 3.6 million cubic yards of material from the waterway during that period, depositing it as fill in Cape Coral and in the rose garden area. In some places the dredging left holes more than ninety feet deep in the river bottom where the natural depth was approximately twenty feet. Besides this violation of state law, it was determined that all but four acres of the gardens apparently had been constructed on public land. The 1872 survey of the area by Samuel Hamblin had incorrectly noted the meander line, a commonly used boundary between private property and public lands near a river. The state of Florida was entitled to recover any such land illegally sold or given away by the Internal Improvement Trust Fund trustees.[47]

In its offer, GAC proposed that it should pay a fine of $300,000, give title to the state of 4,835 acres of undeveloped environmentally sensitive land on Cape Coral's western boundary, transfer ownership of the Cape Coral Gardens to the state, and in return be allowed to open seven additional channels from Cape Coral into open water. With clear title to all lands in question, Assistant Attorney General Steve Slepin described the offer as "more of a challenge than an answer." Florida Secretary of State Tom Adams said that he felt confident from his study that all but four acres of the gardens were on state-owned land. He also estimated that it would cost Florida about $490,000 to operate the gardens for the next six months as a state park.[48]

With unclear title and apparently high operating costs, neither the state nor a dozen interested groups were able to take over the management of the gardens. The attraction's heavy financial losses resulted in GAC's announcement in August 1970 that the park was closing. The Cape Coral Gardens were officially closed on September 8, 1970, but were not dismantled. All displays were carefully boarded up at an estimated cost of $7,000, although no future plans for the attraction were anticipated.[49] At the time, the Waltzing Waters display was purchased by its builder and operator, Gunter Przystawik, and set up as a separate attraction at the German-American Club on Pine Island Road. When that facility closed in April 1982, the equipment was transferred by Przystawik to his indoor Waltzing Waters display on U.S. Route 41 in Fort Myers. Dolphin trainer Jack Scarpuzzi bought the dolphin show, moving it to Fort Myers Beach. Although he eventually joined Przystawik's attraction on Pine Island Road, numerous dolphins died and the presentation was abandoned.[50]

Jack and Leonard Rosen had tried various promotions and events during the 1960s to draw attention initially to Cape Coral and later to their other developments. A major problem, however, was the company's lack of credibility with the American public. Many people suspected that the company was trying to sell unusable swampland to them as other promoters had done.[51] In order to counter this suspicion, the Rosens hired several individuals to handle publicity for Cape Coral. The goal of these staffers was to convince third parties such as newspapers and magazines to write positively about Cape Coral. Eventually the publicity staff evolved into a complete news bureau.[52]

At Cape Coral's inception, publicity for the new community was managed by Connie Mack, Jr., and by Eileen Bernard, an early employee. As Mack became busier with public relations, Bernard inherited most of the publicity duties at Cape Coral. Encouraged to move to a warmer climate because of her husband's poor health, Bernard was hired in early 1958 at Fort Myers by Leonard Rosen to answer letters from potential customers. When that operation was moved to the Miami office in early 1959, Kenneth Schwartz asked her to start a newsletter in order to reduce the number of customer inquiries. The result was the *Cape Coral Sun,* a promotional newspaper that included any news items of interest to Cape Coral residents and nonresident lot owners. Eventually the paper was sent to all the prospects on Gulf American's computerized mailing lists, and it was given out at dinner sales parties throughout the country. According to Bernard, the *Cape Coral Sun* had one of the largest circulations of any publication in Florida during the mid-1960s.[53]

Written entirely by Bernard, the *Cape Coral Sun* presented the benefits of living in southwest Florida and particularly in Cape Coral. Articles described the area's tarpon fishing, new businesses, and recently arrived residents. It displayed numerous photos of tropical Florida living. It also shared the dreams of new residents about building a city. Emphasizing the positive, Bernard said: "You never mentioned anything like mosquitoes or heat or dirt roads. You didn't mention them or you said they were being fixed." Her biggest problem, however, was pressure from staffers in the Baltimore and Miami offices to reduce the factual content and increase the sales push in the articles. "It wasn't that they wanted to lie, they just got carried away," said Bernard. With an eventual budget of $100,000 annually, the paper continued publication until cutbacks led GAC Corporation to cancel it in 1971. Bernard noted the paper's impact on the company's success by remarking, "A lot of people came to Cape Coral because they read that magazine and it made everything look so wonderful."[54]

As the publicity efforts increased in number, Gulf American officials decided that a full-time news bureau was necessary for Cape Coral. Some of Bernard's publicity duties had been taken over by community relations director Richard Crawford and public relations director Robert Finkernagel. In October 1964 Richard Sayers was hired to set up a news bureau in Cape Coral for the company and to handle any media relations. Sayers previously had worked for the *Miami News* as chief copy editor and had been contacted by Mert Wetstein about working for Gulf American at Cape Coral. Wetstein was a vice-president of Woody Kepner and Associates, the public relations firm that created many of the company's Florida promotions and advertisements. The Cape Coral news bureau was set up on the third floor of the Gulf American building in Cape Coral, directly above the offices of Mack and Finkernagel.[55]

The news bureau included a complete photography lab. Photographers who worked for the bureau included William Mahler, Edward Farrell, Richard Wylie, and Robert South. Susan Jones and Vincent Smith wrote articles for release to newspapers. Jerry Schomp was responsible for putting out an internal publication called *Impact*. The *Cape Coral Sun* was primarily the work of publications editor Eileen Bernard, who worked almost independently of the news bureau but was technically under its direction.[56]

Because the goal of the news bureau was to get newspapers to write articles about Cape Coral, Sayers in Cape Coral and Freiberg in Baltimore engineered a program whereby newspaper writers and editors, particularly those with bylines, were invited to visit the property. These journalists were guided and entertained by Gulf American staffers such as Sayers, Bernard, and Peggy Tanfield. The object of such a visit was to show the group that a beautiful, real community was being developed. In 1968 a group of 270 writers was brought to Cape Coral to see the city. At an earlier meeting, Sayers was introduced to the executive editor of the *Cleveland Plain Dealer*, who was on vacation in Fort Myers, and arranged several successful charter fishing trips for him while he was there. The newspaperman was so impressed that he wrote an editorial on Florida's new communities, particularly Cape Coral, and another article on sportfishing in southwest Florida. It was this kind of free publicity from a respected third party that guided many of the news bureau's actions.[57]

In addition to the visiting journalists program, Sayers was responsible for publicizing any major event in Cape Coral. Press releases were sent to targeted newspapers throughout the country. Using computers located in offices on the floor above them, news bureau staffers were able to pinpoint newspaper audiences, depending on the subject of the article. For example, they could arrange to send an article on the presence of churches in the community to all of the religion editors of weekly papers in Ohio. During Sayers's eight-year tenure, the Cape Coral news bureau averaged 100,000 column inches of publicity a year in newspapers and magazines.[58]

In the early 1960s a publicity scheme was initiated that grew into a separate organization. In mid-1964 Gulf American launched a non-profit Florida corporation called the National Hobby Institute (NHI) under the direction of Joseph Miller, who had initially been hired to manage various new projects that the Rosens wanted to start. The motivation behind the creation of the NHI was to generate new sales leads from the estimated 24 million American hobbyists and to gain free publicity for Cape Coral. For example, communication between an NHI-sponsored model railroad club in Cape Coral and a similar club in Atlanta provided an inexpensive mailing list of hobbyists for future Gulf American marketing efforts. In order to house the operation, a National Hobby Center was set up in a building at the western end of the Cape Coral shopping plaza. Eventually, the center was moved to a building at the rose gardens.[59]

The National Hobby Center attracted nationwide publicity by sponsoring a wide range of hobby events. Model powerboat regattas, model airplane races, rocket competitions, stamp conventions, model drag races, and matchbook cover conventions, among other events, highlighted the calendar. The Cape Coral news bureau made sure that media and hobby editors were notified of all these events and were sent articles with photographs. On one occasion, Miller promoted the idea of shooting down a model airplane with a model rocket. Practice firings of the rocket prompted a complaint by a National Airlines pilot, who claimed that his plane was nearly hit, and a call to Miller from the Federal Aviation Administration. Despite the problems, a photograph of the event appeared in approximately 400 publications throughout the United States.[60]

The goal of the majority of Gulf American promotions and publicity was to gain recognition for Cape Coral and southwest Florida. Two promotions, however, were designed to encourage people to come to Cape Coral and take the sales tour. Early in the history of Gulf American, sales managers hired roving salespeople (OPCs) to drive or fly tourists from their vacation spots elsewhere in Florida to Cape Coral. The estimated average cost of bringing a couple to Cape Coral in this manner was $120. In order to reduce the costs, a new marketing strategy was employed in 1961 called the "Very Important Traveler" or VIT program.[61]

The VIT program, headed by a longtime associate of Leonard Rosen named Murray Grossman, offered rebates to tourists for driving to Cape Coral and taking the sales tour. Travelers were offered a $15 rebate per family to help pay for gasoline, meals, and motel room. Visitors were greeted at a welcome center on U.S. Route 41 in North Fort Myers and introduced to a salesperson. Under the direction of Grossman and his assistant, Joseph Miller, the VIT program offered additional prizes to visitors that included a chance at winning an automobile, fur coats, and other gifts. Coupons or "passports" for the rebates were offered throughout Florida by gasoline stations, restaurants, motels, and tourist-oriented shops. In return for distributing the "passports," these business owners received a fee or "spiff," as it was called, from Gulf American. The cost of delivering a potential customer to Cape Coral was reduced, therefore, from an estimated $120 to approximately $30, which included the $15 rebate to the prospective customers and fees to the coupon distributors. The program was so cost effective at Cape Coral that it was incorporated into the sales program at each of Gulf American's Florida properties.[62]

While the VIT strategy was successful, a vastly larger program was started that involved the flying of potential customers to Cape Coral. Bringing prospective buyers to a land sales project was not new in Florida. In the early 1900s Henry M. Flagler had offered inexpensive transportation to Florida on his Florida East Coast Railway to home seekers wanting to purchase some of his lands. Induced to make the trip by seeing advertisements and a specially outfitted railway car named "Florida on Wheels," potential buyers were given discounts of up to 50 percent on fares.[63] During the 1920s land boom in Miami, George Merrick employed a large fleet of buses, emblazoned with "Coral Gables" on the sides, to transport potential property buyers to Coral Gables from Miami.[64] The factor that made Gulf American's flight program unique was its huge volume.

Since the beginning of Cape Coral sales in January 1958, Gulf American had employed airplanes in its land sales operation. Originally, customers who visited the sales office at Cape Coral and purchased a homesite were flown over the property to inspect their lot. Piloted by Edward F. Wilson, Granville Petrie, Harry Hirsh, or Joseph Gibson, among others, the six small aircraft flew from 7:30 A.M. to dark, six days a week, carrying an average total of 500 passengers per day. The planes, mostly Cessna 172s, were supplied by Wilson's Fort Myers Airways, and many had "Cape Coral" painted in large letters on the fuselage. The first runways for the short flights were Coronado Boulevard and Cape Coral Parkway until increased automobile traffic forced the company to move its "airport" one street north of Cape Coral Parkway to Southeast Forty-seventh Terrace. A large building in the Cape Coral shopping plaza, which later temporarily housed the National Hobby Center, served as the terminal.[65]

As Cape Coral grew, the Cape Coral airport was moved to a location on the west side of Del Prado Boulevard, near the present site of St. Andrew's Catholic Church. The airport featured two 4,000-foot runways, one running east-west and one running north-south, control tower operation, a temporary terminal building, and lighting for night conditions. By 1963 the airfield ranked as the 225th busiest in the nation. In the same year, Southeast Airlines began flying ten-passenger twin-engine Beechcrafts into Cape Coral for twice-a-day Cape Coral—to—Miami air service for a round-trip fare of $28. According to company officials, Cape Coral was the first major Florida land development to have commercial air service.[66] The busy airport was closed in 1965, and Gulf American air traffic was transferred to Page Field in Fort Myers. Page Field had become more accessible because of the opening of the Cape Coral bridge in 1964. The runways beside Del Prado Boulevard were torn up and the area was sold as homesites.[67]

Besides the observation flights at Cape Coral, Gulf American had routinely arranged to fly prospective buyers to Cape Coral as part of its OPC program. Couples were flown from the east coast of Florida to the site in small planes owned by salespeople and later in six chartered thirty-two-passenger DC-3 aircraft and a fleet of buses. Extremely costly, the flights were eventually abandoned in the early 1960s as the VIT program proved to be a less expensive way to get Florida tourists to Cape

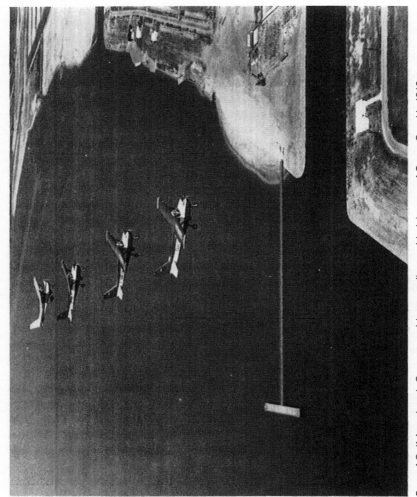

Four of Gulf American's Cessnas cruising over the yacht club area of Cape Coral in 1960.

Coral.[68] As more people throughout the United States and Canada began to purchase lots in Cape Coral, Gulf American sales managers discovered that these homesite owners were prime prospects for future sales of houses and additional land. They were already convinced of the product and many purchased additional property. The major obstacle was bringing them to Cape Coral to see the community.

Beginning in the housing division in Cape Coral, a marketing operation was started in the early 1960s called the "Fly and Buy" program. Independent brokers in large northern cities recruited and screened homesite owners for a flight to Cape Coral to consider purchasing a house for their lot. A broker would call the head of the program in Cape Coral, Milton Green, an energetic salesman and a longtime associate of the Rosens, or his assistant, Raymond Meyer. They then arranged to fly a couple to Fort Myers. The customers made a down payment of several hundred dollars and were given a tour of the area along with a three-day and two-night stay at Cape Coral. If they bought a house, the money became their first payment. If no sale was made, it was refunded.[69]

The program started small, averaging only three to five couples per week. Within a short time, however, the number of homesite owners involved was so great that the airline ticket bill for National Airlines reached $68,000 in one month. National was the only major air carrier that serviced Fort Myers. The Miami office of Gulf American subsequently limited the expenditures for the flights. The success of the operation was shown by its estimated closing rate of over 90 percent and low cancellation or "burn" rate. The normally high cancellation rate in the housing division had always been a problem for the company. The major drawback in the Fly and Buy program was its high cost, largely due to the combination of paying for airline tickets and substantial commissions to the independent brokers and the housing salespeople.[70]

Ordered to cut the flight costs, Green began chartering planes to transport his housing customers. While the strategy was potentially less expensive, he found that it was difficult to fill all of the seats, even though the planes stopped in three or four cities before they reached Fort Myers. In order to fill the remaining places, Green approached the directors of the land sales division about bringing customers to Cape Coral who had purchased their lots but had not visited the property. Because buyers had a six-month inspection and cancellation privilege in their homesite contracts, land salespeople hoped to solidify their sales and possibly interest their clients in purchasing more property or upgrading to a more expensive lot. The land sales division experienced a dramatic decrease in the cancellation rate and subsequently took over the Fly and Buy operation from the housing division. As Raymond

Meyer said: "These boys [land salesmen] are not stupid. They know a good thing when they see it."[71]

During the early 1960s, Gulf American had been accelerating its dinner party sales program in eastern American cities. As a result of the company's aggressive marketing policies, several states, including New Jersey, New York, and Wisconsin, began restricting out-of-state sales of real estate. Without the freedom to solicit customers in states outside Florida, a large part of Gulf American's market potentially was eliminated. The problem was solved by a unique concept developed by Charles Hepner and Jack Rosen in 1965. While company salespeople and brokers were not allowed to market homesites in a particular state, they were not prevented from soliciting people to join a travel club. Hepner and Rosen envisioned signing up people for the travel club and including a reduced-price vacation to Cape Coral as part of the package. As an inside observer on much of the process, Meyer commented: "Once again, Gulf American took a lemon and turned it into an exotic bar drink, not just lemonade."[72]

All company marketing and sales executives were called to Baltimore by Jack in early 1965 for a secret meeting to discuss the proposal. The trouble-shooting session lasted several days and resulted in a proposed program called the Travel Guild of America. Although Jack kept pushing the idea, many of the assembled executives remained skeptical. On the final day of the meeting, Jack went around the conference table, asking for comments. As he proceeded across the room, he eventually reached Charles Cavanagh, who had been hired by Jack to fill various management positions as needed by the company. He had previously worked in a number of marketing positions in New York City and had held management jobs with Prudential Insurance Company.[73]

Cavanagh responded to Jack's questions by standing up and stating: "Jack, I guarantee you that the people will go absolutely ape. They'll throw fifty dollar bills at you. They'll throw checks at you. You will not be able to handle it." His enthusiastic support for the new program resulted in numerous snickers and derisive comments from the assembled group. Cavanagh could tell by Jack's broad smile that he loved the evaluation. Jack immediately turned around, facing Cavanagh, and said: "You're in charge. It's your baby. You are going to set it up for me."[74]

The location for the trial effort of the Travel Guild of America (TGA) was Wisconsin, a state where Gulf American had had little success getting its Florida property approved for sale. Attorney Ronald Sandler, brother of Gulf American board member Solomon Sandler, was sent to Wisconsin to satisfy various state and legal requirements for the new plan. A promotional film was developed in Baltimore from Gulf American's standard sales film, featuring Florida and Cape Coral but removing the sales pitch. Cavanagh flew to Wisconsin in July 1965 to set up, at the Red Carpet Inn in Milwaukee, the initial dinner presentation, which was organized similarly to the land sales dinner parties. The speakers promoted the beauty and benefits of Florida and talked about the advantages of joining TGA. All soliciting for land sales at the meeting was excluded. Careful attention was given to details to ensure that the guests had an enjoyable evening. Brokers invited the same people to the dinner that they would have chosen for a land sales dinner. Many of the brokers and salespeople later served as travel guides, accompanying the members on the flights to Cape Coral.[75]

The first two dinner parties in Wisconsin yielded dramatic results. For a membership fee of $79, customers were entitled to free travel bags, complimentary shirts, discounts at hotels, and a free three-day trip to Cape Coral on a chartered airplane. The only requirement was that they attend a sales presentation in Cape Coral if they took the vacation. The enthusiasm for the program surprised Cavanagh and other Gulf American executives present at the dinners. Because Cavanagh forgot to bring contracts, guests signed up for the program on business cards, hotel napkins, checks, and paper currency. Cavanagh later described the scene: "I had two shopping bags of money and pieces of paper. . . . I had to remember and try to set up the three separate flights." A total of three planeloads of customers enrolled.[76]

The flights were scheduled back to back, leaving Milwaukee on November 20, 23, and 26, 1965, with food and alcohol served during the trip to Florida. Gulf American entertained the guests at the Nautilus Inn in Cape Coral. About 60 percent of the group purchased homesites. Leonard Rich, director of sales promotion, attributed the sales success to Gulf American's honesty with vacationers about the upcoming sales pitch. Cavanagh recalled that the first flight generated $141,000 in sales, the second brought in $132,000, and the third produced $168,000. The program was expanded quickly throughout the country, eventually requiring approximately sixty charter flights per month.[77]

By December 1965 the Travel Guild promotion had grown so fast that Cavanagh threatened to resign because of the heavy workload. Jack Rosen responded by promoting him to national flight director and convincing him to go to Cape Coral to oversee all the flights. At that time, the Rosens decided that it would be considerably cheaper to buy an airplane than to charter all of the flights. In February 1966 Gulf American began purchasing stock in Modern Air Transport, a small supplemental carrier operating out of Trenton, New Jersey. Gulf American received approval in May 1966 from the Civil Aeronautics Board to complete the $807,500 purchase. Company officials were particularly interested in Modern Air's previous CAB authorization to fly charters throughout the country.[78]

Immediately after the purchase was complete, Gulf American transferred the firm's operations to the Miami International Airport and announced a $17.3 million equipment-expansion program. In order to transport customers efficiently from throughout the United States to Gulf American properties in Florida, Leonard Rosen believed that an all-jet fleet was needed. Five 135-passenger Convair 990 fan-jets were ordered from American Airlines, three of which were delivered in early 1967.[79]

Within a year of the airline's acquisition, the staff had grown from 47 to 532 employees. As a result of this growth and the new jet purchases, Modern Air lost $2.5 million during the fiscal year ending August 1967. While he began selling off the slower DC-7, Martin 202, and DC-3 aircraft during the latter part of the year, Leonard publicly acknowledged that the airline was still losing $200,000 a month by early 1968. He and Solomon Sandler, who had been named vice-president of the airline, secured additional charters in Canada and Germany in an effort to bolster the carrier's lagging revenues. These contracts included some seven hundred flights from Berlin, West Germany, to holiday resorts in southern Europe and a few transatlantic flights. Despite the charter contracts and some transport work for the United States military, Modern Air's losses mounted, due largely to the 20,000 customers per month that it flew to Gulf American sales presentations in Florida.[80]

Flying into Miami International Airport, customers were transported to Cape Coral and Golden Gate on a fleet of large commercial buses that initially numbered twenty-six. During a typical stay, vacationers were taken to a local attraction such as Sanibel Island, the Shell Factory, or the Cape Coral Gardens, eventually ending up at a company-sponsored luau in the evening. The following day was set aside for the sales presentation and tour of the property. The customers were often taken shopping in Fort Myers on the third day before returning to Miami. Cavanagh's task was to feed, house, and entertain the customers during their stay. Estimating the peak number of buses at sixty, Raymond Meyer remarked, "You couldn't go anywhere in Cape Coral without being behind a bus." By 1967 Cavanagh's staff of more than 300 were servicing an estimated 50,000 people per month from all sources, including the VIT program. The busiest month recorded 80,000 visitors throughout the travel promotion.[81]

The most critical problem with the vast size of the Travel Guild program was keeping the various busloads of people separate once a group had heard the sales presentation. For this reason, meals were served in locations throughout Cape Coral, including the Surfside Restaurant, the country club, and temporary locations protected by tents. Needing a more permanent structure for cookouts, Cavanagh pressed company officials for a building on the beach at the yacht club. The result was a $45,000 pavilion in front of the clubhouse, complete with a bandstand. The necessity of keeping groups separate resulted in expensive situations for Gulf American if departing flights were delayed. In such a case, busloads of vacationers were housed throughout Miami or given free three-day cruises to the Bahamas.[82]

As the number of patrons increased, the cost of the Travel Guild program rose dramatically. After estimating that the cost of Coca-Cola alone for the bus ride to and from Cape Coral would amount to more than $500,000 annually, the Rosens concluded that the flights had to land in Fort Myers at Page Field. The Rosens' original plan for the flight program had always been to bring the flights into Fort Myers and not Miami. Before the first group had left Milwaukee, Gulf American representatives appeared before a special meeting of the Lee County Commission on November 18, 1965, to secure a ten-year lease for a terminal site at Page Field. Gulf American was allowed to construct a wood-frame building with the agreement that the temporary terminal would not exceed $85,000 in value and that it would be demolished by July 1966 in favor of a more permanent structure.[83]

As the terminal neared completion in late spring 1966, Leonard arrived to inspect the new facilities. He had already been negotiating with American Airlines to purchase several new four-engine Convair 990 jets to land at Fort Myers. He was informed, however, by company engineer Thomas Weber that, according to the FAA, the runway was too short to accommodate the larger jet aircraft and that Lee County did not have the funds to lengthen it. Furious at the prospect of another delay, Leonard asked Weber for the estimated cost of the improvements. Without hesitating, he instructed the assembled Gulf American executives to schedule the flights because he planned to pay for the extension. An agreement was reached with county officials for the $134,000 project, with Rosen promising to provide one-half the funds. On November 15, 1967, Gulf American paid Lee County $78,000 for its part of the expenses. During this period, the flight program continued to operate out of Miami.[84]

With the Page Field runway extension nearly finished by late 1967, Gulf American officials set January 15, 1968, as the target date for landing Modern Air jets in Fort Myers. In December 1967, however, the FAA advised Gulf American that it would not be allowed to land four-engine jet aircraft at the airport until a control tower was built. After numerous negotiations, the requirement was temporarily waived, and a traffic controller was stationed on the roof of the new passenger terminal. The first Convair 990 made a trial landing at Page Field in January 1968, carrying only a flight crew. Although the large jets were forced to brake hard and to use the entire length of the runway, they were approved to carry passengers to Fort Myers. The first planeload of prospective land buyers arrived February 1, 1968, and Gulf American flight operations were transferred to Fort Myers from Miami.[85]

The Travel Guild promotion continued to grow, averaging two to three flights a day at Fort Myers and requiring an operating budget of $250,000 per month. Company officials allowed the huge expenditures because of the large number of sales that was generated. Optimism about the program ran throughout the company. Cavanagh explained, however, that it was difficult to make the promotion cost efficient. He said: "We, the corporation, I'm sure we all felt the same way, that there was no end to the dollar, that there was never going to be a day of reckoning, that we were building a city and people were going to move in and it was growing and growing and growing." While the flight program produced large numbers of land and housing sales, its high cost made it a primary target during cost-cutting measures by GAC Corporation officials after 1969. GAC curtailed the flights and eventually cancelled the program in the early 1970s to save money.[86]

The promotions and publicity by Gulf American from 1958 to 1969 had a profound effect not only on the development of the company's properties but also on the economic growth of the entire state of Florida. Gulf American, along with General Development Corporation and other large land development companies, had increased interest in Florida through aggressive advertising and by pioneering the sales strategy of presenting homesites in the state as strong investments.[87] Previously, salespeople had tried to convince customers to buy a lot for their dream home or as a retirement place. In order to show the investment potential of the company's properties, Gulf American needed to demonstrate the growth and economic strength of Florida. Much of the publicity by the company, therefore, focused on Florida's growth trends and the desirability of living in Florida.[88]

A typical example of Gulf American's strategy was a booklet called *Golden Gate Estates: Your Golden Opportunity for a Prosperous Future.* Developed in mid-1963, the large eleven-by-seventeen-inch gold-colored brochure vividly described Florida's rapid population growth and the resulting increase in land values. Statistics were shown that predicted that the Sarasota-to-Naples area was going to have the fastest growth rate in the state. The literature also told how a $1,000 investment in Cape Coral property in January 1958 was worth $3,560 in 1962, far oustripping a similar investment in a savings account or a stock portfolio. Job opportunities and the growth of new industries within Florida beckoned to potential customers. Nearly one-half of the twenty-five-page brochure emphasized the benefits of buying land and living in Florida. Portraying homesites as an excellent investment was also a common selling strategy at Cape Coral.[89]

Although the investment potential of Gulf American homesites was an important factor in sales presentations, publicity for the company most often focused on Florida living. Newspaper editors were brought to Cape Coral and Golden Gate to fish, hunt, and enjoy the warm climate. Often the resulting articles described Florida primarily, but the "Cape Coral" dateline on an article carried an indirect message to readers. A sixteen-page color magazine supplement called "The Gulf American Story" was placed in the *New York Times* and six other major newspapers on Sunday, June 25, 1967. Showing the beauty of Florida, the advertisement reached an estimated 20 million readers. In addition to printed advertisements, color films of southwest Florida were shown to thousands of people at dinner parties and Travel Guild sign-ups throughout the United States and Europe. Similar commercials aired on NBC's "Tonight" and "Today" shows during the mid-1960s.[90]

While sales were of primary importance to the Rosen brothers, publicity efforts and various promotions educated people about Florida in general and southwest Florida in particular. Bernice Freiberg, who worked extensively on Gulf American's magazine, newspaper, and television advertising, estimated that the company was spending between $8 million and $10 million annually during some years in the 1960s to promote Florida and Gulf American properties.[91] Hundreds of thousands of people were flown into the state at subsidized prices to see Cape Coral, Golden Gate, and River Ranch. Many were visiting Florida for the first time. The result was an increased awareness by people throughout the United States and Canada of the benefits of living in Florida.

The company's promotion of Florida in the late 1950s and 1960s was designed to help sell land just as Henry Flagler and Henry Plant had reduced rail fares for settlers to encourage land sales along their respective railroads in the early 1900s. Gulf American's advertising of rising land values in the 1960s was similar to reports and advertising in northern newspapers of boom times and profitable investments in Miami in the mid-1920s. While the direct result was the sale and resale of land, the indirect consequence was the increased movement of northerners into the state.[92] People who did not purchase homesites in Florida in the 1960s at least became aware of Florida's benefits for the first time as a result of Gulf American's promotions. While it is difficult to calculate the precise result of Gulf American's advertising, as well as the promotions of smaller companies, the impact of these presentations on Florida tourism and subsequent migration into the state cannot be overlooked.

8

Growing Pains: 1964 to 1967

Dramatic growth characterized the Gulf American Land Corporation from 1964 to 1967. During these years, the company showed its most pronounced increase in sales, reaching a peak in 1966. Even more remarkable was the rapid development of Cape Coral and Golden Gate, both in population and in construction. At Cape Coral, as well as at other Gulf American properties, development was critical to the credibility of the company in the eyes of the buying public. Therefore, the Rosens stressed construction, along with sales, during those years.

Sales volumes increased rapidly from $94,363,985 in August 1964 to a high point of $143,862,440 in August 1966. Although the total dropped off to $131,381,196 by mid-1967, sales figures placed Gulf American at the top of all land development companies in the nation during the mid-1960s.[1] Gulf American had sold a total of 55,000 homesites at Cape Coral as of February 1964 to residents of the United States, Canada, and fourteen other countries.[2] By July 1, 1967, salespeople at the community had written more than 92,000 land contracts for customers in all fifty states and in fifty-eight foreign countries. Based on an average of three and one-half homesites per acre, 92,000 lots represented approximately 50 percent of all available homesites at Cape Coral.[3] As Leonard Rosen confidently restated the company's sales totals in 1967, "We're selling $750,000 worth of land a day and we're collecting on those sales at the rate of $280,000 a day."[4]

Gulf American's sales increases also resulted in a complete change in the relationship between the largest of Florida's land development companies. In 1959 General Development Corporation was headed by Louis Chesler in association with the Mackle brothers of Miami. During that year, their corporation sold 49,933 homesites in eight Florida communities for a total sales revenue of $67,237,864.[5] For the same period, Gulf American recorded approximately $20 million in sales at its only development, Cape Coral. Within six years, however, Gulf American's aggressive sales approach began to dominate the market. The company recorded sales of $104,214,000 for 1965, nearly twice the combined total of the next two competitors, General Development and Deltona Corporation. For the same year, General Development, without the Mackle brothers since 1962, showed total sales of only $29.4 million. Deltona sold $15,604,000 in homesites and houses in 1965 while participating in $14.4 million in revenue from a half-owned affiliate at Marco Island, Florida, near Naples.[6] In addition to its clear lead over other land companies, Gulf American ranked sixth in 1965 among all publicly held, Florida-based corporations, as determined by sales, net income, and assets. Ranked ahead of it were Southern Bell Telephone, Florida Power and Light, Atlantic Coast Line, Winn Dixie Stores, and Florida Power Company.[7]

As Gulf American sales rose from 1964 through 1967, Cape Coral showed dramatic growth during the same period. By late 1963 Cape Coral had grown to a community of 2,850 people. Scattered throughout the southeastern part of the city were, 1,100 completed homes and business establishments with more than 200 others under construction. The population increased rapidly so that by August 1964 the community boasted 3,825 residents, 817 of whom were children. Construction had been completed or was proceeding on a total of 1,722 buildings. Homesite owners continued to move to the city, and in August 1967 Gulf American recorded a total of 8,331 permanent residents. The number of children in the community had more than doubled to 2,084. The number of structures, including residential, multifamily, and business, nearly doubled in three years to a mid-1967 total of 3,070 buildings with another 182 under construction. By comparison, General Development's main project, Port Charlotte, grew much faster to 14,000 residents in 1966 because of General Development's emphasis on housing over land sales.[8]

Gulf American continued to pursue the transformation of raw acreage at Cape Coral into salable homesites. Under the direction of resident engineer Thomas Weber, the company had completed the building of roads, canals, and homesites on 3,500 acres by November 1963, with 4,000 acres in various stages of development; 53,500 acres re-

Table 2 Residents and Structures in Cape Coral, 1963–1967

Year Ending	Total Residents	Families	Children	Buildings (completed or under construction)
July 1963	2,850	N/A	N/A	1,300
August 1964	3,825	1,445	817	1,722
August 1965	5,200	N/A	1,200	2,370
August 1966	7,000	2,630	1,665	2,814
August 1967	8,331	3,107	2,084	3,252

Sources: Fort Myers News-Press, November 12, 1963; Gulf American Land Corporation, *Annual Report*, 1964, 8, 1965, 7, 1966, 8; Gulf American Corporation, *Annual Report*, 1967, 17.

mained undisturbed. Weber disclosed in 1963 that the company had spent $4.36 million on development during the year and a total of $9.7 million since the community's beginning in late 1957. He estimated that $83 million would be required to complete the entire system of roads, waterways, and site preparations. Ninety miles of paved roads had been finished in the city along with seventy miles of canals. In November 1963 Gulf American employed 357 workers at Cape Coral in road and canal construction and used heavy machinery valued at $3.5 million.[9]

During the following four years, Gulf American nearly tripled the finished area of Cape Coral to 9,549 acres. In July 1967 the company's construction subsidiary, Fort Myers Construction Company, had completed a total of 229 miles of paved roads and 95 miles of waterways. An additional 68 miles of roads and 22 miles of canals were under construction. The vast majority of Cape Coral's 61,000 acres were yet untouched by Gulf American, however, though the company emphasized the work that was being accomplished through regular release of information and updated aerial photographs of the city in brochures and advertisements.[10]

During Cape Coral's early history, the Rosens' foremost goal was to increase the company's sales volume. In order to persuade people to buy homesites, however, the brothers soon realized that it would be necessary to start a viable city with many of the normal community services. If customers also did not find a city built with quality construction, no amount of aggressive marketing would convince them to buy. Early in the city's history, Leonard Rosen settled the issue of quality road construction in a meeting at Cape Coral with Kenneth Schwartz and a county official. He emphasized to Schwartz that all roads were to be built at or above county specifications. Associates attributed Rosen's action to his farsighted thinking. Unsure of how fast the project would sell, he wanted the roads, as well as other improvements, to be acceptable to the public years in the future. As he later stated, "Everything we did, we tried to do in very fine ways."[11]

A major objection for many early visitors to Cape Coral was the community's relative remoteness to larger communities. The distance from Cape Coral Parkway to the nearest shopping in North Fort Myers and Fort Myers was twenty to twenty-five miles each way by road. At some point during the development's first year, Leonard became convinced that a bridge across the Caloosahatchee River to Fort Myers was necessary for the community's growth. According to Kenneth Schwartz, Leonard was motivated not only by a desire to increase the flow of customers into Cape Coral but also to make access to Fort Myers easier for the community's residents. At the time in Lee County, the only bridge across the river at Fort Myers was the two-lane Edison Bridge, which had been completed in October 1930. The span connected Business Route 41 in North Fort Myers with Fowler Street on the south bank.[12]

For many of the people who knew the situation, Leonard was the driving force behind the building of the Cape Coral bridge. Connie Mack, Jr., doubted that the bridge would have been constructed without Leonard's single-minded determination. Schwartz viewed the bridge as a typical case of Leonard's power to achieve an objective. Describing Leonard's determination on the issue, he said: "He was a guy who would not allow any opposition to stand in his way. I always felt that Leonard Rosen could have put us on the moon five years earlier than we ultimately got there."[13]

As early as 1959, Leonard sponsored a bridge feasibility study by Rader and Associates of Miami to determine the best location. The report concentrated on two sites, site C connecting Everest Parkway in Cape Coral to Colonial Boulevard in Fort Myers and site B connecting Cape Coral Parkway with the Braden-Sutphin Road in south Fort Myers. The cost of constructing the span at site B was estimated by the engineering firm at $1.3 million while the more northerly site C was estimated at $2.5 million. Because of the lower cost and its proximity to Cape Coral's initial growth area in 1959 and 1960, Leonard recommended site B as the best location.[14] Privately pledging to associates to pay for the entire project if the county would not, he began the task of acquiring the rights-of-way for the bridge.[15]

The property for the right-of-way on the Cape Coral side was owned by two men, Sam Nahama and John C. O'Han. Nahama had been recruited in Rivervale, New Jersey, by Charles Hepner to relocate his

Early stages of construction of the Cape Coral Bridge in 1963, looking toward the Fort Myers side of the river.

sporting goods business in the Cape Coral Industrial Park, which he eventually did. He and his brother-in-law, O'Han, had also been persuaded to buy a riverfront parcel by their good friends Kenneth Schwartz and Edward Pacelli because of its investment potential. They had purchased the approximately 1.25-acre parcel for $45,374 in January 1961. Leonard later found that he needed all of that parcel for the bridge approach. Schwartz was chosen to negotiate a repurchase because of his close friendship with the two men. As weeks passed, O'Han and Nahama, particularly O'Han, continued to escalate their demands, eventually demanding 100,000 shares of Gulf American stock for the land. Between 1961 and the end of 1962, Gulf American common stock ranged between 3⅝ and 56⅞ per share, making the request worth at minimum $362,500.[16]

Feeling that the price was unreasonable and that O'Han and Nahama had already agreed to a much lower price, Schwartz arranged a meeting in one of Gulf American's offices in North Fort Myers. Swept up in the emotion of the situation and believing that O'Han's demands were outrageous, Schwartz charged: "You can describe your change of mind any way you want to, but there's only one word that I would apply to it. You're a welsher!" Schwartz continued to call him "welsher" because he knew that the word deeply bothered O'Han. Finally, O'Han advanced on him and a fistfight ensued. Even though Nahama tried to break up the two men, the fight was violent enough to be heard throughout the entire wooden office building, alerting a salesman and secretary working in an outer room who helped to separate the two men. O'Han brought charges and later a civil suit against Schwartz, but both actions were later dropped. Eventually, an agreement was reached with Nahama and O'Han and the property was sold to Gulf American on July 6, 1962, for $75,000.[17]

The site on the Fort Myers side of the right-of-way to the bridge was owned by Al Sutphin, a wealthy businessman from Cleveland, Ohio. Sutphin felt that the bridge would destroy the tranquillity of his Braden-Sutphin Farms, a resort and truck-gardening enterprise located where the Landings condominiums were later constructed. Under pressure to sell his right-of-way to the Rosens, Sutphin repeatedly contacted Connie Mack, Jr., to urge him to stop Leonard from building the bridge. After Sutphin learned that Mack was unable to alter Leonard's determination, he angrily criticized Mack by letter and phone. Emotions on both sides were heated, but Sutphin eventually sold some of his property to Gulf American in 1961, although he continued to oppose the bridge.[18]

While Leonard was trying to purchase the rights-of-way, he also had started negotiating with the Lee County Commission for approval to build the bridge and to charge tolls to pay for it. Leonard's main contact on the commission was Mack H. Jones, the commissioner whose district included Cape Coral. While Jones was generally supportive of Gulf American projects, the majority of the commission took a conservative stance on new capital improvements. In mid-1961 the commission finally authorized Wilbur Smith and Associates to make a feasibility study of the bridge proposal and to see if present traffic volume would provide enough toll revenues.[19]

After examining both sites B and C, the Smith company presented a report to the commission on May 9, 1961. According to the study, the more northerly Everest Parkway site C would be the more useful location once the city of Cape Coral became fully developed. At the time of the study, however, site B at Cape Coral Parkway was closer to the heaviest concentration of the community's population. Although not specifically recommending either site, the report predicted that bridge tolls would fall far short of meeting maintenance, operation, and bond-interest costs. Estimating annual traffic at 480,000 trips and yearly costs of $150,000, the study calculated that a fifteen-cent toll would generate only $66,000 and a twenty-five-cent charge would produce only $110,000. The study predicted that the bridge would be entirely self-sustaining financially in five years but significant shortfalls in revenue were likely in the early years. The result was that the county commission became increasingly reluctant to take on the project.[20]

Unwilling to accept financial responsibility for the bridge, the county commission proposed that a special bridge taxing district be created to issue the bonds and guarantee any shortfalls in revenue. The district was to include all of Cape Coral and a small area near the Fort Myers entrance to the bridge. Concerned that Cape Coral voters would not approve the taxing district in a referendum, Leonard made a bold proposal to the commission in October 1961. In order to ensure that Cape Coral residents would not have to pay any toll deficits, he offered to deposit $100,000 in an escrow account with the county. If at any time toll revenues fell short of costs, the county would use the Gulf American funds and the account would be replenished by the corporation up to its original total. The proposal also called for the permanent removal of tolls when payment for the bridge was complete. The plan was announced by Leonard at a public meeting in Cape Coral at the Surfside Restaurant on October 12, 1961. He explained to the crowd of more than 400 persons that Gulf American was guaranteeing the finances of the bridge with its $75 million in assets and that the bridge taxing district was a formality to satisfy the county commission. Of the 283 registered freeholders in the proposed district, 143 signed a petition to the commissioners that night in support of the new taxing district.[21]

The escrow agreement by Gulf American was officially proposed to the Lee County Commission on October 20, 1961, and on October 30 a letter by Harry Fagan of First National Bank of Fort Myers confirmed that $100,000 had been deposited in an escrow account. Based on these actions, the commission set an early December 1961 date for the tax district referendum. The six weeks preceding the balloting was a period of sharp division among the residents of Cape Coral. Kenneth Schwartz's attitude was typical of many residents; he saw the conflict as a struggle that he had to win. As he explained it: "I didn't know much about grays. Everything was black or white."[22]

Many residents, though supportive of the new bridge, feared that the entire cost of paying for the structure might revert to the small Cape Coral population. Several opponents of the span were motivated by economic factors. Chester Berry, an outspoken opponent, owned a number of commercial buildings at the corner of Del Prado Boulevard and Pine Island Road. With the opening of the bridge, most Cape Coral traffic would no longer pass in front of his businesses. H. M. Fiori, a former attorney from New York, also feared that the bridge would divert the majority of customers away from his North Fort Myers businesses. Energized by his opposition to the bridge and to Gulf American in general, Fiori started a weekly newspaper called the *Cape Coral Times,* launched one week ahead of the *Cape Coral Breeze.* Although never a resident of Cape Coral, Fiori continued to oppose Gulf American projects and to publish his paper until late 1963.[23]

The division in the community was easily seen in the disunity of the Cape Coral Taxpayers Association. Formed in 1960, the organization had initially been active in representing the interests of the residents. In the fall of 1961 a slate of officers led by Chester Berry was elected to head the association. The new leaders took a stand adamantly opposed to the Cape Coral Roads and Bridge District. Many association members resigned out of dissatisfaction with the new officers. Richard Crawford, a former officer of the association, commented that Berry and his followers got elected because "we didn't watch what we were doing closely enough."[24]

The referendum for the taxing district, held in early December 1961, narrowly passed with 174 voting in favor and 124 against. The first issue of the *Cape Coral Breeze* on December 14, 1961, announced the voter approval. The referendum had been held because the county wanted a safety feature should Gulf American for any reason default on its $100,000 pledge. With the tax district approved, Crawford suggested in an editorial in the *Breeze* that Chester Berry and his fellow officers resign from the taxpayers association. Berry refused and, as a result, eighteen residents organized a committee for a new civic organization in early February 1962. A near-capacity crowd met on March 1, 1962, at the Cape Coral shopping plaza and formed the Cape Coral Civic Association with 228 charter members.[25]

The taxpayers association declined in membership and influence for two important reasons. Primarily, Berry's opposition to the bridge was a minority opinion among Cape Coral's residents. The referendum results and the rapid growth of the civic association demonstrated that fact clearly. But Berry's forces had another crucial problem. Because Berry had refused to resign at Crawford's suggestion, Crawford refused to print any news in the *Breeze* concerning the taxpayers association. When association members demanded that he also print news from opponents of the bridge, Crawford replied that he would not. He later noted that "The nice thing about having your own newspaper, you can print what you want." Weakened by the resignation of many members, the taxpayers association continued for nearly two more years before disbanding.[26]

The next task facing Leonard Rosen was to arrange financing for the bridge construction. Because Lee County did not have the funds available, he began soliciting a bonding agent to fund the huge project. With the unfavorable report by Wilbur Smith and Associates in May 1961, finding a willing bonding agent was difficult. Rosen met with company secretary Joseph Maddlone about the problem because of Maddlone's extensive experience with the Wall Street financial community. For some reason, Maddlone happened to be irked at something Leonard had done recently, and he refused to direct the financing effort unless Leonard gave him a bonus. When Leonard protested, Maddlone told him, "If you want the bridge built, call the engineer and tell him to do it." Leonard relented and agreed to a $5,000 bonus.[27]

Maddlone was placed in contact with a bonding agent named James Sims of Herbert J. Sims and Company of New York. Maddlone flew to New York City, met with Sims, and found the company willing to provide the financing. The bond issue was agreed to be $2.6 million, although the construction estimates had not been finalized. Sims asked Maddlone to write the prospectus, a document used to sell the bonds to investors. Maddlone had previously written a number of successful prospectuses for other companies and was skilled in the process. Sims also required that Rader and Associates not be used for engineering of the bridge. While Maddlone insisted that Rader was one of the top firms in Florida, Sims countered with the comment, "They are not Wall Street engineers, Joe." A more acceptable firm, J. E. Greiner and Company of Tampa, was selected and Maddlone arranged for its supervision of the project.[28]

Leonard's local efforts at arranging financing helped to speed up the governmental process. At a May 16, 1962, meeting of the Lee County Commission, the commissioners voted to dispense with the Cape Coral Roads and Bridge Taxing District and to approve the bridge as a county project. Commissioner Mack Jones noted that the district was no longer necessary because of the bonding agreement arranged by Rosen. However, the district, according to Jones, "served a useful purpose in that it allowed us [the commissioners] to proceed with the engineering studies." A special referendum validating the bond issue was deemed not necessary because of Gulf American's $100,000 escrow account. An engineering report by J. E. Greiner and Company was accepted by the commission one week later. The study estimated that the entire cost of land and construction for the bridge would amount to $2.2 million. An additional report by Goodbody and Associates, fiscal agents for the project, upgraded the pessimistic Smith calculations of the previous year by stating that revenue from the tolls would be sufficient to retire the thirty-year bond issue in fourteen years, leaving a $345,000 surplus.[29]

With the county government no longer responsible for raising the funds for the bridge, the project moved ahead rapidly. On August 8, 1962, Herbert J. Sims and Company officially agreed to become the bonding agent for the bridge. With a taxing district no longer necessary, the Cape Coral Roads and Bridge District was abolished by special referendum on October 2, 1962, by a vote of 321 to 2. Official groundbreaking ceremonies took place on December 21, 1962, for the mile-long structure. Construction firms working on the bridge included J. E. Greiner and Company, Hardaway Construction, and Alonzo Cothron. Actual construction costs included $1,245,594 for the bridge itself and $200,459 for the approaches.[30]

The formal opening ceremonies were held on March 14, 1964, with Kenneth Schwartz and his family, the first residents of Cape Coral, cutting the ribbon. Leonard Rosen addressed the crowd about his vision for the bright future of the city, and then the spectators were allowed to drive free across the bridge. Tolls were set at twenty-five cents per car with a reduced ten-cent charge for commuters. Traffic on the bridge far exceeded even the optimistic annual estimates of 730,700 by Goodbody and Associates in 1962. From its opening in 1964 until June 30, 1968, 5,572,380 vehicles passed through the tollgates, paying $1,162,788 in tolls. In 1967 construction began on College Parkway, a four-lane highway that eventually connected the bridge with U.S. Route 41 in south Fort Myers. The county continued to charge a fee for crossing the causeway until 1973 when all tolls were removed.[31]

The building of the Cape Coral bridge virtually assured the rapid future growth of the city. During the community's early years, salespeople had repeatedly promised a bridge to customers although company management forbade the ploy. Some salespeople were fired because of their continued guarantees of a causeway, but as it became more evident that a bridge was necessary, the promise became a standard promotion by salespeople. The resulting bridge also made access to Cape Coral easier for curious vacationers who might become customers. Most sources agreed, however, that in all likelihood the bridge would have taken at least another five years to complete without the determination and financing of Leonard Rosen.[32]

Another important milestone in the city's growth was the building of schools. In fall 1958 only five school-age children were recorded in Cape Coral. They attended J. Colin English School in North Fort Myers after a bus ride of more than ten miles. With the steady increase in the number of young children in the city, an elementary school was planned by the Lee County School Board for Cape Coral. Located on Vincennes Boulevard in the southeastern part of the city, Cape Coral Elementary School was completed in summer 1964 at a cost of $347,000. The twenty-classroom school was opened for the academic year 1964–65 with 212 children registered. Junior high and high school students had to travel to North Fort Myers and Fort Myers for their education.[33]

In order to present Cape Coral as a city of all ages, Gulf American regularly released statistics on the number of children under twenty-one years of age living in the community. One such notice pointed out that Cape Coral had about 1,200 children while only 1,100 members of the American Association of Retired Persons were residing there in 1965. Many customers considered Cape Coral's educational facilities a key factor in purchasing a homesite. The community's elementary school grew rapidly so that several additions had to be completed in order to house the 502 students enrolled in 1967. Older students continued to attend classes outside the city until the building of the Caloosa Middle and Elementary School complex on Del Prado Boulevard in 1971. The first high school, named Cape Coral High, was finished in April 1979; the student body of approximately 1,400 students had been attending classes during a special afternoon session at North Fort Myers High School since August 1978.[34]

As Cape Coral grew during the mid-1960s, residents also needed banking facilities within the community. The idea of organizing a bank in Cape Coral originated with Col. Lowell H. Mills, a World War I veteran and retired employee of the Army Corps of Engineers. Mills had purchased property at Cape Coral in 1958 and moved to the city in January 1961. Shortly after arriving, he went to Tallahassee to discuss with the state banking commissioner the starting of a bank in the southwest Florida community. Receiving little encouragement, he returned to Cape Coral to garner support. Gulf American officials enthusiastically approved of the idea, and some company employees believed that highly-placed persons in Gulf American may have first suggested the idea to Mills.[35]

Upon his return from Tallahassee, Mills formed a group to discuss the organization of a bank. By October 1961 the bank boosters included Mills, H. D. Anderson, Clarence Duffala, Jack Topley, Charles M. Blackburn, Cliff Hanson, Cort Pohle, L. T. Ahrenholz, John Holmes, Frank Noland, and Aage Schroder. Committed to launching the bank project, the committee began offering on January 15, 1962, subscriptions for the sale of stock at $14.50 a share. By February 13 the stock had been oversubscribed by $30,000.00. The group received a state charter in May 1963, along with approval for insurance from the Federal Deposit Insurance Corporation. A bank building was constructed by the Duffala Construction Company on Cape Coral Parkway immediately east of Del Prado Boulevard. The structure was completed and equipped for an overall cost of $240,000.00. With Mills as bank president and William F. Baker of Daytona Beach as executive vice-president, the bank opened in February 1964. By November deposits from more than 2,000 accounts amounted to $2.4 million.[36]

Although the establishment of the Cape Coral Bank was important to the life of the community, the Rosens wanted to have greater access to the financial resources of the residents and to the growing mortgage market in Cape Coral. Therefore, Leonard sent company attorney Richard D. DeBoast to Washington, D.C., in October 1967 to investigate the possibilities of securing a charter for a savings and loan institution for the city. DeBoast was selected by Leonard to become one of the founding directors of the new Gulf American subsidiary. To qualify for the position, DeBoast moved from Fort Myers to Cape Coral, where his rent was paid by Gulf American. Several presentations were made in Washington before the Federal Home Loan Bank Board, but the authorization was opposed by W. Thomas Howard, president of First Federal Savings and Loan Association of Fort Myers.[37]

The federal agency finally denied Gulf American's request and subsequently granted permission on January 5, 1968, for First Federal to open a branch office in Cape Coral. Howard had made application for the branch office the previous May because he saw the potentially large mortgage market in the community. Also, First Federal already had more than 1,000 depositors from the Cape Coral area and had invested $9.2 million in home loans in the community. By late 1968 First Federal Savings and Loan Association of Fort Myers and Cape Coral Bank served as the only financial institutions for a population of more than 10,000 Cape Coral residents.[38]

During the mid-1960s, Gulf American directed the building of water and sewer facilities for Cape Coral. Previous to this time, residents had drilled their own wells for water and had installed septic tanks. On October 18, 1961, the Lee County Commission granted a franchise to the Gulf Utilities Corporation to supply a central water and sewage system for Cape Coral. Gulf Utilities was a wholly owned subsidiary of Gulf American. In 1963 construction was completed by Gulf Utilities on a $1 million water treatment plant in Cape Coral. The facility had a capacity of 1 million gallons of water per day and was boosted by a 200,000-gallon storage tank located north of the golf course. When it opened, the plant was connected to approximately 1,200 customers.[39]

Homebuilders in Cape Coral by the mid-1960s typically bought homes from Cape Coral Construction Company, the residential construction division of Gulf American. In order to obtain water and sewer service, customers were charged $356 for a well and pump on their property and about $200 for a septic tank. Because central utilities were unavailable in most areas of the development, customers had no other alternatives. In addition, Gulf Utilities charged homebuilders an $800 betterment fee for the future construction of central water and sewer systems. According to the franchise agreement of October 18, 1961, Gulf Utilities was required to begin work on a central sewage system within twelve months.[40]

Problems arose in 1965, however, when several Cape Coral residents challenged Gulf American's handling of water and sewer construction in the city. By autumn of that year, most residences were still unconnected to city water, and little had been done about a central sewage disposal system. Therefore, at the September 1965 meeting of the Cape Coral Civic Association, Edward Tohari accused the company of misusing and illegally profiting from the betterment fees collected from homeowners in Cape Coral. A native of Poland, Tohari was a veteran of the Polish underground during World War II and had earned degrees at the London School of Economics and the University of Geneva, Switzerland, after the war. Tohari was joined in his accusations by independent Cape Coral realtor Granville Petrie and retired Rear Adm. Kenneth Loveland, a resident of the community.[41]

Responding to the charges, Robert Finkernagel, along with several other high-ranking Gulf American officials, appeared before the October 4, 1965, meeting of the civic association. With a capacity crowd present at the Cape Coral yacht and racquet club clubhouse, a number of company officials explained the handling of the funds in the betterment fee trust fund. They also commented on unnamed residents who made charges that were not true or factual. After a lengthy speech by Finkernagel, Tohari requested permission to reply. The chairman granted him only three minutes, adding that "two of those minutes are already gone." As a result of this and other actions, Tohari and his associates clearly believed that the civic association leadership was more supportive of the Gulf American position and labeled the chairman's actions as "a shocking outburst of bad manners and hostility."[42]

Tohari took his fight before the Lee County Commission two days later, when he demanded that the commissioners revoke the franchise of Gulf Utilities Corporation. The sewer problem was of much greater concern to many of the residents of Cape Coral than the legal issue of Gulf American's delays. Granville Petrie reported a situation in which many septic tanks within the city were no longer functioning and raw sewage was running off into the Caloosahatchee River. Although Gulf American officials publicly denied such a problem, Petrie noted that the company had recently drilled approximately 500 dry holes to keep down the overflow from the septic tanks. Leonard Rosen later acknowledged that problems did exist. Responding to a question from a resident, he stated, "If you are having a problem with your septic tank, I suggest you see Tom Weber [resident engineer]. We will try to help solve your problem."[43]

Believing that Gulf American had forfeited its franchise contract, Tohari, Petrie, and Loveland wanted the existing water and sewer facilities confiscated by the county. As an alternative, Tohari proposed that a utilities district be organized for Cape Coral. Quoting expert sources, he estimated the actual cost of sewer and water construction to be $1,500 per residence and not the $800 collected by Gulf American. Assuming that Gulf American's major problem was a lack of adequate funding, Tohari was convinced that a governmental unit would be able to finance the project easier by being able to issue bonds bearing tax-exempt interest. Insinuating that Gulf American was stalling on its commitment to build the facilities, he stated, "Gulf American has yet to prove it can finance such a system."[44]

Tohari's charges were immediately denied by company vice-president Connie Mack, Jr., who acted as Gulf American's chief representative to the Lee County Commission in most situations. He rebutted Tohari's arguments by pointing out that Gulf American had spent $2.7 million on water and sewer construction since 1957. He added: "There have been so many statements [about Gulf American] that were not true facts. All we have to do is live up to our contract and that's what we want to do." Commission chairman Julian L. Hudson agreed with Mack, noting, "I think so many of the facts brought out [by Tohari] may be slightly strained." The commissioners, however, agreed to study carefully the charges leveled by Tohari.[45]

In reality, Gulf American had made some progress toward a comprehensive water and sewer system. The million-gallon-per-day water treatment plant was completed in 1963 as a first step. Connected to more than 1,200 customers, the facility served the majority of residences in the city. By 1963 Gulf Utilities also had built two 75,000-gallon sewage plants, costing $85,000 each. These facilities were connected, however, primarily to commercial customers and apartment buildings in the city. The vast majority of residences remained on septic tanks. By late 1965, little had been done to improve the situation. As Tohari noted, "The present two primary plants cannot by any stretch of the imagination, either legally or technically, be considered as a central sewage system."[46]

The conflict between Gulf American and Tohari and his associates continued to escalate during late 1965 and 1966. Because of comments attributed to Gulf American officials in the press about their critics, Tohari filed a libel suit against various company representatives. In December 1965 Gulf American responded by filing suit against Tohari and Cape Coral resident Kenneth Loveland. The action sought $1 million in damages from each man and charged them with making false and malicious statements about the company concerning the water and sewer situation.[47]

The conflict reached a peak at the January 1966 meeting of the Cape Coral Civic Association. Leonard Rosen was invited to speak on the issues facing Cape Coral and then to answer questions from the audience. When Tohari attempted to make an unscheduled rebuttal speech, he was jeered and booed by the audience. When he paused, Rosen said: "Mr. Chairman, I must say that I will not answer questions from a man I am going to court with. I am sorry but I did not know him by sight." After Tohari was asked to sit down by civic association president A. L. McMillian, the general atmosphere of the meeting was positive toward Rosen and Gulf American. Although Tohari and his associates were a minority, they continued to press their demands in the community.[48] With the county health department also displeased about the sewer situation, Gulf American made an agreement with the county in January to accelerate the construction of residential sewer lines. The company agreed to have 250 more houses connected to the system by September 1966 and to expand sewer treatment facilities. By late 1966 a new $187,000 plant was opened as the first stage of a five-stage project. Although the facility was ultimately to accommodate a population of 70,000, the initial phase served only 4,000.[49]

While Gulf American was having difficulties with several vocal residents of Cape Coral, the company enjoyed generally a positive relationship with Lee County officials through 1966. The governmental officials found company representatives cooperative and competent in most matters. Although all initial road construction was made to county standards, the head of the county engineering department, F. James DeLozier, Jr., convinced Gulf American to increase those standards as the county increased its specifications. Therefore, all new roads were to be spread with two layers of asphalt and rock, not just one. From the beginning of Cape Coral, Leonard Rosen had insisted that all roads meet or exceed county specifications, although some advisers did not see the need; Leonard saw it as a major selling point of the property. He also did not know how long his company would have to maintain the roads it built. As it turned out, Gulf American continued to service most existing roads in the city into the late 1960s.[50]

County commission chairman Julian Hudson and county attorney Frank Pavese were skeptical of the company at its beginning in 1957, but they changed their minds. Both men noted Gulf American's positive economic effect on Lee County and its completion of all obligations with the county. DeLozier added to this optimism: "The continued growth of Lee County will no doubt depend to a considerable extent on the growth of the community of Cape Coral." Douglas Taylor, director of the building and zoning department, found no violation with the county's master zoning plan because the county had none. The commissioners did not feel that the budget was large enough to afford a planner, and all zoning matters that affected the county were handled by Taylor. Gulf American was allowed to direct nearly all details of the building of Cape Coral, using its own engineers.[51]

The greatest motivation for Gulf American's positive reception among Lee County officials was the dramatic impact on the county's economy and tax base. Leonard noted that by January 1966 Gulf American had spent $19 million to advertise Lee County all over the world and had brought more than 250,000 visitors into the area to look at Cape Coral. In addition, more than 2,000 homes had been built in the community, generating revenues for Lee County residents and businesses. County tax assessor Harry Schooley estimated that for every 500 houses built there, business worth about $3 million per year was generated in Fort Myers. Although Schooley had some concern over the excess number of vacant platted lots in the county, he was more upset over the governmental obstacles placed in the path of Gulf American that slowed its progress. He applauded Cape Coral's growth because of the subsequent increase in the value of the taxable property in the county.[52]

While some county commissioners were skeptical during the late 1950s of the Rosens' ability to complete their plans for Cape Coral, they soon became convinced of the developers' economic benefit to the county. The company not only provided hundreds of jobs to Lee County residents but also helped increase the taxable value of much formerly agricultural property in the county. With rapidly increasing land values in Cape Coral, the commissioners would have a greater tax base from which to draw tax revenues. In a 1968 statement, county commissioner P. A. Geraci commented, "In the five years that I have been a county commissioner, the only real difference that has arisen on any of their commitments was in regard to their sewage plans and plant." As a result, the commissioners were supportive of most Gulf American operations.[53]

At the same time, the commissioners seldom exposed the county government to any risk for the sake of Gulf American. When the issue of funding the Cape Coral bridge developed in the early 1960s, the commission refused to consider financing the project unless a taxing district was established to guarantee sufficient revenue. In addition, the maintenance of roads and the establishment of parks were viewed as responsibilities of the developer and not of the county government. Even into the late 1960s, the county was reluctant to assume the maintenance of some major streets in Cape Coral.[54]

A major factor in the company's success in dealing with the county was the significant number of people working for the Rosens who had personal contacts with Lee County officials. In addition to acting as a spokesman for Gulf American in public, Connie Mack, Jr., represented the company in most major matters of business with the commission. Mack was well known and respected by the commissioners, and Leonard often used him in the 1960s to pursue a particular governmental goal. Cape Coral general manager Kenneth Schwartz also established friendships with various county commissioners, including W. Wilson Piggott and Mack Jones. As a result, he was appointed to the first panel charged with creating a zoning and planning concept for Lee County. After the chairman, surveyor Carl E. Johnson, resigned, Fort Myers developer J. Foster Pate became chairman and Schwartz was elevated to vice-chairman. Besides these connections, Leonard hired several county officials to work for Gulf American, among them Stanley W. Hole, the head of the county's engineering department, and county attorney William Carmine.[55]

Carmine had been a local attorney in private practice in Fort Myers when he was named as the county attorney in the early 1960s. As county attorney, he represented the Lee County Commission in all legal matters. Leonard hired Carmine in 1962 to serve as legal counsel for Gulf American in all local matters because he needed a legal voice with some local authority. Eventually, Carmine moved to Gulf American's Miami office and became a vice-president for legal affairs. Upon leaving the Fort Myers area, he arranged for all local legal work for Gulf American to be handled by Richard DeBoast, a Fort Myers attorney. DeBoast remained the company's Lee County counsel throughout the 1960s.[56]

Carmine remained with the corporation for several years, but he never fully accepted the aggressive sales approach of the company. If customers had complaints of any kind, he simply issued a refund. Many of these refund requests were brought to his attention in Miami by Connie Mack, Jr. Although Leonard liked him and respected his work, Carmine eventually sued the company for $1 million in fees to which he claimed he was entitled. As part of his contract with Gulf American, Carmine was to receive a commission on all title insurance written for nearly 40,000 lots sold in Cape Coral and Golden Gate. As DeBoast observed, "Gulf American often signed things and didn't read them, and in this case, they didn't understand that Bill [Carmine] was to get this money and so he had to sue them." Leonard eventually agreed to settle the case, and Carmine was paid $500,000. Interestingly, the original contract was never found, and Leonard's decision to pay was based on an unsigned copy of the agreement shown to him by Carmine.[57]

While Gulf American enjoyed a generally positive relationship with the Lee County government, the residents of Fort Myers had mixed feelings about the Rosens and Cape Coral. The business community supported the new development because the increase in population meant additional volume in most Fort Myers businesses. Harry Fagan, president of First National Bank of Fort Myers, encouraged Leonard in the late 1950s to pursue the Cape Coral project and assisted him with some early financing. Leonard also received support early in Cape Coral's history from Homer T. Welch, Jr., the president of the Lee County Electric Cooperative, and from John N. Johnson, president of the Inter-County Telephone and Telegraph Company. These three individuals were critical to the success of the Cape Coral project because they provided necessary aspects of any new development: financing, electricity, and telephone.[58]

Another major reason for the acceptance of Gulf American by many Fort Myers residents was the personality and community beliefs of Leonard Rosen. He displayed an energy and charm that was attractive to most people he met. He and his brother also believed that when they came into an area they accepted community responsibilities. As Kenneth Schwartz observed: "You didn't go into a community just to take. You also had to make your contribution."[59]

As the Rosens' personal representative in the early years, Schwartz was active in local affairs, serving as cochairman of the United Way, president of the synagogue, and member of the boards of the Girl Scouts, Fort Myers Symphony, and a county-wide biracial commission. He explained the Rosens' attitude: "If there was a ballet company that would start in Fort Myers, I would have the authority to make a pledge, because I knew that that would be what the Rosen brothers wanted. Not because it would help them to sell more land or that it would help us to become heroes in the community, but because it was the right thing to do." Ruby E. Watson, executive director of the United Fund of Lee County, also emphasized this point: "The most gratifying part of Gulf American's success in this community is their leadership and philanthropic leanings in showing other people how to give."[60]

Much of the goodwill toward the Rosens was attributed by Schwartz to Fort Myers businessman Samuel Posner, who owned and operated a five-and-ten-cent store called American Variety Store (later the American Department Store). Posner was one of the few Jewish residents of the community and was well liked and respected. His friendship enabled Schwartz and the Rosens to benefit from much of the goodwill he had built up. Because the Rosens were Jewish and aggressive in their business dealings, the potential for anti-Semitic feelings among Fort Myers residents was high. But with Posner's friendship, the Rosens and Schwartz experienced generally positive reactions from the community. Posner and Schwartz continued their relationship in a joint business venture after Schwartz left Gulf American in 1964.[61]

Despite the generally warm reception, elements of hostility were present in Fort Myers. Resident engineer Thomas Weber attributed the anti-Rosen, anti–Cape Coral sentiment to a minority of people in Fort Myers who simply did not want to see rapid growth in their small, quiet, southern town. Raymond Meyer, who joined Gulf American in the mid-1960s, remembered one hostile reception he encountered in Fort Myers. After selecting several hundred dollars' worth of household items at J. C. Penney's in downtown Fort Myers, Meyer prepared to pay for his purchases. After learning that he was from Cape Coral, the saleswoman closed her salesbook and stated, "I'm not going to wait on you trash from Cape Coral." When the manager arrived, he added to the saleswoman's remarks: "There's 28,000 people in Fort Myers and we don't need any more trash."[62]

For many Fort Myers residents, Cape Coral represented a large influx of undesirable blue-collar northerners. Millard Bowen, a Cape Coral resident since 1965 and a past president of the Cape Coral Civic Association, related an incident that occurred to him soon after his arrival. After purchasing some merchandise at a Fort Myers store, the clerk discovered that he had a Cape Coral address. Her comments were pointed: "I don't know why you people came down here to Cape Coral. We had a nice area before you built this place. You should have stayed up there where you belonged." Bowen received his purchases, but the experience left a vivid impression.[63]

The opposition to the Rosens and to Gulf American had various sources, but some of it took on anti-Semitic overtones. Edward Pacelli commented that many Fort Myers people did not want to cooperate with people that they referred to as "those Jew boys." Attorney Richard De-Boast suspected that much of the resentment against Gulf American and the Rosens could be attributed to anti-Semitism, and he believed that Gulf American's aggressive sales approach at Cape Coral fed much of the resentment. Fort Myers residents, who frequently visited Cape Coral, were often stopped by official-looking uniformed men on Del Prado Boulevard and urged into company sales offices. Many bad feelings resulted. In a separate encounter, Fort Myers residents were overheard commenting that Connie Mack had to be Jewish even though he publicly denied it. Mack in fact was Catholic. Anti-Semitic attitudes and feelings were not at all uncommon but rarely were they made public.[64]

Anti-Semitism was an issue about which Leonard Rosen was extremely sensitive. According to Schwartz, he had no tolerance for it in his corporation. "If you said 'good morning' to Leonard in the wrong way," noted Schwartz, "he would assume it was because you were an anti-Semite." In fact, Leonard felt that many of Gulf American's difficulties with the Florida Land Sales Board during the late 1960s were due to anti-Semitism. Some of the largest competitors to Gulf American in Florida were seen by Leonard to be headed by individuals with anti-Semitic attitudes.[65]

The relationship between Gulf American and the residents of Cape Coral was generally positive. While a vocal minority disliked the Rosens and opposed anything their company wanted to do, the majority viewed Gulf American as a parent that would take care of them and their community problems. The majority of residents also saw Leonard Rosen as trying to improve Cape Coral. Although often unknown to the public, he helped residents with special needs. When the young grandson of Marguerite J. Garretson developed leukemia, Thomas Weber notified Rosen that the child needed to travel to Miami for treatments every week or two. Leonard made the company's executive plane available to the family for the next two years at no cost. No public announcement of the kindness was made until a letter of thanks from the family to the editor of the *Fort Myers News-Press* in 1967 revealed the story.[66]

Besides the vast amount of construction activity in the city, Cape Coral grew in several other ways. In November 1962 a small library was opened for use by city residents. Located in a small room in the Cape Coral shopping plaza, the 700-volume library was largely the result of the efforts of Madge and Robert Yoak, along with the aid of several other volunteers. Relying entirely on donations, the new library received some tax support the next year as the result of a 1963 Lee County referendum establishing a county-wide library system. The growing library needed to expand to a new building but funds were not available for a move.[67]

Cape Coral Shopping Plaza, located on Cape Coral Parkway, was the first shopping center in the city.

Responding to the need, Dallas Darling provided a site on Coronado Boulevard just north of Southeast Forty-seventh Terrace for the project. In addition, Leonard and Jack Rosen donated and transported to the site "the Rotunda," a round building formerly used as a sales office. After remodeling efforts, the library moved into its new location in 1965. Growing rapidly, the library needed still larger facilities by the late 1960s. Although the community rejected a referendum in 1969 that would have provided a civic center/library combination, the city of Cape Coral eventually purchased (in 1976) the Cape Coral Medical Clinic, a building located next to the Rotunda on Coronado Boulevard. The new facility was opened for business in summer 1977, although the official dedication was not held until October 16, 1977.[68]

Another area of growth for the city was the building of houses of worship in the community. By 1966 six churches and one synagogue had been built with another church still under construction. The first church in Cape Coral had as its pastor a retired Lutheran minister, the Reverend Henry Dickert. Services were held in the lounge of the Nautilus Inn. By 1961 Christ Lutheran Church and Faith Presbyterian Church were organized. The Lutherans and their pastor, the Reverend Everett P. Bunck, met in various storefronts in the Cape Coral shopping plaza. The Presbyterians purchased a house for their meetings, which were led by the Reverend Richard Grey. Following in quick succession, additional Protestant, Catholic, and Jewish congregations were organized including Epiphany Episcopal Church, Temple Beth-El, St. Andrew's Catholic Church, First United Methodist Church, and Cape Coral Baptist Church, a mission of First Baptist Church of Fort Myers. Gulf American provided assistance to all these groups by opening company facilities for their use and by selling them land at their cost of development. While the Rosens were community minded in these actions, the establishment of houses of worship gave potential customers a stronger impression of Cape Coral's high quality of life.[69]

By the mid-1960s Gulf American was attempting to persuade residents to take more responsibility in community projects. With no city government in existence in Cape Coral, Gulf American was forced to retain many of its "parental" functions, such as road maintenance, water and sewer maintenance, and police and fire services. In 1965 residents and businesses voiced a need for street lighting, particularly in the downtown area of Cape Coral Parkway. Based on a feasibility study initiated by the civic association, residents launched a petition drive to establish a street lighting tax district for the community. The referendum passed with the voters, and in November 1966 seventy-five new streetlights illuminated major intersections in Cape Coral for the first time. The project was accomplished due in large part to the efforts of the civic association and the Cape Coral Chamber of Commerce.[70]

While citizen groups were pushing for various capital-improvement projects, Gulf American continued to build new commercial and housing units between 1964 and 1967. Located at the corner of Cape Coral Parkway and Del Prado Boulevard, the four-story Gulf American sales and office building was completed in 1964. The structure featured a modern design, a spiral stairway in the lobby, and a gold-anodized plate-glass exterior. During December 1966 Gulf American opened the plush clubhouse of the Cape Coral country club, estimated to have cost more than $600,000. The facilities included banquet rooms, restaurants, and a pro shop for the company's championship golf course. The 100-unit Country Club Inn had opened in November 1965. Other projects included the Del Prado Inn motel ($216,000), the Gulf American terminal at Page Field ($50,000), Neisner's Junior Department Store ($160,000), and a sewage treatment plant ($183,000).[71]

In 1964 Gulf American launched an ambitious $16 million construction venture in Cape Coral that featured condominium apartments instead of single-family residences. On May 13 of that year, the Florida legislature had passed the Condominium Act, allowing individual ownership of apartment units. Within a few weeks, Gulf American officials had instructed their attorney, Richard DeBoast, to prepare condominium documents for the new projects in Cape Coral. After trying to decipher the statute for more than a week, DeBoast contacted the Florida Bar Association for assistance.[72]

DeBoast was subsequently referred to Fort Lauderdale attorney Russell McCaughan, one of four authors of the bill. Although none of the authors was a legislator, they anticipated that the real estate industry would be receptive to the new form of ownership. McCaughan later commented on the finished law: "If the real estate advertisements in the daily newspapers are a criterion, then the Florida Condominium Act is a raging success." Because of increasing questions about the complex law by local attorneys like DeBoast, McCaughan also wrote an article explaining the act in the *University of Florida Law Review* in summer 1964. Based on the information that DeBoast received from McCaughan, he wrote the documents for the Newport Manor condominiums in Cape Coral, one of the first such arrangements in Lee County.[73]

With the legal questions answered, Gulf American pressed forward with condominium construction. By 1967 six condominium complexes had been completed in the city. The most visually dramatic project was the six-story $1 million Harbor South, which was opened in spring 1966. The fifty-nine units, located near the Cape Coral bridge approach, featured a boat dock and heated pool. Others included the Newport Manor, Breezeswept Manor, and Freedom Manor. By early 1967 condominium sales were so strong that the company had compiled a construction backlog totaling $3.5 million.[74]

While growth at Cape Coral was dramatic, development and construction at Golden Gate proceeded even faster. Criticized by the Collier County commissioners for selling land that would not be developed for years, Gulf American vice-president Thomas Weber responded by telling the commission of company plans to purchase additional construction equipment worth $1 million by February 1965. In addition, he promised that the company would be able to increase greatly its development schedule by March 1. He explained: "We are presently completing 350 acres a month. We will be developing 800 acres monthly by March 1 through the use of large equipment and by working double shifts." The new equipment nearly doubled the productive capacity of the construction crews and raised the weekly payroll at Golden Gate to $14,491. Based on the increased development rate, Gulf American representatives presented the commission with forty-one square miles of new plats in Golden Gate Estates for approval for sale.[75]

At the same commission meeting, commissioner Wes Downing questioned Weber's plans, noting that development would take at least six years to finish the already platted seventy-seven square miles, even at the accelerated rate. He wanted the firm to purchase even more equipment so that the project could be completed in three years. The three-year period had been designated in a bonding agreement between Gulf American and Collier County. The company had posted more than $20 million in bonds to ensure completion of all road and drainage construction in Golden Gate. Anxious over Gulf American's ability and willingness to finish the project, the commissioners wanted the firm to provide additional security by setting up an escrow account that would contain all sales proceeds from Golden Gate. This new bonding procedure had been first offered to Collier County by the Mackle brothers' Deltona Corporation for its 10,100-acre Marco Island development. By August 31, 1967, Gulf American had worked out an alternative agreement in which the company pledged $91.2 million of contracts receivable to Lee and Collier counties to guarantee development.[76]

Officially dedicated on July 15, 1964, Golden Gate grew rapidly with the accelerated pace of development. By August 1967 the community had expanded to include more than 240 families for a total population of more than 600 people. Patterning the city of Golden Gate after Cape Coral, Gulf American built a country club with a championship golf course, a motel and restaurant complex, an airport, a fifty-unit shopping plaza, and a monthly newspaper. Development crews had completed more than eighty-three miles of nonpaved roads and had an additional eighty-two miles under construction. Dredges had finished more than sixty-two miles of drainage canals and were working on twelve additional miles. By late 1967 Collier County engineer Harmon

Turner reported that Gulf American was ahead of schedule by 10 percent on the development of the 114,406-acre project.[77]

While construction at Golden Gate proceeded rapidly, the population did not grow as fast as at Cape Coral. A major reason for the slower rate was the small size of the city of Golden Gate. According to the Rosens, Golden Gate was designed to be a "tremendous showcase" of Gulf American's land and housing products in Collier County. Consisting of only 2,640 acres out of a total of 114,406 owned by the company, the city was the only part of the project that Gulf American intended to develop as fully as Cape Coral. The remainder was to be partially developed into acreage tracts that would eventually be subdivided by the new buyers. This scheme enabled the company to sell land without incurring the high cost of development that they had experienced at Cape Coral.[78]

During the mid-1960s Gulf American also proceeded with other acreage sales at River Ranch Acres in Polk County and Remuda Ranch Grants in southeastern Collier County. Beginning with Golden Gate Estates, these new sales programs were significantly different from Cape Coral, Gulf American's first project. The Rosens pursued the new projects because acreage sales yielded a much higher profit than the marketing of developed homesites. Much of the cost of development of the acreage tracts was left to the buyer, who would subdivide the land at some later date. Because the company was offering little in the way of development at these later projects, salespeople often resorted to exaggeration to sell the parcels. They also typically used Cape Coral as a primary example of the appreciation potential of Gulf American properties, particularly acreage tracts. Problems arose, however, when customers discovered that costs of bringing telephone, water, and sewer lines to their parcels were prohibitive and that little resale market existed for their lots.[79]

The success of acreage sales caused the Rosens to focus the majority of their energies on those projects and away from Cape Coral in the mid-1960s. By 1967 the profitability of the new promotions was readily apparent. Including development expenditures, payroll, commissions, taxes, and the cost of the land, Cape Coral yielded a profit of 549 percent over Gulf American's total investment. By comparison, Golden Gate Estates and Remuda Ranch Grants combined produced earnings of 581 percent over cost. Although higher profits had been expected from these Collier County projects, the potential was reduced by the high cost of digging drainage canals in Golden Gate and by the fact that Remuda had started sales only in May 1966. By early 1967, however, River Ranch Acres demonstrated the advantage of acreage sales by posting a profit margin of 804 percent over the company's total investment.[80]

During the mid-1960s, Gulf American Land Corporation continued to increase its sales volume while proceeding with construction at the various sites. One former Gulf American salesman who analyzed the atmosphere said that the company was so successful in Florida that many company executives became drunk with power. He stated: "At first we sold Cape Coral in Florida as a legitimate community, and today it is a community. Then we sold Golden Gate with roads, then River Ranch with nothing, and finally Remuda Ranch under water. Everything worked. One of the bosses said one time that eventually we'll reach the point where we'll just mail contracts and the people will send them in and we'll tell them where we'll put them."[81]

Despite dramatic growth in all areas, problems with the company's sales program continued to surface. As the Florida state government increased its regulation over land subdividers between 1964 and 1967, a major confrontation appeared certain between the state and the largest land development company in the United States.

Regulating the
Land Giants

By the mid-1960s Gulf American Land Corporation had become the largest land development
firm in Florida, dwarfing the sales of all its competitors. Much of the reason for the company's
meteoric rise was attributable to Leonard and
Jack Rosen. Both men were determined continually to push the sales staff to new record levels. By 1966 Gulf American had grown into the
largest operation of its kind in the entire country.
All the time, the Rosens were planning other
projects in order to expand sales still further.[1]

The aggressive sales philosophy of the Rosens
resulted in salespeople pressuring customers to
achieve results. While it is doubtful that Leonard
or Jack directly instructed salespeople to lie or
misrepresent, they both believed that people had
enough willpower of their own to refuse a deal
even in the face of high pressure. Therefore, aggressive sales pitches at the project sites and at
luncheon or dinner parties were encouraged if
they yielded additional closings. Although the
company attempted some regulation of its staff,
sales commissions and encouragement from the
Rosens resulted in abuses that eventually drew
the attention of state governmental agencies.[2]

Throughout the 1960s, Gulf American and the
Rosens came under increasing scrutiny by various governmental bodies, culminating in the
thirty-day suspension of their license to operate
in late 1967. The brothers' bitter feud with Florida
Governor Claude R. Kirk, Jr., also contributed to
the corporation's problems with the state. Al-

though Leonard refused to acknowledge that the suspension had any discernible effect on Gulf American, the conflict undoubtedly influenced the Rosens' decision to sell the company.[3] In order to understand the causes and consequences of the suspension, it is necessary to examine Florida's history of regulating land developers.

Throughout the first half of the twentieth century, Florida land developers operated without much state regulation. The most serious intervention by the state into the industry involved the licensing of real estate agents. However, little was done to monitor advertising or the daily activities of land corporations. As land sales giants Lehigh Acres Development Corporation, General Development Corporation, and Gulf American were formed in the mid-1950s, many observers called for increased governmental regulation to protect the consumer.

Florida's basic land sales law, enacted in 1953, was designed to supervise sales within the state through a real estate commission. Brokers were licensed by that agency and could have their licenses revoked or suspended for fraudulent activities. The statute specified the abuses as being adjudged guilty of "false advertising in, on or by signs, billboards, newspapers, magazines, periodicals, books, pamphlets, circulars, radio, telephone, telegraph, or other means of communication or publicity of such character as to deceive or defraud investors or prospective investors."[4] Despite the legislators' clear attempt to outlaw false advertising in the state, unscrupulous sales practices continued in Florida.

As a result, the *Miami Herald* launched a series of articles in the mid-1950s that outlined the abuses and outright fraud going on in mail-order land sales in Florida. The articles were written by Stephen Trumbull, a reporter who had previously written about crime in Al Capone's Chicago. After traveling throughout south Florida in 1956, Trumbull discovered that many developers were selling submerged homesites in communities where improvements promised in company brochures had yet to be started. After describing many of the most flagrant abuses, he suggested that *Herald* readers warn their northern friends about real estate sales brochures that came in the mail. As a consequence of the publicity, Governor LeRoy Collins called a meeting of the Florida Real Estate Commission in his office on July 5, 1956, to hear allegations and to examine the state's advertising regulations.[5]

Persuaded that the situation needed immediate attention, Governor Collins called an emergency session of the state legislature on July 23, 1956, to address it and several other issues. In a message to that session, Collins noted that "a fringe group of mail order real estate operators have launched a series of promotions which threaten us with national scandal," and he recommended corrective legislation. The

Florida Advertising Act was passed in that 1956 special session; it included stiff criminal penalties, providing a fine of up to $100,000 plus imprisonment for up to five years for any person publishing false or misleading information for the purpose of inducing any other person to purchase Florida real estate. The act required all advertising materials that concerned Florida property—including Florida subdivisions that were advertised outside of Florida—to be submitted to the Florida Real Estate Commission for approval. While the law was designed to halt misleading advertisement of Florida real estate, enforcement was lax, partly due to the real estate commission's limited staff of twenty-six.[6]

As before, Stephen Trumbull investigated the situation after the passage of the law, and in August 1957 he published his findings in a *Miami Herald* article entitled "Land Dealers Thumb Nose at Lax Officials." Although nearly a year had passed since the passage of the tougher land law, Trumbull noted that not a single prosecution under the law had been started by the Florida Real Estate Commission. In a letter to Governor Collins on August 6, he criticized the commission for the lack of "vigorous prosecutions." Two developments, Lakeville and Tropical Gulf Acres, both located between Fort Myers and Punta Gorda, were accused of having none of the paved roads and lakes that were advertised in their color brochures. Those developers had been investigated by the state, but Florida officials related that "There isn't a thing we can do about it under the new law. Their out-of-state advertising is clean and that is all we can control."[7]

Convinced that the 1956 law was not being adequately enforced, Governor Collins appointed Walter S. Hardin as the new chairman of the real estate commission in mid-1957. In a letter to Hardin on August 26, 1957, he referred to the 1956 law, stating, "I anxiously want to see the purpose, spirit, and intent of the law enforced to the maximum." Replying to Collins on September 9, Hardin agreed: "I assure you that it is this commission's ambition and purpose to enforce this advertising act to the maximum degree supported by our statute." Despite the agreement, Hardin was already suggesting changes to make the law more inclusive.[8]

As a result of Trumbull's revelations, the state legislature passed the Interstate Advertising Law on May 30, 1959. Although the old law had provided criminal penalties, it had not given adequate protection for the purchasers. John W. McWhirter, Jr., executive director of the Florida Installment Land Sales Board from September 1963 to January 1965, observed in his testimony before a U.S. Senate subcommittee in 1964: "The Interstate Advertising Law, passed in 1959, was designed not only to continue criminal penalties, but also to exercise some control over advertising before it was distributed, to nip an incipient fraud in the bud."[9] Although developers were required by this law to be more specific in their claims and to submit advertising to the real estate commission before it could be distributed, deception continued.

In the summer of 1962, articles began to appear in national publications that dramatized the abuses in the installment land sales business. Many of these articles were directed at developers in Florida. Fearing that the scandal would severely damage Florida's public image and the many legitimate operations, Governor C. Farris Bryant appointed a committee on January 12, 1963, to examine interstate land sales with particular focus on installment sales. Reporting back on March 29, the committee members recommended, with Bryant concurring, that the legislature set up a separate state agency to regulate the installment land sales business in Florida. Describing the Florida Real Estate Commission as a "toothless tiger" in the area of enforcement, the *Miami News* called for the committee's recommendations to be passed into law by the legislature. As a result of this and other newspaper editorials, the Installment Land Sales Act was passed on May 21, 1963, establishing the Florida Installment Land Sales Board (FILSB).[10]

John McWhirter, in his Senate testimony in 1964, summarized the law and the three basic functions of the FILSB:

> First, to give every purchaser full and fair disclosure in advertising, free from deception. Secondly, to see that there are reasonable assurances to purchasers that they will receive marketable title to the land they buy and that the improvements which have been promised will be completed. Finally, the law hopes to foster a healthy economic climate in which a legitimate land developer can sell his property to a willing buyer with the least possible governmental interference.[11]

An important first step toward full disclosure was the requirement that all developers in 1964 supply the FILSB and all prospective buyers with a property report, a uniform document describing the land under consideration.

With the authority to revoke licenses and to seek court injunctions against developers, the FILSB had the power to regulate the industry. The board's power was limited, however, because of a stipulation that three of the five board members were to be directly involved in land sales and development. In addition to Marshall M. Criser, a Palm Beach attorney and later president of the University of Florida, Broward Williams, the first chancellor of higher education in the state university system, and Donald Bradshaw of Inverness, Gerald Gould and Elliott Mackle were given terms of office on the new board. Gould, a former advertising executive from Miami, was the president of Lehigh Acres

Development Corporation, developers of Lehigh Acres near Fort Myers. Elliot Mackle, along with his two brothers, had built General Development Corporation before leaving the company to form the Deltona Corporation. Although Bradshaw was an attorney, he had also built several small subdivisions.[12]

The board became more heavily influenced by the major developers as more appointments were made. When Williams resigned in February 1965, Howard R. Hirsch, a Miami attorney who had formerly represented Gulf American, replaced him. Later, on October 29, 1965, Governor Haydon Burns appointed Leonard Rosen to replace Bradshaw. When Rosen stepped down on September 21, 1966, he was succeeded by Robert Finkernagel, vice-president for Gulf American. Therefore, for much of its existence in the mid-1960s, the board was controlled by three of the largest development companies in Florida. This fact did not go unnoticed by the *Miami Herald,* as well as other newspapers. As Morton C. Paulson, business editor for the *Daytona Beach News-Journal,* noted, "The foxes were guarding the chickens."[13]

The FILSB's effectiveness as a regulatory agency was severely limited by the presence of so many developers on the board. Other shortcomings in the 1963 law that established the board were addressed when the state legislature passed the Florida Uniform Land Sales Practices Act in June 1967. The law accomplished two basic objectives. First, the FILSB was replaced by the Florida Land Sales Board (FLSB), thus recognizing the new board's jurisdiction over more than just installment sales. The legislation also increased the board's size from five to seven members with only two members allowed from the real estate industry. This was an attempt to limit the influence of developers. Second, the law enabled the FLSB to require developers to demonstrate adequate financial resources to complete their promised subdivisions.[14]

The FILSB had originally been formed in 1963 because of newspaper and magazine exposés of fraud in mail-order land sales. While writers frequently pointed out abuses in Florida, widespread deceptions also occurred in the southwestern part of the United States, particularly in Arizona. Because of the national scope of the problem and the seeming inability of state governments to come to grips with it, U.S. Senator Barry Goldwater of Arizona proposed in January 1963 a full-scale Senate investigation of fraudulent land promotions in Florida, Arizona, and other states. The Senate Special Committee on Aging, under the chairmanship of Senator George Smathers of Florida, began making inquiries later that year. The Special Committee on Aging addressed the situation because developers often targeted retirees for sales presentations and mailings.

Before the committee's work could begin, a federal grand jury in

Phoenix, Arizona, indicted three developers for misrepresenting their property, Lake Mead Rancheros, to customers. The land, located in Mohave County, Arizona, was advertised through newspaper and magazine notices by Miamians Dory Auerbach, David Prosser Randell, and Irving Gottlieb. The illegal activities occurred between September 1962 and January 1963 and involved more than 3,000 customers. Uncovered by postal inspectors, the situation prompted U.S. Attorney General Robert F. Kennedy to warn the public "to exercise precaution in buying land by mail." He added that in 1961 and 1962 the country had "experienced a sharp increase in the sale by mail of nearly worthless land for greatly inflated prices."[15]

During the committee hearings in Washington, it became apparent that a more in-depth study of mail-order land frauds was necessary. Although many buyers still were being misled or duped by unscrupulous subdividers, committee member Senator Harrison A. Williams, Jr., of New Jersey believed that progress was being made, noting that "Federal investigations since their hearings [1963] have resulted in indictments and several convictions." Of twenty-two prosecutions listed for the Senate record, however, only two involved Florida land or developers. Although Williams felt that the most blatant excesses had been modified, he remarked in 1964 that "some old techniques, however, appear to have long lives."[16]

As a result of these preliminary hearings, the Senate formed in 1964 the Subcommittee on Frauds and Misrepresentations Affecting the Elderly, to be chaired by Senator Williams and to report directly to Smathers's committee on aging. While the subcommittee did not focus specifically on land frauds in Florida, much of the testimony did relate to activities within the state. Twenty-two witnesses were called on three days of hearings from May 18 to May 20. Experts from Florida included Morton Paulson, business editor of the *Daytona Beach News-Journal;* Robert Doyle, planning director for the East-Central Florida Regional Planning Council; Warren L. Greenwood, former president of the Daytona Beach Board of Realtors; John McWhirter, executive director of the FILSB; and Marshall Criser, chairman of the FILSB.

At the outset, Williams stated that the hearings were intended to help the senators learn more about various land promotions throughout the country. Williams personally wanted to determine if the previous year's publicity and enforcement activity had "resulted in a significant reduction of misleading advertising and sales promotions or are some shady developers merely finding more subtle ways to mislead the buyer." Williams believed that much had already been accomplished to clean up the industry and that "the high standards of the many should not be endangered or clouded by the actions of the minority."[17]

As the subcommittee discovered, the selling of swampland in Florida was not a rare occurrence. Morton Paulson and Warren Greenwood detailed the questionable promotional efforts of Florida Ranchettes (Volusia County), First America Development Corporation (Volusia County), and Webb Realty Company (Collier County). Greenwood said, "We are still confronted with many of these corporations which are still dealing in swamplands even though their advertising brochures are now being edited." He added that approximately $15 million had been spent each year on advertising by promoters but less than one-third of the companies had registered with the FILSB as the law required. Paulson acknowledged that swamp merchants were in the minority, however, and that companies like General Development, Deltona Corporation, and Del Webb were building attractive, well-planned communities.[18]

Many sellers of submerged lands were not simply anonymous corporations. First America Development Corporation, the developer of University Highlands, a 9,420-acre tract of swampy woodland near Deland, Florida, was represented by several prominent individuals. Officers of the corporation included Frank S. Cannova, a Florida assistant attorney general from 1949 to 1952; T. Frank Hobson, a former chief justice of the Florida Supreme Court; and Fuller Warren, former governor of Florida. Warren, in a letter to the committee, vehemently denounced Paulson's and Greenwood's testimony. Although engineering reports stated that much of the land was swampy, he called such claims a "deceitful bag of half-truths and half-lies" and described Paulson as "a pliant hireling of a vicious and untruthful so-called newspaper." Warren provided no evidence to support his attack on Paulson's testimony.[19]

Despite words of warning to the subcommittee, official representatives of the state of Florida were reluctant to portray the situation in anything but a positive light. John McWhirter and Marshall Criser, both of the FILSB, testified at length to the ability of the FILSB to regulate the land sales industry in the state. They opposed increased federal regulation of the industry because many sales did not involve interstate transactions and because federal legislation meant loss of control of a major Florida industry that was largely beneficial to the state's economy. With the new board less than one year old, Criser argued, "We feel that we should be given an opportunity to prove that the FILSB can do the job that it was created to do." Besides, he reasoned, "if a person reads the [property] report and has had an honest representation, then that is as far as government should go. You cannot protect a fool against himself."[20]

Although most of the witnesses urged Congress to increase its regulation of the industry, several Florida public officials opposed federal interference in Florida land development. Most prominent among these officials was the full committee's chairman, Senator George Smathers. During his questioning of Criser, Smathers made clear to all present that even if swamp peddling was still happening, the problem had been greatly reduced by recent Florida legislation. He felt that the federal government should not interfere. He saw the issue as "a human problem of overselling," and he said, "most developers in our state are a credit to the business."[21] Besides his obvious reasoning, Smathers had been directly involved in several Florida land promotions himself. As Smathers observer Robert G. Sherrill noted, "Senator Smathers has always been keen for land promotion in Florida."[22] The subcommittee ultimately recommended that federal legislation supplement state regulation by requiring full-disclosure statements from all developers and proposed that the legislation be administered by the Securities and Exchange Commission.

While no significant federal legislation resulted from the subcommittee hearings, other states were beginning to regulate out-of-state mail-order land sales firms. As of September 20, 1963, California refused to allow any sales of subdivided Florida real estate within the state. In that year, at the insistence of Governor Pat Brown, the legislature enacted a law that reclassified out-of-state land offerings as securities. As a result, land companies such as Gulf American were required to issue a full-disclosure report on their subdivisions and to prove that their land offerings were valued in a "fair, just and equitable" manner. Believing that the investment potential of most Florida subdivisions was grossly overstated, California officials banned sales of all Florida real estate within their state's borders.[23] In New York, Florida land was allowed for sale, but a July 1, 1963, law required a full-disclosure report on the property and required that all advertising be approved by the state.[24]

Florida's regulation of the installment land sales industry focused on several areas. A major area of concern among state officials, as well as developers, was the lack of clear guidelines for advertising. This problem was stated in a report from Governor Bryant's Committee on Interstate Land Sales in April 1963.[25] As the FILSB gradually clarified its stand on false and misleading advertising, hundreds of proposed advertisements from Gulf American and other developers were edited or banned. Bernice Freiberg, then the Gulf American vice-president who handled much of the company's advertising, commented about those regulations: "Life became very difficult. We had no fault with that. It was there to protect the buyer and it was a great selling point with us on land. They [buyers] would say, 'How do we know that the land is there? How do we know that it's what you say?' And we'd say, 'Because the state of Florida says it's there and the state of Florida allows us to say it.'"[26]

Several other states, including New Jersey, required that all mail-order materials and advertisements also be approved by their agencies.

The FILSB also investigated the financial backing of various land companies to determine if they would be able to fulfill their promises to buyers. In January 1964 the management consulting firm of Fails, Willis, and McCall of Tampa was chosen by the board to examine Gulf American in order to test a new method of analyzing the finances of major subdividers. The FILSB wanted to determine if Gulf American was adhering to responsible business practices and would be able to meet mortgage payments. A major reason for this interest involved the bankruptcy of numerous promotions, which left many subdivisions without enough improvements to make the homesites buildable. In its report, Fails, Willis, and McCall concluded that while Gulf American had declined in profitability over the previous three years, it would have enough cash to make its necessary payments.[27]

An example of a failed project was Harbour Heights in Charlotte County. The developers, Charlotte County Land and Title Company, approached the New York City Patrolmen's Benevolent Association (PBA) about putting its seal of approval on the company's advertisements in return for a 10 percent discount on a lot and house for each police officer who became a customer. The PBA visited the 2,080-acre site on the Peace River and found a flourishing development with a country club, pool, and houses. Several hundred police officers, as well as other New York City workers, purchased lots. One day the owners each received a newspaper clipping in the mail notifying them that Harbour Heights had gone into bankruptcy and that the parent company could not reimburse the owners or finish the improvements.[28] Interestingly, the president of the Harbour Heights promotion was Milton Mendelsohn, who subsequently went to work as a consultant for Leonard Rosen at Cape Coral.

For the next year, the FILSB continued to ask for additional financial guarantees from Gulf American. Throughout 1964 Gulf American officials were required to report proposed loan agreements to the board for approval. The purpose of that ruling was to prevent Gulf American from borrowing more than it could reasonably expect to be able to repay. In order to satisfy the board, the company deposited $600,000 with the state in escrow against its outstanding mortgages. Therefore Gulf American not only had to borrow money for development but also had to post $600,000 to guarantee that the firm would repay it.[29]

The FILSB felt nevertheless that Gulf American had not provided sufficient guarantees that it would complete all improvements. Although the company had already posted performance bonds with the

Lee County Commission by mid-1963 for completion of streets and drainage, the FILSB wanted assurances that all improvements would be finished. In December 1964 Gulf American set up another escrow account into which the pro rata cost of developing each lot was funded from installment payments. On January 25, 1965, the FILSB called on Gulf American to supply a $1 million performance bond to the state. During the early part of 1965, Carl A. Bertoch, the new executive director of the FILSB, made a personal inspection of Cape Coral and Golden Gate. He concluded that construction was being completed on schedule, the company's financial condition was considerably improved, and the corporation would retain a positive cash flow. Concerns over Gulf American's financial situation lessened thereafter as other issues received more attention.[30]

Beginning in April 1964, the FILSB received numerous complaints about Gulf American sales practices and promotions. Other companies were also accused of infractions, but Gulf American began to receive the largest number of complaints. Purchasers objected to an unclear refund policy, a requirement that buyers pay for documentary stamps that the seller was actually supposed to purchase, refusal or neglect in providing a property report, and numerous instances of misrepresentation by salespeople. In describing some of the sales practices, the board noted that "there was substantial evidence indicating an atmosphere of deception."[31]

In order to see the problem in better perspective, it is important to understand how the FILSB handled letters from the public. While large numbers of people who sent letters to the FILSB wanted information about Gulf American and other companies, others had legitimate complaints. During a sample period from July 12, 1966, to February 12, 1967, the FILSB found ninety-one complaints against Gulf American worthy of investigation. These complaints represented sales from 1961 to 1967. Although this was a significant number of accusations for such a short space of time, it was relatively minor when compared with Gulf American's land sales of more than $76 million for the same seven-month period. Many of those complaints were settled eventually by refunds from the company.[32]

The FILSB faced a serious obstacle in trying to regulate Gulf American and the other companies operating installment sales programs in the state. The entire budget for the board in 1966 was $120,000, which allowed for eleven staff members, including a janitor and typists. These few individuals were responsible for regulating 233 companies that operated about 300 subdivisions in Florida containing 850,000 acres of land. Because its resources were limited and the board was attempting to control sales practices for the entire industry, it was logical that the largest firm would receive the greatest amount of attention from the board's staff.[33]

Faced with continuing complaints, Bertoch called Leonard Rosen, Gulf American attorneys Bernard Herzfeld and William Carmine, Jr., and treasurer Joseph Maddlone to appear before the FILSB on July 15, 1965, to explain the complaints. After discussion, the board was convinced that Gulf American management was aware of the seriousness of the charges. Company officials did not dispute the findings and proposed various corrective measures. Gulf American officials were primarily concerned that the board's show-cause order would adversely affect the company's standing with the Securities and Exchange Commission and thereby damage its ability to borrow development money. A show-cause order indicated that an investigation by the board had already revealed violations of state law and the firm was required to provide reasons that the board should not take disciplinary action. The order was dismissed when the board was convinced that Gulf American was taking corrective action. Concerned over the potential of the board to affect Gulf American, Leonard Rosen subsequently secured a gubernatorial appointment to the FILSB on October 29, 1965.[34]

Despite Rosen's appointment, the FILSB continued its investigation in January 1966 to determine if Gulf American was complying with the board's requirements. Most of the investigation focused on sales at Golden Gate Estates. Company officials assured the board that all buyers were provided with property reports on the land they were buying and that signs in the closing rooms encouraged customers to ask for a property report. By the August 5, 1966, meeting, however, Bertoch had discovered otherwise. He delivered his preliminary findings then, and on October 10, at a four-hour closed-door board meeting, he presented an extensive report outlining abuses. Bertoch concluded that since the July 1965 board action, misrepresentation by Gulf American continued and buyers were not getting property reports, which were required by state law. A property report provided a complete description of the property for sale and had to answer a uniform list of questions specified by state officials. Bertoch recommended that accused salespeople be suspended, that Gulf American mail property reports to all buyers during the previous year, and that money be refunded if buyers sensed misrepresentation.[35]

Gulf American officials agreed to all conditions set down by the board. A spokesman for the company said the charges involved only two of thirty to forty salespeople at Golden Gate, noting that the two would be "suspended" if the land board brought proceedings against them. He added: "But, I think it's only fair they should be proven wrong before they're fired. We believe there was no intentional misrepresentation on the part of the salesmen. We didn't get this big by misrepresenting land." Despite protests of innocence, public confidence in Gulf American was beginning to unravel.[36]

As a result of the findings of the FILSB, the New Jersey Real Estate Commission imposed a ban on November 10, 1966, on all sales by Gulf American within the state. It prevented the company from conducting dinner parties, initiating vacation sales trips, or promoting its properties in any way. The commission showed concern over Gulf American's switching of lots without notifying owners of the newly purchased land. The ban remained in effect until May 9, 1967, when New Jersey officials were persuaded that Gulf American was making restitution with refunds.[37]

Even before the FILSB heard Bertoch's report, the U.S. Senate was again holding hearings on June 21 and 22 and August 18, 1966, concerning federal regulation of the promotional land industry. A subcommittee of the Banking and Currency Committee, chaired by Senator Harrison Williams, called witnesses to testify about the proposed Interstate Land Sales Full Disclosure Act (ILSFDA). The committee wanted more information about numerous cases of alleged misrepresentation using the mails that did not fall under federal postal fraud statutes. Promoters had received careful scrutiny during the early 1960s with 358 land fraud investigations launched by the Postal Inspectors Office from July 1962 to May 1964. Convictions were obtained in only 7 of those cases, and many unscrupulous developers managed to avoid federal postal prosecution. The wide variety of state statutes further complicated the situation; thirty states had no laws regulating the sale of out-of-state land developments. Senator Williams was pushing for the new ILSFDA because it would require most mail-order land sales firms to register with the Securities and Exchange Commission.[38]

Among other witnesses, the subcommittee invited Leonard Rosen to testify. According to Senator Williams, "Numerous statements have been made by other witnesses regarding Gulf American and it seemed only fair to give Mr. Rosen an opportunity to respond to some of the allegations and statements made in previous hearings." Originally scheduled to appear on August 18, 1966, Rosen had notified Williams's office that he was unable to attend due to the airline strike and the press of business. While Rosen answered several of the committee's questions in writing, Williams caustically noted that Gulf American had a main office in Baltimore and that "the trains were running."[39]

Rosen's testimony was rescheduled for September 7, 1966, and a Williams staff aide arranged a meeting in Baltimore with Gulf American chief counsel Bernard Herzfeld to discuss the line of questioning. Shortly after the meeting, Herzfeld called Williams's office and said that

Rosen would not appear because he felt "nothing productive could be obtained by his appearance." Williams commented on the canceled appearance: "I regret very much that Mr. Rosen has refused to appear before the subcommittee."[40] A further evasive action was Rosen's quiet resignation from the FILSB in early September 1966. Governor Haydon Burns replaced him with Robert Finkernagel, a Gulf American vice-president.

On a local level, accusations of wrongdoing by Gulf American accelerated. In September 1966 Naples realtor Vince Conboy petitioned the circuit court for a grand jury investigation of corruption in Collier County government as it related to unhindered sales abuses by Gulf American employees at Golden Gate. In December a grand jury was called in Collier County to look into an unrelated gunshot death. Because a grand jury could investigate any matter it chose, Conboy requested and received permission to appear before it. On December 20, 1966, he testified with three others concerning what he called the "deception, misrepresentation, and fraud by Gulf American."[41] Appearing with Conboy were realtor W. A. Burton; Claude Grimm, a former Gulf American sales manager; and Harry Morrison, a former Gulf American office manager.

In addition to these accusations, the *Miami Herald* carried a damaging story on Gulf American two days before Conboy's testimony. Written by former *Herald* real estate editor Fred Fogarty, the article quoted an admission by Gulf American assistant vice-president Edward R. Bryan "that there had been lot switching in the north end of Golden Gate Estates." According to the writer, lot owners who purchased specific parcels were assigned other lots. Bryan was also quoted as saying "the 1,300 owners were not notified prior to the switch."[42]

The grand jury reported its findings on January 4, 1967, in what Conboy described as a "whitewash." In reality, the grand jury sidestepped the whole issue of fraud by Gulf American, stating that "testimony from various witnesses indicates a need for further investigations" and unanimously recommending that a new grand jury be formed to focus on land fraud. The grand jury also recommended that the effectiveness of the FILSB "leaves much to be desired" and that five new members should be appointed from one of the five following categories: realtor, banker, mortgage banker, land title attorney, and land developer. The majority thus would have no past or present connections with land developers. Another grand jury was impaneled in January 1967, but it did not mention land sales fraud in Collier County.[43]

Despite the two grand juries' lack of interest in the land sales industry in southwest Florida, Gulf American faced a major new threat to its freedom to operate in the state. In November 1966, Claude R. Kirk, Jr., of Jacksonville was elected governor of the state, the first Republican governor since Reconstruction. Throughout the 1960s, Florida's governors were outspoken in their support of business expansion in the state. C. Farris Bryant, governor from 1960 to 1964, openly promoted Florida tourism. Governor Haydon Burns (1964–66) proclaimed that "when people, money and industry pour into a state, that state will prosper and offer unlimited opportunities." Burns's support of the land sales business, and of Gulf American in particular, was evidenced by his appointment of Leonard Rosen to the FILSB in 1965 and by his eventual position as a consultant for Gulf American after he left politics.[44]

Burns faced a reelection bid in 1966 because of a change in the state constitution, and Leonard and Jack Rosen wanted to keep a sympathetic friend in the governorship. As a result, the Rosens contributed heavily to his campaign, which spent nearly $1.5 million. Besides financial resources, the Rosens gave the Burns staff free access to Gulf American's massive phone rooms in Miami and even supplied personnel to staff them. When Burns was defeated by liberal Miami mayor Robert King High in the Democratic primary, the Rosens threw their support and resources to High. Consequently, bad feelings developed between Kirk and the Rosens.[45]

In the gubernatorial election, conservative Democrat Burns gave strong support to Republican Kirk over High. Nevertheless, Kirk, upon taking office, split sharply with the previous administration. So bitter was the split that, according to the *St. Petersburg Times,* Kirk personally visited the Disney offices in California to try to block Burns's plans to link his consulting business with the new Disney World attraction at Orlando. Burns's deal with Disney eventually fell through. Kirk's intense opposition to the former governor may have been partly the result of Burns's business association with the Rosens. While Burns's support for Kirk was not rewarded, Elliott Mackle aligned himself with the Republicans and consequently was named chairman of the new Florida Land Sales Board in August 1967.[46]

Kirk's intentions had become obvious in January 1967, when he requested the resignations of all FILSB members because of their alleged sympathy with the land sales industry and with Gulf American in particular. Only Mackle and Gerald Gould agreed to resign, but their offers were refused because Kirk could already count on their support. Board chairman Gould, who knew Kirk well, explained the new governor's reasoning to the board. Kirk had made it known to him "that no single issue, other than crime, was of more importance to him than the functions of the Installment Land Sales Board." The governor advised him that he had received many letters about the land sales industry and a large number questioned the board's composition.[47]

In addition to Mackle and Gould, the board consisted of several individuals with direct ties or sympathies with Gulf American. They included Robert Finkernagel, Gulf American vice-president; Howard Hirsch, a Miami attorney who had handled the land purchases in 1962 for Gulf American's corporate headquarters at Seventy-ninth Street and Biscayne Boulevard; and attorney Joseph F. Chapman, Jr., vice-president for a business consulting concern that at the time still did work for Modern Air Transport, a Gulf American subsidiary. The consulting firm, Haydon Burns and Associates, was owned by former Governor Burns, who described his involvement with GAC: "I handle management problems for the airline." Specifically, he had many contacts on the state level, and he was able to advise the Rosens on what they could and could not do legally and politically. Burns also had appointed all five of the current board members. With Gulf American control of the board assured and most of the board members refusing to resign, Kirk attempted to replace the FILSB altogether.[48]

In April 1967 Governor Kirk initiated a proposal in the legislature to create a new Florida Land Sales Board (FLSB) and abolish the old FILSB. Not content to allow a potentially crippling law to pass, Gulf American sent numerous lobbyists to Tallahassee. At one point, the company offered to transport Dade County legislators to and from Tallahassee in the company plane. On several occasions, company representatives attempted to meet with Kirk to discuss the firm's problems. After waiting for several hours on one occasion in the governor's office, one Gulf American vice-president was told the governor was not interested in talking to him.[49]

Responding to the governor's pressure, the legislature passed the Florida Uniform Land Sales Practices Act in June 1967. The new law, strongest in the history of Florida land regulation, expanded the new board from five to seven members and designated that only two could be connected in any way with the industry. The new law also regulated the whole field of land sales, not just installment and mail-order sales. "This is a good strong law with lots of teeth," commented Elliott Mackle. Under the law, willful violations by corporations became a felony for which the officers and directors could be jailed for up to two years and fined $100,000. The law also gave the board authority to suspend salespeople who misrepresented land.[50]

Impatient with the lack of action by the old board, Kirk wanted the new law to take effect July 1, 1967. When opponents urged that the date be September 1, a compromise determined that it would take effect on August 1, 1967. The governor, who was reported to have said he would not stand for a "whitewash" of Gulf American, requested that the FILSB defer any action until the new publicly dominated board took office on

August 1. While the FILSB had started an investigation of Gulf American's sales practices in January 1967, the board had shown little desire previously to consider the findings. However, an urgent meeting was called by the current board for June 30 to handle the proceedings itself before the new board convened. One unnamed observer quoted in the *Wall Street Journal* commented on the turn of events: "It was seldom anything you could put your finger on, but in the time these three [Finkernagel, Hirsch, and Chapman] were on the board, the Gulf American hearing just never seemed to get anywhere. Somebody always was sick or tired or had to catch an airplane."[51]

The June 30 meeting was questioned by observers at the time for two other reasons. Some close observers believed that Mackle and Gould were unlikely to attend the meeting in order to prevent a quorum. Without them, only board members with Gulf American ties would be present to hear the evidence. In addition, the board's rules required that Finkernagel, as a Gulf American vice-president, disqualify himself from voting. Subsequently, the board would be left without a quorum. Besides the quorum issue, a three-month-old ruling by the Florida attorney general's office allowed the Gulf American case to be examined behind closed doors, an unusual circumstance in such investigations.[52]

Sensing that Kirk planned further problems for the company when he gained control of the FLSB, Gulf American officials went on the offensive. In a June 22, 1967, letter to Carl Bertoch, executive director of the FILSB, Gulf American senior vice-president James Layden accused the board and Bertoch of harassing Gulf American while other major developers were guilty of the same or worse infractions. Layden specifically accused the Lehigh Acres Development Corporation of not having posted the proper bonding with the county and the state to ensure that development of purchased lots would be completed. Furthermore, he charged that the board had not exposed this violation because of active collusion by Bertoch and the board chairman, Gerald Gould, who also was a senior officer at Lehigh. Layden noted that when these charges were brought to the public's notice, Bertoch and Gould would be able "to share some of the feelings and have a little understanding as to why the officials of Gulf American have reacted as they have when they have received what we consider to be unfair amounts of publicity."[53]

Even before these accusations, Gould had been called to answer to the board in May 1967 concerning several instances of alleged misrepresentation by Lehigh salespeople. Apparently, several salespeople had promised improvements in the Lee County development to which the Lehigh Acres Development Corporation had not agreed. Gould maintained that the developer was not guilty of failing to fulfill the contracts but that the problem was one of better regulation of the sales staff.[54] Although Lehigh and other developments were being scrutinized by Florida government officials, few received the attention of Gulf American.

During the first half of 1967, Gulf American had succeeded in keeping the results of the FILSB's investigation behind closed doors. Convinced that the old board planned to censure the company for its activities, which involved only a reprimand, Governor Kirk decided to bring public pressure on the FILSB. On June 15 of that year, James Wolf, Kirk's press secretary, talked to reporters at the *Wall Street Journal* for about one and one-half hours, describing in detail his knowledge of the secret FILSB report on Gulf American. Although Wolf denied releasing the contents of the secret report, within two weeks, on June 28, the *Journal* published a front-page story by Kenneth G. Slocum that accused Gulf American of "grossly immoral and unethical sales activities." Wolf later explained that he had contacted the *Journal* because "they've had a big interest in this thing."[55]

The *Journal* article, which quoted numerous unnamed sources, outlined many of the findings of the FILSB's undercover investigation. According to these sources, the board's exhaustive study of Gulf American included going to such lengths as hiding investigators in car trunks, taping sales pitches, and meticulously comparing various site maps. The report accused Gulf American of grossly misrepresenting the investment potential of some of its land, concealing key information from the FILSB, and switching lot numbers. Specifically, the lot switching involved the selling of lots bearing specific numbers and then changing the lot numbers to other land, often miles away. The report also questioned the practice of refusing to refund the payments of people who defaulted on the lots whose numbers had been changed.[56]

In addition, the article noted the many complaints received by the FILSB concerning the firm. According to the FILSB report, "throughout the board's history, Gulf American has been the greatest single source of complaints. To date [June 1967], the staff is unaware of any positive action taken by management to control the situation." At the time of the article, Gulf American accounted for approximately 25 percent of the land business in Florida, which included at least 200 other firms. From 1963 to 1967, however, complaints to the board naming Gulf American ranged between 39 and 64 percent of the total. Leonard Rosen's explanation of the figures was: "Our complaints are higher because we do more business and a lot of complaints are generated by competitors and newspapers. . . . We give back more money than most of the industry takes in." He added, "We may soft soap customers to death but we didn't get this big by beating them over the head." When confronted with the accusation that salespeople were not supplying buyers with the required property reports, Rosen called the charge "an outright lie. We have private detectives calling on other developers and they also come away without property reports."[57]

Of all the accusations made in the *Wall Street Journal* article, the most damaging was the charge of lot switching. During 1962 and 1963 the company sold some 1,300 lots in Golden Gate Estates and then in 1963 relocated these properties on company maps to different land, retaining the same lot numbers. Often the new locations were several miles away. Neither lot owners nor the FILSB were notified of the change until early 1967. Complicating the matter further were the several hundred buyers who had purchased such lots and forfeited their contracts by stopping payments but who in 1967 were asking for refunds. According to Rosen, the switch had been necessary because the company had discovered muck under the land, making it unbuildable. He claimed that the customers had received better lots as a result of the trade.[58]

In a separate instance, a similar switch occurred at Cape Coral for different reasons. Gulf American had sold nearly 600 lots in Unit 44, Part 1, in southwestern Cape Coral by 1963, when it discovered a valuable deposit of marl under the site. Marl is a rocklike material used in road building that was in great demand by Gulf American because of road construction needs. Chief engineer Thomas Weber made the discovery and proposed to Leonard the possibility of mining it in order to cut the company's costs. Lot changes were made without any notification to owners or even the Gulf American sales staff. Edward Pacelli, vice-president of sales at Cape Coral and later at Golden Gate, emphasized the point: "We didn't know. . . . We discovered it when people started coming to the property. People started saying, 'Here's my property, why is it there?'" The marl was mined, and the site can be identified today as the Eight Lakes area in southern Cape Coral.[59]

Although the motivation for the switches was higher profit, most observers noted that the Rosens had no intention of financially harming any purchasers. Kenneth Schwartz, general manager for Cape Coral who left the company in 1964, commented later on the Rosens' involvement in the lot changing. He noted that the brothers would never ask their employees to "do anything dishonest. That doesn't mean that they didn't screw things up . . . but I know there was no plan. There was never a call for selling the property to Jones and then switching him over and giving the same property to Smith." Schwartz was referring to an illegal practice within the land sales industry called "double-decking," whereby a lot was sold twice. The theory behind double-decking was that during the term of the installment contract on a lot, at least one of the buyers would default on payments. If one did not, then one of the buyers was given another parcel. Gulf American was not accused of double-decking, but it did admit to switching the lots in question.[60]

By February 1967 Gulf American had already begun to contact owners of lots about restitution, due to increased FILSB interest in the subject. Buyers were either offered another parcel or they could have their money refunded. Many Cape Coral lot owners did not want the refunds or to be switched to yet another homesite. In either case, Gulf American had already refunded $669,000 to purchasers so affected by the time of the *Wall Street Journal* article.[61]

The lot-switching episode in Cape Coral appears to have been the result of an error in judgment on the part of Leonard Rosen. When Weber presented his findings to Leonard about the marl deposits, Leonard discussed the matter with a close associate. The unnamed associate persuaded Leonard that if lot numbers were switched, none of the property owners would know the difference. According to Edward Pacelli, this individual "was a most persuasive man, too. He had to be to overcome the Rosens. You couldn't win an argument with him." He was also the same man who convinced the Rosens, against their strenuous objections, that the best way to ensure the future growth of their community was to include a "Caucasian-only" clause in the early sales contracts at Cape Coral. The clause was later deleted.[62]

In all likelihood, the unnamed associate was Milton Mendelsohn, a paid consultant who had advised the Rosens on early development at Cape Coral and other Gulf American projects. Mendelsohn acquired considerable experience in land development through his project at Harbour Heights near Punta Gorda. But his brilliant, creative mind was constantly coming up with innovative sales schemes that potentially could get the Rosens in legal difficulties. Mendelsohn had already acted as an adviser to Gerald Gould when they worked together in an advertising agency in Miami. Gould and Mendelsohn later helped Lee Ratner start Lehigh Acres. Despite his creative genius, Leonard Rosen recognized Mendelsohn's potential to harm the company. Early in Kenneth Schwartz's tenure with Gulf American, the first instruction Leonard gave him was that Mendelsohn was never to sign anything or make any commitments for the company. Recognizing Mendelsohn's brilliance, however, Leonard also urged Schwartz to listen to Mendelsohn and learn all that he had to teach. In that respect, Schwartz acknowledged that Mendelsohn served as a kind of mentor to him during those years.[63]

Another example of Mendelsohn's powerful influence in the corporation occurred at Remuda Ranch Grants. By late 1966, construction had

Advertising executive Bernice Freiberg and Milton Mendelsohn (left) discuss a layout of Cape Coral's further development.

commenced on two hotels at the project, each located on opposite sides of the Tamiami Trail. As engineer for the development, Thomas Weber did not understand the purpose of two similar facilities just across the road from each other. When Mendelsohn was questioned by Weber, he told the engineer that two separate facilities were necessary, but he did not elaborate on the reason. Because Mendelsohn and Leonard Rosen often conferred on such subjects, Weber assumed that Mendelsohn knew what he was talking about. After construction was under way, Weber discovered that an irritated and surprised Leonard had never ordered two separate lodges. Although Weber had received a written order signed by Rosen for the facilities, Leonard apparently had not been aware that the project had been designed in this way until he visited the work site. Because Mendelsohn was personally involved in the design and concept of most of the Gulf American projects, the dual facilities were likely his idea. Leonard undoubtedly did not notice the unnecessary building in the crush of projects he was authorizing until it was too late, and Mendelsohn's concept remained.[64]

Investors reacted quickly to the Gulf American story in the *Wall Street Journal* on June 28, 1967. Listed on the American Stock Exchange, Gulf American stock closed on Tuesday, June 28, at $11.75 per share, down 25 cents for the day. As a result of the story, trading in the issue was halted by the exchange on Wednesday because of a large number of sell orders. Trading resumed on Thursday, June 30, and by the end of the session Gulf American stock had dropped to $9.00 a share, down $2.75 from Tuesday's closing. The decline represented a paper loss of almost $17 million to Leonard and Jack Rosen, who owned more than 66 percent of the outstanding shares.[65]

Aware that investors and the financial community would be alarmed by the publicity, Leonard had quickly issued a calming statement on June 28. He indicated that he did not believe that the FILSB would suspend or revoke Gulf American's license to do business in Florida. He noted that the confidential report quoted in the *Journal* article "related largely to transactions which took place prior to the formation of the FILSB. There is no proceeding pending before the board which in any way affects Gulf American's right to do business."[66]

FILSB chairman Gerald Gould reinforced that point by stating that the board had never heard the matter fully and that Gulf American "has never been found guilty of anything." Gould also expressed concern about "newspaper accounts which told only half the story." Critical of the *Journal* account, he added, "It is unfortunate to have someone tried and convicted because of insufficient information having been released to the press."[67]

Leonard issued a second public statement on the article on June 29, maintaining that the story in the report was "seriously distorted." He rebutted the alleged information, stating that the land board had actually received only 609 complaints about Gulf American between January 1963 and February 1967. The rest were, according to Rosen, requests for information. Compared with the 150,000 contracts signed with customers during that period, he called the number of complaints "an insignificant percentage." He added that "all except three had been satisfactorily discharged." Consequently, he assured investors, "In my opinion, there is no exposure whatsoever regarding the information released in newspapers and if there should be any liability or exposure, it would be much less than $100,000, which in terms of company assets or volume of business would be inconsequential."[68]

Although Leonard attempted to depict the article as little more than a temporary nuisance, Florida state officials thought differently. Carl Bertoch, FILSB executive director, notified the press the day after the article appeared and announced that the FILSB did have authority to revoke a company's right to sell property. He also advised the officials at the American Stock Exchange that no suspension or revocation was "imminent against Gulf American—that is, within twenty-four to forty-eight hours." In an interview in early July 1967, Governor Kirk commented on the article: "We don't want to shut anybody down. We just want to clean up a bad situation." However, Kirk made it clear that he did not believe the current FILSB would clean up anything. Rather, he planned to make every effort to prevent any other meetings of the FILSB until August 1967 when the new board would take over.[69]

With Kirk having forbidden the FILSB to assemble, Gould cancelled the June 30 meeting. The governor had stated clearly that he wanted the next meeting to be in his office where he would again ask for the resignations of all five members. He made sure that the board would not be able to address the Gulf American case by ordering its chief investigator, Carl Bertoch, to go on vacation until the new board met.[70]

In addition, the governor and his aides refused to meet with any Gulf American officials. Hoping to reach some sort of settlement, Leonard attempted to call Kirk at his office on July 7, 1967, but was unable to reach him. In a letter to Kirk on the same day, Leonard stated that he wanted a personal meeting with him so that he might present Gulf American's side of the alleged misdeeds. Leonard explained in his letter, "In the rapid growth of our company, we have made a mistake or two but, by far, have done many, many good things on the positive side of the ledger." The meeting never occurred, prompting Leonard to observe the partiality of the governor toward his competitors: "Elliott Mackle can go in and out [of the governor's office] any time he pleases."[71]

Mackle's connections with Governor Kirk became clear when the Florida Land Sales Board (FLSB) was filled on August 2. Not only was Mackle the only appointee from the old board, but he was named chairman. The other land development representative on the board was Joseph P. Taravella, president of Coral Ridge Properties Corporation of Fort Lauderdale. The five nominees representing the public included Jon C. Moyle, an attorney from West Palm Beach; Phillip N. Smith, an Orlando attorney who was resident counsel for Compass East Company, a subsidiary of Walt Disney Productions; Charles W. Johnson, Jr., a certified public accountant from Jacksonville; Tom Courtney, a vice-president for securities at Peninsular Life Insurance Company in Jacksonville; and J. Norman Rosmoser, Jr., a St. Petersburg realtor.[72]

Throughout July 1967 Kirk continued the pressure on Gulf American. He met in early July with Governor Jack Williams of Arizona at the Western Governors' Conference in Wyoming, after which Williams requested that Kirk send his Gulf American files to Phoenix. Kirk readily agreed. Coincidentally, Gulf American officials were pursuing well-publicized plans to begin construction on Rio Rico, a large multicity development near Nogales, Arizona. On July 6, Leonard Rosen submitted plans for the project to Santa Cruz County officials and completed the purchase of the 55,000-acre Baca Float Ranch for $3.4 million. The next day, Williams's probe made headlines in Nogales, and several articles appeared in the *Arizona Republic* and the *Arizona Daily Star*. A *Daily Star* editorial revealed the problems that Kirk's efforts had caused the company and described Gulf American's "badly damaged image." Despite the bad publicity, Rosen pledged that his company would spend more than $30 million on the development over the next ten years.[73]

The new FLSB held its first meeting August 8, even before the state senate had confirmed the appointments. Governor Kirk addressed the board, saying that there would be "no more winking at shoddy sales practices." Within minutes, the board asked Gulf American to waive its right to a confidential hearing of the charges against it. When Gulf American officials responded on August 23 and refused to comply, the company and the board became embroiled in a legal fight over the issue, a fight that lasted more than two months. While the conflict continued, the FLSB refused to certify any additional Gulf American plats of land for sale.[74]

At conflict were two opposing sets of regulations. According to a rule of the old FILSB, complaints against developers were to be kept confidential without disclosure to the public until the board took action. Conflicting with this regulation was the "government in the sunshine" law passed by the 1967 legislature that forced governmental bodies to keep their discussions public. The board requested Florida Attorney General Earl Faircloth to rule on the legal delay. He stated on October 6 that the secret report on Gulf American could be heard behind closed doors. He indicated that the investigative hearing seemed to parallel a grand jury and should be afforded the same kind of confidentiality.[75]

Two separate incidents in autumn 1967 further complicated the situation. Earlier in the year, Leonard had hired Barry Horenbein, a Tallahassee lobbyist, to help smooth relations between Gulf American and the governor's office. Horenbein recommended to Leonard that the company needed additional legal counsel with legislative and political experience. In late September, Gulf American had hired Mallory Horne, a state senator from Tallahassee, to provide legal assistance in preparing court appeals from any judgment the FLSB might issue. At the time, it was not uncommon for state legislators to represent clients before state agencies while retaining their positions in the state legislature.[76]

While Lawton Chiles of Lakeland, chairman of the Florida Senate Ethics Committee, saw no conflict of interest in Horne's new employment, other state officials did. Governor Kirk called on Horne to withdraw from the arrangement, describing the situation as "a carefree lack of ethics" and a "clear and unmistakable conflict of interest." Horne, as one of the authors of the law that had created the new FLSB, was a member of the governmental reorganization committee and had access to the confidential files of the FLSB.[77]

In a second more bizarre incident, on October 13 Governor Kirk accused a representative of Gulf American of trying to blackmail the governor's staff into suppressing the FLSB's investigation of the company. According to a Kirk aide, the unnamed representative approached several members of the governor's staff and offered not to disclose embarrassing information about a Kirk appointee if the governor would induce the FLSB to halt its investigation of Gulf American. The appointee was C. Shelby Dale, a longtime friend and political associate of the governor who had been named chairman of the Florida Development Commission. Dale denied the allegations of wrongdoing but was suspended anyway by Kirk pending an investigation.[78]

Ultimately, Kirk fired Dale on November 8 because of "a too close relationship between his law practice and state involvement." The governor based his decision on information obtained by investigations handled by the Wackenhut Corporation. On January 3, 1966, Kirk had announced that he was hiring George R. Wackenhut and his Miami-based private security company to investigate organized crime and corruption among public officials in the state of Florida. During his 1966 gubernatorial campaign, Kirk had made crime and corruption major issues. In appointing the conservative Wackenhut, Kirk pledged that his attack on corruption would be privately financed so as to be under his control. Many observers feared that a private police force that was independently financed would amount to the formation of a secret state police. By May 1967, however, critics claimed that the Wackenhut investigation was inept and that it deceived the governor and the public and focused most of its 356 individual investigations on political subversives and opponents of the Kirk administration.[79]

Kirk turned Dale's Wackenhut file over to State Attorney Russell B. Clarke of Broward County for further investigation, but the case was dropped.

The Florida Development Commission was originally intended to promote Florida's image throughout the nation, but its focus was redirected by the governor in an effort to gain publicity for Kirk in the national press for a possible upcoming campaign for the U.S. presidency or vice-presidency. When criticized about his personal use of the commission's $4 million annual budget, the governor insisted that he was one of Florida's natural assets. He maintained that everything spent to publicize Kirk also benefited the state's image.[80]

According to Dale, an attorney approached him in early October 1967 about going to work for Gulf American. Although he was unsure as to whether the attorney had any authority to speak for the company, Dale claimed: "I told him I couldn't because of my position in state government." Leonard Rosen denied any attempt to hire Dale to smooth relations with the Kirk administration. Dale observed that he was the victim of a rumor but, by the time the governor's office had determined that it was groundless, "it was a question of getting out of it in some way." Suspicion also focused on Dale's legal representation of Rader and Associates, a highly respected Miami engineering firm whose clients included the state road department and Gulf American. As a result of the publicity, Dale was removed from his position on the commission.[81]

The alleged blackmailer was identified several weeks later by sources in the governor's office as Tallahassee lobbyist Barry Horenbein. Horenbein, who had grown up in Miami Beach, moved to Tallahassee in 1961 and started his own public relations/lobbying firm, Florida Consultants, in 1962. During the 1967 legislative session, Horenbein worked as a registered lobbyist for Minnesota Mining and Manufacturing Company (3M), Remington Rand Company, and Florida horseracing interests. Although he was not a registered lobbyist for Gulf American, Horenbein said later that he did represent the land sales firm but had started working for them after the end of the 1967 legislative session.[82]

According to the allegations reported in the *Wall Street Journal,* Horenbein approached two Kirk aides, repeating his proposition twice. The lobbyist said, "I got a call from Leonard Rosen, and I'm just doing what I'm told." The aide recalled that Horenbein "told me Gulf American had the goods on Shelby Dale and if the [FLSB] meeting wasn't called off, they would tell all." On the previous day, another official reported that Horenbein advised him that "Gulf American had information concerning Shelby Dale and certain contracts. He gave the idea a delay by the board might not be a bad idea."[83]

When questioned about the incidents by a *Wall Street Journal* reporter, Horenbein denied that he made any offers for Gulf American, but he added, "I was there [October 13] and I talked to the governor's aides, but it was on business for 3M, not Gulf American." In another instance, Horenbein stated that it was he who was responsible for Gulf American's hiring of Mallory Horne to represent the company during its troubles with the FLSB. Commenting on his function with Gulf American, the lobbyist explained that the Gulf American people were "politically immature."[84]

Despite the allegations by Governor Kirk, Horenbein had another explanation for the events of October 1967. Early in the month, the governor's office notified Leonard Rosen that the governor was going to hold a press conference in several days to announce the evidence that had been put together on Gulf American misdeeds. Horenbein related in a later interview that he received a 3 A.M. phone call on October 11 from Leonard, who was in England on business. After a brief greeting, Leonard told him, "Now, if the governor is getting ready to play hardball with me, I'm prepared to play hardball." With that, Horenbein was instructed to take notes while Leonard outlined various improprieties in the Kirk administration, particularly involving Shelby Dale and key Kirk supporters in the legislature. In addition, Leonard stated that he had evidence that Elliott Mackle, who was chairman of the FLSB at the time, was in close contact with Kirk and that it appeared to him to be a conspiracy to put Gulf American out of business. Leonard had obtained much of the information by hiring a private investigator to examine the governor's office. After forty-five minutes of dictating information to Horenbein, Leonard concluded with a challenge that if the governor held a press conference, he would hold his own and present his evidence. He then instructed Horenbein to present the information to the governor's office in an attempt to halt the news conference.[85]

Aware that the information could have had serious political implications for several of his legislative friends, Horenbein called the governor's office at 7 A.M. the same morning. After he related some of the evidence, an aide suggested that they set up an 8 A.M. appointment. The meeting lasted for one hour and was attended by Governor Kirk and several aides, including Thomas Ferguson. After reading the information to them, Horenbein suggested to the governor that some other solution be found for the conflict between Rosen and the governor's office. Horenbein was thanked for not going first to the newspapers and was told that the governor hoped something could be worked out. Horenbein then called Leonard and Leonard suggested that they wait to see what would happen.[86]

The next day Horenbein received a phone call from a reporter from the *Wall Street Journal* wanting an interview. On the pretext of doing a story on the five most powerful lobbyists in the South at the time, the reporter conducted a two-hour interview on Horenbein's background and lobbying history. No questions about Gulf American were asked. After the lengthy session, the reporter admitted that he had just come from the governor's office and that Horenbein was being accused of blackmailing the governor. He added that the information from the interview was going to be part of the story on the alleged blackmail attempt. Horenbein denied that any blackmail had occurred. Acknowledging that he had been with the governor the day before, he later admitted that he told the reporter that he had been discussing 3M business at the meeting because he did not want to make any further statements to the press before he found out what the governor's office was going to do. He later explained: "I know I didn't try to blackmail them. I told them exactly what Leonard said. 'Here's what Mr. Rosen is going to have at his press conference when you have yours.'" The next day, October 13, Governor Kirk publicly charged an unnamed lobbyist with trying to blackmail him to "take the heat off" Gulf American.[87]

While Kirk's accusations were carried in several newspapers across the United States, Horenbein's name never surfaced until November 9. On that date, the *Wall Street Journal* published a front-page story on Horenbein, naming him as the alleged blackmailer. Much of the information in the article was obtained during the October 12 interview one day before Kirk made his accusations. Although blackmail was a serious crime, no formal charges were ever brought against Horenbein.[88]

Horenbein received some insight into the motivations of the governor's actions about two years later. After Gulf American was sold to GAC Corporation in early 1969, one of the first actions by GAC president S. Hayward Wills was to hire Thomas Ferguson, Governor Kirk's executive assistant, and Richard Warner, the governor's public relations director, for high-level positions at GAC. About one month later, Horenbein received a call from Ferguson. Apologizing for the problems that the blackmail allegations had caused Horenbein in his lobbying business, Ferguson explained that the governor's office was afraid that Leonard Rosen was going to hold a press conference to embarrass the governor. Fear of Leonard's revelations prompted the aggressive attack on Gulf American with the claim that Horenbein had attempted to blackmail the governor. After further explanation, Ferguson, representing GAC, offered to hire Horenbein to lobby for GAC in Tallahassee. While Horenbein doubted the offer at first, he soon joined GAC at twice his former salary.[89]

When questioned about Horenbein's relationship with the company, Leonard Rosen refused to verify if he had been employed by Gulf American. In an interview after the October 13, 1967, FLSB meeting, Rosen said, "To my knowledge, we have not tried to entrap anybody." At that point, his attorney, Bernard Herzfeld, interrupted and advised him to say no more. By early November, Rosen refused to talk at all with reporters from the *Wall Street Journal*. During a telephone call from the paper, Rosen was quoted: "I don't want to talk to you. After what the *Wall Street Journal* did to Gulf American, you're distasteful to me. I don't want to talk to you. You're distasteful, is that plain enough?" He then slammed the receiver.[90]

At its October 13 meeting, the FLSB issued an "order to show cause," calling on Gulf American to answer five specific charges at a November 10 meeting or face revocation or suspension of its license in Florida. In the previous four and one-half years, the FILSB and the FLSB had issued 148 show-cause orders.[91] While the type of order was not unusual, it did prepare the way for legal action against Gulf American. Whereas the previous board had rarely gone beyond this measure, the new board had been specifically appointed by Kirk with the Gulf American investigation in mind.

The seriousness of the action was noted by investors on the American Stock Exchange, where Gulf American stock opened on October 13 at $9.00 a share. As sell orders poured in, it rapidly dropped to $8.00 when trading was halted at 1:27 P.M. by the exchange. On the following Monday, the issue closed at $7.125.[92]

In response to the board's order, Leonard Rosen said that he welcomed the fact that the charges, which had been circulating unofficially for months, were being brought into the open. Although the company "had been forced to operate under a cloud" of suspicion since the June 28 *Wall Street Journal* article, Rosen said the fiscal year ending August 31, 1967, was the second best in the company's history. He also pointed out a potential legal problem by stating that "most of the events in the show cause order issued by the board dated back to events of 1963 and even earlier." The inference was that the FLSB did not have jurisdiction over those events. Rosen added that "almost all of the customers' complaints . . . have been resolved by the company voluntarily and with the payment to customers not otherwise satisfied of nearly $700,000 in cash refunds."[93]

Although Rosen felt certain that he could answer all charges against the company at the November 10 FLSB meeting, a compromise agreement with the board was negotiated sometime in the preceding two weeks. The *Wall Street Journal* somehow obtained a preview of the proposed settlement and, on the morning of November 10, published a detailed outline. According to the article, Gulf American would admit to the board's five allegations of deceiving and misleading thousands of site buyers. The counts included accusations of lot switching and of misrepresentations by many salespeople. The article said that the FLSB would appoint a five-member board to monitor the company for a specified period. The *Journal* also predicted that Jack and Leonard Rosen would step down from active management of the company: "It is no secret in Florida that politicians and regulatory officials consider the Rosens personally responsible for what these people call the 'over-aggressive' sales practices of Gulf American."[94]

The previous week, the FLSB had discussed possible actions against Gulf American. The options ranged from censure, which had already occurred to the company in 1965 and which carried no penalties, to revocation of its license to sell property in the state. For Governor Kirk, the direction was clear: "The thing we're determined to do is bring the scoundrels under control." However, many state officials believed that the option of shutting down the company permanently would damage the economy of southwest Florida. One regulator explained: "So what the hell do we do? If we shoot them [Gulf American] out of the water, what happens to the 150,000 buyers who have done nothing wrong? The company has obligations of $65,000,000 in improvements to those people." A *Miami Herald* article described specifically Gulf American's deep impact on Lee and Collier counties.[95]

Another factor in the board's decision revolved around the high level of publicity that the case had received in the press. On the day of the hearing, Gulf American attorney Herzfeld severely criticized the *Wall Street Journal* for publishing confidential agreements and reports. Because of the company's "trial by press," Herzfeld noted that Gulf American had "sustained shock after shock but we're still in business." FLSB counsel Stewart D. Allen agreed that there was great merit to Herzfeld's claim that the company had been tried by the media. He added, "I don't condone Gulf American's actions but there has been too much publicity and they couldn't get a fair trial anywhere." Allen told FLSB members that "if we continue to delay this case, you'll be trying a corpse." Hoping to salvage the situation, he added, "it is not the job of the board to force companies out of business."[96]

Although a preliminary agreement had been reached for a thirty-day suspension of the company's sales activities, the accord was nearly cancelled by Gulf American. A week before the November 10 session, Rosen and Herzfeld had met with board members in a Tampa hotel room and worked out an agreement for the rehabilitation of the company. On the morning of November 10, however, the *Journal's* article predicted that the company would plead guilty and Leonard Rosen would resign. Incensed by yet another news leak, Gulf American officials were nevertheless persuaded in a closed-door session of the FLSB to attend the hearing. As a consequence, however, Rosen did not offer his resignation.[97]

The meeting was held on schedule and, as expected, Gulf American pleaded guilty to five violations of the law rather than allow itself to be further damaged by the testimony of unhappy customers. The penalty, accepted by Herzfeld, included a 30-day sales suspension from December 10, 1967, to January 9, 1968, a $5,000 fine, the acceptance of monitors to observe the company's operations for 150 days, and payment for any costs incurred by the board in enforcing its regulations. Leonard Rosen commented on the guilty plea: "We consented to today's order by the land sales board first and foremost for the protection of our customers, shareholders, financial backers, and employees." He added that the settlement would get Gulf American "out from under the cloud that has hung over the company since late June."[98]

Despite the acceptance of the penalties, Herzfeld, answering for Gulf American, addressed all five charges in a forty-five-minute presentation. Concerning the lot switching of more than 1,300 parcels in Golden Gate Estates in 1962 and 1963, Herzfeld claimed that company engineers had found that it would be impossible to develop the land because of a thick layer of muck under the surface. "We gave the purchasers better land than they had bought," he stated. Herzfeld said that $688,000 in refunds had been made since February 1967, but "the company was derelict in not clearing up the matter when it happened." He said, "We did a good thing in a poor way." He did not condone the lot switching, admitting, "We can't defend that situation." In Cape Coral the maneuver involved some 320 acres that had been purchased as homesites. The buyers were given new lots one-half mile away with the same lot numbers. The marl discovered under the homesites was mined and used for road building in Cape Coral.[99]

Another charge by the FLSB involved selling land from a preliminary plat, resulting in buyers losing 150 feet of their land in Golden Gate Estates to the new Alligator Alley cross-state highway without prior knowledge that would happen. Herzfeld rebutted the accusation, explaining that no one paid for land they did not receive. The plat had simply been in error, and buyers had been offered their money back.[100]

A major infraction claimed by the FLSB concerned the changing of plats at Golden Gate Estates already conditionally accepted by the board and not notifying that state agency of the modifications. Herzfeld said that the board routinely accepted both the original plat and the revised version when they were presented and "we started to sell the land. The board should have caught the error."[101]

The most serious charge involved the unethical sales practices of Gulf American salespeople. Recalling a 1965 censure ruling against the company, the FLSB said that Gulf American had failed to give property reports to buyers as required. Customers were also told of excellent resale values for their land when, in reality, resales at any price were often impossible. Without trying to defend the company, Herzfeld remarked: "Salesmen are a problem to all Florida land companies. This is because salesmen work on commissions and are eager to make sales. I'm not here to deny they did do it."[102]

Following the November 10 FLSB meeting, Leonard Rosen issued a public statement to calm nervous investors, homesite owners, and employees: "Gulf American Corporation will continue all of its business activities with one exception. That one exception, for a period of thirty days, beginning December 10, will be the selling of Florida land." All employees were kept on the payroll for the entire suspension period although no new sales were made. Altogether, the company maintained a worldwide staff of more than 2,800 employees during the suspension. This number was partly reduced from a high total of 5,500 by a continuing strike by 425 employees of the Fort Myers Construction Company at Cape Coral; the strike had started October 16.[103]

Public reaction to the suspension was mixed. By November 12, Gulf American stock had ebbed to $7 per share. Because many investors were selling their stock, the American Stock Exchange halted trading of the issue for the third time that year. Newspapers with a statewide circulation, however, responded positively to the board's decision. The *St. Petersburg Times* called the guilty plea of Gulf American "a major victory for the people and a magnificent precedent for the legislature to continue." An editorial in the *Miami Herald* said the decision "marks the fresh start sorely needed and overdue." The paper added that "A state of six million must not be libeled by the greed of a handful of men." Most observers agreed with the FLSB's Carl Bertoch, who called the action a "landmark decision" that "demonstrates that offenders will be punished swiftly and certainly for their derelictions, regardless of size and position."[104]

As a consequence of the FLSB investigation, federal authorities became interested in Gulf American's sales activities. Assistant United States Attorney E. J. Salcines, chief of criminal prosecution in Tampa, met on November 9 with postal authorities regarding the company's violation of state laws. Of particular interest to Salcines was the possible effect of the Gulf American probe on other states where the firm operated. He promised to study the case to see if postal inspectors should consider possible mail-law violations.[105]

Others who showed an interest in the outcome of the case were the residents of Lee and Collier counties. Fearing an economic recession in the region if Gulf American was put out of business, the residents of Lee County, and particularly the 8,677 residents of Cape Coral, were relieved at the announcement of only a thirty-day suspension. Warren Whiteside, editor of the *Cape Coral Breeze,* described the attitude in Cape Coral as "watchful waiting" with no rush to sell homesites. Gulf American's impact on Lee County had been great, with the firm paying out $27.5 million in salaries and commissions from 1957 through 1966.[106]

As a sign of support, three prominent Lee County business leaders addressed the FLSB in early December, asking the board to lift its upcoming suspension of Gulf American because of its damaging impact on the county's economy. The three leaders were Charles M. Blackburn, executive vice-president of the Cape Coral Bank and president of the Cape Coral Chamber of Commerce; Harry Fagan, president of First National Bank of Fort Myers; and Samuel Posner, president of Fort Myers American Department Stores. Fagan, one of the earliest supporters of Leonard Rosen's efforts in Lee County, summarized the group's plea: "You [FLSB] are really penalizing 30,000 people [in Lee County]. This is Christmas and they are being hurt tremendously." He added that between 1,000 and 1,400 Gulf American employees and subcontractors would be put out of work temporarily.[107]

FLSB chairman Elliott Mackle responded that the board could not remove the suspension but assured the three men that the board would see that construction continued on the development. Board member Joseph Taravella said that the effect of the suspension on the economy of Lee County was regrettable but that Florida's six million residents would be harmed if abuses went unchallenged by the state. "There comes a day when these things must be faced," he said.[108]

The *Wall Street Journal* continued its coverage of the case by describing how Gulf American's wayward sales practices had been checked. Kenneth Slocum, the reporter who had broken the story on June 28, recalled the anecdote of a mule that was returned to a farmer by its owner because it refused to budge on command. Slocum related: "Unceremoniously, the farmer picked up a heavy two-by-four, slugged the mule over the head and told it to 'Giddiap'—and it did. 'What in tarnation was that all about?' demanded the astounded owner. 'That mule minds fine,' explained the farmer, 'but first you have to get its attention.'" In view of the FLSB decision, Slocum added, "The Florida land sales industry, like the farmer's mule, at long last is paying attention."[109]

By the end of November 1967 the initial clamor over the suspension had quieted. On November 27 the FLSB named five monitors to oversee the operations of Gulf American for 150 days after November 10. According to the board's penalties, Gulf American would also be required to pay for the monitors, at a maximum rate of $1,000 per day or a total of $150,000. The five overseers included Stewart Allen, the legal counsel for the FLSB who had helped investigate Gulf American; Donald Reed, a Boca Raton attorney who also served as Republican house leader in the Florida legislature; Charles Crumley, an Atlanta accountant; Dermitt Noonan, a New York certified public accountant and management consultant; and William D. Davis, a Kansas City property appraiser.[110]

Although a *Fort Myers News-Press* editorial announced, "Cloud Lifted from Gulf American," company officials were not content to accept all of the penalties. On December 5 the FLSB learned that Gulf American had refused to open financial records to the five monitors.

FLSB director Bertoch said that a review of the company's finances was "of vital importance" because it would reveal Gulf American's ability to make refunds and pursue promised development construction totaling $90 million. The FLSB ordered company officials to step out of the way of the monitors or face further prosecution.[111]

The board was concerned about the firm's ability to make refunds. A portion of the alarm came from the 2,770 letters received by the board in the previous fifteen working days concerning Gulf American. About half of the letters requested additional information and half concerned allegations. Between November 11, 1967, and March 1, 1968, the board received 7,588 complaints or inquiries about Gulf American or approximately 86 percent of all such FLSB correspondence. The large number of inquiries and complaints about the firm were described by Bertoch as the "darndest deluge of letters I've seen in three years." In order to handle the increased correspondence, the board hired more workers at a cost of $10,000 for the year. The great increase in correspondence was largely attributable to widespread news coverage of Gulf's suspension.[112]

Another issue taken up by the board at its December 5 meeting was an investigation of Travel Guild of America. Although it posed as a travel company, Travel Guild actually was operating as a lead-procuring subsidiary of Gulf American. According to Leonard Rosen, Gulf American had entered into an agreement with Travel Guild whereby Gulf American sponsored and Travel Guild attempted to sell to its members tours of Gulf American properties. The FLSB had written to Travel Guild in October and November, inquiring about its close relationship with Gulf American. The agency, managed by the Rosens' cousin Paul Venze, refused to answer the board's letters and, as a result, its advertising was banned by the board. Gulf American was also instructed to break its national advertising ties with the company. Board member J. Norman Rosmoser, Jr., described the relationship between the two companies as "just another dodge."[113]

Because the FLSB did not halt its suspension of Gulf American, company officials prepared the firm to stop all sales activities on December 10. On December 8, however, a minority shareholder in Gulf American filed suit in the District Court of Appeals, Second District, in Lakeland, Florida, to have the firm's thirty-day suspension set aside. The shareholder, Frank J. Florik of Chicago, charged that the FLSB did not have jurisdiction over events that had occurred prior to August 1, 1967, the date that the FLSB took office. Florik, a former Internal Revenue Service employee, owned 118,000 shares of stock in the company, representing an investment of $832,000. He also claimed that the suspension had cost him financial losses as the stock dropped in price; he told a

Wall Street Journal reporter, "You . . . cost me half a million dollars with those damned articles."[114]

Some observers suspected that Gulf American was actually behind the suit, pointing out that Florik's Miami attorney was Marion E. Sibley, who had represented Gulf American in a case the previous year. Gulf American officials denied any connection with the suit. A company spokesman stated, "We didn't recommend him [Sibley] to Mr. Florik and we aren't paying his fees." Subsequently, the district court of appeals issued a stay order to the FLSB, preventing enforcement of the thirty-day suspension until a full hearing was held on the issue. Beginning December 10, however, Gulf American voluntarily started its thirty-day suspension. In response to the legal confusion, the FLSB withdrew the monitors until the suit could be resolved.[115]

On December 28 the three-judge district court of appeals dismissed Florik's case, citing numerous reasons. In a thirteen-page decision, Judge William P. Allen stated that Florik could not originate his case at the appellate level and that he would have to file at the circuit court level. Otherwise, Allen responded positively to Florik's argument that the FLSB was not empowered to appoint monitors to oversee the activities of the firm and said that the use of monitors in a private company was "particularly disturbing." He said he could find no legal basis for it and added that it would set a dangerous precedent for other state regulatory agencies. Despite the judge's misgivings, Carl Bertoch responded to the decision of the court by saying, "The dismissal of the suit means the return of the monitors."[116]

Before Bertoch could send in the monitors, Florik refiled his suit in the Circuit Court of Hillsborough County in Tampa on January 2, 1968. As with his first action, he attempted to block the FLSB from punishing Gulf American. By Friday, January 5, Judge Roger D. Flynn had issued a temporary injunction against the FLSB's sanctions, pending a hearing. Within an hour, FLSB attorney Stewart Allen had filed an appeal in the second district court of appeals in Lakeland. "The appeal supercedes the lower court's action, and legally, this means we can resume our monitoring of the company's operations," he said. The monitors, however, were refused admittance to Gulf American offices on Monday, January 8, by company secretary Joseph Maddlone, who told the monitors that he was acting on direct orders from Leonard Rosen.[117]

Governor Kirk, angered by Florik's two suits, announced on January 5 that the FLSB would be forced to appoint a receiver for Gulf American if lawsuits continued to challenge the board's authority. "I'm very disturbed that a minority shareholder is trying to create some strange new law," he said. Claiming no responsibility for Florik's suit, Bernard Herzfeld, newly appointed Gulf American board vice-chairman, said that the suit had done nothing more than cause the company additional trouble. He also described Kirk's comments as "unfair."[118]

Up to January 8, 1968, Gulf American officials had adopted the position that the company would basically accept the FLSB's punitive measures, serve its suspension, and return to business on January 10. As the monitors continued to press for access to all financial records, Gulf American reversed its position and began to fight the measures. Although it is doubtful that the company initiated Florik's suits, Gulf American filed suit itself on January 8 in the second district court of appeals in Lakeland, challenging the FLSB penalties. The suit claimed that the company had agreed to the penalties because of threats and "economic duress." It also asked that all penalties be quashed. Interestingly, Gulf American had already voluntarily served all but one day of its thirty-day suspension.[119]

The firm's petition offered several reasons for nullifying the board's actions. It primarily challenged the constitutionality of the act that had established the FLSB, claiming that it restricted the governor's appointive power by limiting to two the number of development representatives on the board. The suit also said that the law did not authorize the board "to suspend the petitioner from carrying on its lawful business." In addition, Gulf American claimed that the monitors exceeded their authority when "they demanded information not relevant to any justifiable inquiry but concerning the inner and confidential workings of the petitioner [Gulf American]."[120]

Gulf American officials further claimed that the company's credit standing was damaged by Kirk's and Bertoch's implication that the appointment of a receiver for the company was imminent. The injury to its credit, according to the company's petition, would "prevent it from carrying out development plans which are in progress." The constant claim by FLSB members that Gulf American had hurt thousands of lot buyers was not only distorted, according to the suit, but also "false and untrue." The legal petition also accused Elliott Mackle of singling out Gulf American for investigation because he was president of the firm's largest competitor. During the month of December 1967 Mackle's company, Deltona Corporation, recorded its best month in the firm's history, reporting $6.4 million in sales out of a total for the year of $26.5 million. These sales occurred during the Gulf American suspension. Gulf American also warned in its suit that its legal action was likely to elicit an "act of reprisal" from the state.[121]

Evidence did exist to suggest that Gulf American had been singled out for special emphasis. According to FLSB officials, the monitors, working in key locations within the company, were essential to the state's goal of bringing Gulf American within suitable legal and ethical bounds. State officials maintained that unless the largest company was disciplined, the unruly Florida land sales industry could not be controlled. Although other reasons may have motivated some FLSB members, Gulf American's immense size made it the likely first target.[122]

Gulf American faced several additional hazards as a result of its suspension by the FLSB. Responding to the Florida board's action, the New Jersey Real Estate Commission instituted a second ban, halting all sales of Gulf American properties indefinitely within the state as of November 1967. In addition, the Pennsylvania Real Estate Commission suspended the firm's sales in that state for thirty days. While Pennsylvania officials allowed Gulf American to resume sales within a month, New Jersey refused to allow the company to operate anywhere in the state throughout the spring of 1968.[123]

Although sales virtually dried up from December 10, 1967, until January 10, Gulf American maintained most of its staff. Employees at sales outlets and at the properties received a furlough pay, which was an undisclosed percentage of their regular pay. While the exact number of employees paid was not revealed, Gulf American had 2,800 workers and salespeople at the time of the suspension. The ban on advertising necessitated the closing of the Cape Coral Gardens because "every souvenir in the gift shop is stamped 'Cape Coral,'" said company vice-president Robert Finkernagel.[124]

The Gulf American Very Important Traveler (VIT) program, a lead-procurement scheme, employed 136 people and subcontracted with 3,500 others. Program chief Tom Kolar commented that they faced "a bleak December." Estimates of the loss of salaries, commissions, and business in Lee and Collier counties ranged as high as $1.1 million for the month of the suspension. Much of the potential business was to come from tourists who planned to visit Cape Coral and the other sites. (The VIT program had prompted 7,233 tourists to visit Cape Coral during the previous December.) The FLSB refused to change the sentence even after the appeals by three Fort Myers businessmen, prompting Finkernagel to observe, "Governor Kirk missed a good chance to play Santa Claus."[125]

In addition to lost revenue from the suspension and the cost of keeping employees on salary until January 1968, Gulf American faced another critical pressure from the FLSB. A major ingredient in the company's formula of high sales volume involved the constant preparing of new lots for sale. While construction and dredging continued, the FLSB began to refuse to allow any new Gulf American parcels for sale. Gulf American officials repeatedly filed with the state board to have new land units approved but were refused. Board members specified that no new lots would be authorized until Gulf American's conflict with the board was resolved.[126]

The problem grew serious as lot inventories shrank. Salespeople did not have as many lots or the variety of lots they needed to offer to potential buyers. Even before the problems with the FLSB, Gulf American had experienced periodic shortages of land inventory. Edward Pacelli, a vice-president for sales, explained: "You were either pushing for sales or you were pushing for [land] inventory. And we just had so many problems in keeping up with the inventory. Our sales were exceeding what we could produce, which forced the Rosen brothers to keep buying and buying more property."[127] The net effect of the inventory problem was to strangle Gulf American.

The lack of salable land for the company prompted a full-scale attack on the FLSB by Gulf American and some observers. In hearings conducted by the second district court of appeals on January 16, 1968, Gulf American attorney Thomas Anderson charged that Elliott Mackle was attempting to force Gulf American out of business. Leonard attacked further: "This is a conspiracy by the land board and Elliott Mackle." He added, "I'm convinced Elliott Mackle is behind this to do our company an injustice." Rosen also contended that the conspiracy was being aided by unnamed persons in Governor Kirk's office. While all accused persons denied the charge, the FLSB asked the legislature to appropriate $100,000 or more to finance its side of the legal struggle with Gulf American.[128]

Many outside observers agreed with Rosen. The *Apalachicola Times* of January 11, 1968, published an editorial that not only questioned the state's right to monitor private corporations but also accused Mackle and Kirk of cooperating to "break Gulf's back." Describing the situation as the "rawest shakedown I have ever seen," writer Jay P. Lord accused FLSB attorney Stewart Allen of conflict of interest because he also was appointed a monitor. The *Tampa Tribune* added its comments in a January 12 opinion that stated that the FLSB had clearly overstepped its powers when it appointed monitors for Gulf American. A *Fort Myers News-Press* editorial attacked the FLSB's harassment of Gulf American, describing the board as "vindictive." *Forbes* magazine raised tempers further by publishing a one-word editorial in the January 1, 1968, issue that described Governor Kirk as a "jerk."[129]

The FLSB responded to the accusations at its January 19 meeting by directing Bertoch to expand his investigation of Gulf American. The board members denied approval for sale of eight new areas in Gulf American projects and began questioning the corporation's financial stability. In a statement issued shortly thereafter, Leonard Rosen called on the Florida legislature to "investigate the FLSB, particularly the possibility of a conspiracy between a major Gulf competitor and certain board staff members." Bertoch responded, "We would welcome a legislative investigation of the FLSB, particularly if it goes back to the time Mr. Rosen was on it."[130]

Within a week, Rosen retaliated by filing a suit against Dow Jones, two aides of Governor Kirk, Carl Bertoch, and a newspaper reporter, asking for $16 million in damages. The suit accused Kirk's aides, Thomas Ferguson and James Wolf, and FLSB director Bertoch of providing confidential information about the company to *Wall Street Journal* reporter Kenneth Slocum. Wolf served as the governor's press secretary and Ferguson worked as Kirk's executive assistant. Gulf American charged that revelation of confidential information about the company had resulted in a $26 million drop in the value of the corporation's stock.[131]

Adding to the legal snarl, Gulf American filed another suit in the second district court of appeals on January 30, 1968, in an effort to force the FLSB to approve eight sections of land the company wanted to market. The parcels totaled about 5,000 acres in Cape Coral and Golden Gate. The issue became critical because of the rapid depletion of the company's inventory of salable lots. In other court action, the company asked that a FLSB subpoena to hand over financial records be blocked.[132]

On February 2 the second district court of appeals ruled that all the penalties imposed on Gulf American by the FLSB were illegal. That same day a Dade County circuit court blocked the board's subpoena, which had called for the release of company financial records. While the rulings were a major victory for the beleaguered corporation, Bertoch said that Judge William P. Allen's decision would have serious effects beyond the Gulf American case: "All cases prior to August 1 [1967] have been shot down. . . . It is a very serious blow to the board and hinders our ability to clean up land sales practices." He expected the FLSB to seek new ways to control Gulf American. Although generally good news for the company, two additional suits by lot owners were filed in the Circuit Court of Dade County. Claiming fraudulent misrepresentation by Gulf American, the cases asked for a total of $4.125 million in damages.[133]

With its penalties voided and its subpoena blocked, the FLSB voted unanimously to turn all records on Gulf American over to grand juries in Lee, Collier, and Polk counties for possible criminal prosecution. According to FLSB attorney Stewart Allen, the board "had no alternative." He noted that the three counties were selected because Gulf American did most of its business there. The board also refiled a subpoena for Gulf American financial records. The first order was thrown out by the Dade County circuit court because it had been signed by Bertoch instead of all members of the board. Board member Charles W. Johnson, Jr., an accountant, had pushed for disclosure of the company's financial records. "I don't want this to be considered harassment but we just want to protect the public," he said.[134]

Gulf American responded with a statement claiming that it welcomed the investigation by local grand juries. Company officials, however, characterized the announcement by the board as another attempt to try Gulf American in the press. Taking the offensive, Gulf American's statement said: "We also are going to suggest that the grand jury investigate the action of the board."[135]

By February 1968 the company had blunted most attempts by the board to control its activities. The FLSB had seized an effective strategy when it refused to approve any new land for sale by Gulf American. Because selling new lots was the lifeblood of the firm's operation, slow strangulation was certain unless the situation could be resolved.

Irregularities in Gulf American's sales operation were the primary reason that the FILSB and later the FLSB focused on the company. While some selling problems existed in all corporations of this type, Gulf American continued to have problems with its sales staff after years of admonishment by state authorities. The conclusion was that Gulf American leadership had either consented to the abuses or it was not fully in control of its sales employees.

Solomon Sandler, a member of Gulf American's board of directors and a company vice-president, provided some insight into the situation: "We tried to control our [sales] people. . . . It's just that you can't watch everyone all the time and we had a lot of people." According to Sandler, the company had hired the Wackenhut Corporation of Miami to pose as buyers at various Gulf American sales offices. Written reports were provided to company officials of any infractions. Sandler observed: "When your business is small, you don't have problems. . . . I would say about the middle of the 1960s, the company started to go to hell. . . . We were the biggest. We took a lot of heat. Some of it was deserved."[136]

Kenneth Schwartz, who knew both Rosens well, said they would never have consciously defrauded or deceived any customer. They became, however, "enslaved to increasing their volume." In order to finance their ventures, the Rosens had to increase their earnings; high earnings meant that they needed ever higher sales volumes. "I just know that they were the victims of their own greed, their own overambition, their own absence of moderation. I think that everyone got swept up in that," explained Schwartz. He contrasted this atmosphere of constant pressure from the Rosens to sell with that of Coral Ridge

Properties and Arvida Corporation: "They were both much more soberly managed without that pressure."[137]

The Rosens, according to Schwartz, never intended to take customers' money and leave without delivering the property and improvements as promised. They were living their dream of building a city, particularly at Cape Coral. Schwartz supported his contentions by noting that the Rosens never lived lavishly, receiving annual salaries of $100,000 each during the peak later years of the company. In the mid-1960s Leonard still drove a white two-door Ford. The Rosens also owned nearly two-thirds of all common stock in Gulf American. Unlike many unscrupulous developers, however, the brothers refused to sell their shares or to consider selling the company. But with the rapid growth of the firm and the pressure to increase sales, "the Rosen brothers' original control was lessened as the company got bigger. . . . There was too much aggressive salesmanship," Schwartz observed.[138]

Leonard Rich, sales promotion manager at Gulf American from 1961 to 1969, provided his own analysis:

> Your real problem with these salesmen was that the salesmen would tell lies. I hate to think of how many salesmen there were who said to people, "Look, if you don't like it [homesite], the company will take it back because it's so valuable." The company wasn't going to take anything back. If there was a lie that could possibly be told to hoodwink people, these salesmen would tell it. . . . They were all like that. When new men would come in, these guys always chose the easy way to sell. It takes a good man to sell and sell responsibly. We did a lot of training. We made a lot of effort. We didn't want these problems with people saying, "But the salesman told me you would take it back," and all the other problems they created. That is one element of control that is almost impossible to cope with.[139]

Rich noted that the sales philosophy also contributed to Gulf American's problems with the FLSB because of its portrayal of homesites as investments rather than as places to build a house. "They were selling resale," he said. "Lester [Engle] would do a pitch up front where he'd show them their paper profit, so to speak, and he used the words, 'paper profits'. . . . When they showed Golden Gate, for example, their slogan was 'Buy by the acre, sell by the lot.' They would show the customer how you could buy a five-acre tract and get twenty lots out of it." As Rich summarized the tactic, "They were tempting people with greed," and the whole industry, not just Gulf American, adopted the same philosophy.[140]

The problem with those tactics was that the profit could be shown only on paper. As Gulf American officials constantly raised the selling price of lots in new sections, customers realized that earlier buyers had purchased their lots at bargain prices. Unfortunately, no resale market existed for their lots because the company continued to push new home-sites to potential buyers. Gulf American also tried to keep independent realtors out of its developments because they had to resell lots at a significant discount in order to attract any buyers. By the mid-1960s, for example, independent Cape Coral realtor Granville Petrie was adver-tising lots at 40 percent off Gulf American's prices on new lots.[141]

A major cause of Gulf American's problems began when the company started to sell raw acreage to customers without any promises of im-provements. At Golden Gate Estates, the acreage surrounded a core city that was to be built like Cape Coral. The Rosens had successfully started the city of Cape Coral by the early 1960s and visitors were impressed with what they saw. Based on the company's performance there, people were induced to purchase unimproved acreage at Golden Gate Estates, River Ranch Acres, and Remuda Ranch Grants. In order to sell these properties, salespeople often either convinced customers of their invest-ment potential or misrepresented them in some way. When buyers real-ized the high cost of constructing roads and utilities to their property, they often demanded a refund.[142]

Most of the property at Remuda Ranch Grants stood underwater a large part of the year; even the property reports stated that fact. Be-cause of protests by some officials within the company, Jack Rosen made a personal pledge to drain the region and set up a $7 million reserve fund for that purpose. Many salespeople then promoted the land based upon its value once it was drained. As Leonard Rich stated: "It wasn't that we were malicious or put profit above all else. We thought we were doing good [by draining the land]. It was only in later years that we learned we weren't doing good on that score."[143]

When the draining of Remuda was ultimately blocked by Collier County for environmental reasons, all of the promises made to custom-ers became invalid. Charles Hepner, a company vice-president, said that when drainage was halted, "then we became the bad guys because they [Collier County officials] didn't let us do it." The customers, while not expecting another Cape Coral, hoped that something could be built on their land one day. Without the capability to build structures, the acreage was worthless except for hunting areas, and all statements about its investment potential were incorrect. The result was an outcry from customers to the company and to the state.[144]

Another main factor in Gulf American's conflicts with the state cen-tered around its enormous size. The company by the mid-1960s had emerged as the largest land developer in Florida, producing more sales volume than its next four competitors combined. The FLSB knew, therefore, that if Gulf American could be brought under control, the smaller developers would fall in line. Company secretary Joseph Maddlone agreed: "The [FLSB members] were going for the big ones." Leonard Rich added: "If they [FLSB] could control Gulf American and knock us on our ear, they would be hitting a substantial part of the whole industry."[145]

According to most sources within the company, the FLSB's investigation of Gulf American was at least partly justified by various abuses by salespeople. The vigorous way in which the company was pursued by the state beginning in 1967, however, can be traced to several sources. The political feud between the Rosens, who were Democrats, and Claude Kirk, a Republican, started during the 1966 gubernatorial campaign, when the Rosens had placed their Miami phone rooms, complete with personnel, at the disposal of Robert King High, Kirk's opponent. But the intensity of the bad feelings grew because of the perception of Leonard Rosen's arrogant attitude. As Rich observed: "Leonard thumbed his nose at them. He was arrogant as hell. We were the prime target and, of course, he managed to antagonize them [Kirk and the FLSB]."[146]

When asked in early 1968 if Kirk had ever sought money from Gulf American, Leonard Rosen said, "I have no comment on that." He did say that "the governor tried to call me in Palm Beach four or five days before the election." Without elaborating, Rosen said that Kirk aides had also made some contact after the election. Rosen refused to comment on his relationship with the governor, but Gulf American officials privately questioned Kirk's use of Elliott Mackle on the FLSB to attack Gulf American and the Rosens.[147]

While Leonard made few public comments about Kirk's fund-raising efforts at Gulf American, he related several incidents to Barry Horenbein, the Tallahassee lobbyist hired by Leonard in 1967 because of his political contacts. Leonard acknowledged that he was called by the governor's office before the election about a donation but he said that he was supporting Robert King High. After the election, several high-placed aides in the governor's office contacted Leonard and asked him for a $25,000 contribution to Kirk's campaign fund to make up for a deficit. At the time, Elliott Mackle, a Republican, was on the governor's campaign finance committee. Leonard agreed to the request, at which point they asked that the donation be made in cash. Leonard agreed, but he balked when they wanted to come to Miami and pick it up for the governor. He wanted to deliver it personally to the governor in Tallahassee because he wanted to make sure it would get to the governor and that he would be given credit for it. When Leonard refused to back down, communications between the governor's office and Gulf American were broken off. As Horenbein observed, "For some reason, they didn't want Leonard and the governor to get together."[148]

Later, Kirk's antagonism toward Gulf American was seen as antagonism toward the Rosens. An article in the *St. Petersburg Times* observed in early 1968 that "the governor has been taking unusual interest in a running battle between his land sales board and Gulf American." After the Rosens sold the company to GAC Corporation in early 1969, the leadership of GAC brought together the entire management of the newly acquired subsidiary, along with bankers and other financial people, at a resort in the Pocono Mountains of Pennsylvania. By that time, however, Kirk no longer wanted to force the company into receivership but rather was more friendly toward it. GAC chairman Hayward Wills, a close friend of Kirk, arranged for the governor to be the guest speaker. Later, Kirk had so changed his attitude that he helped Charles Hepner, by then president of GAC Properties, cut the ribbon at the opening ceremony of a movie theater in Cape Coral. The change in Kirk's attitude indicates that his objections concerning Gulf American during the late 1960s were more personal than substantive.[149]

Often Leonard Rosen proved to be his own enemy in the area of political relationships. Although the Rosens were competitors of the Mackle brothers in the early 1960s, they had cooperated for a time on various efforts, including a self-policing board of land developers. Later, when Elliott Mackle, a Republican, was the only person reappointed by Kirk to the new FLSB, Leonard sensed a political conspiracy against him. Leonard's verbal attacks on Mackle in early 1968 widened the gap between the two men.

Leonard Rosen attributed the attacks on Gulf American by the FLSB to anti-Semitism. He, as well as others in his company, suspected that the Mackles held anti-Semitic feelings. Kenneth Schwartz later commented on the situation: "As the Rosen brothers were falling, I think it's fair to say that some of the people who particularly enjoyed their fall were some of the people who were seen as anti-Semites."[150]

Many times Leonard Rosen antagonized even his supporters, including the Lee County government, which had generally supported the Rosens' efforts. In a speech before the Cape Coral Chamber of Commerce on January 23, 1968, Leonard began with a tirade against the FLSB members, calling them "bums." "They are nothing," he stated, "sucking on the blood of those who produce." The monitors, he said, were "the last straw. We thought they [FLSB] wanted a pound of flesh. But they wanted our blood, they wanted everything." Responding to a ruling that Lee County wanted Gulf American to renew a $500,000 surety bond each time a new plat was recorded, Rosen charged that the county commission "doesn't treat Cape Coral much better than the Land Sales Board does. They sit there with straight faces and decide what is good for Lee County. As if I don't know what's good for Lee County! I've put every dime I own into Lee County."[151]

County commissioner P. A. Geraci responded quickly to the charges:

"If we don't treat Cape Coral any better than the land board, are we also a bunch of bums? I'd like to know." Geraci answered other numerous charges, including accusations of favoritism and fraud. Rosen also irritated candidates for the commission by stating that Gulf American would approve of Cape Coral electing its own representative to the county government. He predicted further that Fort Myers would someday become a suburb of Cape Coral. Edward Tohari, a candidate for the commission, rebutted Rosen's contentions: "That is not my feeling. . . . The residents of Cape Coral are not braggarts and want to live in perfect harmony with all the other citizens of Lee County." He and Millard Bowen, another commission candidate, declined Gulf American's support in the election. Rosen, in an effort to reconcile the breach, offered an apology to the commission members, which was accepted.[152]

The conflict between Gulf American and the state of Florida evolved from an issue of misleading sales practices to a battle of personalities. Many of the members of the FLSB had come to view the Rosen brothers as personally responsible for the overly aggressive sales practices of the company. As a result, they believed the company would never reform itself while the Rosens were still in control. Therefore, the secret FLSB deal with the brothers, which included their guilty plea, also required that they step down from Gulf American's leadership. However, with the publication of the confidential agreement in the *Wall Street Journal* prior to the FLSB's meeting on November 10, 1967, the Rosens felt betrayed and refused to concede to that requirement.

The brothers, particularly Leonard, lashed back at the FLSB. The Rosens wanted to make Gulf American the largest land development company in the world, and their personal drive toward that goal resulted in the push by salespeople for ever-higher sales. Less than a month after Gulf American's suspension order, Leonard vented his frustration in an interview by the *Miami Herald.* Unable to contain his anger at the FLSB and other state officials, Leonard stated: "Do you realize that was a secret report [by the FLSB]? Why isn't something done to the man who made it public? . . . Bad publicity makes me angry more than anything else." Leonard saw the problems with the state as personal attacks. But he confidently noted: "It doesn't affect our sales. Why, after the *Journal* story [June 28, 1967] was published, we had the best month in our history." In character, he added: "I can outsell any competitor at four o'clock in the morning or any other time."[153]

Leonard's personality determined the direction of much of Gulf American's actions in its conflict with the state. When he focused his attention on a particular goal, he seldom allowed opposition to slow him down, let alone stop him. During June 1967, when revelations about the company were appearing in the press, Leonard directed a fund-raising campaign for Israeli relief. An ardent Zionist, Leonard felt the need to aid the Israeli cause during and after the Six Day War in early June. For one of the benefit events, he convinced Bob Hope to act as master of ceremonies. The total effort raised $3 million within a few weeks after the end of the war, due largely to Leonard's direction and powers of persuasion.[154]

The campaign won him praise and support from several different groups. When the Dade County Metro Commission voted overwhelmingly in 1967 to ban sidewalk land salespeople (a move aimed primarily at Gulf American canvassers who worked on tourists in Miami), Commissioner Alex Gorden abstained. He explained, "Mr. Rosen of Gulf American Land just gave $150,000 to Israel and I don't feel I can vote against him now." Later that year and shortly after Gulf American's suspension was announced, Leonard appeared before the directors and friends of the Hebrew Academy of Miami, for which he served as chairman. After a rousing ovation by the group, Rabbi Alexander Gross exclaimed, "Leonard, we're with you all the way."[155]

Yet even among his most ardent supporters, Rosen's ambition to succeed created resentment. One reluctant donor was reported as saying: "Rosen didn't solicit funds; he demanded them. It was a case of 'You give or else!'" Jewish officials at one large Miami company were sternly reminded that some of its best customers were active in the fundraising campaign and would be quick to recognize an inadequate gift.[156]

Although the Rosens, and in particular Leonard, protested that the conflict with the state had barely affected Gulf American, the company's revenues began to decline. As profits eroded, the brothers acknowledged that the situation and the strain it was causing on Gulf American's finances needed to be resolved. Leonard, however, refused to accept limitations on himself or his company. According to Kenneth Schwartz, "There was a certain arrogance in Leonard Rosen. Almost a self-defeating stubbornness." He added, "There were a handful of people who provoked Leonard to the point where Leonard had to get revenge."[157] The Rosens seemed incapable in some disputes of just stepping aside and letting an issue pass. As Gulf American resisted state regulation and aggressively tried to block it at every turn, the conflict was pushed from the relatively unnoticed arena of state bureaucracy to the public press. This switch came as a result of Kenneth Slocum's *Wall Street Journal* exposé and the action by individuals in the governor's office who had given him confidential information.

The Rosens would not drop the struggle. Without doubt, the usually pragmatic brothers could have settled their differences with state regulators, reached a peaceful accord with the governor's office, and continued to sell thousands of homesites. Instead, they refused to concede any point to regulators without a fight. "None of which was typical or even necessary from the Rosens," Kenneth Schwartz concluded.[158] As a result, the Rosens were faced with their most important decision: whether to keep on fighting or to sell Gulf American to the highest bidder.

10

The Takeover of Gulf American

By February 1968 Gulf American had successfully blunted most efforts of the FLSB to bring the land sales giant under state control. A flurry of legal actions by the corporation had managed to slow down or stop the board's attempts to supervise Gulf American's business practices. The struggle focused on the board's attempts to obtain the financial records of the corporation. A series of reverses in the courts, however, altered the situation dramatically for Gulf American. The Rosen brothers became convinced that the political climate in Tallahassee would not allow them to continue their land sales business. As a result, they began to look for alternatives and, ultimately, a corporate customer to purchase the entire company.

The second district court of appeals in Lakeland ruled on February 2, 1968, that the FLSB had no authority to enforce penalties against Gulf American. This action, the result of a suit initiated by the land company the previous month, effectively erased the board's restrictions on Gulf American. The court's ruling was so potentially serious for the FLSB that executive director Carl Bertoch assessed the situation negatively: "All cases prior to August 1 [1967] have been shot down." Although he quickly appealed the ruling, Gulf American officials believed that they were finally beginning to win in their fight with the board.[1]

Shortly before the ruling, Gulf American had continued its offensive against the FLSB by filing a $16 million civil suit against *Wall Street Journal* reporter Kenneth Slocum, Kirk aides James Wolf and Thomas Ferguson, Dow Jones, and Carl Bertoch for releasing confidential information about Gulf American. Naming only Bertoch out of all FLSB personnel, company officials hoped that the suit would further tie down Bertoch and other state officials and force them to negotiate a settlement more in favor of Gulf American. Although Bertoch denied that he released information from the confidential Gulf American investigation to the press, he interpreted the motives of Gulf American officials: "They hope this will make me less interested in the Gulf American case. . . . It appears to be an effort to intimidate me." The suit apparently had an impact on Bertoch because he lamented about Florida Attorney General Earl Faircloth's reluctance in defending him. "I may be forced to retain private counsel," he said.[2]

The only major problem remaining for Gulf American was the FLSB's refusal to approve any new sections of land for sale by the company. In late January 1968 the company had filed suit in the second district court of appeals to have the legislation forming the FLSB in August 1967 declared unconstitutional. After hearing oral arguments, however, the court dismissed the case on February 20 without giving any grounds. The decision dealt a critical blow to Gulf American's expansion plans in Cape Coral, Golden Gate Estates, and River Ranch Acres. Without new lots to sell, the company's sales operation was increasingly being strangled.[3]

In an effort to further curb Gulf American's sales program, the FLSB rejected several new pieces of company advertising over the next month. The board argued that the promotional materials were "misleading" and did not completely describe the property. Reviewing the recent dismissal of Gulf American's court action, the FLSB again rejected the company's application to register new land for sale. In addition, the board received $43,000 in funds from the legislature to be used principally for legal costs in pursuing Gulf American.[4]

The seriousness of the situation became evident as Gulf American refiled the suit in the Hillsborough County circuit court. Although the corporation charged that the FLSB was prejudiced against Gulf American and that it discriminated unfairly against the company's advertising, Judge Roger D. Flynn threw out the case on March 25, denying all of Gulf American's allegations. Company attorney Thomas Anderson said that Gulf American had not been allowed to register any new land since July 1967. "The board is in effect putting us out of business," he argued, adding, "Our inventory is getting lower and lower because of the unreal, unjustified, and untrue statements of the board."[5]

With a legal victory in hand, FLSB attorney Stewart Allen took the offensive on March 28, announcing his plans to appeal an earlier reversal to the Florida Supreme Court. Earlier in the year, the second district court of appeals had ruled that the board's fines and other penalties were invalid. Responding to the news, Gulf American attorneys refiled two other suits on March 29 in the second district court of appeals and in the Hillsborough County circuit court. Both actions were aimed at forcing the FLSB to approve eight new parcels of land for sale by Gulf American. They also attempted to bar the FLSB from any further punitive actions against the company.[6]

"This is just two different ways of forcing the board to register these lands," commented Carl Bertoch regarding the petitions. "They're just pouring it on." While company officials complained that Gulf American was suffering financially from the board's refusal, Bertoch disavowed any responsibility. He said that he had no way of knowing the effect the registration rejection was having on the company's sales. "Because of all of this litigation, we have not been able to police them," he said.[7]

The FLSB's ban on registering new Gulf American lands had a far-reaching impact even outside the state boundaries. In November 1967 the New Jersey Real Estate Commission for a second time banned all Gulf American sales within the state in response primarily to the Florida board's investigation. In an effort to reverse the decision, Gulf American requested in early April 1968 that the prohibition be lifted. During hearings, company officials stated that they had refunded $1.4 million to customers and had dismissed forty-three employees in an attempt to correct sales irregularities. Carl Bertoch, however, in a letter and in testimony to the commission, stated that it was the opinion of the FLSB that Gulf American had not been "rehabilitated." He added that he "had no direct knowledge that restitution has been made or that misleading sales practices have been eliminated" by the company. As a result of such testimony, New Jersey's four-month-old ban remained in effect for another month. The New Jersey commission finally lifted its restrictions on May 8, 1968, noting that Gulf American "is presently working diligently toward the goal of rehabilitation of the corporation."[8]

With a rapidly shrinking inventory of land to sell, Gulf American received a final decisive blow. Hillsborough County circuit court judge Roger D. Flynn denied a motion by Gulf American on April 5 to block the FLSB's attempts to examine the company's financial records. The board had subpoenaed Gulf American treasurer Harry D. Schloss to appear before the board with the records. With few other legal maneuvers left, Gulf American chairman Leonard Rosen and vice-chairman Bernard Herzfeld met informally with FLSB member Charles W. Johnson, Jr., in the hallway of the courthouse in Tampa and agreed to release the records. Johnson and the board wanted to examine Gulf

American's ability to finance future development and to find out if restitution had been made to victims of lot switching. "We have a right to determine whether the firm is financially able to carry out its commitments," Johnson said. Rosen had always felt that the request was an unfair invasion of the private workings of his sales organization and that his trade secrets would become public knowledge.[9]

Apparently believing that agreement to the board's demands would rapidly resolve the situation, Leonard Rosen opened company records to FLSB accountants. The board appointed Charles Crumley, an Atlanta accountant, to make a preliminary inspection of the financial accounts of Gulf American. (Crumley had earlier been named to the five-man team of monitors that was to oversee Gulf American beginning in January 1968.) During the investigation, the dramatic impact of the five-month-old struggle on the company became evident. On April 14, 1968, Gulf American reported steep declines in sales revenues and earnings for the six months preceding February 29. Sales had dropped from $63,977,000 the previous year to $44,742,000. Net earnings showed a 73 percent drop from $7,384,000 to $2,026,000. Company officials would not comment on any reasons for the decline, but the thirty-day suspension, the New Jersey ban, and the lack of inventory all reduced company sales.[10]

Although Charles Johnson promised that the investigation would not develop into a "witch hunt," the poor financial showing by Gulf American prompted further action by the board. Based on the preliminary study by Crumley, the FLSB voted on May 3 to spend $17,500 for a full financial investigation of Gulf American. Noting the company's "cash flow situation," the board hired Crumley's firm, Arthur Young and Company of Atlanta, to do the study. The board also voted to enlarge the investigation by looking for any lot switching that had taken place since August 1, 1967.[11]

As the investigation continued, the board refused to approve any new Gulf American plats for sale. According to board attorney Stewart Allen, the FLSB could not act on Gulf American's bid to register new acreage so long as the two groups were locked in court battle. The $16 million civil suit and various other actions by Gulf American were pending at the time. When the financial examination was finally completed in early June 1968, Gulf American officials still feared that litigation could continue for months without any new land being registered. As a result, company vice-chairman Herzfeld proposed a settlement that called for the FLSB to approve 15,000 acres of Gulf American land for sale in return for a dropping of all lawsuits by the company. Because board members stated that they had not seen the accountant's financial review of Gulf American, however, the board refused to take action on the proposed settlement until a later date. The sentiment of the board was clearly to continue the investigation. The conflict, therefore, remained stalemated.[12]

While the Rosens attempted to put pressure on the FLSB through lawsuits, another strategy was developed in early 1968. The FLSB maintained that any new Gulf American acreage could not be registered for sale until the company's financial health was evaluated by monitors. In order to prove their financial stability without the monitors, the company moved to have Lee County approve new plats. Under a long-standing agreement, the Lee County Commission had required the posting of accounts receivable as assurance that all improvements would be completed. Gulf American attorney Curtis Bader explained that the maneuver was designed to put pressure on the land board by "packing its shelves" with unfinished business. Commission chairman Julian Hudson responded with a complaint: "You are indirectly attempting to involve Lee County in the land sales board controversy with Gulf American." Bader replied, "Indirectly, yes, but we've got to do something."[13]

The maneuver might have been successful except that the commission required accounts receivable from the sale of Lee County land as collateral. Gulf American had already pledged all of its Lee County land sales as security for other plats. With no new land being registered for sale by the FLSB, the company had no alternative but to offer other land as collateral. On February 14, 1968, Gulf American pledged $4 million in accounts receivable on sales from Golden Gate Estates in Collier County. The commissioners refused and agreed to approve the plats only tentatively. A cash bond was required if full approval was to be granted. The constant publicity from the conflict with the FLSB had made financiers nervous about Gulf American and had thus dried up many of its money sources. Without full approval of the new plats, the maneuver left Gulf American officials with few weapons in their fight with the FLSB.[14]

The main alternative left to the Rosens was to sell their interest in Gulf American. By late 1967 the Rosen brothers owned 5.4 million shares of company stock, out of 9,664,164 outstanding. In a speech on January 23, 1968, before the Cape Coral Chamber of Commerce, Leonard Rosen disclosed that he and his brother might consider selling out their interest in the company. He said that "two fine firms want to pay a great deal more than market value" for his holdings and those of his brother. Although he declined to name the firms, the news reached investors on January 24, sending Gulf American stock up $1.75 in two days to close at $9.625. "I have a big decision to make," Rosen said.[15]

The rumors of a Gulf American sale were not new. As early as March

20, 1967, a *Wall Street Journal* article reported that Leonard Rosen was engaged in "exploratory merger negotiations" with several companies. One of the firms involved in those early discussions was Gulf and Western Industries, a conglomerate looking to further diversify. Gulf American vice-president Charles Hepner noted that a deal with Gulf and Western had been close but was never completed. Hepner also said that by the time of Gulf American's suspension in December 1967 and January 1968, the Rosens were firmly committed to selling the company because they saw few alternatives.[16]

During the spring of 1968 the Rosens began negotiating in earnest with a firm called GAC Corporation of Allentown, Pennsylvania. Looking to diversify its finance operations, GAC believed Gulf American's land sales program fit neatly into its philosophy. As GAC vice-president W. R. Strothman noted: "After all, the guy who buys land is the same consumer we've been dealing with all along. It just so happens that historically, finance companies have not been involved in the land segment of the finance business."[17]

GAC's history began in 1933, when Francis Reed Wills launched it as a small loan company under the name of General Acceptance Corporation. Wills bought other finance concerns and several small insurance companies in order to enlarge. In 1961 he developed a new concept called "private brand financing." Under that program, GAC organized and operated captive finance operations for companies that for various reasons did not want to operate financial captives themselves. These finance firms bore the client company's name but were actually GAC subsidiaries. The numerous clients included Sylvania, RCA, Fisher Radio Corporation, and the Coleman Corporation. Private brand financing rapidly became the fastest growing part of GAC, accounting for $72 million in receivables during 1968.[18]

Although GAC's growth was steady, it was far from dramatic. The growth rate soared, however, after Wills's son, Hayward Wills, took over in 1964. The new super-aggressive forty-three-year-old president of GAC directed the company to constantly expand into new fields but with one important qualification. All new acquisitions were to provide further opportunities for GAC to do what it did best—handle installment loans of various types. GAC had been known to sell off healthy profitable subsidiaries because they did not do any credit business. Wills saw land sales as perfectly suited to GAC's expertise in credit and he pushed the corporation in that direction. GAC financial vice-president Delbert D. Reichardt echoed the sentiment: "Land happens to be a product you sell on an installment basis."[19]

Before looking to real estate financing, Wills embarked on a dramatic series of acquisitions. GAC first diversified into manufacturing in the mid-1960s, purchasing numerous companies involved in the production of truck trailers, cargo containers, construction equipment, and library shelves. GAC moved into computer leasing in March 1968, reaching a total of computers worth $38 million out on lease by the end of the year. Two chains of retail stores specializing in auto parts and accessories were also added.[20]

GAC also began to purchase troubled financial institutions. Beginning in 1967, Pioneer Finance Company of Detroit, New Hampshire Finance Corporation, Atlantic Acceptance Corporation, Commonwealth, and Equitable Savings and Loan Association of Portland, Oregon, were acquired in rapid succession. While some of these lenders were only experiencing declining earnings, many had become insolvent. GAC acquired the companies, liquidating the remaining assets if necessary or restructuring the firms for higher profits. Investment analyst Ernest Widmann of Drexel Harriman and Ripley described the method: "There are a lot of companies that with a little work can be turned around and GAC had found more than its share of them."[21]

The result of Hayward Wills's ambitious diversification plan was spectacular. Between 1963 and 1968, GAC net receivables soared from $383 million to approximately $900 million. Net receivables were considered a reliable assessment of a finance company's assets. Earnings for the same period jumped from $4.4 million a year to $11.2 million. While GAC's manufacturing businesses recorded a slight loss on sales of $45 million, the company's finance and insurance operations remained highly profitable. With that in mind, Wills looked to expand into a still more profitable field such as the financing of real estate sales.[22]

The initial point of contact between GAC and Gulf American was largely unknown, but it appears that an individual named Gordon W. Mallatratt had some influence in the discussions. Mallatratt was named executive vice-president and a director of Gulf American on January 12, 1968, shortly after the company finished serving its thirty-day suspension. His function within the firm was to oversee all operations except sales. He replaced Edward Bryan, whom Kenneth Schwartz believed was forced out in December 1967, along with James Layden, in an effort to appease a vindictive land sales board. Layden handled most of the administration of the Miami office and answered directly to Leonard. Bryan oversaw phone sales among other matters. Leonard brought Mallatratt into the company because of his good record as a top corporate administrator.[23]

Mallatratt, an attorney, had been a vice-president and a director of Rheem Manufacturing Company, a New York–based maker of heating and air conditioning equipment, for seventeen years. Near the end of his tenure at Rheem, Mallatratt had assisted in the sale of Rheem to another firm. According to Connie Mack, Jr., Mallatratt made the initial contact with GAC for Gulf American and helped to make the deal for Gulf American's purchase. He also believed that Mallatratt received a finder's fee for his efforts.[24]

By early summer 1968, Gulf American sales volumes were dipping lower as a result of the FLSB's ban on registering any new company lands. Undoubtedly, discussions with GAC had already begun. With the imminent announcement of a sale, Leonard Rosen resigned as chairman of the board and chief executive officer of the company. The fifty-two-year-old promoter left his $100,000-a-year position, he said, because he wanted to devote more attention to education and philanthropy. Although stepping down from top management, he noted, "I will be available as needed from time to time for consultation, and I will remain as an officer and director." Rosen was succeeded by Gulf American board vice-chairman Bernard Herzfeld. The Rosen brothers retained majority stock ownership in the company.[25]

Another indication that the Rosens were preparing to sell the company during the spring was the closing of the Baltimore office. During the previous ten years of the corporation's existence, all marketing and most advertising were directed from the Baltimore headquarters, which was under the direction of Jack Rosen. All other operations were handled from the Miami office complex. Leonard Rich, sales promotion director assigned to the Baltimore office, took notice of the consolidation, assuming that it was in preparation for the sale of the company. Rich told Jack Rosen that he would not move with the company to Florida unless Jack made him an officer. Rich reasoned that unless he was an officer, the new owners of Gulf American might believe he was expendable. Rosen made Rich an assistant vice-president for sales and Rich moved with the company to Florida in 1968.[26]

Another indication that a sale was imminent was a rapid increase in the price of Gulf American's stock. In late February 1968 the company's common shares were trading at just above $8.00 per share. By July 17, 1968, the issue had soared to $17.50 per share. Rumors of a buy-out were the likely source of the high demand for Gulf American stock because earnings were sliding during 1968. Most other news about the company that reached investors concerned the prolonged fight between Gulf American and the FLSB. With questions routinely coming from the FLSB about the company's financial stability, investors were responding to the buy-out rumors. As late as July 9, the FLSB had responded negatively to a Gulf American proposal to settle the long-standing feud, tabling the proposal for additional study.[27]

Within days, however, GAC Corporation announced an agreement to acquire Gulf American for more than $200 million in GAC stock.

According to the contract, each share of Gulf American common stock would be exchanged for 0.416 share of GAC common or 0.188 share of a new GAC voting preference convertible stock. Each new preference share would be convertible into 2.13 GAC common shares after four years. Anytime after five years, the preference shares would be callable at $100.00 and would yield an annual dividend of $1.06. They would also be entitled to 0.1 vote each. The terms of the agreement were subject to the approval of both firms' directors and shareholders, although no date was selected for the votes.[28]

The GAC buy-out was a potentially lucrative deal for the Rosen brothers, who owned a combined total of nearly 56 percent of the 9,664,164 outstanding shares. When the agreement was completed, each brother was required to take approximately 413,000 shares or 80 percent of his payment in GAC preference stock. According to the revised numbers, neither brother could convert his preference stock into GAC common stock for three years from the closing of the sale. By the time the merger was completed in January 1969, each brother's stock was worth approximately $63 million with an annual dividend payment of $1.64 million once it had been converted to GAC common. During the three-year period, dividend payments would be approximately $544,000, which was considerably more than the brothers had earned as corporate officers of Gulf American. They each had a salary of $100,000 during Gulf American's later history but received no proceeds from their stock during that time because Gulf American never paid dividends.[29]

In addition to the stock trade, Jack and Leonard Rosen resigned from their positions in the corporation and each received a $100,000 consulting fee from GAC for one year. In reality, the Rosens were removed from any control over the new owners and were not asked for advice in managing the company. According to the agreement, the brothers were bound to limit their voting power in GAC. In addition, the Gulf American art collection, acquired by Leonard, went to GAC. The Rosens, however, were permitted by the contract to repurchase the artworks "at their appraised value, which is in excess of their cost to Gulf American." Many of the pieces in the collection, now valued at $2 million, were eventually bought back by Leonard.[30]

For GAC chairman Hayward Wills, the proposed acquisition of Gulf American was "a natural step" in the diversification of GAC. During May 1968 the corporation adopted a holding company status to facilitate its expansion into the land sales field. In that move, GAC Corporation was formed to acquire all of the assets of General Acceptance Corporation and its subsidiaries. Gulf American's declining profits and its ongoing impasse with the FLSB seemed ideally suited for a GAC restructuring program. Selling costs were considered an indication of profitability in the land business. The selling expenses—commissions, promotion costs, and advertising costs—of Gulf American had reached a horrendous 47 percent of sales revenues. With effective management, GAC officials saw the situation not only as worth salvaging but also as highly profitable.[31]

At first glance, the takeover appeared to be an example of the mouse swallowing the cat. At its height in 1966, Gulf American made more than $22 million in net earnings on revenues of $124 million. The combination, however, was potentially of benefit to both corporations. The biggest installment land sales operation in the country was combined with one of the nation's larger finance companies that specialized in installment loans. Bernard Herzfeld of Gulf American agreed that the move would be "a mutually beneficial combination."[32]

Despite the potential, the FLSB remained a major obstacle to the success of the takeover. Without the freedom to register new land for sale, Gulf American's land holdings would be of little use to GAC. It is highly doubtful that a purchase of the magnitude considered would have proceeded without some assurance from the FLSB that registrations and sales would be allowed to continue without serious interference. Many Gulf American observers believed that Hayward Wills's close personal friendship with Governor Claude Kirk proved to be the key factor in that assurance. After the sale was completed, the securities brokerage firm of Goodbody and Associates assessed the situation: "Under GAC management, there seems little likelihood of additional conflict [with the FLSB]."[33]

The future of Gulf American's conflict with the FLSB was probably settled sometime during the three months following the takeover announcement on July 17, 1968. After that date, both Gulf American and GAC were required by law to go through a process called due diligence. Before the sale was final, each company's officers were liable to the stockholders to determine if the other company had honestly represented itself. Acting on behalf of all stockholders, company officials traveled to the other's headquarters and evaluated the strength of the other firm. Primary concerns for Gulf American officials focused on GAC's plans for Gulf American management after the takeover. Joseph Maddlone, Gulf American secretary, remembered that GAC officers planned no changes immediately in Gulf American's management because the Allentown firm had little expertise in land sales.[34]

GAC sent in a team of investigators that varied in number between twenty and thirty different people. Included in the group were accountants, attorneys, marketing experts, and public relations people. According to company officials, the GAC representatives were given open access to anything in the company and they spent more than three months researching Gulf American's strengths and weaknesses. As vice-president Charles Hepner observed: "They went through our company with a fine-tooth comb. . . . They questioned everybody in the company, went through all the books, went through all the records, went through everything." At the end of the due diligence process, both boards of directors officially authorized the merger on October 24, 1968.[35]

After the July 17 announcement of the takeover, Gulf American officials greatly reduced their pressure and attacks on the FLSB. On July 24, Gulf American dropped two of its lawsuits against the board. The suits, both in the second district court of appeals in Lakeland, asked that the law creating the FLSB be declared unconstitutional. Despite the conciliatory gesture, the board refused to take action on Gulf American's request to register more land. Because the board did not have a quorum at its July 26 meeting, executive director Carl Bertoch gave temporary authority to put 8,000 acres on the market. The action was meaningless, however, because Bertoch did not have the legal authority to make such a move in a case as significant as the one against Gulf American.[36]

In a final peacemaking move, Gulf American dropped its $16 million damage suit against Dow Jones, two Kirk aides, reporter Kenneth Slocum, and Bertoch on September 3, 1968. The suit charged that the defendants had conspired to violate a Florida law on confidentiality by publishing a secret FLSB report on Gulf American in November 1967. The action was dismissed "with prejudice," meaning that the charges could not be brought again. Within days, the FLSB approved 4,540 acres of Gulf American land for sale in its existing developments. The clear intention of the board, however, was to keep tight control over the land firm because requests for an additional 3,292 acres were refused.[37]

While the due diligence process was being completed in early autumn 1968, Gulf American announced on October 22 its financial figures for the year ending August 31. As expected, the company recorded lower sales of only $95.7 million, down from the previous year's total of $131 million. More seriously, the earnings fell to a net loss of $1.6 million for the year as opposed to a profit of $16.8 million for the same period a year before. Gulf American board chairman Bernard Herzfeld attributed the deficit directly to the "year-long controversy and litigation with the FLSB." Despite the financial setback and unclear political climate for Gulf American, GAC directors authorized the purchase of the company on October 24. Gulf American and GAC stockholders were scheduled to vote on the agreement in early February.[38]

With GAC directors firmly committed to the takeover, the company sent a transition team to Miami to begin the transfer of functions to GAC's top officials. The goal was to be able to function at top efficiency once the takeover was approved by stockholders.[39] GAC chairman Hayward Wills was so confident about Gulf American's potential profitability that he directed his corporation to immediately expand its land

holdings. The purpose was to replace Gulf American's depleted inventory of Florida land.

An agreement for GAC to purchase a huge 265,000-acre tract in central Florida for $100 million was announced by Wills on December 30, 1968. The property was owned by Zion Securities Corporation of Salt Lake City, Utah. Zion Securities was a wholly owned subsidiary of the Church of Jesus Christ of Latter-Day Saints (the Mormon Church). The company had held the property since 1950 and had operated it as a cattle ranch under the name of Deseret Farms of Florida, a Jacksonville corporation. The tract was located east and southeast of Orlando, mostly in Osceola County but partly in Orange and Brevard counties. At the time of the agreement, Deseret Farms included sixty modern homes, various warehouses, a 1,800-acre orange grove, a 240-acre grapefruit grove, more than 51,000 acres of heavy pine timber, and 63,779 head of cattle.[40]

In order to pay for the massive tract, GAC planned to finance most of the $100 million price. GAC vice-president Delbert Reichardt said GAC would pay Deseret Farms $10 million in cash, issue $10 million in convertible debentures, assume a $25 million seven-year 7 percent interest mortgage and a $55 million ten-year noninterest-bearing note. GAC president Wills believed that the purchase was important to GAC. "The acquisition of this property will help us to replenish Gulf American's land inventory much more quickly than otherwise would be possible," he said.[41]

GAC officials envisioned the eventual development of the rural property into a complex of light industrial centers surrounded by residential and service areas. Wills said, "It is beautiful land and its closeness to Cape Kennedy and the future Disney World and Orlando should make it especially attractive to future residents and businesses." Wills was not alone in his assessment. Governor Claude Kirk described the purchase as "one of the most significant developments in Florida's history." He also said that the sale would be the largest single land transaction between private parties in the nation's history. *Miami Herald* financial editor James Russell noted that the purchase would make GAC the second-largest owner of land in Florida behind the St. Joe Paper Company, headed by Edward Ball.[42]

The final sale of the land rested on two conditions. First, the buy-out of Gulf American by GAC had to be approved by stockholders in early

1969. In addition, Zion Securities was awaiting a ruling to determine the tax consequences from the sale. Despite the delay, GAC officials felt confident enough to announce the offering of $80 million of convertible subordinate debentures. Some of the cash raised was designated for the Deseret Farms purchase.[43]

On February 10, 1969, Gulf American stockholders voted to approve the sale of the company to GAC. The approval was all but assured by a GAC agreement with the Rosen brothers that they would "cause not less than 5,000,000 shares" or approximately 50 percent of Gulf American's stock to be voted in favor of the transaction. The next day, GAC stockholders voted in favor of the takeover at a meeting in Allentown, Pennsylvania. They also approved GAC's $30 million buy-out of Equitable Savings and Loan Association of Portland, Oregon. February 24 was set as the official date for the Rosens to relinquish control of Gulf American.[44]

GAC inherited the liabilities as well as the assets of Gulf American. Gulf American had pledged certain of its accounts receivable, equal to 110 percent of the estimated cost of development, to various county governments in order to guarantee projects would be finished. The company had assigned $64 million of those accounts to Lee County and $23 million to Collier County. GAC also took over Gulf American's fight with the trustees of the Internal Improvement Fund (IIF) concerning the right to use 2,400 acres of waterfront property in Cape Coral near Matlacha. On July 19, 1967, the Lee County Commission had fixed the bulkhead line at one foot seaward from the mean high-water mark. The move was clearly designed to protect sensitive marine estuaries by preventing their development by Gulf American. The ruling cut off the company from land that might otherwise have been approved for development by the IIF. The case ended up in court and remained unsettled at the time GAC took over the company.[45]

A major problem that resurfaced in 1968 focused on the maintenance of Cape Coral's vast canal system. The canals, most of which did not have seawalls, were filling in because of the erosion of their banks. As early as August 29, 1967, Cape Coral residents asked the Lee County Commission to require all waterfront property owners to install seawalls. Property owner Harry R. Jacobsen said at the time, "The land is filling up canals to such an extent that some of the canals are no longer navigable." Because the commissioners wanted to study the problem, little was done until June 1968, when the issue returned to the commissioners' agenda. The Cape Coral Waterway Committee, headed by retired Maj. Gen. H. Freeman Bigelow, wanted the commission to make seawalls in Cape Coral mandatory and to determine whether Gulf American or Lee County was responsible for canal maintenance. Bigelow claimed that fourteen other organizations had endorsed his committee's request and that those groups represented more than 3,500 people. The issue remained a problem for Gulf American with GAC ultimately faced with providing a solution.[46]

Cape Coral continued to grow throughout 1968, with the population topping 10,000 by midyear. As it expanded, the community began to take on responsibilities independent of Gulf American. After long-running discussions among residents, a memorial arch was planned to honor war veterans. The arch was located in the median on Cape Coral Parkway immediately east of Del Prado Boulevard, with construction begun on December 7, 1968, and dedication on May 8, 1969. Cape Coral also saw the completion of a second golf course, which was a nine-hole executive course, and the dedication of a new post office. In the business community, numerous new ventures were started, including the community's second financial institution, a branch office of First Federal Savings and Loan Association of Fort Myers. The total number of businesses in Cape Coral was more than 250.[47]

To observers outside the company, the sale of Gulf American to GAC made sense when the strengths of both companies were examined. Gulf American's strongest areas were its sales force and its plan of installment purchases of land. As one spokesman for Gulf American pointed out in 1966, "We're financing a little bit of our customers' future and carrying it in the form of receivables." GAC's strength was management and the financing of consumer purchases. The combination appeared to have the makings of an ideal business marriage.[48]

Observers within Gulf American noted that other matters took precedence for the Rosens and motivated them to sell. The FLSB appeared intent on bringing the company's wayward sales practices under state control. Board members saw the obvious solution as removal of the Rosens from control of the company. With Claude Kirk's animosity toward them, the Rosens found themselves in a no-win situation. While it is probable that they would not have sold out if profits had remained high, they understood that steadily decreasing sales revenues after 1967 would be the most likely result of their conflict. Therefore, they looked for buyers for their company while there was still something left to sell.

Another major factor in the Gulf American sale was that the price suited the Rosens. In fact, the offer for the company was higher than what they thought Gulf American was worth on the open market. As early as January 1968, Leonard had said that "two fine firms want to pay a great deal more than market value" for the brothers' holdings. In the political climate of Florida in 1968, the offer from GAC was well received by the Rosens.[49]

A final factor in the brothers' decision to sell involved Jack Rosen's health. Jack had suffered for years from recurring heart problems. At one point, a heart attack had sidelined him for months in the mid-1960s. Jack's constant competition with his brother within the company added to his stress; indeed, many inside observers pointed to this conflict as the source of Jack's heart problems. In any case, Jack's impaired health probably contributed to the decision to sell.[50]

With the sale of Gulf American, the Rosen brothers concluded their twelve-year leadership of the company. Between late 1957 and February 1969, the brothers had taken a $125,000 personal investment and parlayed it into a fortune worth potentially more than $115 million. They successfully built the largest land sales operation in the United States and had assembled one of the strongest sales staffs in the country. Other companies entered the field, but Gulf American remained the industry leader throughout the 1960s.

From the mid-1950s to 1969, Florida experienced a dramatic rise in the number of large developers that was unique in Florida's history. These subdividers stood out from previous land sellers, such as the developers in the 1920s Florida boom, because of the immense size of their developments. Lehigh Acres Development Corporation began Lehigh Acres, a 60,000-acre project. General Development Corporation launched several projects in the state in the late 1950s and the 1960s, with Port Charlotte's 90,000 acres topping the list. Deltona Corporation, owned by the Mackle brothers after they left General Development, pursued housing in communities such as Deltona (15,000 acres) and Marco Island (10,100 acres). Smaller operators included Arvida Corporation, which built housing subdivisions throughout the state. Coral Ridge Properties was credited in the 1960s with developing about one-third of Fort Lauderdale.[51]

Although other entrepreneurs contributed to the flurry of land sales activity in Florida in the late 1950s and the 1960s, Gulf American dwarfed the sales of the next four competitors in the state combined. Other companies copied their techniques, as the Rosens often did from their competitors. Gulf American's huge size also made it the obvious target for the FLSB in its struggle to control the industry. Of all of the reasons for the success of Gulf American, company officials unanimously pointed to the dynamism and ambition of Jack and Leonard Rosen. While other developers were content with smaller goals, Connie Mack, Jr., said, "Leonard and Jack were never going to be satisfied with Cape Coral and doing a beautiful job with that. . . . Jack had to be the head of the greatest land sales company that ever was on this earth. That was his goal." It was also Leonard's goal and, in large measure, they succeeded.[52]

11

GAC's Demise

With the sale of Gulf American to GAC in February 1969, the future for GAC looked bright. Confident that sales could be increased and costs lowered under new management, Hayward Wills prepared to expand his newly acquired land development empire even further. Originally, Wills was attracted to Gulf American because of its accounts receivable. Although he wanted to refinance the installment contracts through GAC, he soon began to look to even greater profits in land sales and housing construction.

In the spring of 1969, GAC changed Gulf American's name to GAC Properties. At the time of the takeover, Gulf American had already sold more than 67 percent of its property at its four Florida developments. The best sales record belonged to Golden Gate Estates, which had sold nearly 91 percent of its 114,406 acres. Sales for the entire company had increased to more than 225,000 purchasers in all fifty states and many foreign countries. The figures indicated to Wills that GAC needed additional properties in order to maintain or expand its sales levels.[1]

Even before the takeover was completed, Wills had agreed to purchase the 265,000-acre Deseret Farms near Orlando. While that deal was still being worked out in early 1969, GAC acquired two smaller parcels on Florida's southeastern coast in July. The first tract included 418 acres in Hollywood near Hallandale, and the other consisted of 500 acres located about fifteen miles away in another part of Broward County. GAC officials reported that the total price was $37.7 million, of which $4.7 million was cash. A spokesman for the company said that the tracts were going to be used for condominium apartments, golf courses, and other recreational facilities. By September 1969 GAC had also purchased an oceanfront Miami Beach hotel, which it planned to demolish and replace with a seventeen-story $20 million condominium building.[2]

With its new emphasis on high-rise condominiums and other such construction, GAC began looking for a builder with that experience. In June 1969 GAC paid $4 million in cash for the Miami contracting firm of Robert L. Turchin, a well-known builder of many of Miami's hotels and apartment buildings. Robert L. Turchin, who founded the contracting firm in 1946, had erected Southgate Towers, one of Miami Beach's early high-rise apartment buildings. He also had served as a Miami Beach councilman and vice-mayor. According to the agreement with GAC, he became president of GAC Realty, an independent subsidiary that would help guide the development of new GAC projects. His first task was the 418-acre condominium project in south Broward County.[3]

GAC Properties' emphasis on building as opposed to Gulf American's concentration on selling land was a significant change in the company's focus. Gulf American had entered the housing market only reluctantly so that its salespeople could show prospective customers that a city was being built at Cape Coral. The Rosens had virtually abandoned any idea of expanding their housing construction division by the time Golden Gate Estates opened because of the high costs involved and the lower profit margins associated with housing. They even found their development costs at Cape Coral too high and subsequently began to sell unimproved acreage at later projects. GAC financial vice-president Delbert Reichardt explained, however, that land sales would not be enough for the new management: "Construction is an important part of the real estate business and we should be in it."[4]

Hayward Wills saw no limits to what GAC Properties could do financially. According to Leonard Rich, who stayed with the company after the takeover, Wills expected at least a 20 percent increase in sales each year. Believing that the conflict with the FLSB was virtually over by 1969, he wanted to expand sales even further. By the middle of the year, Wills decided that Allentown was too far removed from the financial centers of the United States. In order to improve the company's image as a major corporate force, he directed that GAC move its headquarters to an office building it owned near Wall Street in New York City.[5]

During 1969 GAC management began to bring GAC Properties' selling expenses back to a reasonable level. Gulf American had allowed selling costs to reach an unprofitable 47 percent of sales volume by the mid-1960s. GAC had reduced that indicator to 30 percent by September 1969. While Gulf American had shown a net loss of $1.6 million for 1968, GAC Properties earned $9.6 million in the first half of 1969 and expected to complete the year with profits of $23 million to $25 million on sales of $180 million. The predictions proved basically correct although sales only topped $150 million for 1969. GAC Properties accounted for 85 percent of GAC's total profits. Confidence within the company remained focused on its land sales subsidiary, as shown by newly appointed GAC Properties president Charles Hepner, who boasted of the company's broad perspectives: "We plan to introduce no less than six new developments in 1970."[6]

With definite plans for future growth, GAC began to acquire large tracts of land in late 1969. At this time, efforts to buy the 265,000-acre Deseret Farms near Orlando were abandoned although the reasons remain unclear. On December 24, 1969, however, GAC announced its purchase of the 35,000-acre Empire Ranch in Arizona for $7.7 million, of which $2 million was in cash. Located some forty miles southeast of Tucson, the property had originally been part of a ranch owned by Walter Vail Empire and had once covered more than 1,000 square miles. GAC officials said that the land would be developed as homesites with an emphasis on recreational facilities. The project was to be modeled after Rio Rico, the 55,000-acre development (started by Gulf American) located about forty miles southwest of the new acquisition. Sales at Rio Rico had started in mid-1968. In another unrelated purchase, GAC bought a 4,700-acre tract in central Florida for $3.1 million. Located fifty miles northeast of Ocala, the property was acquired by GAC in order to increase its inventory although there were no immediate plans for it, according to vice-president Robert Finkernagel.[7]

At the same time that it was buying new tracts of land for development, GAC's confidence began to erode as the company experienced numerous setbacks in its GAC Properties subsidiary. The first major problem involved a condominium project planned in late 1969 for the 418-acre parcel in Hollywood, Florida. Consisting of a series of islands in a bay, Wills named the project Three Islands and planned the construction of 18,000 high-cost luxury condominiums in addition to commercial buildings. Wills and other GAC officials were advised by Charles Hepner and Joseph Maddlone, both formerly with Gulf American but then working for GAC, that the project should be modified or abandoned. They reasoned that sales would be difficult, citing Gulf American's unprofitable experience with selling condominiums at Cape Coral. Wills remained unmoved and pushed the project forward.[8]

Three Islands received a major setback when the Hollywood City Commission approved an ordinance reducing the number of apartments and hotel rooms that could be built on an acre of land. Surprised at the city's lack of enthusiasm for the development, Wills threatened to sue Hollywood mayor David Keating and the city commissioners personally for any losses suffered by the company due to the ordinance. Keating responded publicly, accusing GAC officials of trying to pressure the commission. By this time, GAC had spent millions of dollars on the project, including $5 million that went just to engineering. In December GAC ended up writing off a loss on Three Islands that exceeded $16 million. Company vice-president Delbert Reichardt summed it up by saying, "Obviously, the project isn't as attractive today as it was two years ago." In assessing the situation, Charles Hepner expressed it more bluntly: "They just lost their ass on that." Hepner had opposed the project because he did not think it would sell. GAC officials did not get the chance to find out if he was correct.[9]

A second financial disaster for GAC involved a grandiose project in the early 1970s on the island of Eleuthera in the Bahamas. The property was located on the southern tip of the island at Powell's Point. Wills had negotiated a deal with Juan T. Trippe, the former president of Pan American Airways, to purchase 5,800 acres of Trippe's land on Eleuthera. Trippe had stepped down after more than forty years of active management of Pan American in 1968 and had become involved in numerous real estate ventures. The GAC plan called for the development of an entire resort with hotels, condominiums, seawalled harbors, and airstrips. A lack of adequate fresh water and the inability to market the condominiums in the United States resulted in losses in the millions of dollars.[10]

Although Wills stubbornly pushed the project ahead even when it showed signs of failure, he undoubtedly was influenced by other developments starting in the region. In early 1968, a $10 million construction program was launched by Roberts Realty on the island of Great Harbour Cay in the Bahamas. Located about 100 miles east of Miami, the tourist resort was to include a hotel and golf course. In an unrelated transaction, Willard F. Rockwell, Jr., board chairman of North American Rockwell Corporation, paid $2 million for Cat Cay, a 186-acre island in the Bahamas. In addition, officials at North American Rockwell began making preliminary plans for a $50 million development on 700 acres on the north end of Bimini Island. Such large-scale activity in the area encouraged Wills, as did his personal enjoyment of deep-sea fishing, particularly around the Bahamas and other Caribbean islands.[11]

The Three Islands and Cape Eleuthera failures caused financial problems for GAC during the early 1970s. A deeper conflict arose, however, from two opposing directions within the company. Because of Gulf

American's history with the FLSB, Wills wanted to make sure that sales irregularities were cleaned up so that GAC would not face similar scrutiny. While that was a solvable task, Wills created a near-impossible situation by expecting land sales to leap at least 20 percent each year. According to Leonard Rich: "Hayward expected too much. If he wanted us to clean up the operation, we couldn't keep going up at 20 percent a year. And if he wanted 20 percent a year, we couldn't really clean up the operation. You can't do it overnight."[12]

To complicate matters further, Wills and the upper-level management of GAC had little or no experience in land development and sales. During the due diligence process in 1968, Joseph Maddlone, secretary for Gulf American, asked GAC officials about proposed changes in management after the takeover. They responded that no changes were anticipated because GAC knew little about the real estate business.[13] Wills himself was weak in his knowledge of the field although he was strong in the areas of finance and insurance. Charles Hepner doubted that Wills fully understood Gulf American's sales strategies or the people who worked in that field.

> He [Wills] was naive to the type of people it takes to run it. Nobody is going to walk up to you and say, "I need to buy a piece of land"; it just doesn't happen. I mean you have to find that person. You have to seek him out. Then you have to twist him one way and the other way, back and forth. It's hard to sell. . . . If you've got a conscience, it's difficult to sell a piece of land sometimes. These guys have no conscience. They want their commission and that's it. Hayward didn't understand them.[14]

Furthermore, Wills and other GAC officers did not like the type of people that made up their sales organization. They felt that it was nearly impossible to control most of the salespeople who had been recruited by Gulf American. For many of the salespeople, successfully completing a sale was paramount. Leonard Rich admitted: "We built a company on street fighters." Although they could be ruthless in closing a sale, the sales staff members kept sales volumes high. As Rich said: "We [sales staff members] were really, in essence, paying their [GAC officers'] salary because without the generation of sales, these people would not have been paid."[15]

The conflict went deeper than simply differences over sales techniques. Rich noted: "They looked on the old Gulf people as really being people without morals . . . in their eyes, there was a great social gulf between the lords of the manor and the mercenaries." Part of the difficulty stemmed from differing backgrounds of the two groups. Wills emphasized conservative thinking, strong educational background, and management experience, whereas the Rosens had counted more heavily on creative thinking, practical street skills, and sales ability in their subordinates. While there were exceptions, Rich observed: "In various conversations, I found out that these people [GAC officials] thought that we were real dirt. They had the utmost contempt for us."[16]

When GAC took over, most of the top Gulf American management went with GAC although some left to join in new ventures with the Rosens or other companies. Within a year of the sale, some of those who had stayed with GAC had resigned for various reasons. In December 1969 Charles Hepner, formerly a vice-president of marketing for Gulf American, was named president of GAC Properties. According to Wills, the choices for the position were narrowed to Hepner; James M. Browne, GAC vice-president for operations; and Gordon Mallatratt, GAC vice-president for industrial development. Hepner's marketing experience gave him the inside track. Wills explained: "The company is mainly a marketing company and the one in charge of marketing should be in charge of the company." Hepner had also been successful at greatly reducing consumer complaints against GAC and in increasing sales volumes during 1969.[17]

Midway through 1970, Wills recommended to Hepner that he fire several of his top vice-presidents and managers, all of whom had previously worked for Gulf American. One of Wills's greatest concerns was to get rid of misleading sales practices. He felt that the sales managers directly influenced the salespeople in the field, and he did not believe that these officials could be rehabilitated. In recalling the situation, Hepner said: "He [Wills] just didn't like these guys. . . . He felt they were too aggressive and doing things that they shouldn't do."[18]

Hepner refused to fire the employees because of their long tenures and proven record with Gulf American and GAC. He promised instead to rehabilitate them. At that point, Wills hired a whole new marketing group with a new marketing vice-president to operate parallel to the people Hepner had refused to fire. In February 1971 Hepner was replaced as president by Frank M. Steffins, a former senior vice-president with Arvida Corporation. Hepner was named vice-chairman of the board, which effectively removed him from any policy decisions.[19]

In April 1971 Steffins called Hepner into his office and gave him the option of resigning with one year's severance pay or getting fired. Hepner resigned, and eight other former Gulf American vice-presidents also were fired or forced to resign on May 3. Included in the shake-up were Morton Rolnick, marketing; Robert Finkernagel, community relations; Lester Morris, creative sales promotion; Ronald D. Nitzberg, North American and Florida sales; Vic Sanders, research sales and reception division; Leonard Rich, advertising; William Baron, audiovisual division; and Morton Lesser, North American and Florida sales. Steffins publicly explained the changes by stating that the company's higher management had philosophical differences with the former executives concerning sales methods and the customer. The new company philosophy, according to Steffins, included more concern for what would happen to the property and customer relations after a sale was completed.[20]

Wills and Steffins soon found out that the sales levels recorded by Gulf American were difficult to duplicate without the type of salespeople Gulf American had recruited. By autumn, sales were down almost 10 percent since Steffins had taken over. A spokesman for GAC explained: "We expect our salesmen to sell one contract a week, or four a month, but they've been well below that lately." The cost of sales had also risen above the desired 25 percent level.[21]

In November 1971 Wills called Hepner on the phone and asked him to return as executive vice-president for sales and marketing. Wills explained that sales were in a shambles and that he needed help. Receiving some vindication for his forced resignation, Hepner added later: "At that point, I probably made the biggest deal of my life." The factor most enticing to him, Hepner said, was the increase in his salary. Another source estimated the new contract to be double Hepner's former salary, to extend for five years, and to include a lavish expense account.[22] Hepner remained with the company until June 1975. Several former Gulf American personnel had also returned with him, including Robert Finkernagel.

GAC not only forced out Hepner and other former Gulf American executive staff members but reshuffled its entire sales operation during 1971. With sales ebbing and the Three Islands project draining off excess cash, Wills ordered the sales staff at GAC Properties to be reduced and made more efficient. By the end of 1971, total company personnel at Cape Coral had declined from a high of 3,000 workers to approximately 600. The worldwide sales force for GAC was cut during the summer of 1971 from 2,250 to 1,550. In addition, it revised its sales training program and increased its volume of construction.[23]

During the same year, GAC began to close many of its related operations at Cape Coral. The company had already sold off two of its hotel holdings, the Nautilus Inn and the Parliament House. The Nautilus Inn, Cape Coral's first business, went for a reported $1.04 million. GAC was also negotiating with a Swiss concern to buy the 100-room Del Prado Inn complex. The local GAC public relations department was abolished, and all promotional flights to Cape Coral for customers were halted. The GAC personnel office was closed as the company shut down all operations at the GAC building at the corner of Del Prado Boulevard and Cape Coral Parkway in Cape Coral. By December 31, 1971, the *Fort Myers News-Press* reported, only two original Gulf American executives remained on the GAC payroll: Paul Sanborn, director of community relations, and Charles Cavanagh, community sales director.[24]

Despite the cutbacks, GAC went into the red by $56 million for 1971. The loss was the first for the corporation in its thirty-nine-year history. Wills blamed the losses on setbacks within its land subsidiary, GAC Properties. At the time, GAC Properties accounted for more than two-thirds of GAC's total revenues. The company elaborated on the loss by explaining that it was taking a number of after-tax write-offs totaling $29 million. The write-offs amounted to nearly $6 per share for the year. The cause of much of the losses was the Three Islands project. "The high-rise luxury condominium market has faded very seriously and hasn't really come back," noted vice-president Delbert Reichardt. The *New York Times* assessed the situation: "What happened to Three Islands is a comment on the overbuilding of condominiums in Florida . . . which already has scads of the kind of high-rise buidings GAC wants to put up."[25]

GAC also faced a problem in 1971 with restoring investor confidence in its land operation. During 1969 and 1970, GAC Properties had borrowed large amounts of money from other GAC subsidiaries in order to support the sales operations and to develop real estate already sold. By November 1970, GAC Properties was in debt to GAC Finance Corporation for $83 million. Because GAC's credit subsidiaries could not supply additional funding due to recurring losses, GAC was forced to seek financing from outside sources. As a result, GAC marketed $50 million in debentures on November 12, 1970. The extent of GAC's problems with investor confidence was demonstrated by the 12 percent yield needed to sell the bonds when the highest yielding bonds at the time had dropped to 8.6 percent.[26]

Another reason for the lack of investor confidence in the company stemmed from a change in the financing of homesite sales. During most of Gulf American's history, installment contracts for real estate permitted payment over six to nine years with a down payment of between 5 and 10 percent. During 1969 and 1970, GAC had allowed salespeople to push longer-length contracts in order to increase sales volumes. The new terms permitted full payment over a seven- to fourteen-year range. By early 1970 the average maturity of installment contracts had jumped from eight to twelve and one-half years. With a minimum down payment of 1.25 percent, the purchaser would not have paid more than 10 percent of the contract at the end of the first year. Because the cost of selling those homesites had again risen above 30 percent of the selling price, the situation further reduced GAC's cash flow.[27]

Despite the low initial return, GAC, as well as most land companies, recorded the entire price of the sold real estate as current revenue. The result was dramatic overstatement of the company's net earnings in official reports. In addition, the longer contracts provided more opportunities for default by the buyers. Stock analysts began questioning in 1971 the high returns that land industry stocks in general were showing on paper. One observer, Robert Merz of the *New York Times*, noticed GAC's poor cash position and openly doubted the company's ability in 1971 to cover its annual dividend of $1.50 per share.[28]

In order to improve its cash reserves in 1971, Wills announced in October that GAC would sell three profitable finance institutions, including Equitable Savings and Loan Association of Portland, Oregon, and two mortgage banking firms. Wills stated that he believed the cash raised from the sales would enable GAC to compete better in its largest activity, land development. The sales were estimated to bring in more than $40 million in cash. Other factors in bringing about the sales were undoubtedly GAC's slow condominium sales and its continuing difficulties in getting the Three Islands project in Broward County fully approved.[29]

Harried by losses at Three Islands and by lower land sales revenues, Wills began negotiating in late 1972 with the Bank of America Corporation to purchase GAC Finance. The GAC subsidiary consisted of 471 consumer loan offices in forty-two states and had assets of $700 million. While GAC Properties had lost $4.5 million in the previous year, GAC Finance had turned a $5 million profit. *Miami Herald* financial editor James Russell noted that "it is well known in financial circles that GAC needs cash and the sale of its profitable units will provide considerable cash." By late 1972 GAC's total long-term debt was estimated at $628 million, some of it with interest rates as high as 12 percent. The Bank of America purchase was an all-cash deal but would leave GAC with only its land development and utilities operations. By December the deal was approved by GAC stockholders, but the sale price of $100 million in cash was considerably lower than the subsidiary's reported assets.[30]

A major indicator of the lack of investor confidence was the price of GAC stock, which had soared to a high of $67.25 by mid-1969. As late as early 1970, the issue had traded on the New York Stock Exchange above $60.00 per share. However, as the high earnings of land development companies were openly questioned by many analysts, the stock plummeted. By the end of 1971 the shares traded for only $10.75. Although a company spokesman predicted that the worst was behind them, investors were not convinced, and the stock recovered little. By November 1972 the stock had sunk to $6.50 per share.[31]

GAC encountered other problems, particularly with the physical development of its various properties. During the period between 1959 and 1965, Gulf American had dredged 3.6 million cubic yards of material out of the Caloosahatchee River in order to build up the area in Cape Coral around the rose gardens. Three million yards of the fill were dredged without permits and, as a result, the state claimed the acreage as state land. Because much of the 172-acre tract in question had already been sold as homesites, GAC inherited the problem of getting clear title to the land from the state of Florida.[32]

In May 1969 GAC proposed a settlement in order to gain permits for new dredging. According to the proposal, GAC offered to pay $400,000 for the illegal fill, donate 4,835 acres of coastal land in Cape Coral to the state as a park, purchase the 172 acres of filled land with clouded title, and donate the Cape Coral Gardens to the state. The proposed park on Matlacha Pass consisted of 2,740 acres north of Pine Island Road and 2,095 acres south of Pine Island Road. In return, GAC wanted permission to dredge seven channels into open water in northern Cape Coral. Richard DeBoast, a Fort Myers attorney who represented GAC in 1969 before the trustees of the Internal Improvement Fund, commented on the overdredging: "The whole thing need never have happened because approval was pretty much automatic. You just went up there [to the trustees in Tallahassee] and paid them the money for what you wanted to dredge and they gave you a permit. Somebody just forgot to do this."[33]

The negotiations between GAC and state officials were complicated further in October 1970. Florida secretary of state Tom Adams accused GAC vice-president Thomas Ferguson of political meddling. Specifically, Adams stated that a third party had called him to offer a deal from Ferguson. He said, "I got it [the phone call] last night to the effect if Tom Adams would back off the Cape Coral situation, it would be very helpful politically." Adams, as a member of the state cabinet, was one of the trustees of the IIF. He was also campaigning as the Democratic candidate for lieutenant governor with Reubin Askew against Republican Claude Kirk. Ferguson, the former chief aide to Kirk, denied any knowledge of the call to Adams. When asked about the situation, Kirk's only reaction was to ask, "Anything else in the melodrama?"[34]

While environmental matters had not been a major state concern in the early 1960s, by 1968 local conservation groups were beginning to organize to stop destruction of sensitive ecological wetland areas. One such southwest Florida example was the meeting of all Naples, Florida, conservation groups in January 1968 to discuss the future of private lands surrounding the Audubon Society's Rookery Bay preserve.[35] The IIF began addressing ecological issues in the late 1960s and in the 1970s before it issued any new dredging permits.

The environmental records of Gulf American and later GAC were lamentable. Many of the companies' subdivisions were located in wetland areas and required dredging and filling in order to create dry lots. While no regulatory authority existed in the late 1950s to assess adverse environmental effects, Charles Lee, vice-president of the Florida Audubon Society, described Cape Coral in 1977 without reservation: "No question it was an environmental tragedy. They had obliterated thousands of acres of mangrove habitat." INFORM, a nonprofit New York research group, studied nineteen subdivisions in the United States in a three-year survey of land development practices. The 1977 report described Cape Coral as "barren, lifeless tracts on which nothing will grow because of the infertility of the dredged soil." Overall, INFORM rated Cape Coral as having the worst environmental record of any subdivision in the nineteen studied.[36]

With GAC wanting to proceed with development in the early 1970s, negotiations continued between the company and the state with the dollar amounts of proposed settlements rising accordingly. Secretary of State Adams considered $2 million an appropriate price for the dredged land in question. He felt that GAC "should not be allowed to profit" on the sale of state land. A settlement was finally reached, based more on issues of environmental protection than on law. The 4,835 acres of wetlands on the western coast of Cape Coral were donated to the state as well as 9,523 acres in Collier County. The Collier County land included much of an environmentally sensitive area called the Fahkahatchee Strand. The state also took a five-year option on 17,500 additional acres in Collier County but refused to accept the rose gardens because of high maintenance costs. GAC received clear title to the filled land in Cape Coal.[37]

The state of Florida had become vitally interested in the fate of the Fahkahatchee Strand area. The unique wetland was an area twenty miles long, and three to five miles wide lying northwest of the Big Cypress Swamp. Its significance was described in a biological report in 1973:

> The ecological values of the Fahkahatchee Strand are probably greater than any area of comparable size in the state of Florida. It contains the largest stand of royal palms and the largest concentration and variety of orchids in the continental United States, and many species of plants and animals now rare and becoming extinct. It is the principal drainage slough of the southwestern Big Cypress Swamp and the unimpeded flow of its waters is essential to the continued health of the estuarine ecosystems lying immediately to the south of it, including those in the western portion of Everglades National Park.[38]

GAC's request to dredge seven channels to open water in Matlacha Pass and Charlotte Harbor met resistance from the IIF trustees on the grounds that the dredging would cause significant damage to the marine environment. The proposed canals would empty excess runoff water and silt from Cape Coral into the Matlacha Pass Aquatic Preserve, which was designed to protect the highly productive estuaries in the pass. Marine biologist Allen Burdett of the Florida Department of Natural Resources described it as "easily one of the most valuable marine habitats in the state." Wildlife biologist Curtis A. Laffin pointed out GAC's deplorable environmental record to date in Cape Coral: "They've developed a Sahara Desert down there. Everytime the wind blows, the dust flies. They've completely denuded the land of every bit of vegetation. It's a bad one—an abortion."[39]

GAC countered with the argument that much of the destruction occurred before its takeover in 1969. "This isn't exactly virgin wilderness," said Richard Warner, GAC vice-president for public affairs and former public relations director for Governor Claude Kirk. "You have 20,000 people living there." He went on to point out that by July 1973 Cape Coral already had 841 miles of roads, with another 291 miles under construction, and 241 miles of waterways with 13 miles being built. Although state officials admitted that GAC's alternate proposal of a peripheral waterway would cause less environmental damage, they did not want runoff water from private development dumped into publicly owned waterways. The peripheral waterway was to be a canal running along the western edge of Cape Coral that would allow boaters access to the Gulf of Mexico through locks. While the IIF trustees recommended a lengthy hydrographic study of the involved area, state officials showed no inclination to approve the project. The result left thousands of already-sold Cape Coral waterfront homesites with no gulf access, even though that access had been promised at the time of sale.[40]

When GAC took over Gulf American, Wills had an opportunity to transform the land company's image from a high-pressure amoral sales team into a well-managed, controlled builder of communities. Although Wills gave explicit instructions that sales methods were to be cleaned up, he inadvertently sabotaged his own efforts by requiring that sales revenues increase by 20 percent a year. Most former Gulf American managers who knew what it took to achieve high sales realized that the cleanup would suffer. GAC, however, had a reputation for sound management. The company also had the appearance of cooperation from Governor Claude Kirk. Shortly after the takeover in 1969, the governor's chief aide, Thomas Ferguson, accepted a high-level position at GAC. (Ferguson was one of the aides accused by Gulf American of releasing the secret FLSB report on Gulf American to the *Wall Street Journal* in 1967.)[41]

The impression that GAC had cleaned up its misleading sales practices was smashed on May 2, 1971, when the *Miami Herald* released an article on the subject entitled, "They Went on Land Firm's 'Fun Tour'." Reporters Wood Simpson and Cynthia King had posed as tourists in Fort Lauderdale and had taken GAC's bus tour of Golden Gate Estates in April 1971. The article related various instances of misrepresentation and high-pressure sales techniques. Despite the fact that many tourists on the tour were initially unaware that a sales pitch was going to be made, GAC land worth $79,500 was sold to various members of the group.[42]

Responding to the publicity, Wills said that any offending salespeople involved in misrepresentation would be fired. While he did not think the problems were widespread, he said: "I'm not saying that GAC is perfect. I'm not saying there isn't misrepresentation. I'm not saying there aren't mistakes being made. I am saying we're attempting and have made a fantastic improvement." Despite Wills's assurances, the executive director of the FLSB, Lowell Steve, announced that the board had started an investigation into the sales practices of GAC at Golden Gate based on the allegations in the *Herald* article.[43]

GAC received more unfavorable publicity on January 26, 1972, when a Miami federal judge ruled that the 1963 and 1964 sales contracts on four Cape Coral lots were void because of misrepresentation. Judge James L. King pointed out in the ruling that the GAC officials did not contest the evidence "which showed that at the time the contracts were executed, the value of the land was only a small fraction of the purchase price and that at the present time—eight to nine years later—the land value is far less than the purchase price." Specifically, the four contracts totaled $28,094, but evidence indicated that the value in 1972 was only $2,500. The lots had been sold and misrepresented by GAC's predecessor, but the ruling placed public doubt on GAC's current sales operation.[44]

GAC took a major step toward eliminating potential problems with the FLSB when it decided to stop sales altogether at Remuda Ranch Grants and to phase out River Ranch Acres sales. Both projects had been a chief source of complaints for Gulf American because no finished development was planned or practical at those operations. GAC, however, had a difficult time halting the River Ranch sales program. In late 1971, when asked if offering unimproved acreage to the public was fair, GAC Properties president Frank Steffins had replied: "Yes, I would say so. It's unimproved acreage, and it's sold as unimproved acreage."[45]

While Rio Rico had just been started when the Rosens sold Gulf American, the 55,000-acre development caused repeated difficulties for GAC management. Sales began on the project in mid-1968. In the fall of 1969, the California Department of Real Estate filed suit for civil penalties and an injunction against GAC Properties. The suit accused GAC salespeople of misrepresenting the property to customers and soliciting sales in California without a state permit. In another action in the federal court in Tucson, Arizona, a class action suit accused GAC of fraud, deceit, and misrepresentation in sales of land at Rio Rico. The suit, on behalf of 20,000 Rio Rico customers, asked for $100 million in damages.[46]

GAC faced additional difficulties with public officials in the state of Rhode Island. John R. Assalone, Jr., head of the Rhode Island Consumer Protection Council, had spent six months as a salesman with GAC, earning $17,000 in commissions from his long-distance sales of property in GAC's Barefoot Bay mobile home community near Melbourne, Florida. "I thought at first it was a pretty good thing. But I kept running into people who had bought property before from GAC [in other developments] and had been unable to sell it," said the Rhode Island native. After confronting GAC officials with the problem and receiving no satisfactory answer, he filed charges of misrepresentation against GAC with the Rhode Island Department of Business Regulation in 1971. A series of hearings was held in late 1971 in Providence with numerous GAC customers describing various forms of deceit and misrepresentation. An estimated 1,100 Rhode Island residents had purchased land from GAC. The company's attorney, Peter Kennedy, made no attempt to refute the charges, noting: "We don't feel there is anything to be gained by the individuals or the state of Rhode Island were these hearings to continue."[47]

GAC agreed to a Rhode Island consent order in November 1971 under which the company would reimburse victimized Rhode Island customers and stop any future misrepresentations. After GAC failed to grant the refunds, the Rhode Island Department of Business Regulation halted all GAC land sales in the state for seven weeks beginning December 11, 1971, and continuing through January 1972. The ban was lifted when GAC refunded $235,000 to eighty-six customers. Within weeks, the Council of Better Business Bureaus issued a news release throughout the United States stating that a survey of local Better Business Bureaus had turned up a "consistent pattern of complaints" against GAC. Despite the repeated conflicts with regulatory agencies, GAC Properties president Steffins maintained in early 1972 that the company had cleaned up its sales operation. He said: "In an age of consumerism, those things simply cannot be allowed to continue. We don't feel that high pressure is necessary any longer. We feel that the caliber of our product makes razzle-dazzle unnecessary."[48]

Throughout 1973 GAC's major problem centered around its inability to secure enough cash to run its operations. The company's finances had reached a critical point. Forced to sell its major profitable subsidiary, GAC Finance, the company hoped also to sell its insurance firm. Although the sale of GAC Finance to the Bank of America Corporation was approved by stockholders in December 1972, the Federal Reserve Board had to approve the sale because it involved a bank. The antitrust division of the Justice Department filed strong objections to the sale in July 1973, stating that the takeover could lessen competition in the consumer finance market, particularly in California. Further study of the concerns by federal officials delayed the sale until late in 1973.[49]

When the sale was finally completed, the price had dropped 20 percent to $80 million. A major reason for the drop was that Bank of America Corporation was forced to sell immediately 128 of the GAC Finance offices because of the terms of the agreement with the Federal Reserve Board. In addition, GAC sold its insurance subsidiary, Stuyvesant Insurance, in early January 1974 to H. F. Ahmanson and Company of California. The $36 million proceeds combined with the $80 million raised from the sale of GAC Finance proved to be crucial for GAC. In April 1973 GAC had been rocked by rumors that it would not be able to meet its May 15 interest payments on its 12 percent bonds. Although the payment was made, GAC faced the refinancing of $60 million in short-term loans by the end of 1973. Without the sales of the subsidiaries, GAC would have defaulted on the loans.[50]

The sale of various subsidiaries reduced GAC's long-term debt from more than $600 million to $375 million. Wills explained that the reason for the reduction was that much of the corporation's debt was attached to its finance operations at GAC Finance. Although the sale improved GAC's cash situation, the company's still shaky financial condition prompted federal authorities to threaten to suspend GAC's land sales activities. In December 1973 the Department of Housing and Urban Development (HUD) began proceedings that would ban GAC sales unless the firm disclosed its poor financial condition to prospective buyers. According to GAC officials in a proxy statement to stockholders in early December, the failure of the sale of GAC's subsidiaries would have devastating effects for the company. According to the proxy statement quoted in the *Miami Herald,* "Under such circumstances, GAC would have no alternative but to place itself under the protection of the courts in bankruptcy or reorganization."[51]

Although the crisis passed, George Bernstein, interstate land sales administrator for HUD, noted that the fact remained that GAC Properties had a negative cash flow. After months of negotiating, HUD officials accepted a settlement offer from GAC on March 27, 1974. According to the agreement, the company would provide customers with more information about GAC's profitability and cash flow situation. The information would enable customers to determine if GAC was going to be able to complete development of its projects.[52]

While the HUD agreement did not have a great impact on GAC, another ruling by the Federal Trade Commission (FTC) during the previous week had far-reaching consequences for GAC as well as the entire land sales industry. In autumn 1971 the FTC had launched an investigation of GAC's reportedly deceptive advertising practices. After more than two years of negotiations, GAC agreed to a consent decree that would protect future land buyers and remedy some of the past abuses. According to the agreement, GAC was not to use the word *investment* in any future advertising about its lands. In addition, salespeople were required to "clearly disclose in contracts the uncertainty of the future value of the land." The FTC was referring to a common practice in the land sales industry of promoting homesites or acreage with specific emphasis on future resale value. The method had been extensively used by Gulf American, as well as by GAC and other land companies, from the early 1960s on. Problems arose, however, when buyers of homesites found that their property had little or no resale value.[53]

In another part of the agreement the FTC noted that, in a significant number of cases, the lots offered by GAC were not excellent investments as claimed by company advertising. The FTC order affected a minimum of 6,500 GAC buyers. In addition, the regulatory agency found that salespeople had misrepresented that all lots of River Ranch Acres, Remuda Ranch Grants, and Golden Gate Estates would be developed as homesites. In order to settle the conflict, GAC consented to an exchange program for buyers of land at River Ranch and Remuda in which they would be able to trade their land for buildable homesites at Cape Coral or at GAC's new development near Orlando called Poinciana. GAC also promised to make cash refunds when misrepresentation could be shown and to develop further Golden Gate Estates. The estimated cost to GAC over eight years was $17 million. Although GAC officials claimed that the ruling only formalized changes they had been trying to make since 1969, the agreement did not help the company's already poor cash flow position.[54]

The settlement with the FTC had a far greater impact, however, on the land industry as a whole. According to one government spokesman, "The shock wave that will go through the industry is going to be enormous." The FTC's action against GAC was not an isolated investigation. J. Thomas Rosch, director of the FTC's Bureau of Consumer Protection, elaborated: "An industry-wide nationwide investigation of about thirty other land sales companies, some bigger and some smaller than GAC, is under way and action is expected soon on these." The agreement with GAC, when approved by the full FTC, would have the force of law for all land sales operations with possible penalties for each violation of up to $10,000.[55]

Many GAC officials hoped that the company's problems with regulatory agencies were over. One GAC spokesman noted in late March 1974: "We're happy to have the FTC and HUD matters resolved so that we can get on with our development programs." Some consumer groups, however, felt that the FTC had not prosecuted the company severely enough. John Assalone, Jr., head of the Rhode Island Consumer Protection Council, said that the settlement agreement was "ridiculous" because it did not provide refunds for all affected lot owners, particularly some Rhode Island buyers. He added that his organization was one of those that originally brought GAC's sales practices to the attention of the FTC in 1971. Wanting a more severe judgment, Assalone said, "We're looking for prosecution of the principals." The lenient terms of the agreement were also attacked by the Iowa attorney general and the interstate land sales office of HUD. The FTC, however, approved the agreement on September 3, 1974.[56]

In order to reduce conflicts with state and federal regulators, GAC officials began making radical changes in the company's sales organization. Wills, among others, did not believe that high-pressure tactics were necessary to maintain satisfactory sales volumes. Wills said that his salespeople would pursue prospects only when they visited property sites or in their homes when they indicated an interest in hearing about GAC's homesites. Among other changes, Wills ordered the reduction of the sales staff from 2,200 in mid-1970 to 570 at the end of 1972. Further layoffs resulted in a total sales staff of 250 by early 1974. In addition, he planned to pay salespeople a base salary of $12,000 by mid-1974 in order to relieve the reliance on sales commissions and thereby to reduce much of the motivation to make exaggerated claims. GAC also terminated its telephone land sales operation and sharply curtailed its high-pressure dinner party program. While sales abuses were greatly reduced, sales volumes slumped.[57]

A major financial problem arose for GAC when its charter airline, Modern Air Transport, continued to lose money. Originally purchased by Gulf American to carry prospective customers to company land sales projects in the mid-1960s, the charter service had grown rapidly. GAC, however, became alarmed at the high cost of shuttling customers to the various developments and in 1969 began phasing out that aspect of Modern Air's business. Although the airline quickly expanded its commercial charter flights, financial losses mounted. By 1971, the deficit for Modern Air had reached an annual rate of $3 million.[58]

In an administrative shake-up, GAC replaced Modern Air president James Browne with Thomas Ferguson, GAC vice-president for public relations and former chief aide to Governor Claude Kirk. In an effort to stem the losses at Modern Air, Ferguson announced in November 1971 that the charter service was shifting most of its operations to Europe. Focusing primarily on its profitable charter flights between West Berlin's Tegel Airport and the rest of Europe and North Africa, the switch resulted in reducing the number of employees in the United States from 300 to 100. The Berlin staff was increased, however, from 263 to about 400, mostly because of the addition of German flight attendants. In a promotional move, some Modern Air flights from Berlin featured topless German showgirls. Although Ferguson maintained that the restructuring "will increase our yield and minimize our exposure to loss," one former employee noted: "It's just a case of a big corporation getting involved in a business that it doesn't understand."[59]

The U.S. layoffs at Modern Air enabled company officials to project that despite huge losses in 1971 the airline would be able to cut its 1972 losses from $4 million to near the break-even point. Despite the optimism, Ferguson admitted in early 1972 that Modern Air was still financially unstable and GAC would have difficulty selling the ailing airline. He said, "We feel that Modern Air is not a salable product at this point in time." The pressure from the parent corporation for profitability increased because GAC announced in late December 1971 that it was writing off $43 million in losses on several projects.[60]

By February 1972, however, Ferguson announced another dramatic shift for the company. Predicting that the airline would be profitable again by 1973, he disclosed that the company would once again enter the U.S. charter market. The new base of operations was going to be New York instead of Miami. Accompanying the announcement was news that several key European officers had resigned. When questioned about the rapid changes in company policy and personnel, Ferguson responded: "It was a difficult problem to be given an assignment in a company whose financial problems were so profound." Ferguson's efforts did not solve the airline's problems, and in May 1973 he resigned from Modern Air and from his vice-presidency with GAC. Ferguson explained that he wanted "to pursue other business interests" in the Miami area. By March 1976 he had filed for bankruptcy, listing his debts at $529,000 and his assets at $252,000.[61]

The financially troubled carrier faced another major blow when the Civil Aeronautics Board (CAB) charged the airline in April 1974 with 859 violations of CAB regulations. Although the violations concerned bookkeeping procedures and not safety problems, Modern Air potentially could have received fines totaling $859,000. While the airline had settled its dispute with the CAB by August 1974, GAC had virtually shut down Modern Air because of continuing losses. The losses would normally have been written off by GAC, but the parent company had already written off the full value of Modern Air in 1971. Its declared value was $15.4 million. With nothing left to gain, GAC searched for a buyer.[62]

Although the Modern Air organization continued for another year, the airline had almost stopped flying. In November 1975 the CAB voted to revoke its operating certificate. A CAB official explained: "There is not a future for Modern and, in its present condition, Modern cannot be resurrected by anyone." To emphasize the bleak picture, a striking Modern pilot noted: "We wouldn't even know where you'd picket." With GAC in serious financial difficulty and unable to rescue itself, Modern Air dissolved as a business organization and its remaining assets were sold.[63]

As a result of declining sales in 1974, GAC was forced to sell off more of its assets. In December 1974 the company sold its Empire Ranch property in Arizona to Anamax Mining Company for an undisclosed price. The transaction involved 32,000 acres and a leasehold on another 15,000 acres. In another cost-saving measure, GAC announced in early 1975 that it planned to move out of its eleven-story Miami headquarters building at Seventy-ninth Street and Biscayne Boulevard by midyear. The building previously had served as headquarters for Gulf American. The new location, a reduction of one-third in office area, was the new Ponce de Leon building in Coral Gables. Despite efforts to save money, GAC faced a major crisis in August 1975.[64]

During the first half of 1975, GAC, as well as other land firms, recorded declining sales due to a downturn in the national economy. By midyear many Florida land firms reported sharply reduced earnings or even losses for the previous six months. GAC's sales revenues slumped, and its profit statement recorded a loss of almost $9 million in the first half of 1975 as compared with a profit of $4.6 million for the same period of 1974. The shortage of cash resulted in a financial crisis for the firm because it had $36 million in bonds due on November 15, 1975. GAC announced in August 1975 that unless something changed, "There will not be sufficient cash available to repay the outstanding debentures in full at maturity." To make matters worse, GAC also had $43.65 million of 12 percent debentures due in 1977. The second set of bonds, however, became immediately due if GAC defaulted on the first set of bonds.[65]

The impact of the announcement was immediately understood in the financial community. As a result, the New York Stock Exchange halted trading in the bonds on August 8, 1975, until a pay-back plan was presented. A company spokesman indicated that a water utilities subsidiary, worth $17 million, was being offered for sale. The spokesman bluntly explained that the reason was "to raise cash." Emphasizing GAC's financial difficulties, the company refused to reimburse some $500,000 in payments to customers in September 1975, claiming that the FTC was pressuring the company to repay money it did not owe. Responding to the company's financial difficulties, HUD officials ordered GAC in mid-October to stop all installment land sales.[66]

In an effort to prevent default, Wills proposed two exchange offers for the debentures coming due. Under the plan, GAC Properties Credit would exchange an old bond worth $1,000 face value with a new 12 percent $1,000 debenture due in 1980, or with $200 in cash plus new bonds worth $700. Problems arose, however, when many bondholders refused the exchange. By November 14 fewer than 60 percent of the bondholders had accepted the offer, far below the 80 percent needed by GAC to make the plan successful. Wills assessed the situation: "If 80 percent of the bonds are not turned in, GAC will default. We will be forced into bankruptcy and will have to sell our assets."[67]

Desperate to make the exchange work, Wills held four bondholder meetings in Miami, New York, Chicago, and Los Angeles. He was concerned that the debenture holders were waiting for a better offer. Appearing personally at each meeting, he explained to reporters that the bondholders were assuming that if 80 percent of the debenture holders turned in their bonds, then GAC would be forced to pay the remaining 20 percent at full face value. As Wills noted, "Everybody wants to be in the 20 percent." For whatever reason, only 62 percent of GAC bondholders accepted the offer, and on November 18, 1975, GAC announced that GAC Properties Credit had defaulted on the bonds.[68]

Although technically in default, GAC extended the deadline for the bond exchange three times and made a third proposal of trading $600 in cash for the old debentures. By early December 1975 only 65 percent of debenture holders had exchanged their bonds. With few options open to corporate officials, GAC voluntarily requested on December 11 that the Securities and Exchange Commission suspend trading in GAC stock on the New York Stock Exchange. At the time of the suspension, the stock was trading at fifty cents per share. Shortly thereafter, two of GAC's major subsidiaries, GAC Properties Credit and GAC Properties, filed for bankruptcy under chapter 11 of the federal bankruptcy laws. By mid-January 1976 GAC Corporation, the parent company, had filed for protection from bondholders and other creditors under chapter 11 proceedings.[69]

Under the provisions of chapter 11, GAC's management was entitled to continue managing while the company was being reorganized by court-appointed receivers. Federal bankruptcy judge Paul Hyman appointed David Hughes and Frank Callahan to oversee the GAC case.

Hughes, a Miami businessman, had previously served as a bankruptcy receiver and trustee in more than 300 cases, while Callahan, also of Miami, had extensive corporate business experience in boat-building and metal firms. By June 1976, however, the Securities and Exchange Commission had convinced the court that GAC needed closer regulation, and the proceedings for GAC were moved into chapter 10 of the bankruptcy laws. As a result, the top management officers of GAC, including Wills, were dismissed, and the court-appointed trustees took over. With the change, Hughes and Callahan, not GAC management, were responsible for forming a plan to pay off the company's debts. Although Wills was officially removed from the company, he was retained as an expert consultant because of his overall knowledge of the vast company. Hughes said of Wills: "We're going to pick his brains."[70]

The first major decision facing the trustees was to choose between two different courses of action. With the goal of benefiting both creditors and people who had purchased GAC lots, Hughes and Callahan abandoned the easiest course of selling off GAC's assets because it would help only the creditors. Instead they chose to try to reorganize and operate the company so that development could continue. Many of the homesites sold by GAC had yet to be developed and their owners would likely have never been able to build on them. Because Gulf American and GAC had guaranteed development by posting bonds secured mainly by the contracts yet to be paid off by purchasers, the dissolving of GAC meant that more than 78,000 lot buyers would be left with worthless land.[71]

In order to cut costs, the trustees devised a plan during mid-1976 for consolidating development in Florida at three sites. According to the proposal, much of the development construction would halt at Golden Gate Estates, North Golden Gate, and River Ranch Acres to save money. In return, some 18,000 owners in those subdivisions would exchange their undeveloped property for usable homesites of equal value in Cape Coral in Lee County, Barefoot Bay in Brevard County, and Poinciana in Polk and Osceola counties. Poinciana consisted of 47,300 acres, and sales had begun in November 1971. Plans for that community called for a completely developed city of 60,000 residential lots, similar in concept to Cape Coral. The court-appointed trustees believed that the consolidation move would reduce GAC's development commitments from $218 million to $148 million. The plan was formally approved in Miami by Judge Hyman on October 14, 1976, after two days of hearings.[72]

The planned exchange program, however, ran into opposition from state and federal environmental agencies. Because many of the lot owners involved in the exchange were opting for Cape Coral homesites, much of the yet undeveloped property in northern Cape Coral needed to be dredged and filled. The Florida Department of Environmental Regulation, along with the U.S. Army Corps of Engineers, informed GAC that any dredging permits would be denied because of probable damage to the coastal ecosystems. In a petition in a U.S. district court, GAC trustees argued that without the dredging the exchange program would fail and GAC would probably have to be liquidated. An editorial in the *Miami Herald* on August 10, 1976, described the situation as a "new twist" in Florida history because bankrupt GAC had received a "temporary order restraining the state from forcing the company to obey Florida laws." Despite protests from state officials, some dredging was allowed because of GAC's hardship situation. The editorial protested the fact that GAC was allowed to violate the law. By mid-1977 the legal disputes had been resolved and GAC continued some dredging at Cape Coral.[73]

After one and one-half years under the direction of the bankruptcy court, GAC appeared to have recovered financially. On June 17, 1977, trustee Frank Callahan announced "a spirit of new confidence coming out of the ashes and I can see the light at the end of the tunnel for GAC." He added: "The specter of liquidation is gone." In order to meet its development commitments, GAC would, Callahan explained, spend $25 million on construction during 1977, including $12 million to $14 million at Cape Coral. The spending rate was to continue through 1980. Callahan also noted that 80 percent of the necessary lot owners had agreed to the exchange program.[74]

While GAC's financial situation was improving, various groups placed the blame for the bankruptcy of the billion-dollar conglomerate on its top executive management. In mid-January 1977 the Securities and Exchange Commission charged Wills with violations of federal fraud statutes. In addition to Wills, the court action named Russell E. Kemmerer, former chief financial officer; Paul R. Stuken, former chief accountant; and Marvin R. Hartung, a New York attorney who was GAC's legal counsel. The SEC charged that the GAC executives illegally transferred $39 million from one subsidiary to another in an attempt to conceal the extent of the company's financial problems from bondholders and investors in 1974 and 1975. Wills later commented on the accusations: "We ran the company as one entity. Whatever was necessary to provide the capital to run the company, we did, and we believe everything we did was legal."[75]

By late August 1977 the number of legal actions against former top GAC executives had grown to five. Three suits by bondholders and banks that had issued the bonds also accused the officers of disguising the poor financial condition of the company. On August 30 the court-appointed trustees filed the fifth suit against the officers for "gross neglect, willful abuse, and misappropriation of funds." In addition to the executives, the lawsuit named Lloyds of London, which had insured the officials against misdeeds in office. The civil action asked for $135 million in damages.[76]

A sixth damage suit was filed against Wills and thirteen other former GAC directors on July 27, 1978, by the trustees, Frank Callahan and Herbert S. Freehling. (Freehling had been appointed when David Hughes died in 1976.) The case accused the directors of "profiteering" from the sale of company bonds by selling off GAC assets to benefit large lending firms to which the corporation was indebted and by paying cash dividends when the company was already in a serious cash-poor situation. Believed by the *Miami Herald* to be the largest damage suit of its kind in Florida, the trustees sought $1.2 billion in damages from the directors.[77]

Because most of the lawsuits were for damages, the SEC fraud charges were important to all the cases. On December 15, 1978, U.S. District Court Judge Gerhard Gesell ruled that Hayward Wills and Paul Stuken had violated federal securities statutes but had not defrauded GAC bondholders. Gesell explained that while the company's true financial situation was not disclosed by the officers, the men did not intentionally deceive stockholders and bondholders. Wills, who at the time of the decision was operating a mortgage brokerage firm in Coral Gables, was reported as being elated at the outcome. He said: "I think that we won a tremendous victory. What they accused us of was being a bunch of crooks. What the judge said was, 'You weren't crooks.'" He added, "I felt the SEC was under pressure to find a scapegoat and I didn't want to be a scapegoat." The two other defendants, Russell Kemmerer and Marvin Hartung, previously had signed consent orders neither denying nor admitting guilt.[78]

While various court cases were being argued, pressure increased on the GAC trustees to complete the reorganization of GAC. Although November 15, 1978, was mandated as the deadline for the plan, discussions with creditors and the FTC delayed the presentation until mid-1979. On June 27, 1979, trustees Callahan and Freehling filed a reorganization plan in federal court that would result in a new corporate name, new stock, and new management. After public hearings in September, four other companies offered their own reorganization plans for GAC and their offers to purchase the new corporation. By mid-April 1980 bankruptcy judge Thomas Britton selected the plan presented by the trustees, calling it the "fairest" of all those proposed. With the ruling, the largest bankruptcy case until that time in Florida history had ended.[79]

According to the plan, bondholders and other unsecured creditors would receive the following for each $1,000 in claims against GAC: $35 in cash, $135 in twenty-year 8 percent bonds, and 25 shares of common stock. While the bondholders received some of their investment back, stockholders were excluded totally. Believing that GAC's remaining debts of $391 million left few assets for distribution, the trustees recommended that GAC be declared insolvent. The move cancelled all outstanding GAC common and preferred stock, making it worthless. The stock had plunged by this time to less than twenty-five cents per share. The 20,000 persons with some 7.5 million shares of stock in the company were left with nothing; for all practical purposes, the 40,000 creditors and bondholders emerged with the entire assets of GAC. One broker described the situation of GAC stockholders: "An investment is a gamble. They [the old stockholders] lost."[80]

After the reorganization plan was approved by the bankruptcy court, a majority of the creditors agreed to it. Elections for corporate officers were held in September 1980, and GAC Corporation became Avatar Holding on October 1. Edward F. Swanson, Jr., became the new chairman of the board, and real estate developer Peter Sharp was selected as president and chief executive officer. Former trustee Callahan predicted that the Miami-based Avatar would complete all commitments made by the old GAC and would soon be profitable again. Basically, the company was to continue as a land sales and community development operation but with a stronger commitment to the property owners.[81]

The financial failure of GAC could be attributed to several causes. Many observers have claimed that GAC inherited its most important problems from the Rosen brothers and the old Gulf American Corporation. Gulf American had been targeted by the FLSB in order that the company, and ultimately the entire industry, might be brought under tighter state regulation. One of the primary reasons that the Rosens sold the company was because they saw increasing regulation in Florida and therefore lower profits. While GAC was held responsible for sales problems that dated to before February 1969, GAC officials still had difficulties controlling its own sales staff.

GAC also had little control over existing developments that Gulf American had started. While Cape Coral and parts of Golden Gate were designed as finished residential subdivisions, developments such as Remuda Ranch Grants, River Ranch Acres, parts of Golden Gate Estates, and Rio Rico were sold as undeveloped acreage. Although salespeople extolled the land's investment potential, many prospective buyers believed that the property might have little or no resale value. With increased publicity of Florida land scams in nationally distributed newspapers and magazines, potential buyers became more wary of high-pressure land promotions. State and federal regulators eventually ruled that sales methods used to promote raw acreage tracts were inherently deceptive and ordered GAC to finance a massive exchange program. In response, GAC phased out the acreage sales in order to prevent more complaints.

Another problem facing GAC was the increasing awareness of the public concerning the destruction of the natural environment by dredging and filling. Although Gulf American had proceeded with much of its dredging during an era when environmental concerns were not a high priority for state officials, GAC received increasing attention during the ecologically conscious period of the 1970s. Of particular concern for the public were the numerous wetlands slated by GAC for development at Cape Coral and other projects. During 1970 GAC dramatically increased the rate of development at Cape Coral. Out of a total of some 60,000 acres, GAC more than doubled the developed area of the community from 17,761 to 36,770 acres. The ensuing conflicts over dredging permits, mostly at Cape Coral, were costly, particularly for a company with financial problems. While noting that Gulf American had had few such conflicts, GAC officials seriously misjudged the regulatory climate during the early 1970s in Florida.[82]

Although GAC's inherited difficulties were significant, the company's overall failure can more readily be traced to several serious miscalculations on the part of Hayward Wills and GAC management. Wills wanted to expand the company's land development subsidiaries at a rate of 20 percent per year while at the same time eliminating sales abuses. As pressure increased on the company to control its aggressive sales force, Wills ordered cuts in the sales staff. With fewer and less aggressive sales personnel, revenues slumped. Without regard to his declining income, Wills pushed forward with several large new projects, including Three Islands and Cape Eleuthera. According to Charles Hepner, Wills used up much of GAC's cash reserves on the two abortive projects. Wills's ambition caused him to continue to push the developments despite opposition from sales and development advisers. At one point, Wills wanted the Eleuthera project so much that when Hepner openly opposed it at a top-level meeting, Wills became so infuriated that he refused to speak with him for six months.[83]

Part of the miscalculation on Three Islands and Cape Eleuthera centered on Wills's lack of background in sales. Gulf American had developed a sales organization that recruited people who were able to close land sales deals. Describing that type of person, Hepner explained: "If you have a conscience, it's very difficult to sell a piece of land sometimes. These guys have no conscience." In the selling of land, Gulf American realized that most people do not feel a need to buy land as they might other necessities of life. It was therefore necessary for salespeople aggressively to pursue prospective customers. According to Hepner, Wills "was naive to the type of people it takes to run it [the sales operation]."[84]

Joseph Raso, a sales manager at Cape Coral and at the Gulf American office in Rome, Italy, agreed that GAC had a different philosophy about sales. Pointing to GAC's background, Raso noted that in the consumer loan business, customers came to GAC's finance centers because they needed the loans and therefore loan officers did not have to be extremely courteous. In the land sales industry, however, customers did not have the intrinsic need for the product, and salespeople had to persuade the buyers in other ways. According to Raso: "Being nice to them [customers] is what we prided on. When GAC took over, I think it changed a little. I think that's probably the downfall of this thing. Sales began to drop. People were having more trouble. Nobody was taking care of them. That's all you need. Just a little disagreement here and there and it spreads."[85]

GAC's sales problems increased further during the recession that hit the housing industry in Florida during the early 1970s. As interest rates soared, consumers were more reluctant to invest in a retirement homesite. The subsequent lack of sales resulted in a severe cash flow shortage for the company. Forced to borrow at high interest rates, GAC's cash reserves were depleted still further. A surplus of condominiums on the Florida market further complicated GAC's situation because Cape Eleuthera and Three Islands were designed as condominium communities. Despite the poor economy in the 1970s, GAC might have survived if such large new projects had not been allowed by Wills to drain money from the company.

Despite GAC's later dismantling of the once powerful Gulf American sales organization, the impact of Gulf American on southwest Florida, as well as the entire state and the eastern part of the United States, was important. With the help of its smaller competitors, Gulf American introduced residents of the Midwest and Northeast to the climate, low cost of living, and casual life-style in Florida. Between 1957 and 1969, the company spent millions of dollars advertising its developments and Florida in general. Hundreds of thousands of people were given discounted or free transportation to Florida to hear a Gulf American sales presentation. Regardless of the methods used, more than 225,000 customers purchased land by 1968, and many moved from other parts of the country to settle in Florida.

While people were already being attracted to Florida on their own by the 1950s and 1960s, Gulf American's sales efforts provided many of them with an affordable piece of Florida real estate on which to settle. Paul Sanborn, an early executive with Gulf American at Cape Coral, noted that the Rosens gave people of modest means their only chance to live in a waterfront home in Florida. The ease with which a person of average income could purchase a lot increased sales for the company, but it also promoted more migration to Florida.[86]

Gulf American had an impact not only on the state's demographics but also on the regulation of subdividers within the state and throughout the nation. While the FILSB was created in 1963 because of the sales abuses within the whole industry, the FLSB was formed in 1967 specifically to gain control over Gulf American. Because Gulf American had wielded enough influence on the previous board to prevent serious prosecution, the new board singled out the company for particular attention. During U.S. Senate hearings in 1964, 1966, and 1967, testimony concerning interstate land sales abuses focused in large part on Florida land sales and specifically on Gulf American's activities. Some observers partly attributed the passage of the Interstate Land Sales Full Disclosure Act of 1969 to Leonard Rosen's refusal to testify before one of the subcommittees.

During the 1970s, GAC Corporation pursued Hayward Wills's grandiose plan for expansion in the land industry only to discover the many pitfalls in the field. While Wills was battling to keep GAC solvent after several major project failures and a national housing recession, Jack and Leonard Rosen began other business ventures soon after the sale of Gulf American to GAC in February 1969.

After Gulf American

According to the purchase contract between Gulf American and GAC Corporation, the Rosen brothers were paid $100,000 each for one year after the sale to act as consultants to GAC. Although the company paid the salaries, GAC officials ignored the Rosens immediately after the sale was final. Solomon Sandler, a brother-in-law to the Rosens and a director of Gulf American, observed that the abrupt break hurt the brothers personally, particularly Jack. In describing the younger Rosen's feelings, Sandler said: "He was very upset. They were just not consulted on it, on any major decisions. GAC delivered what they promised. They just didn't consult with them. And Jack felt hurt, ignored." Jack was so upset by the situation, according to Sandler, that he "would have bought the company back because they [GAC officials] were running it into the ground." No negotiations were ever started to repurchase Gulf American, however.[1]

When it became obvious to the Rosens that they would no longer play any role at GAC, Jack set up a marketing company in Miami. Located across the street from the old Gulf American building, the business began working on an arrangement with GAC company officials to provide prospects for GAC's land sales operation. Some of the former Gulf American marketing and management people were hired by the new firm. The venture was barely started, however, when Jack suffered a fatal heart attack at his home in Miami Beach on November 22, 1969. He died at the age of fifty.[2]

The settling of Jack's estate provided some insight into the Rosens' financial condition as a result of the sale of Gulf American. According to the *New York Times,* Rosen left an estate worth more than $10 million, not including outstanding debts totaling $1 million. His will left 50 percent of his estate to his widow Claire, 20 percent to two funds, 90 percent of the balance to his four minor daughters, and the remainder to thirty-three other persons. An initial compilation of his entire estate within a short time after his death, however, revealed a net worth of $46,446,047. At the time of the sale of Gulf American, media accounts estimated his and his brother's shares of the sale to be about $63 million each.[3]

The rapid decline in Jack Rosen's net worth was directly attributable to the sale agreement with GAC. According to that contract, the brothers took 80 percent of their payment in a special convertible stock share that had limited voting rights. In addition, they were not allowed by the agreement to exchange or sell any of those shares until February 1972. By that time, however, GAC stock and its special convertible shares had begun to fall dramatically in value. The decline was so steep that the value of Jack's estate had dropped to $18,981,170 within one year of his death. Leonard's stock holdings in GAC were similarly affected. At the time of the sale, each brother's convertible shares were worth only $51,047,716 when exchanged for GAC common at $58.00 per share. The price dropped to $10.75 by the end of 1971, yielding only $9,461,429. Because 80 percent of their receipts from the sale of Gulf American were in the convertible shares, which they could not sell, the brothers lost much of the return from the sale.[4]

While Jack pursued marketing after the sale, Leonard went to Europe to live. In late 1969 Leonard set up a Luxembourg-based mutual fund known as Preferred American Realty Security Fund, or Parfund. The investment fund sold shares in American real estate to West German citizens. Although he hired many salespeople, Rosen presented the fund personally, guaranteeing charter investors an annual rate of return of 15 percent for the first eighteen months. They were also told that a $100,000 investment would grow to $858,727 in twenty years. According to the promotional brochures, "The Parfund investor is in the enviable position of having his financial planning in the hands of one of America's richest men and greatest financial geniuses."[5]

With much of his net worth tied up in GAC stock that he.could not sell for several years, Rosen needed to raise cash for a new venture. Within a year, Parfund had taken in an estimated $20 million, a large percentage of which ended up in other companies controlled by Rosen. By late 1970 the West German government had suspended sales of Parfund, citing problems it had with similar overseas investment funds. By that time, however, the money had been reinvested in Rosen's new project in Nevada called Calvada.[6]

As early as 1969, Leonard Rosen had begun purchasing land in the Pahrump Valley in Nevada under the corporate name of Preferred Equities Corporation (PEC). The Pahrump Valley was located approximately sixty miles west of Las Vegas, and PEC eventually purchased more than 18,000 acres of land there. Sales of homesites began at the Calvada development in 1970. Modeled after Rosen's former sales operations in Florida, tourists in Las Vegas were encouraged to take the one-hour van ride to Calvada and to buy a lot. From its inception, PEC faced criticism from various public agencies for misrepresenting the value of the land. In 1974, for example, the state of Nevada ordered PEC to stop telling sales prospects that the Calvada-area population would soar by 50,000 because the state itself projected a net addition of only 4,000 people by the year 2020. Despite the problems, Rosen built an effective marketing organization, selling more than 26,700 parcels in the Pahrump area by 1986; 2,700 of those lots were sold to foreigners.[7]

With the West German government putting Parfund out of business in late 1970, Leonard Rosen faced the legal wrath of some 900 Germans who had purchased shares in the fund. Within three months after the shutdown, investors received a letter from a Rosen-controlled company that offered to settle their claims. In exchange for each $10 worth of claims, the company would give them $11 worth of land in Calvada. Seven hundred twenty-three investors agreed to the limited-time offer only to discover that their property was worth only a fraction of its list value, primarily because the land was located sixty miles from Las Vegas, not on the outskirts of the city as they had been led to believe. When Nye County, Nevada, tax bills were sent out, some of the Germans defaulted on their lots, not wanting to pay taxes on worthless land, and the property was auctioned off for delinquent taxes. PEC repurchased the lots for an average of $800; these were the lots that had been traded to the Germans at $5,000 in value.[8]

More than 200 Germans who had traded for the land ultimately took action against Rosen personally. Forming the Calvada Protective Association, they sued the promoter for $100 million in damages, charging that there was no resale for the lots. Represented by San Francisco attorney Gregory Stout, the Germans settled out of court in 1983 for $10 million. A source involved in the negotiations reported that the Germans recovered 100 percent of their original investment, which was an unusually successful settlement. In 1973 several hundred Parfund investors who had refused the exchange had negotiated a settlement from Rosen amounting to 70 percent of their claims.[9]

While the money that originally was invested in Parfund by West

German citizens undoubtedly ended up in Rosen's other businesses, Rosen was probably the only one who knew for sure. During the 1970s the Nevada Real Estate Division (NRED) looked into the Germans' claims of fraud. During the investigation, NRED attorney James Barnes confronted Rosen in Caesar's Palace in Las Vegas and asked him about the Germans' money. Barnes quoted Rosen's response: "He laughed and said, 'I put the money in my pocket and you can watch me spend it at Caesar's Palace,' and he pointed at the gambling tables."[10]

While his Nevada business ventures were being investigated, Rosen faced more serious personal challenges. On April 13, 1977, a federal grand jury in Miami accused Rosen of falsifying his 1970 income tax return by placing $5,579,999 in profits in a bank account in the Bahamas to avoid paying some $500,000 in income taxes. The profits had come from real estate that he had sold in Dade County and in Las Vegas. Shortly before his trial was to start in January 1978, Rosen pleaded no contest, and Las Vegas federal judge Roger Foley put him on three years' probation and fined him $5,000. The unusually light sentence was part of a plea bargain that required Rosen to tell federal agents how he was able to move the money out of the country to the Bahamas. Federal officials wanted to learn how he did it in order to catch other wealthy Americans who were illegally avoiding taxes in the same way. The officials, however, later admitted that Rosen gave them little useful information.[11]

Rosen began to have serious heart problems in the mid-1970s. Always an active, athletic man, he had played tennis nearly every morning since moving to Florida in 1957. Ultimately he had a quadruple heart bypass operation in order to restore his health. For Rosen, however, the thought of being incapacitated physically was almost more than he could handle emotionally. Later, after the operation, he remembered: "Because I am so physical, I actually got to the point that I thought for a minute of taking my life." Rosen attributed his recovery to his friends and associates because they kept calling him to encourage him. He said: "They helped me maintain some semblance of a reasonable attitude toward life. I never thought I would again be so strong . . . to take on any challenge. I feel there are so many things I want to do, want to conquer."[12]

After recovering from his surgery, Rosen expanded his company from land sales into the rapidly growing time-share resort business. He began in 1977 to sell weekly occupancy rights at the Grand Flamingo Resort, a 187-unit hotel in Las Vegas. According to the contracts, buyers were entitled to seven-day visits each year for thirty years. Rosen administered the venture under the name of Grand Flamingo Corporation, which was a subsidiary of PEC. By 1980 he had expanded his operation to include the 95-unit Reno Spa Resort in Reno, Nevada, and the 80-room White Sands Waikiki Resort in Honolulu, Hawaii. Eventually, he wanted to have twelve such operations.[13]

While the novelty of time sharing had left many customers wary of the new form of ownership, several time-sharing promoters were openly skeptical of Rosen's involvement in the new industry. They suspected that he just wanted to cut himself in on time-sharing sales that were expected to grow to more than $1 billion annually by 1980. Carl Burlingame, publisher of *Resort Time-Sharing Today* and one of the most respected men in the industry at the time, wanted proof of Rosen's sincerity. He said: "When I first heard that Rosen was getting into time-sharing, I was mighty suspicious. I have a memory back to the Florida days." After investigating Grand Flamingo thoroughly, Burlingame admitted: "The way Rosen has it set up, it would be impossible for him to pick up the money and go to Argentina. It's the most solid practical trust arrangement I've seen." He said further, "You can say whatever you want about Rosen's other activities, but his time-share operation is ironclad."[14]

Leonard Rosen himself wanted the public to know that his new time-sharing business was stable. During a promotion for it in Las Vegas, he emphasized the point in a public statement in 1980: "As you can see, we're a highly organized, laid-back organization. So if you came in here looking for some kind of high-pressure organization, we don't know anything about it." Despite his pronouncements of a change in sales methods, Rosen's salespeople at Calvada continued to promise high investment potential from Calvada homesites. One salesman confidently proclaimed: "This Calvada is going to be another Las Vegas strip." Notwithstanding the high-pressure sales, Rosen's time-sharing venture appeared to be on firm financial ground. His son Ronald Rosen, who was in partnership with him in PEC, stated: "We put up $6,750,000 to guarantee anything we've promised people in time-sharing."[15]

Looking to expand his company into a major national corporation again, Rosen needed increased financing. In an agreement announced on June 28, 1979, Rosen's Grand Flamingo Corporation was acquired by Scottish Inns of America, a small, nearly bankrupt chain of economy motels located in the southeastern part of the United States. In return, Rosen's primary corporation, Preferred Equities, received 80 percent of Scottish Inn's common stock. In the nearly cashless deal that had Preferred Equities pledging some of its accounts receivable, Rosen ultimately gained control of both Scottish Inns and Grand Flamingo. While many observers were unclear as to his purpose in the merger, Carl Burlingame assessed his motives: "Rosen sure as hell didn't buy Scottish Inns because he wanted hotels in Tennessee. He'll probably sell off most of them and use the public stock listing for financing future sales projects."[16]

Burlingame's assessment proved accurate. On January 28, 1981, Scottish Inns registered 12.5 million additional common shares with the Securities and Exchange Commission for sale to the public. Company officials announced that the proceeds from the sale would be used to improve facilities and to pay debt to its parent company, Preferred Equities. Virtually admitting that the funds were destined for speculative ventures, company spokespersons said that its securities "involve a significant degree of risk" and "should be purchased only by persons who can afford the risk of loss of their investment." Because Rosen apparently was only interested in expanding his time-sharing operations and real estate holdings and not in operating economy motels, the name of the company was appropriately changed from Scottish Inns of America to Vacation Spa Resorts on June 30, 1981.[17]

While sales of lots at Calvada continued throughout the 1970s and early 1980s, Rosen expanded into other real estate ventures. In the early 1980s, PEC started two large recreational vehicle parks in the southwestern section of the United States. In addition, the company began developing condominium projects for time sharing in Gatlinburg, Tennessee, at a site north of Myrtle Beach, South Carolina, and on the Gulf coast of Alabama. Although the latter two were eventually dropped before construction started, the Gatlinburg project was finished in the late 1980s. In order to ensure that Calvada and Gatlinburg were built properly, Rosen called on Thomas Weber to serve as chief engineer. Weber had worked for Gulf American and GAC until 1972 when he retired and went to work for Rader and Associates in Miami. Before becoming associated with Rosen again in Nevada, Weber had directed the construction of a greyhound racing track in Hallandale, Florida. Weber remembered later that construction at Calvada had to be carefully engineered because much of the valley floor consisted of loose sand that frequently settled. The shifting sand often resulted in structural failures in the buildings.[18]

Charles Hepner also returned to work for Leonard Rosen, joining PEC to help start the recreational vehicle parks. Within a short time, Rosen switched Hepner to the Gatlinburg project. Named the Gatlinburg Golf and Racquet Club, the development was located on a ridge east of Gatlinburg called Cobby Knob. By the mid-1980s the project was in deep financial trouble. Calling Hepner, Rosen admitted: "I've got a big problem and you've got to help me. It's Gatlinburg. I can't sleep at night. We've already lost somewhere between $2.5 million and $3 million on the project." Despairing that the development would ever be finished, Rosen wanted to abandon it. Hepner convinced him that the cheapest option was to finish it, and the project was ultimately completed and sold out in 1987.[19]

By 1986 Rosen's Calvada development was facing increasing criticism from Nevada officials. Since 1971 PEC had split more than 26,000 lots from the farms and ranches of Pahrump Valley. Free Las Vegas show tickets, champagne breakfasts and lunches, and tours of local attractions were used to draw thousands of tourists to the sales offices. Local developers subdivided an additional 14,000 lots in the valley, hoping to sidetrack some of the tourists to their developments. Of special concern to the Nevada authorities were salespersons' claims that Calvada's homesites would have high resale potential. The salespeople also made unsubstantiated predictions of an eventual population for the valley of 300,000.[20]

The entire Pahrump Valley had grown to only 5,200 residents by 1986, but it was admittedly one of the fastest growing areas in Nevada. Of the 1,800 lots that had been developed, only 377 had been sold by Preferred Equities. The major obstacle in using the lots was the lack of water. The vast majority of the company's homesites were without water, electricity, and sewer hookups. Aware that the land was useless without water, the Nye County government began requiring performance bonds from PEC to ensure that water and sewer systems would be built on the company's twenty-nine square miles of subdivision.[21]

Coinciding with Leonard Rosen's increasing conflict with Nevada authorities were his continued heart problems. In the early 1980s he underwent another quadruple heart bypass operation. His normal health, however, did not return. Hoping to restore his good name before he died, Rosen appealed to U.S. Senator Paul Laxalt to help him receive a pardon for his 1978 conviction on tax evasion charges. Officials in Laxalt's office recommended that Rosen's civil rights be restored in Nevada before application was made for a pardon from President Ronald Reagan. Represented by Nevada state senator James Bilbray, Rosen's case came before the Nevada Pardons Board in 1986. The board consisted of Governor Richard Bryan, five Nevada supreme court justices, and the state attorney general.[22]

The pardons board took only minutes to vote to pardon Rosen in Nevada. Bilbray noted that numerous communications had been received by the board that recommended that Rosen be forgiven, including letters from Rosen's Las Vegas rabbi and U.S. senators Paul Laxalt and Chic Hecht. Governor Bryan acknowledged that the pardon was not out of the ordinary. He explained that a pardon "is routinely granted . . . to persons who have served their sentences and have been out in the community for a number of years."[23]

Rosen did not appear at the board's session because of his heart condition. The sixty-nine-year-old Rosen appeared so ill that Bilbray said, "I am not familiar with how to give CPR and I felt the way that it was going, that there was a likelihood that would happen." Bilbray assessed Rosen's motives in the pardon request: "I think he wants to make peace not only with God, but with his country and to put it bluntly, he wants to go out with a clean slate." He added, however, that Rosen had decided not to pursue his pardon on the federal level but he did not give any reason for this decision.[24]

Although he continued working, Rosen's health never returned. On Friday, August 14, 1987, he died in Valley Hospital in Las Vegas at age seventy-two; he was buried in Baltimore. He was survived by his wife Sonia, former wife Dorothy Rosen, and three children—Linda Sterling, Ronald Rosen, and Sandy Raymond. Also surviving him were two step-children and six grandchildren. The size of Rosen's estate at the time of his death was closely connected to his business. Because most of his assets were included in his Preferred Equities Corporation, of which he was the primary stockholder, and that company was purchased on February 1, 1988, for $10,513,000 by Mego Corporation, Rosen's estate could be concluded to be somewhat near that value.[25]

Leonard Rosen's impact on Nevada is still difficult to evaluate, but his life and the life of his brother had a tremendous effect on the development of Florida during the 1960s. The brothers' entrepreneurial ability and promotional skills introduced thousands of people in the United States and around the world to the benefits of living in Florida. The enormous size of Gulf American and its unabashed aggressiveness in sales resulted in increased state and federal legislation regarding land sales and promotions. Despite accusations of misrepresentation, the brothers left several thriving communities in Florida that continue to grow.

Of all the Rosens' residential projects, Cape Coral remained their most significant development. With the sale of Gulf American in 1969 and the subsequent departure of the Rosens, however, residents of Cape Coral became convinced that they needed to incorporate their subdivision as a city if they were to develop further as a community. While other events contributed to the drive for incorporation, the takeover by GAC spurred many citizens to action. Throughout the Gulf American years, Cape Coral had been treated as a company town by the developers. Most services, such as police protection, fire protection, and the supplying of roads, sewers, and water, were provided by Gulf American. By the mid-1960s Gulf American officials began trying to persuade residents and the county government to take over the financial burden of providing many of these services. Throughout the time period, many Cape Coral residents appeared before the Lee County Commission in attempts to force Gulf American to provide services such as sewer and water. By 1968 the responsibility for the maintenance of the waterways in Cape Coral also became a hotly debated issue.

During the late 1960s, the Cape Coral Civic Association actively began to look out for the interests of Cape Coral. Millard Bowen, association president from 1968 to 1969, described the attitude of the group: "We developed the idea that we would be the watchdog for the community and the community's relationship with the county commission and Gulf American. There wasn't anybody else around." As a result of this philosophy, Bowen started sending members of the association's board of directors to attend every county commission meeting. Whenever a matter of interest to Cape Coral residents came up, the observer relayed the information to the civic association, which in turn publicized it. Community interest soared in 1968 with more than 500 people attending civic association meetings and with membership exceeding 2,000.[26]

During 1968 and 1969, Bowen became aware that the Lee County Commission was going to do as little as possible for Cape Coral as long as Gulf American was still operating in the community. As an example, citizens grew increasingly irritated at the county's lack of road maintenance in Cape Coral, a responsibility that had been taken over from the developer. Justifiably, Gulf American wanted to turn over maintenance of roads and canals, and other services, to the county government so that taxes, not company revenues, would pay for them. Paul Fickinger, a Cape Coral community leader and eventually the first mayor of the city, described the county's attitude:

It appeared to the residents that the county fathers were most happy to see the growth in assessment value and what it meant to the financial structure of the county and the increase in tax income. But when it came to the matter of supervising the development, providing law and order, development of parks, fire protection and other services to the residents of the community, there was little inclination to meet such needs.[27]

Residents grew more apprehensive in July 1968 when the takeover of Gulf American by GAC was announced. With Gulf American reducing its efforts in Cape Coral and the county commission reluctant to assume responsibility for most services, Cape Coral residents discussed ways of protecting their interests. The idea of incorporating the community into a city was increasingly suggested. Millard Bowen noted that the issue of incorporation was raised continually at civic association meetings in late 1968.[28]

During the same time, the civic association, as the major public forum in the community, began holding a series of programs on the pros and cons of incorporation. The association was officially neutral at the time and served as an information-gathering organization. Various speakers from around Florida were invited to present opposing views, particularly on the issue of increased taxation under incorporation. In an effort to gather more local publicity and information, Bowen, with the aid of Connie Mack, Jr., arranged for all five county commissioners to come to Cape Coral at one time and tour the development. Leonard Rosen agreed to guide the officials, and he enthusiastically provided a bus for the tour and hosted a luncheon at the country club. The commissioners met residents and Gulf American officials who presented Cape Coral's unique benefits and problems. According to Bowen, it was the first time all five commissioners had visited Cape Coral together. Later the commissioners spoke to a crowd of more than 500 people at the civic association meeting at the yacht club. The officials presented their views on incorporation and then the meeting was opened for questions. Although no firm results came from the meeting, it served to clarify many issues for Cape Coral residents.[29]

By the middle of 1969 the incorporation drive had gained momentum. As more residents began to view the county commission as insensitive to Cape Coral's needs, they increasingly supported incorporation. Richard Crawford, editor of the *Cape Coral Breeze,* kept the issue before the public's attention in the newspaper. After the benefits and hazards of incorporation had been discussed for several months, the civic association took a vote among its members on the issue. The organization voted strongly for incorporation. As a result, in the summer of 1969 an executive committee was formed by the association to pursue incorporation. The five-member committee selected 100 residents to fill several other subcommittees that focused on, among other matters, fire and safety, law enforcement, finance, building and zoning, and public works. The first official meeting of the executive committee was September 2, 1969, at the Cape Coral Italian-American Club.[30]

According to Paul Fickinger, who was a member of the executive committee, the next step of the process toward incorporation was the establishment of boundaries. Although some residents wanted a smaller area, the boundaries included all areas where development had occurred or was proposed by GAC. Throughout the fall of 1969 and into 1970, the committee began developing a city charter. GAC provided its attorney, Richard DeBoast, to assist in drawing up the document. With the incorporation of Cape Coral, GAC would be relieved of the high cost of maintenance in the community. The finished charter was presented to the state legislature, and it was enacted into law in June 1970, subject to a referendum by Cape Coral voters.[31]

A brochure was prepared by the executive committee outlining the results of all the feasibility studies, the proposed budget for the first year, and an estimate of income from various sources. The brochure was delivered by hand to every house in the proposed city. Several town hall meetings were held to discuss the benefits and hazards of the incorporation. While most residents supported the measure, many were apprehensive. GAC supported incorporation but did not want to risk a backlash by trying to force the issue on the residents. Fickinger remembered: "All was not 'sweetness and light' during this period. There were definite and honest fears as to what might happen if the community was incorporated." The fears included skyrocketing taxes and the belief that perhaps the executive committee was not presenting the whole picture. Despite these hesitations, the referendum was held on August 11, 1970, and the incorporation measure passed by a vote of 2,067 to 1,798.[32]

An election was held during the fall of 1970 to select seven council members. Those elected were: District 1, Cleo Snead; District 2, Paul Fickinger; District 3, Chandler Burton; District 4, Robert South; District 5, Gordon Berndt; District 6, Lyman Moore; and District 7, Casey Jablonski. The first city council meeting was held on December 3, 1970. Because of his extensive work on the incorporation process, Fickinger was selected by the council as the city's first mayor; Burton and Moore later served as mayors of the city. Fickinger commented on the event: "We are starting from scratch. We don't often get an opportunity to participate in a historic occasion like this." After nearly thirteen years of being administered by other governmental bodies and by Gulf American, Cape Coral's 15,000 residents were able to plan for their own future.[33]

Of all the results of the Rosens' efforts, one of the most important was the founding of the city of Cape Coral. Cape Coral was designed by Gulf American to be a showplace that would eventually help to sell other less-developed projects. Because of that goal, Cape Coral residents witnessed the building of country clubs, golf courses, and a yacht club. With hundreds of miles of canals, the community was unique, even among Florida cities. Residents of Cape Coral had a plaque made to honor the Rosens and had it placed in the lobby of the old Gulf American building in Cape Coral. It reads: "In honor of Jack and Leonard Rosen, whose courage and leadership enabled the dream of a magnificent city to become a reality."[34]

In the final analysis, Gulf American would not have come into existence or accomplished what it did without Jack and Leonard Rosen. Without exception the Rosens' closest associates attributed the company's success to the brothers' ambition and personal drive. In addition, they both had an extraordinary gift for sales. They were the heart of the company, and many employees were fiercely loyal to them. At a reunion dinner in 1979 in his honor at Miami Beach, Leonard Rosen remarked that the greatest dreamer of the two brothers was Jack. Many of Gulf American's most innovative ideas came from the younger Rosen. Leonard even downplayed his efforts: "I'm just a pitchman, an old peddler trying to work my way through this life and sometimes, luckily, people help me out."[35]

The Rosens had accomplished a great deal since they began selling pots and pans on the streets of Baltimore as young teenagers. They had made a fortune in cosmetics and installment real estate sales. Jack did not live long enough to enjoy much of his wealth. Leonard witnessed his fortune, most of it tied up in GAC stock that he legally could not sell, dwindle to less than 10 percent of its former size. Commenting on GAC's collapse, he said in 1977: "I never dreamed in my wildest dreams the company could have so much trouble." The loss did not seem to dishearten him. He explained, "It would be very easy for me to sit down and cry about the money I lost in the stock market, but I would rather go out and do something." Commenting on his success, Rosen noted: "I'm not disappointed in Cape Coral. What we set out to do is build a nucleus of a fine community and we did that." He added: "We would have done even better if we'd continued to run the company, but it's very difficult to go back. I'm always moving forward."[36]

Many employees remembered that even though they were not sure that Gulf American would be able to accomplish what it set out to do, they stayed with the company because of the excitement that the Rosens created. No one was more amazed at the accomplishments of the Rosens than their mother Fannie Rosen. On a visit to Cape Coral in early 1958, she was escorted around the new development by Kenneth Schwartz. At the conclusion of the tour, she commented about her son Leonard: "I can't get over it. My son building a city. He couldn't keep his room clean and now he's building a city."[37]

Although the Rosens successfully sold the dream of living in Florida to thousands of people in the United States, many buyers saw their dream turn into a nightmare. They purchased land from Gulf American as an investment only to find that they had grossly overpaid for the property. Lawsuits from lot owners pursued Gulf American and, later, GAC for years after land sales had been completed, eventually resulting in court decisions that crippled a cash-strapped GAC in the mid-1970s.

While misrepresentation undoubtedly did occur, the Rosens cannot be dismissed as yet another example in a long line of unscrupulous Florida swamp sellers. On the one hand, they did sell undeveloped or unusable land to individuals who probably had little idea of what they were getting. The Rosens also forever altered the physical environment of several parts of Florida by their draining of huge tracts of land with hundreds of miles of canals. Their well-publicized struggle to prevent state regulation of their company resulted in stronger legislation concerning land sales. At the same time, however, Gulf American spent millions of dollars promoting Florida, its climate, and its casual lifestyle to people throughout North America and Europe. The brothers' company also provided thousands of people with their first trip to Florida with their Fly and Buy program. The installment purchase plans developed by the Rosens enabled many Americans to buy Florida property who otherwise would not have been able to afford to do so. Ultimately, the cities of Cape Coral, and to a lesser degree Golden Gate, stand as evidence that the brothers wanted to build something lasting in which they and their customers could take pride.

In assessing the legacy of the Rosens and the Gulf American Land Corporation, few observers can overlook the dramatic rise of the brothers from humble beginnings in Baltimore to the top of the corporate world through sheer entrepreneurial ability. Their lives were fleshed-out examples of the "rags-to-riches" American dream. At the same time, many of their customers—not all by any means—suffered financially because of the aggressive sales organization that the Rosens created. While the brothers' company created waterfront homesites in the price range of many blue-collar Americans, Gulf American contributed to environmental damage in large areas of Florida in order to develop those lots. In any appraisal of the Rosens, therefore, an observer must examine the proverbial coin with two distinct, often conflicting, sides. Looking at only one side of the controversial and complex brothers yields a distorted picture of their impact on Florida.

As the Rosens strived to achieve their personal goals, Gulf American played a significant role in the development and urbanization of the state of Florida during the late 1950s and 1960s. Due to their promotion of Florida, their company heavily influenced the migration of people to the state after 1957. Yet behind the promotions, dinner parties, and the building of the largest land sales company in the United States were two men who knew how to ignite the imagination of their co-workers and customers. The building of Gulf American was seen by the brothers as an incredible attempt to do what seemed impossible to most observers. They viewed themselves as salesmen without equal and felt confident of their ultimate success. For the Rosens, the money that Gulf American made was secondary. They loved the thrill of beating insurmountable odds in reaching their goals.

As the Rosens pursued their financial kingdom, they left an environmental and administrative nightmare in many of their developments. Gulf American's method of subdividing land, so common in the post—

World War II era, drew so much public condemnation that such a company will not likely appear again in the state. With the subsequent increase in environmental and subdivision regulations, it would be virtually impossible for the Rosens to be able to duplicate today their meteoric rise with Gulf American. In that sense, the company and the brothers rose to success due to their abilities and to the unique time period in which they lived. Many of the conditions that gave rise to that era in Florida are gone. Yet in the two decades of freewheeling development in the 1950s and 1960s, Jack and Leonard Rosen and the Gulf American Land Corporation were unequaled in Florida land sales, a record that will likely never be broken.

Notes

Chapter 1. Grand Dreams in Southwest Florida

1. Kenneth J. Schwartz, taped interview with author, Hollywood, Florida, November 16, 1987, University of Florida Oral History Archives, Gainesville (cited hereafter as OHA); *Cape Coral Breeze,* April 1983.

2. *Cape Coral Breeze,* April 1983.

3. Gifford A. Cochran, "Mr. Lincoln's Many-Faceted Minister and Entrepreneur Extraordinary, Henry Shelton Sanford 1823–1891," typescript, 291, P. K. Yonge Library, Gainesville.

4. Joseph A. Fry, *Henry S. Sanford: Diplomacy and Business in Nineteenth-Century America* (Reno: University of Nevada Press, 1982), 121.

5. Jerry Weeks, "Florida Gold: The Emergence of the Florida Citrus Industry 1865–1895" (Ph.D. diss., University of North Carolina at Chapel Hill, 1977), 231; Fry, *Sanford,* 101.

6. Fry, *Sanford,* 104.

7. Pat Dodson, "Hamilton Disston's St. Cloud Sugar Plantation 1887–1901," *Florida Historical Quarterly* 49 (April 1971): 357; T. Frederick Davis, "The Disston Land Purchase," *Florida Historical Quarterly* 17 (January 1939): 204–8; Samuel Proctor, *Napoleon Bonaparte Broward: Florida's Fighting Democrat* (Gainesville: University of Florida Press, 1950), 56–57; Alfred J. Hanna and Kathryn Abbey Hanna, *Lake Okeechobee* (New York: Bobbs-Merrill, 1948), 94–95.

8. Hanna and Hanna, *Lake Okeechobee,* 99, 100–101.

9. Dodson, "St. Cloud Sugar Plantation," 365–66; Hanna and Hanna, *Lake Okeechobee,* 102–3.

10. Edward N. Akin, *Flagler: Rockefeller Partner and Florida Baron* (Kent, Ohio: Kent State University Press, 1988), 175.

11. Fort Myers Hotel brochure, 1898, P. K. Yonge Library, Gainesville.

12. Akin, *Flagler,* 184–89.

13. Paul S. George, "Brokers, Binders, and Builders: Greater Miami's Boom of the Mid-1920s," *Florida Historical Quarterly* 65 (July 1986): 28–29; J. E. Dovell, *Florida: Historic, Dramatic, Contemporary,* 4 vols. (New York: Lewis Historical Publishing Co., 1952), 2:769.

14. George, "Brokers," 35; Dovell, *Florida,* 2:775.

15. Philip Weidling and August Burghard, *Checkered Sunshine: The Story of Fort Lauderdale 1793–1955* (Fort Lauderdale: Wake Brook, 1974), 101–2; Stuart B. McIver, *Fort Lauderdale and Broward County* (Woodland Hills, Calif.: Windsor Publications, 1983), 78–79; Virginia S. Young, *Mangrove Roots of Fort Lauderdale* (Fort Lauderdale: Poinsetta Press, 1976), 38.

16. Karl H. Grismer, *Tampa* (St. Petersburg: St. Petersburg Printing Co., 1950), 254–59.

17. James W. Covington, *The Story of Southwestern Florida* (New York: Lewis Historical Publishing Co., 1957), 229–32.

18. Karl H. Grismer, *The Story of Fort Myers* (1949; reprint, Fort Myers Beach: Island Press, 1982), 215.

19. Ibid., 221, 229.

20. *Fort Myers News-Press,* January 23, 1924.

21. Grismer, *Fort Myers,* 222–24, 228.

22. Ibid., 240, 242.

23. R. Lyn Rainard, "Ready Cash on Easy Terms: Local Responses to the Depression in Lee County," *Florida Historical Quarterly* 64 (January 1986): 296.

24. Prudy Taylor Board and Patricia Pope Bartlett, *Lee County: A Pictorial History* (Norfolk, Va.: Donning, 1985), 161; Covington, *Southwestern Florida,* 247; Grismer, *Fort Myers,* 248.

25. *Tampa Tribune,* September 15, 1954. For example, in 1954–55, 19,500 lots at South Venice were sold at $200 per unit.

26. Board and Bartlett, *Lee County,* 183.

27. General Development Corporation, *Your Florida Property and Who's Behind It,* promotional brochure, General Development Corporation vertical file, Miami-Dade Public Library, Miami.

28. Daniel J. Boorstin, ed., *Abstract of the Twelfth Census of the United States 1900* (New York: Arno Press, 1976), 152.

29. E. A. Hammond, ed., "Sanibel Island and Its Vicinity 1833: A Document," *Florida Historical Quarterly* 48 (April 1970): 399–400, 407.

30. Bernard Romans, *A Concise Natural History of East and West Florida* (1775; reprint, Gainesville: University of Florida Press, 1964), 185–88.

31. Hammond, "Sanibel Island," 402–3.

32. E. A. Hammond, "The Spanish Fisheries of Charlotte Harbor," *Florida Historical Quarterly* 51 (April 1973): 377.

33. Hammond, "Sanibel Island," 410.

34. John Lee Williams, *The Territory of Florida* (1837; reprint, Gainesville: University of Florida Press, 1962), 32.

35. James W. Covington, "Seminole Migration into Florida 1700–1820,"

Florida Historical Quarterly 46 (April 1968): 354–55; Charlton W. Tebeau, *History of Florida* (Coral Gables: University of Miami Press, 1971), 150–51.

36. Mark F. Boyd, "Horatio S. Dexter," *Florida Anthropologist* 13 (September 1968): 91.

37. John K. Mahon, *History of the Second Seminole War 1835–1842* (Gainesville: University of Florida Press, 1967), 325–26.

38. George R. Adams, "The Caloosahatchee Massacre: Its Significance in the Second Seminole War," *Florida Historical Quarterly* 48 (April 1970): 376–77. This attack occurred on a small peninsula on the west bank of the Caloosahatchee River that is included in the present city of Cape Coral. It is located near the west entrance to the Cape Coral bridge.

39. Covington, *Southwestern Florida*, 97.

40. Hammond, "Spanish Fisheries," 380.

41. Dovell, *Florida*, 2:131; Tebeau, *History of Florida*, 169–70.

42. Tebeau, *History of Florida*, 168.

43. John S. Otto, "Florida's Cattle-Ranching Frontier: Manatee and Brevard Counties 1860," *Florida Historical Quarterly* 44 (July 1985): 52.

44. Covington, *Southwestern Florida*, 132–33.

45. George H. Dacy, *Four Centuries of Florida Ranching* (St. Louis: Britt, 1940), 52, 57, 59.

46. William W. Davis, *The Civil War and Reconstruction in Florida* (New York: Doubleday Page, 1913), 268–72.

47. Hanna and Hanna, *Lake Okeechobee*, 72–73; Dovell, *Florida*, 2:496.

48. Rodney E. Dillon, Jr., "The Little Affair: The Southwest Florida Campaign 1863–1864," *Florida Historical Quarterly* 62 (January 1984): 325; Covington, *Southwestern Florida*, 146.

49. Grismer, *Fort Myers*, 82.

50. Thomas A. Gonzalez, *The Caloosahatchee* (1925; reprint, Fort Myers Beach: Island Press, 1982), 15.

51. Grismer, *Fort Myers*, 86; Dacy, *Florida Ranching*, 61–62; Hanna and Hanna, *Lake Okeechobee*, 84.

52. Dacy, *Florida Ranching*, 60.

53. *Fort Myers Press*, January 24 and October 31, 1885.

54. Vernon E. Peeples, "Charlotte Harbor Division of the Florida Southern Railroad," *Florida Historical Quarterly* 58 (January 1980): 298–302.

55. Covington, *Southwestern Florida*, 152–53.

56. Betsy Zeiss, *The Other Side of the River: Historical Cape Coral* (Cape Coral: Betsy Zeiss, 1986), 9–11; Grismer, *Fort Myers*, 276.

57. Daniel J. Boorstin, ed., *Abstract of the Tenth Census of the United States 1880* (New York: Arno Press, 1976), 84.

58. *Acts and Resolutions of the Legislature of Florida, First Session 1887* (Tallahassee: State Printer, 1887), 150. The newly created county included all of the territories of modern-day Lee, Collier, and Hendry counties.

59. *Fort Myers Press*, May 5, 1887.

60. Pat Dodson, ed., "Cruise of the Minnehaha," *Florida Historical Quarterly* 50 (April 1972): 400.

61. Daniel J. Boorstin, ed., *Abstract of the Thirteenth Census of the United States 1920* (New York: Arno Press, 1976), 66.

62. Peeples, "Charlotte Harbor Division," 302; Covington, *Southwestern Florida,* 190.

63. (Jacksonville) *Florida Times-Union and Citizen,* December 19, 1897; Dovell, *Florida,* 2:631.

64. *Fort Myers Tropical News,* April 2, 1929; William C. Cray, *Miles Laboratories: A Centennial History* (Englewood Cliffs, N.J.: Prentice-Hall, 1984), 4, 10–11; Louise Miles Bass, interview with Fort Myers Historical Museum staff, Fort Myers, February 29, 1984, Fort Myers Historical Museum Archives. Louise Bass is the adopted daughter of Franklin Miles and came to Fort Myers with Miles and his wife in 1909.

65. Ronald W. Clark, *Edison: The Man Who Made the Future* (New York: G. P. Putnam's, 1977), 152; *Fort Myers Press,* May 5, 1887.

66. Byron M. Vanderbilt, *Thomas Edison, Chemist* (Washington, D.C.: American Chemical Society, 1971), 286–302.

67. Harvey S. Firestone, *Men and Rubber: The Story of Business* (New York: Doubleday Page, 1926), 188; Henry Ford, *My Life and Work* (New York: Doubleday Page, 1922), 240.

68. Marion Godown and Alberta Rawchuck, *Yesterday's Fort Myers* (Miami: E. A. Seeman, 1975), 108; Zeiss, *Other Side,* 98–108. Information contained in this source was based on oral interviews by Zeiss with E. A. "Frog" Smith, a locomotive engineer and machinist at the Slater mill; James A. Sapp, brother-in-law of J. W. McWilliams; Daniel E. Corbett, a guide to McWilliams's timber appraiser; and George M. Thompson, who built roads in the timbered areas.

69. *Fort Myers News-Press,* November 24, 1984. This article about the Slater mill was written by E. A. Smith, a former machinist at the mill.

70. Zeiss, *Other Side,* 107.

71. Ibid., 129–32; Edward K. Hansen, taped interview with author, Fort Myers, May 3, 1989, OHA. The *Virgemere,* a common sight to Fort Myers residents in the 1950s, was well equipped to house the Phipps family. Construction of the boat, along with four others to be used as captains' gigs, had been started during World War II. With the end of the war, the boats were finished as private yachts. Measuring 118 feet in length and only 13 feet at the beam, the boats had an extremely long, narrow hull. One of the crafts was purchased by Ralph Evinrude and another was purchased by Governor George Wallace of Alabama. One of the remaining boats was purchased by Ogden Phipps and named the *Virgemere.* Based on his knowledge of private boats, dockmaster Edward Hansen of the Fort Myers yacht basin estimated that Phipps probably did not pay more than $150,000 for the boat.

The *Virgemere* was docked in Fort Myers for five or six months each winter, although the Phipps family seldom lived there the entire time. During the summer the yacht was taken to New York City, where Phipps spent his summers. He maintained a seven-member crew when no one was on board; the crew was periodically increased to ten or eleven members when the family was in residence. While the *Virgemere* was equipped for entertaining with a resident chef and elegant decor, Phipps located many of his parties at the hunting lodge on his property. From there, guests hunted quail, turkey, and deer in the area that later became western Cape Coral.

72. Raymond Meyer, taped interview with author, Cape Coral, January 25, 1988, OHA.

Chapter 2. Leonard and Jack Rosen

1. Research Associates, *The Economic Impact of Gulf American Corporation on the State of Florida* (Miami: Research Associates, 1967), 3.

2. Solomon S. Sandler, taped interview with author, Hollywood, Florida, February 16, 1988, OHA; Schwartz interview. Edith Rosen died of cancer in early adulthood. In later years, after the Rosens' financial success, Leonard's wife Dorothy set up the Edith Rosen Strauss Organization, a charity that raised money for cancer research. Sylvia Rosen married Solomon Sandler, who later figured prominently in the Gulf American Corporation. Sylvia died of cancer in 1970. Fannie Rosen lived to see the start of Cape Coral and died in 1963.

3. Sandler interview; Schwartz interview.

4. *New York Times,* November 24, 1969; Schwartz interview; Sandler interview; Bernice Freiberg, taped interview with author, Baltimore, January 31, 1988, OHA; Charles K. Hepner, taped interview with author, Miami, January 3, 1988, OHA.

5. Meyer interview.

6. Sandler interview.

7. Freiberg interview.

8. Ibid. Many of the friendships that Leonard and Jack Rosen developed during their carnival pitchmen days remained throughout their lives. Many of these people, including Charles Finkelstein, worked for the Rosens for many years afterward.

9. Hepner interview.

10. *New York Times,* January 13, 1962.

11. Ibid.

12. Ibid., September 4, 1952; Freiberg interview.

13. Freiberg interview.

14. Ibid.; Hepner interview.

15. Hepner interview.

16. Ibid.; Freiberg interview.

17. Freiberg interview; Schwartz interview; Sandler interview.

18. Freiberg interview.

19. Schwartz interview; Sandler interview; Robert H. Finkernagel, Jr., and Paul W. Sanborn, taped interview with author, Cape Coral, September 28, 1987, OHA.

20. Schwartz interview; Edward V. Pacelli, taped interview with author, Fort Myers, December 14, 1987, OHA.

21. Schwartz interview; Hepner interview.

22. Hepner interview; Schwartz interview; Pacelli interview; Sandler interview; Freiberg interview.

23. *Miami Herald, Tropic* magazine, December 3, 1967.

24. Hepner interview.

25. Freiberg interview.

26. Schwartz interview.

27. Ibid.; Joseph N. Kane, *Famous First Facts* (New York: H. W. Wilson, 1981), 638. The first commercial service for car phones in the United States was established on June 17, 1946, in St. Louis, Missouri.

28. Hepner interview.

29. Schwartz interview; Freiberg interview; Sandler interview. An example of this kind of relationship is the fact that Leonard Rosen maintained regular contact with his former wife Dorothy throughout his life, even though he had been remarried for many years.

30. Sandler interview; Hepner interview.

31. Sandler interview.

32. Ibid.; Freiberg interview.

33. Hepner interview; Schwartz interview.

34. *Cape Coral Breeze,* April 1977. This article is based on a 1977 interview with Leonard Rosen by James Stasiowski in Cape Coral.

35. Ibid.

36. Schwartz interview; Freiberg interview; Sandler interview.

37. Meyer interview.

38. *Miami Herald, Tropic* magazine, December 3, 1967.

39. *St. Petersburg Times,* November 25, 1977.

40. Ibid.

41. Ibid.; Richard Austin Smith, "Florida: O.K., If the Brakes Work," *Fortune* 61 (January 1960): 124. Louis A. Chesler controlled 1.5 million of 6.3 million shares of General Development while the Mackles held 535,000 shares. Chesler had made his fortune in Canadian mining stocks, had engineered the controversial sale of Warner Brothers' film library to United Artists, and had been involved in the manufacture of devices that automatically toted up statistics for racetrack betting. He already owned considerable Florida land by the time he met the Mackles.

42. Board and Bartlett, *Lee County,* 183.

43. *Cape Coral Breeze,* April 1977; Hepner interview.

44. *Cape Coral Breeze,* April 1977. This article was based on an interview with Edward F. Wilson by J. B. Wood.

45. William H. Reynolds, Jr., taped interview with author, Fort Myers, December 14, 1987, OHA; Pacelli interview.

46. *Miami Herald, Tropic* magazine, December 3, 1967; *Cape Coral Breeze,* April 1977.

47. *New York Times,* November 24, 1969.

Chapter 3. The First Five Years

1. "They Packaged a Town," *Sales Management,* December 15, 1961, 42–43.

2. *Cape Coral Breeze,* April 1983.

3. Leonard Rosen, "Remarks before the Cleveland Society of Security Analysts," May 7, 1964, Division of Land Sales, Series 141, RG 324, Box 3, File 1, Florida State Archives, Tallahassee; Sandler interview.

4. *Fort Myers News-Press,* March 22, 1978.

5. *Miami Herald,* January 21, 1966.

6. Zeiss, *Other Side,* 140–42.

7. *Cape Coral Breeze,* April 7, 1980; Milton M. Mendelsohn, deposition at Tampa, April 12, 1959, 120–21, Division of Land Sales, Series 384, RG 324, Box 6, State Archives.

8. *Fort Myers News-Press,* March 22, 1978.

9. *Cape Coral Breeze,* April 1983.

10. Hepner interview.

11. *Cape Coral Breeze,* April 1983.

12. Thomas W. Weber, taped interview with author, Avon Park, Florida, March 14, 1988, OHA; Florida Secretary of State, Division of Corporations, letter to author, December 12, 1989.

13. *Cape Coral Sun,* August/September 1959; Weber interview.

14. Weber interview.

15. Ibid.; *Fort Myers News-Press,* April 14, 1963; *Cape Coral Breeze,* April 1978.

16. *Cape Coral Breeze,* April 1978; Schwartz interview.

17. *Cape Coral Breeze,* April 1978.

18. Freiberg interview; Schwartz interview.

19. Reynolds interview.

20. Freiberg interview.

21. *Cape Coral Breeze,* April 1978.

22. Zeiss, *Other Side,* 135; *Cape Coral Breeze,* April 1978.

23. *Cape Coral Breeze,* April 1983.

24. Gulf American Land Corporation, promotional sales brochure (in possession of author).

25. Weber interview; *Cape Coral Breeze,* April 1978.

26. *Fort Myers News-Press,* March 22, 1978; Weber interview.

27. Edward and Gwen McGinn, taped interview with author, Cape Coral, December 10, 1987, OHA.

28. Eileen Bernard, taped interview with author, St. James City, Florida, January 26, 1988, OHA; *Cape Coral Breeze,* April 1978; *Fort Myers News-Press,* March 22, 1978.

29. Bernard interview; *Cape Coral Breeze,* April 1978; *Fort Myers News-Press,* March 22, 1978.

30. Bernard interview; *Cape Coral Breeze,* April 1978; *Fort Myers News-Press,* March 22, 1978.

31. John M. Warren, taped interview with author, Fort Myers, December 10, 1987, OHA.

32. Ibid.; *Cape Coral Breeze,* April 1978.

33. McGinn interview.

34. Gulf American Land Corporation, promotional sales brochure (in possession of author); Warren interview.

35. *Cape Coral Breeze,* April 1978.

36. Gulf American Land Corporation, promotional sales brochure (in possession of author).

37. *Cape Coral Breeze,* April 1983.

38. Ibid., April 1978.

39. *Fort Myers News-Press,* April 14, 1963.

40. Weber interview.

41. *Fort Myers News-Press,* April 14, 1963; *Cape Coral Sun,* June 1, 1962; *Cape Coral Breeze,* November 22, 1963.

42. *Fort Myers News-Press,* April 14, 1963.

43. Ibid., February 10, 1974; *Cape Coral Breeze,* April 1978; Schwartz interview; Meyer interview.

44. Arthur Rutenberg, interview with author, Clearwater, Florida, May 14, 1988.

45. Ibid.

46. Ibid.

47. Meyer interview.

48. "Arthur Rutenberg: Builder of the Year," *Professional Builder* 52 (January 1989): 385; Rutenberg interview.

49. Meyer interview.

50. Gulf American Land Corporation, promotional sales brochure (original in possession of author); Gulf American Land Corporation, *Annual Report,* 1964, 8 (microfilm, University of South Florida Library).

51. *Cape Coral Breeze,* April 1978; GALC, *Annual Report,* 1962, 9.

52. Meyer interview.

53. Ibid.

54. *Cape Coral Breeze,* April 1978.

55. Sandler interview.

56. Ibid.; Schwartz interview; Freiberg interview.

57. McGinn interview; Bernard interview.

58. Sandler interview; Schwartz interview.

59. Schwartz interview; Pacelli interview.

60. Sandler interview; Schwartz interview; Freiberg interview; Hepner interview.

61. Sandler interview; *Cape Coral Breeze,* April 1978; Pacelli interview.

62. Sandler interview.

63. *Miami News,* March 15, 1964; *Miami Herald,* November 11, 1962.

64. GALC, *Annual Report,* 1962, 4; Florida Secretary of State to author, December 12, 1989.

65. *Fort Myers News-Press,* September 11, 1960; *Cape Coral Breeze,* April 1978.

66. *Fort Myers News-Press,* September 11, 13, and 14, 1960.

67. Ibid., September 11–13, 1960.

68. Ibid., September 13, 1960.

69. Ibid., September 12, 1960; McGinn interview.

70. *Cape Coral Breeze,* April 1978.

71. Ibid.

72. Ibid.

73. Mary Anderson Harborn, taped interview with author, Cape Coral, September 29, 1987, OHA.

74. Meyer interview.

Chapter 4. Purchasing a Land Empire

1. *Cape Coral Breeze,* April 1983.

2. Gulf American Land Corporation, promotional sales brochure (in possession of author).

3. *Fort Myers News-Press,* July 28, 1957. The total acreage of the initial tract, according to county records, was 1,724 acres, not 2,100 as noted in newspaper accounts.

4. Pacelli interview.

5. *Fort Myers News-Press,* December 25, 1969; John Sherman Porter, ed., *Moody's Bank and Finance Manual* (New York: Robert H. Messner, 1962), 1248; *Wall Street Journal,* December 20, 1966; Florida Secretary of State to author, December 12, 1989.

6. Schwartz interview.

7. Hepner interview; Joseph S. Maddlone, taped interview with author, Royal Palm Beach, Florida, February 16, 1988, OHA; Pacelli interview.

8. Gulf American Land Corporation, promotional sales brochure (in possession of author).

9. Weber interview.

10. *Cape Coral Breeze,* April 1983; *Miami Herald,* January 19, 1966.

11. Pacelli interview; Reynolds interview.

12. Rosen, "Remarks," May 7, 1964.

13. *Fort Myers News-Press,* July 31, 1960; Schwartz interview.

14. Leonard Rich, taped interview with author, North Miami Beach, January 27, 1988, OHA; Schwartz interview.

15. James S. Fortiner, taped interview with author, Fort Myers, March 28, 1988, OHA.

16. Ibid.; Reynolds interview.

17. Fortiner interview.

18. Reynolds interview.

19. Ibid.; Fortiner interview; *Fort Myers News-Press,* July 28, 1957; *Official Records of Lee County,* Deed Book 278, 472, Mortgage Book 160, 368, Fort Myers.

20. Fortiner interview; *Official Records of Lee County,* Deed Book 278, 472. Baltimore Investment Associates was made up of Julius J. and Claire Rosen, Leonard and Dorothy Rosen, Samuel J. and Frieda Holtzman, Nathan S. and Sylvia Jacobson, Irvin and Jacqueline Kovens, Stanley J. and Rose J. Silberman, Joseph S. and Amelia Jacobson, Gertrude Holtzman, and H. D. and Helen Van Valkenburg.

21. *Fort Myers News-Press,* July 28, 1957, March 22, 1978; Fortiner inter-

view; *Official Records of Lee County,* Deed Book 278, 472, Deed Book 275, 273–74, Deed Book 274, 44, 46, 51, Deed Book 277, 440, Deed Book 276, 420.

22. Pacelli interview; Reynolds interview.

23. Gigi Mahon, "The War of Fortunes: The Wealthy Phipps Clan Is Rent with Strife," *Barron's,* July 31, 1978, 4–5.

24. *Official Records of Lee County,* Deed Book 243, 515, 519; Reynolds interview.

25. Zeiss, *Other Side,* 174–76.

26. *Official Records of Lee County,* Official Record Book 33, 168–99; Reynolds interview; Hansen interview.

27. Reynolds interview; Hansen interview; Zeiss, *Other Side,* 176.

28. Maddlone interview.

29. *Fort Myers News-Press,* July 31, 1960.

30. Fortiner interview.

31. *Miami Herald,* March 14 and August 16, 1962; Gulf American Land Corporation, promotional sales brochure (in possession of author); *Wall Street Journal,* March 19, 1962 (the cutover cypress lands were located north of the Naples/Immokalee Road and southwest of the Audubon Society's Corkscrew Swamp Bird Sanctuary), January 3, 1963.

32. Gulf American Land Corporation, promotional sales brochure (in possession of author).

33. Ibid.; GALC, *Annual Report,* 1964, 11–13.

34. GALC, *Annual Report,* 1964, 11–12; Hepner interview.

35. Pacelli interview.

36. Ibid.

37. GALC, *Annual Report,* 1964, 11.

38. Weber interview; Pacelli interview.

39. GALC, *Annual Report,* 1964, 12, 1965, 11–12; Research Associates, *Economic Impact,* 27–29; Maddlone interview.

40. *Miami News,* October 6, 1962, June 27, 1965; GALC, *Annual Report,* 1965, 18; Richard D. DeBoast, taped interview with author, Fort Myers, May 23, 1988, OHA.

41. *Miami News,* June 27, 1965; Hepner interview; Pacelli interview.

42. Gulf American Corporation, *Annual Report,* 1967, 19 (microfilm, University of South Florida Library).

43. *Miami News,* June 27, 1965; Research Associates, *Economic Impact,* 33.

44. Research Associates, *Economic Impact,* 33; *Wall Street Journal,* February 16, 1966. The *Wall Street Journal* reported the total acreage to be 63,000 acres.

45. GAC, *Annual Report,* 1967, 18.

46. Hepner interview; *Fort Myers News-Press,* January 15, 1967.

47. GALC, *Annual Report,* 1966, 14; GAC, *Annual Report,* 1967, 18.

48. John Hunter, "Selling Land in Florida," *New Republic,* September 2, 1967, 22; Charles Cavanagh, taped interview with author, Cape Coral, November 18, 1987, OHA.

49. Hepner interview; Rich interview; *Wall Street Journal,* January 24, 1969.

50. GALC, *Annual Report,* 1961, 24; GAC, *Annual Report,* 1967, 16; Maddlone interview.

51. Maddlone interview; Sandler interview.

52. *Fort Myers News-Press,* October 3, 1965, January 8, 1967.

53. Ibid., January 22, 1967.

54. GALC, *Annual Report,* 1966, 2–3; GAC, *Annual Report,* 1967, 10–11; *Wall Street Journal,* November 3, 1966; *Nogales* (Arizona) *Herald,* March 27, 1968.

55. GAC, *Annual Report,* 1967, 10–11.

56. Ibid.; Sandler interview.

57. (Phoenix) *Arizona Republic,* July 6, 1967.

58. Ibid.

59. Ibid.; Sandler interview; Weber interview. Milton Mendelsohn quit working for the Rosens in the early 1960s and was deeply involved in the development and promotion of Rocket City, a land sales project east of Orlando.

60. *Nogales Herald,* March 27, 1968.

61. (Melbourne) *Florida Today,* December 30, 1967; *Miami Herald,* September 1, 1971; "Florida's Land Development Giants," *Florida Trend* 13 (August 1970): 29.

62. *Florida Today,* December 30, 1967.

63. "Florida's Land Development Giants," 29; Weber interview.

64. *Miami Herald,* August 1 and December 9, 1971; Finkernagel and Sanborn interview.

65. GAC, *Annual Report,* 1967, 16; Research Associates, *Economic Impact,* 43; Weber interview.

66. Edwin W. Rochon and K. D. Campbell, "Publicly Held Companies: A Sprinkle of Red Ink Dampens Housing's Quest for Capital," *House and Home* 29 (July 1966): 87–91.

Chapter 5. Selling Florida Land

1. Rosen, "Remarks," May 7, 1964.

2. Ibid.; Pacelli interview; Schwartz interview.

3. Rosen, "Remarks," May 7, 1964.

4. Standard and Poor's Corporation, *Standard Listed Stock Reports,* February 11, 1963, 963k; *Miami Herald,* November 8, 1959. It is difficult to compare the revenue statements of Gulf American with other corporations because it used a fiscal year ending August 31, whereas most corporations used December 31.

5. "Florida's Land Boom Gets Down to Earth," *Business Week,* April 13, 1968, 142; Rochon and Campbell, "Publicly Held Companies," 87–91.

6. Rich interview; Freiberg interview; Cavanagh interview.

7. Schwartz interview.

8. *Cape Coral Breeze,* April 1983.

9. Schwartz interview; Rich interview. Rich attributed Jack's death from a third heart attack at age fifty to Jack's personal frustration with Leonard and to Jack's constant need to compete with his brother.

10. Rich interview; Schwartz interview; Pacelli interview; Freiberg interview; Hepner interview.

11. *Cape Coral Breeze,* April 1983; Schwartz interview.

12. Schwartz interview.

13. Rich interview.

14. *New York Times,* January 13, 1962.

15. *St. Petersburg Times,* November 25, 1977.

16. *Cape Coral Breeze,* April 1978.

17. Schwartz interview; Warren interview.

18. Rich interview; Newsletter of Eppler, Guerin, and Turner, November 1966, Division of Land Sales, Series 141, 324, Box 3, File 1, State Archives; Frank J. St. Clair, ed., *Moody's Bank and Finance Manual* (New York: Robert H. Messner, 1967), 1246–47.

19. Schwartz interview; Pacelli interview; Rich interview.

20. Pacelli interview; Schwartz interview; Hepner interview; Cavanagh interview.

21. Pacelli interview; Rich interview; Schwartz interview.

22. Rich interview; Hepner interview; Cavanagh interview. Louis S. Rosen was not related to Leonard and Jack Rosen.

23. Pacelli interview.

24. Ibid.; Hepner interview; Cavanagh interview.

25. GALC, *Annual Report,* 1963, 1; Joseph Raso, taped interview with author, Cape Coral, March 7, 1988, OHA; Schwartz interview; Maddlone interview.

26. Schwartz interview; Maddlone interview; Freiberg interview.

27. Raso interview.

28. Rich interview; Hepner interview.

29. Hepner interview; Schwartz interview; Cavanagh interview.

30. Hepner interview.

31. Ibid.; Schwartz interview; Freiberg interview; Rich interview; Cavanagh interview; *Miami Herald,* January 18 and 19, 1966.

32. Rich interview.

33. Hepner interview; Freiberg interview.

34. Hepner interview.

35. Sandler interview; Cavanagh interview.

36. Pacelli interview.

37. Freiberg interview; Hepner interview.

38. Freiberg interview.

39. Meyer interview; Freiberg interview; Pacelli interview; the *Florida Opportunity Digest* (in possession of author).

40. Hepner interview.

41. Rich interview; Freiberg interview.

42. Freiberg interview.

43. Ibid.

44. Schwartz interview.

45. Freiberg interview; "From the Top Drawer of Gulf American," internal corporate sales memo, vol. 3, no. 2, May 1964 (in possession of author).

46. Freiberg interview; Rich interview.

47. Rich interview; Hepner interview; Morton C. Paulson, *The Great Land Hustle* (Chicago: Henry Regnery, 1972), 142.

48. Freiberg interview; Pacelli interview; Rich interview; Cavanagh interview.

49. Rich interview; Hepner interview; Sandler interview.

50. *Wall Street Journal,* March 15, 1966; Rich interview; Cavanagh interview; Freiberg interview.

51. *Decatur* (Illinois) *Review,* July 18, 1967; Cavanagh interview.

52. Rich interview.

53. *Wall Street Journal,* March 15, 1966.

54. McGinn interview; Bernard interview; Freiberg interview; Rich interview.

55. Freiberg interview; Rich interview.

56. Sandler interview.

57. Hepner interview; Schwartz interview; Freiberg interview.

58. Pacelli interview; Cavanagh interview; Rich interview.

59. Rich interview; Bernard interview.

60. Raso interview; Schwartz interview; Hepner interview.

61. Hepner interview.

62. Schwartz interview; Warren interview.

63. Schwartz interview; Pacelli interview.

64. Raso interview; Warren interview; *Cape Coral Breeze,* April 1978.

65. Warren interview.

66. Al Hirshberg, "Hard Sell in Boom Land," *Life,* November 13, 1964, 67, 74.

67. Warren interview; Freiberg interview; Rich interview.

68. Warren interview; Rich interview; Meyer interview; Connie Mack, Jr., taped interview with author, Fort Myers, July 20, 1988, OHA.

69. Hepner interview; Schwartz interview; Mack interview; Maddlone interview.

70. Rich interview; Warren interview.

71. Rich interview; Warren interview.

72. Meyer interview.

73. Warren interview.

74. Ibid.; *Christian Science Monitor,* March 7, 1962.

75. Rich interview.

76. Hepner interview; Pacelli interview; Raso interview.

77. Pacelli interview.

78. *Wall Street Journal,* March 15, 1966; Hepner interview; Rich interview; Bernard interview.

79. Pacelli interview; *Key West Citizen,* September 23, 1962.

80. Rich interview.

81. Pacelli interview.

82. Rich interview; Raso interview; Hepner interview; Pacelli interview.

83. Meyer interview; Carol McNeely, taped interview with author, Cape Coral, October 30, 1988, OHA.

84. Raso interview.

85. *Fort Myers News-Press,* February 10, 1974; Schwartz interview.

86. *Cape Coral Breeze,* April 1978.

87. Schwartz interview.

88. Meyer interview; Rich interview.

89. *Miami Herald,* September 16, 1962.

90. Trevor Armbrister, "Land Frauds," *Saturday Evening Post* 236 (April 27, 1963): 21.

91. *Miami Herald,* September 16, 1962; Warren interview; Armbrister, "Land Frauds," 22.

92. Pacelli interview; Hirshberg, "Hard Sell," 74.

93. Raso interview; Rich interview.

94. Schwartz interview; Hepner interview; Meyer interview; Cavanagh interview; Freiberg interview.

95. *Cape Coral Breeze,* April 1983.

96. Schwartz interview; Pacelli interview; Meyer interview; Rich interview.

97. *Cape Coral Breeze,* April 1983.

Chapter 6. Financing the Gulf American Corporation

1. *Cape Coral Breeze,* April 1983.

2. Gulf Guaranty Land and Title Company, promotional sales brochure (in possession of author).

3. Pacelli interview.

4. *Miami Herald,* January 19, 1964; *Wall Street Journal,* November 2, 1962.

5. Rosen, "Remarks," May 7, 1964.

6. Rich interview; Schwartz interview.

7. Rich interview; *Wall Street Journal,* November 2, 1962.

8. Freiberg interview; Rich interview; Hepner interview; Schwartz interview; Sandler interview.

9. Rosen, "Remarks," May 7, 1964.

10. *Cape Coral Breeze,* April 1978; Schwartz interview; Finkernagel and Sanborn interview.

11. Gulf Guaranty Land and Title Company, promotional sales brochures (in possession of author).

12. *Cape Coral Breeze,* April 1983.

13. Mack interview; McNeely interview.

14. John Sherman Porter, ed., *Moody's Bank and Finance Manual* (New York: D. F. Shea, 1961), 1253; *Miami News,* December 2, 1960.

15. Meyer interview.

16. *Wall Street Journal,* January 10, June 4, and July 20, 1962; *Miami Herald,* March 9, 1962.

17. Maddlone interview.

18. Ibid.; *Wall Street Journal,* July 24, 1962.

19. *Miami News,* October 30, 1963.

20. *Wall Street Journal,* July 1, 1964; *Miami Herald,* July 3, 1964.

21. *Wall Street Journal,* December 29, 1964.

22. Frank J. St. Clair, ed., *Moody's Bank and Finance Manual* (New York: Robert H. Messner, 1965), 707–8.

23. *Miami Herald,* January 19 and July 3, 1964; *Wall Street Journal,* August 5, 1964.

24. *Wall Street Journal,* June 13 and July 9 and 30, 1963. The four Fenestra directors were Harry Brainin, Irving Taub, Irving Projansky, and F. B. Kaiserman.

25. Ibid., July 30, 1963.

26. Ibid.

27. "Milestones," *Time,* May 22, 1972, 104; *New York Times,* June 14, 1968; "Obituaries," *Newsweek,* February 17, 1986, 43; "How Bob Pritzker Runs a Three Billion Dollar Empire," *Business Week,* March 7, 1983, 64.

28. *Wall Street Journal,* August 22, 1963, January 30, 1964; *Miami Herald,* January 31, 1964; Sandler interview.

29. *Wall Street Journal,* April 7 and November 10, 1966, July 3 and December 6, 1967.

30. *Miami Herald,* July 3, 1964.

31. Ibid.; Meyer interview.

32. *Wall Street Journal,* August 10 and December 20, 1966, January 6 and April 14, 1967.

33. Frank J. St. Clair, ed., *Moody's Bank and Finance Manual* (New York: Robert H. Messner, 1968), 1241–42.

34. *Wall Street Journal,* December 19, 1967; Maddlone interview.

35. *Wall Street Journal,* June 26 and December 12, 1961; *New York Times,* December 15, 1961.

36. *Wall Street Journal,* October 20, November 9, and December 7 and 12, 1961, January 18, 1968; St. Clair, *Finance Manual* (1968), 1241–42.

37. *Wall Street Journal,* May 27, 1968.

38. GALC, *Annual Report,* 1964, 25; GAC, *Annual Report,* 1967, 13; *Wall Street Journal,* December 20, 1966; Florida Secretary of State to author, December 12, 1989.

39. GALC, *Annual Report,* 1964, 25; *Miami News,* July 30, 1963.

40. Meyer interview; Sandler interview; Warren interview.

41. Meyer interview.

42. Ibid.

43. *Wall Street Journal,* May 25, 1966; *Miami Herald,* December 24, 1967; GAC, *Annual Report,* 1967, 14–15.

44. *Wall Street Journal,* February 12 and 13, 1963.

45. GALC, *Annual Report,* 1966, 16; GAC, *Annual Report,* 1967, 12; *Wall Street Journal,* February 24, 1966, November 18, 1965; *Miami News,* March 1, 1966; Hepner interview.

46. Maddlone interview.

47. Rich interview; Schwartz interview.

48. Schwartz interview.

49. Freiberg interview.

50. Meyer interview.

51. Barry Horenbein, taped interview with author, Tallahassee, January 24, 1990, OHA.

52. Maddlone interview.

53. St. Clair, *Finance Manual* (1968), 1241–42.

54. *Miami Herald,* December 11, 1962.

55. *Wall Street Journal,* August 5, 1964; Rosen, "Remarks," May 7, 1964; GALC, *Annual Report,* 1964, 2–3; 1965, 3, 6; Rochon and Campbell, "Publicly Held Companies," 90–91.

56. Schwartz interview; Rich interview.

57. *Cape Coral Breeze,* April 1983.

58. Hepner interview; Sandler interview; Freiberg interview; Rich interview.

Chapter 7. Promoting Florida Living

1. Schwartz interview; Rich interview; Freiberg interview.

2. Freiberg interview; Robert H. Finkernagel, Jr., taped interview with author, Cape Coral, December 11, 1987, OHA.

3. Freiberg interview; *Fort Myers News-Press,* December 18, 20, and 21, 1968.

4. Hepner interview; Rich interview; *New York Times,* advertising supplement, June 25, 1967.

5. *New York Times,* advertising supplement, June 25, 1967; *Miami Herald, Tropic* magazine, December 3, 1967.

6. *Miami Herald, Tropic* magazine, December 3, 1967; Freiberg interview; Rich interview; Horenbein interview; Richard G. Sayers, taped interview with author, Charlotte Harbour, Florida, December 23, 1987, OHA.

7. Finkernagel interview; David W. Neft, Roland T. Johnson, Richard M. Cohen, and Jordan A. Deutsch, *The Sports Encyclopedia: Pro Football* (New York: Grosset and Dunlap, 1974), 286.

8. Finkernagel interview; Mack interview; Ronald L. Mendell and Timothy B. Phares, *Who's Who in Football* (New Rochelle, N.Y.: Arlington House, 1974), 290.

9. GALC, *Annual Report,* 1964, 14–15; Finkernagel interview.

10. Hepner interview; Reynolds interview; Mack interview; Richard G. Crawford, taped interview with author, Cape Coral, December 10, 1987, OHA; Warren interview; Freiberg interview.

11. GALC, *Annual Report,* 1964, 15; Rich interview; Finkernagel interview.

12. Mack interview (the four-story office building is located on the northwest corner of the intersection of Del Prado Boulevard and Cape Coral Parkway); Finkernagel interview; Finkernagel and Sanborn interview; Sayers interview; Bernard interview.

13. Finkernagel and Sanborn interview; Mack interview; *Cape Coral Breeze,* January 4, 1962.

14. Finkernagel and Sanborn interview; *Cape Coral Breeze,* May 3, 1962.

15. Finkernagel interview.

16. Crawford interview; *Cape Coral Breeze,* May 3, 1962.

17. Finkernagel and Sanborn interview; Finkernagel interview; *Cape Coral Breeze,* April 1978, April 1988.

18. *Cape Coral Breeze,* April 1978; Finkernagel interview.

19. Finkernagel interview; Schwartz interview; *Cape Coral Breeze,* May 17, 1962, April 1978, and April 1988. Tate was instrumental in the establishment of the Cape Coral Hospital.

20. Crawford interview; Finkernagel interview; *Cape Coral Breeze,* October 11, 1962, April 1978; *GAC Sun,* Spring 1970.

21. *GAC Sun,* Spring 1970; Crawford interview.

22. Crawford interview; Finkernagel interview; Mack interview; *Cape Coral Breeze,* October 11, 1962. Cassel's radio stations included WBIL in Leesburg, Florida, WCOA in Pensacola, and two stations in Pennsylvania.

23. Finkernagel interview; Mack interview; Crawford interview; *GAC Sun,* Spring 1970; *Editor and Publisher International Yearbook* (New York: Editor and Publisher, 1988), I-383.

24. Schwartz interview.

25. GALC, *Annual Report,* 1964, 8; Finkernagel interview; Finkernagel and Sanborn interview.

26. Finkernagel interview; Finkernagel and Sanborn interview; Sayers interview; GALC, *Annual Report,* 1963, 8, 1966, 6–7; *Cape Coral Breeze,* April 1978.

27. Finkernagel interview; Sayers interview; *Cape Coral Breeze,* April 1978.

28. Finkernagel interview; Sayers interview; *Cape Coral Breeze,* April 1978; Finkernagel and Sanborn interview.

29. Finkernagel interview.

30. Ibid.; Eileen Bernard, *Lies That Came True* (Ocoee, Fla.: Anna Publishing, 1983), 192–94, 195; Sayers interview; *Fort Myers News-Press,* March 22, 1978.

31. Bernard, *Lies That Came True,* 194–95; Joseph Miller and Agnes Miller, taped interview with author, Coral Springs, Florida, January 27, 1988, OHA.

32. Miller interview.

33. *Miami Herald,* January 18, 1966; Miller interview.

34. Freiberg interview.

35. Ibid.; Gunter Przystawik, taped interview with author, Cape Coral, January 25, 1988, OHA.

36. Przystawik interview; *Cape Coral Breeze,* February 26, 1970.

37. *Cape Coral Breeze,* February 26, 1970; Przystawik interview; Freiberg interview.

38. Przystawik interview; *Cape Coral Breeze,* February 26, 1970.

39. Freiberg interview; Finkernagel interview; GALC, *Annual Report,* 1963, 8, 1965, 14–15.

40. Weber interview; Przystawik interview; Cape Coral Gardens brochure (in possession of author); *Fort Myers News-Press,* November 4, 1973.

41. Finkernagel interview; Freiberg interview; GALC, *Annual Report,* 1966, 7; *Fort Myers News-Press,* November 4, 1973; *New York Times,* advertising supplement, June 25, 1967; Cavanagh interview. Jack Rosen's friend, Milt Kessler, was the Gulf American contact with Borglum. The Iwo Jima statue has been restored and is presently located on the corner of Del Prado Boulevard and Viscaya Parkway. The pietà was donated to St. Andrew's Catholic Church in Cape Coral. Various busts are located at the Cape Coral Historical Museum.

42. Finkernagel interview; Freiberg interview; GALC, *Annual Report,* 1965, 13, 15; *Fort Myers News-Press,* March 22, 1978; "McCall's Certified House," *McCall's Magazine,* July 1965, 112.

43. *Miami Herald,* May 20, 1969; *Fort Myers News-Press,* November 4, 1973.

44. Przystawik interview.

45. Meyer interview; Freiberg interview; *St. Petersburg Times,* September 7, 1970; Miller interview; Przystawik interview. Larry Rosen was unrelated to Jack and Leonard Rosen.

46. *Cape Coral Breeze,* December 15, 1966.

47. *Miami Herald,* May 19, 1969; *Fort Myers News-Press,* May 21, 1969, November 4, 1973; *St. Petersburg Times,* May 24, 1969; *Minutes of the Trustees of the Internal Improvement Trust Fund,* vol. 37 (Tallahassee: State Printer, 1971), 304–5; Hansen interview.

48. *St. Petersburg Times,* May 24, 1969; *Fort Myers News-Press,* May 21, 1969.

49. *Fort Myers News-Press,* November 4, 1973.

50. Przystawik interview; *Cape Coral Breeze,* April 5, 1982.

51. *Miami Herald,* July 3, 1956, September 18, 1957; *Miami News,* June 1, 1961.

52. Sayers interview; Finkernagel interview.

53. Bernard interview; Finkernagel interview; Schwartz interview. Bernard was angry for some time over the low wages paid by Gulf American. She had been making $15,000 annually with American Cyanamid in New York but was hired at Fort Myers for only $2,700 a year.

54. Bernard interview; *Fort Myers News-Press,* March 22, 1978.

55. Sayers interview; Crawford interview.

56. Sayers interview; Bernard interview.

57. Sayers interview; Bernard interview; Freiberg interview; Finkernagel interview; *Cape Coral Breeze,* April 1988.

58. Sayers interview.

59. Miller interview.

60. Ibid.; Sayers interview.

61. Miller interview.

62. Ibid.; Raso interview.

63. Akin, *Flagler,* 184–85.

64. George, "Brokers," 38–39.

65. *Cape Coral Breeze,* April 1978; *Fort Myers News-Press,* March 22, 1978; Miller interview; Harborn interview.

66. *Cape Coral Sun,* August/September 1963.

67. *Cape Coral Breeze,* August 10, 1968; *Fort Myers News-Press,* March 22, 1978.

68. Hepner interview; Rosen, "Remarks," May 7, 1964; Miller interview.

69. Meyer interview.

70. Ibid.

71. Ibid.; Cavanagh interview.

72. Meyer interview; Hepner interview.

73. Cavanagh interview.

74. Ibid.

75. Ibid.; Hepner interview.

76. Cavanagh interview; Hepner interview; Rich interview.

77. Cavanagh interview; Hepner interview; Rich interview.

78. *Wall Street Journal,* February 4 and May 25, 1966; *Miami Herald,* December 24, 1967; Sandler interview.

79. *Miami Herald,* December 24, 1967.

80. Ibid.; *Fort Myers News-Press,* February 2, 1968; *New York Times,* advertising supplement, June 25, 1967; Sandler interview.

81. Meyer interview; Cavanagh interview.

82. Cavanagh interview.

83. *Official Minutes of the Lee County Commission,* November 18, 1965, Book 28, 46, December 15, 1965, Book 28, 65, February 9, 1966, Book 29, 20, Fort Myers.

84. Ibid., November 15, 1967, Book 34, 23; Meyer interview; Finkernagel and Sanborn interview; *Miami Herald,* January 6, 1968.

85. *Miami Herald,* December 24, 1967; *Fort Myers News-Press,* January 9 and February 2, 1968; Cavanagh interview.

86. Cavanagh interview; *Fort Myers News-Press,* February 17, 1971.

87. *Miami Herald, Tropic* magazine, December 3, 1967; Louis J. Rolland, "General Development's Plan," *Financial World,* November 2, 1960, 22.

88. Hepner interview; Rich interview; Schwartz interview.

89. Gulf American Land Corporation, promotional sales brochure, *Golden Gate Estates: Your Golden Opportunity for a Prosperous Future* (in possession of author); Hirshberg, "Hard Sell," 73.

90. Sayers interview; GAC, *Annual Report,* 1967, 6.

91. Freiberg interview.

92. George, "Brokers," 30–35.

Chapter 8. Growing Pains: 1964 to 1967

1. See table 1; Rochon and Campbell, "Publicly Held Companies," 87.

2. Rosen, "Remarks," May 7, 1964.

3. *Fort Myers News-Press,* October 1, 1967.

4. *Miami Herald, Tropic* magazine, December 3, 1967.

5. *Miami Herald,* May 18, 1960.

6. Rochon and Campbell, "Publicly Held Companies," 87.

7. Research Publishing Corporation, *Florida Business Letter,* April 15, 1965, 1.

8. *Fort Myers News-Press,* November 12, 1963; GALC, *Annual Report,* 1964, 8; GAC, *Annual Report,* 1967, 17; Lawrence A. Armour, "Sand in Their Shoes," *Barron's,* June 13, 1966, 3.

9. *Fort Myers News-Press,* November 12, 1963.

10. Ibid., October 1, 1967.

11. *Cape Coral Breeze,* April 1983; Rich interview.

12. Schwartz interview; Grismer, *Fort Myers,* 215–41.

13. Schwartz interview; Mack interview.

14. *Fort Myers News-Press,* October 13, 1961. Site A was not mentioned in any of the reports made public by the newspaper, indicating that it was not recommended by the engineering firm.

15. Schwartz interview; Mack interview; Hepner interview.

16. Schwartz interview; *Official Records of Lee County,* January 16, 1961,

Official Record Book 46, 256; Frank J. St. Clair, ed., *Moody's Bank and Finance Manual* (New York: Robert H. Messner, 1963), 855.

17. Schwartz interview; *Official Records of Lee County,* July 6, 1962, Official Record Book 142, 211. Schwartz was represented by William Carmine, a Fort Myers attorney who later went to work for Gulf American.

18. Schwartz interview; Crawford interview; Mack interview.

19. *Fort Myers News-Press,* October 13, 1961.

20. Ibid., October 8 and 13, 1961; *Official Minutes of the Lee County Commission,* May 16, 1962, Book 21, 19.

21. *Fort Myers News-Press,* October 8 and 13, 1961; *Official Minutes of the Lee County Commission,* May 16, 1962, Book 21, 19.

22. *Fort Myers News-Press,* October 8 and 13, 1961; *Official Minutes of the Lee County Commission,* October 20, 1961, Book 20, 17, 18A–F, November 8, 1961, Book 20, 24I; Schwartz interview.

23. Schwartz interview; Crawford interview; *Fort Myers News-Press,* March 22, 1978.

24. *Cape Coral Breeze,* August 10, 1968; Crawford interview.

25. *Cape Coral Breeze,* December 14, 1961, August 10, 1968; Crawford interview. The members of the organizing committee for the Cape Coral Civic Association were Mr. and Mrs. H. L. Weinberg, Col. and Mrs. Lowell Mills, Mr. and Mrs. Leroy Prevellet, Lt. Col. and Mrs. Richard G. Crawford, Mr. and Mrs. Aage Schroder, Fred G. Hulburd, H. James Orefice, Browning Wharton, Clarence Duffala, B. L. Killian, John McEwen, Lt. Col. Kathleen McClure, and Joseph Raso.

26. Crawford interview; *Cape Coral Breeze,* August 10, 1968.

27. Maddlone interview.

28. Ibid.; *Official Minutes of the Lee County Commission,* December 5, 1962, Book 22, 31.

29. *Official Minutes of the Lee County Commission,* May 16, 1962, Book 20, 19, June 2, 1962, Book 21, 19–20A; *Cape Coral Breeze,* May 17, 1962; *Cape Coral Sun,* June 1, 1962.

30. *Official Minutes of the Lee County Commission,* August 8, 1962, Book 21, 47, November 12, 1962, Book 22, 23, November 7, 1962, Book 22, 20–22; *Cape Coral Breeze,* October 11, 1962.

31. *Cape Coral Breeze,* August 10, 1968; *Cape Coral Sun,* June 1, 1962; GAC, *Annual Report,* 1967, 17; *Fort Myers News-Press,* January 1, 1975. With the completion of a second parallel span in 1989, a one-way toll of seventy-five cents was reinstated.

32. Schwartz interview; Warren interview; Mack interview; *Cape Coral Breeze,* August 10, 1968.

33. GALC, *Annual Report,* 1964, 7, 1966, 8.

34. Ibid., 1965, 7; *Cape Coral Breeze,* April 1978, April 1988.

35. *Cape Coral Breeze,* August 10, 1968; Miller interview.

36. *Cape Coral Breeze,* August 10, 1968, February 7, 1964.

37. DeBoast interview; *Fort Myers News-Press,* January 7, 1968.

38. *Fort Myers News-Press,* January 7, 1968.

39. *Cape Coral Breeze,* April 1978; *Miami Herald,* October 7, 1965.

40. *Fort Myers News-Press,* October 7 and 10, 1965.

41. Ibid., June 23, 1983, October 10, 1965; *Miami Herald,* October 7, 1965.

42. *Fort Myers News-Press,* October 10, 1965.

43. *Miami Herald,* October 7, 1965; *Fort Myers News-Press,* October 7, 1965, January 14, 1966.

44. *Fort Myers News-Press,* October 10, 1965; *Miami Herald,* October 7, 1965.

45. *Miami Herald,* October 7, 1965.

46. *Fort Myers News-Press,* November 12, 1963, October 10, 1965.

47. *Cape Coral Breeze,* April 1978; DeBoast interview.

48. *Fort Myers News-Press,* January 14, 1966; *Miami Herald,* January 21, 1966.

49. *Cape Coral Breeze,* April 1978.

50. *Miami Herald,* January 21, 1966; Pacelli interview; Finkernagel and Sanborn interview.

51. *Miami Herald,* January 21, 1966, advertising section, March 27, 1966.

52. *Fort Myers News-Press,* January 14, 1966; *Miami Herald,* January 21, 1966.

53. *Miami Herald,* January 21, 1966; *Fort Myers News-Press,* August 27, 1967; Hepner interview; Sayers interview; Mack interview.

54. Finkernagel and Sanborn interview; Millard Bowen, taped interview with author, Cape Coral, December 14, 1987, OHA. Pacelli interview.

55. Mack interview; Schwartz interview; DeBoast interview; *Miami Herald,* January 21, 1966.

56. GALC, *Annual Report,* 1965, 1, 1966, 1; DeBoast interview; Schwartz interview.

57. Mack interview; Schwartz interview; DeBoast interview; Reynolds interview.

58. Finkernagel and Sanborn interview; Schwartz interview; Mack interview.

59. Schwartz interview.

60. Ibid.; *Miami Herald,* advertising section, March 27, 1966.

61. Schwartz interview; *Miami Herald,* advertising section, March 27, 1966.

62. Weber interview; Meyer interview; Pacelli interview.

63. Bowen interview.

64. Pacelli interview; DeBoast interview; Mack interview.

65. Schwartz interview.

66. DeBoast interview; Bowen interview; Rich interview; *Fort Myers News-Press,* August 29, 1967, January 14, 1966; *Cape Coral Breeze,* April 1978.

67. *Cape Coral Breeze,* April 1978; GALC, *Annual Report,* 1965, 9.

68. *Cape Coral Breeze,* April 1978; GALC, *Annual Report,* 1965, 9.

69. GALC, *Annual Report,* 1966, 9; *Cape Coral Breeze,* April 1978; Rich interview.

70. *Cape Coral Breeze,* April 1978.

71. Ibid., December 15, 1966; *Fort Myers News-Press,* January 1, 1967.

72. *Florida Statutes,* chap. 711, 1963; DeBoast interview.

73. Russell McCaughan, "The Florida Condominium Act Applied," *University of Florida Law Review* 17 (Summer 1964): 1.

74. GALC, *Annual Report,* 1966, 8; *Fort Myers News-Press,* January 1, 1967.

75. *Miami Herald,* November 11, 1964.

76. Ibid.; GAC, *Annual Report,* 1967, 27.

77. GAC, *Annual Report,* 1967, 27; GALC, *Annual Report,* 1966, 12; *Collier County* (Naples) *News,* January 9, 1968.

78. GALC, *Annual Report,* 1966, 12; Pacelli interview.

79. Pacelli interview; Meyer interview; *Golden Gate Estates* brochure; Vince Conboy, *Exposé: Florida's Billion Dollar Land Fraud* (Naples, Fla.: Vince Conboy, 1972), 12–14. Conboy was a realtor and longtime resident of Naples.

80. GAC, *Annual Report,* 1967, 18; Research Associates, *Economic Impact,* 33–36, 43; Weber interview.

81. Thomas W. Pew, Jr., "Peddling the Great West," *Saturday Review,* September 4, 1971, 51.

Chapter 9. Regulating the Land Giants

1. Schwartz interview; Rochon and Campbell, "Publicly Held Companies," 90–91.

2. Schwartz interview; Pacelli interview; Meyer interview.

3. *Miami Herald, Tropic* magazine, December 3, 1967; Schwartz interview; Hepner interview.

4. *Miami Herald,* August 8, 1957; *Florida Statutes,* chap. 475, 1953.

5. *Miami Herald,* July 3, 1956.

6. *Journal of the Florida House of Representatives,* extraordinary session, 1955–56, 6; *Florida Across the Threshold: The Administration of Governor LeRoy Collins, January 4, 1955–January 3, 1961* (Tallahassee: State Printer, 1961), 367; *Florida Statutes,* chap. 475, 1956. The 1956 law amended sections 475.47 through 475.55.

7. Stephen Trumbull to Governor LeRoy Collins, August 6, 1957, Leroy Collins Papers, Series 776, RG 102, Box 75, File 3, State Archives; *Miami Herald,* August 18, 1957.

8. Governor LeRoy Collins to Walter S. Hardin, August 26, 1957, Walter S. Hardin, to Governor LeRoy Collins, September 9, 1957, Collins Papers.

9. Senate Special Committee on Aging, *Hearings before the Subcommittee on Frauds and Misrepresentations Affecting the Elderly,* pt. 2, 88th Cong., 2d sess., May 19, 1964, 166; *Florida Statutes,* chap. 475, 1959. The sections that were amended were 475.51 and 475.52.

10. Senate Committee on Banking and Currency, Subcommittee on Securities, *Interstate Land Sales Full Disclosure Act of 1967,* 90th Cong., 1st sess., February 28 and March 1, 1967, 404; *New York Times,* May 16, 1963; *Florida Statutes,* chap. 478, 1963; *Miami News,* April 4, 1963. The committee had representatives from the land development industry, banking, local government, the legal profession, and chambers of commerce, for a total of thirteen members.

11. Senate Special Committee on Aging, *Hearings,* May 19, 1964, 166–67.

12. *New York Times,* September 5, 1965.

13. Paulson, *Great Land Hustle,* 166; Senate Subcommittee on Securities, *Disclosure Act of 1967,* 293; Senate Committee on Banking and Currency, *Interstate Land Sales Full Disclosure Act,* 88th Cong., 2d sess., June 21 and 22

and August 18, 1966, 134; *Miami Herald,* January 23, 1966. Governor Burns worked as a consultant for Gulf American after leaving office.

14. *Florida Statutes,* chap. 478, 1967; Charles E. Myler, "An Analysis of Promotional Practices of Selected Land Developers in the State of Florida" (Ph.D. diss., University of Florida, 1970), 12.

15. *New York Times,* March 15, 1963.

16. Senate Special Subcommittee on Aging, *Hearings,* May 18, 1964, 242–45.

17. Ibid., 2.

18. Ibid., May 19, 1964, 148–49.

19. Paulson, *Great Land Hustle,* 164.

20. Senate Special Subcommittee on Aging, *Hearings,* May 19, 1964, 161, 173.

21. Ibid., 172.

22. Robert G. Sherrill, "The Power Game: George Smathers, the Golden Senator from Florida," *Nation,* December 7, 1964, 431.

23. Senate Special Subcommittee on Aging, *Hearings,* May 18, 1964, 19.

24. Ibid., 103–4; *New York Times,* September 5, 1965.

25. Senate Special Subcommittee on Aging, *Hearings,* May 19, 1964, 180–81.

26. Freiberg interview.

27. *Minutes of the Florida Installment Land Sales Board,* vol. 1, January 20, 1964, 40, Division of Land Sales, Tallahassee; Fails, Willis, and McCall, report to Florida Installment Land Sales Board, March 25, 1964, Division of Land Sales, Series 141, RG 324, Box 3, File 1, State Archives.

28. Senate Special Subcommittee on Aging, *Hearings,* May 18, 1964, 101–2.

29. Herman J. Hastings, letter to Florida Real Estate Commission, August 28, 1963, Division of Land Sales, Series 845, RG 324, Box 33, File AD63053, State Archives; *Minutes of FILSB,* vol. 1, January 25, 1965, 119.

30. *Minutes of FILSB,* vol. 1, December 14, 1964, 106, January 25, 1965, 119, March 4, 1965, 125.

31. Ibid., April 3, 1964, 58, June 19, 1964, 65–66, 70.

32. Florida Installment Land Sales Board, internal memo, February 12, 1967, Claude Kirk Papers, Series 923, RG 102, Box 49, File 11, State Archives.

33. *Miami Herald,* January 23, 1966.

34. *Minutes of FILSB,* vol. 1, July 15, 1965, 159–60; *Miami News,* November 5, 1965.

35. *Minutes of FILSB,* vol. 1, January 28, 1966, 208, October 10, 1966, 264–65.

36. *Wall Street Journal,* October 12, 1966.

37. *New York Times,* May 10, 1967.

38. Senate Special Subcommittee on Aging, *Hearings,* May 20, 1964, 285, 293; Senate Committee on Banking and Currency, *Interstate Land Sales,* June 21 and 22 and August 18, 1966, 163; *Interstate Land Sales Full Disclosure Act,* 82 stat. 590, sec. 1401, August 1, 1968.

39. *Miami Herald,* September 7, 1966; Paulson, *Great Land Hustle,* 167; Senate Committee on Banking and Currency, *Interstate Land Sales,* June 21 and 22 and August 18, 1966, 472.

40. *Miami Herald,* September 7, 1966.

41. Conboy, *Exposé,* 72–73.

42. *Miami Herald,* December 18, 1966.

43. Conboy, *Exposé,* 74, 76–77; *Fort Myers News-Press,* January 10, 1967; *Miami Herald,* January 5, 1968.

44. *Miami Herald,* advertising supplement, March 27, 1966; *Wall Street Journal,* June 27, 1967.

45. Tebeau, *History of Florida,* 446–47; Schwartz interview.

46. *St. Petersburg Times,* October 18, 1967.

47. *Miami Herald,* June 29, 1967; *Minutes of FILSB,* vol. 2, January 27, 1967, 4, 12.

48. *Wall Street Journal,* June 28, 1967; *Miami Herald,* June 29, 1967; Weber interview.

49. *Miami Herald,* June 29, 1967; *Minutes of FILSB,* vol. 2, April 25, 1967, 37.

50. *Wall Street Journal,* June 28, 1967; *Florida Statutes,* chap. 478, 1967.

51. *Wall Street Journal,* June 28, 1967; *Miami Herald,* June 29, 1967.

52. *Miami Herald,* June 29, 1967.

53. James R. Layden to Carl A. Bertoch, June 22, 1967, Kirk Papers.

54. *Minutes of FILSB,* vol. 2, May 26, 1967, 47.

55. *St. Petersburg Times,* October 10, 1967; *Wall Street Journal,* June 28, 1967.

56. *Wall Street Journal,* June 28, 1967.

57. Ibid.

58. Ibid., *Minutes of FILSB,* vol. 2, January 27, 1967, 12.

59. *Wall Street Journal,* June 28, 1967; Weber interview; Pacelli interview.

60. Schwartz interview; *Miami Herald,* June 29, 1967.

61. Carl A. Bertoch to James R. Layden, June 26, 1967, Kirk Papers.

62. Pacelli interview; Weber interview.

63. Schwartz interview.

64. Weber interview.

65. *Wall Street Journal,* July 1, 1967; *New York Times,* October 10, 1967; *Baltimore Sun,* June 29, 1967.

66. *Wall Street Journal,* June 29, 1967.

67. Ibid., July 1, 1967; *Baltimore Sun,* June 29, 1967; *New York Times,* July 10, 1967.

68. *Wall Street Journal,* June 30, 1967.

69. *Baltimore Sun,* June 29, 1967; *New York Times,* July 10, 1967.

70. *New York Times,* July 10, 1967.

71. Ibid.; Leonard Rosen to Governor Claude Kirk, July 7, 1967, Kirk Papers.

72. *Wall Street Journal,* August 3, 1967.

73. Governor Jack Williams to Governor Claude Kirk, July 10, 1967, Kirk Papers; *Nogales Herald,* July 7, 1967; *Arizona Republic,* July 7, 1967; (Tucson) *Arizona Daily Star,* July 7, 1967.

74. *Wall Street Journal,* August 3, 1967; *New York Times,* August 9 and 23, 1967; *Minutes of the Florida Land Sales Board,* vol. 2, August 23, 1967, 67, Division of Land Sales, Tallahassee.

75. *Orlando Sentinel,* September 22, 1967; *Wall Street Journal,* September 25 and 29, 1967.

76. *Wall Street Journal,* September 29, 1967; *Miami Herald,* October 3, 1967; Horenbein interview.

77. *Wall Street Journal,* October 16, 1967; *New York Times,* October 17 and November 9, 1967.

78. *Washington Post,* October 14, 1967.

79. *St. Petersburg Times,* January 21, 1968; Fred J. Cook, "Governor Kirk's Private Eyes," *Nation,* May 15, 1967, 62; "When a State Opens Its Own War on Crime . . . ," *U.S. News and World Report,* May 22, 1967, 61–62.

80. Ralph de Toledano and Philip V. Brennan, Jr., *Claude Kirk: Man and Myth* (Moonachie, N.J.: Pyramid Publications, 1970), 104.

81. *St. Petersburg Times,* January 21, 1968.

82. *Wall Street Journal,* November 9, 1967; Horenbein interview.

83. *Wall Street Journal,* November 9, 1967; Horenbein interview.

84. *Wall Street Journal,* November 9, 1967; Horenbein interview.

85. Horenbein interview.

86. Ibid.

87. Ibid.; *Washington Post,* October 14, 1967.

88. Horenbein interview.

89. Ibid.

90. *Washington Post,* October 14, 1967; *Wall Street Journal,* November 9, 1967.

91. *Minutes of FLSB,* vol. 2, October 13, 1967, 92–95.

92. *New York Times,* October 17, 1967.

93. *Wall Street Journal,* October 17, 1967.

94. Ibid., November 10, 1967.

95. Ibid., June 28, 1967; *Miami Herald,* November 12, 1967.

96. *Miami Herald,* November 11, 1967; *Miami News,* November 11, 1967; *New York Times,* November 11, 1967; *Baltimore Sun,* November 11, 1967.

97. *Miami Herald,* November 11, 1967; *Wall Street Journal,* January 22, 1968.

98. *Miami Herald,* November 11, 1967; *Wall Street Journal,* January 22, 1968.

99. *Miami Herald,* November 11, 1967; *St. Petersburg Times,* November 11, 1967.

100. *Miami Herald,* November 11, 1967.

101. Ibid.

102. Ibid.

103. Ibid.

104. *St. Petersburg Times,* November 11, 1967; *Miami Herald,* November 12, 1967; *Miami News,* November 11, 1967.

105. *St. Petersburg Times,* November 12, 1967.

106. *Miami Herald,* November 12, 1967.

107. Ibid., December 6, 1967; *Minutes of FLSB,* vol. 2, December 5, 1967, 125.

108. *Tampa Tribune,* December 6, 1967; *Miami Herald,* December 6, 1967.

109. *Wall Street Journal,* November 24, 1967.

110. Ibid., November 28, 1967; *New York Times,* November 28, 1967.

111. *Tampa Tribune,* December 6, 1967; *Miami Herald,* December 6, 1967; *New York Times,* December 6, 1967.

112. *Miami Herald,* December 6, 1967, January 23, 1966.

113. *Minutes of FLSB,* vol. 2, December 5, 1967, 123; *Miami Herald,* December 6, 1967; Senate Committee on Banking and Currency, *Interstate Land Sales,* June 21 and 22 and August 18, 1966, 462.

114. *Wall Street Journal,* December 12 and 20, 1967; *New York Times,* December 13, 1967.

115. *Wall Street Journal,* December 13, 1967.

116. Ibid., December 12, 1967; *Fort Myers News-Press,* June 29, 1967; *Apalachicola Times,* January 11, 1968.

117. *Miami Herald,* January 3 and 6, 1968; *Wall Street Journal,* January 6, 1968; *Miami News,* January 9, 1968.

118. *Miami Herald,* January 5, 1968; *Wall Street Journal,* January 5, 1968.

119. *Fort Myers News-Press,* January 9, 1968.

120. Ibid.

121. Ibid., *Miami News,* January 9, 1968; *Miami Herald,* January 10, 1968.

122. *Wall Street Journal,* January 5, 1968.

123. Ibid., December 8, 1967; *Miami Herald,* January 10, 1968; *Minutes of FLSB,* vol. 2, April 5, 1968, 176–77.

124. *Fort Myers News-Press,* December 9, 1967.

125. Ibid.

126. *Minutes of FLSB,* vol. 2, November 3, 1967, 99–100, January 19, 1968, 138–39.

127. Pacelli interview.

128. *Miami News,* January 20, 1968.

129. *Apalachicola Times,* January 11, 1968; *Tampa Tribune,* January 12, 1968; *Fort Myers News-Press,* January 23, 1968; *Forbes,* January 1, 1968, 37.

130. *Wall Street Journal,* January 22, 1968; *Miami Herald,* January 21, 1968.

131. *Wall Street Journal,* January 29, 1968; *New York Times,* January 27, 1968.

132. *Miami Herald,* January 31, 1968.

133. Ibid., February 3, 1968; *New York Times,* February 3, 1968; *Wall Street Journal,* February 5, 1968.

134. *Minutes of FLSB,* vol. 2, February 7, 1968, 150; *Wall Street Journal,* February 8, 1968; *Miami Herald,* February 8, 1968; *Miami News,* February 7, 1968.

135. *Miami Herald,* February 8, 1968.

136. Sandler interview.

137. Schwartz interview.

138. Ibid.

139. Rich interview.

140. Ibid.

141. *Miami Herald,* January 23, 1966.

142. Rich interview.

143. Ibid.; Hepner interview.

144. Rich interview; Mack interview.

145. Senate Subcommittee on Securities, *Disclosure Act of 1967,* February 28 and March 1, 1967, 402; Maddlone interview; Sandler interview.

146. Rich interview; Sandler interview; Hepner interview; Schwartz interview.

147. *St. Petersburg Times,* January 21, 1968; Schwartz interview; Rich interview.

148. Horenbein interview.

149. *St. Petersburg Times,* January 21, 1968; Hepner interview.

150. Schwartz interview; Rich interview.

151. *Miami Herald,* January 25, 1968.

152. Ibid., January 26, 1968; *Fort Myers News-Press,* February 2 and 3, 1968.

153. *Miami Herald, Tropic* magazine, December 3, 1967.

154. Ibid.; Schwartz interview.

155. *Miami Herald, Tropic* magazine, December 3, 1967.

156. Ibid.

157. Schwartz interview.

158. Ibid.

Chapter 10. The Takeover of Gulf American

1. *Fort Lauderdale News and Sun Sentinel,* February 3, 1968.

2. *Miami News,* February 6, 1968.

3. *Miami Herald,* February 21, 1968; *Wall Street Journal,* February 21, 1968.

4. *Minutes of FLSB,* vol. 2, March 1, 1968, 161; *Miami Herald,* February 21, 1968.

5. *Wall Street Journal,* March 26, 1968.

6. *Miami Herald,* March 29 and 30, 1968.

7. *Fort Myers News-Press,* March 3, 1968.

8. *Miami News,* April 4, 1968; *Minutes of FLSB,* vol. 2, April 5, 1968, 176–77; *Wall Street Journal,* May 9, 1968.

9. *New York Times,* April 6, 1968; *Miami Herald,* April 6, 1968; *Minutes of FLSB,* vol. 2, April 5, 1968, 182.

10. *Miami Herald,* April 6, 1968; *Wall Street Journal,* April 15, 1968.

11. *Wall Street Journal,* May 6, 1968; *Minutes of FLSB,* vol. 2, May 3, 1968, 191.

12. *Wall Street Journal,* June 10, 1968; *Minutes of FLSB,* vol. 2, June 7, 1968, 219.

13. *Fort Myers News-Press,* February 15, 1968.

14. Ibid., February 22, 1968; Hepner interview.

15. *Fort Myers News-Press,* January 24, 1968; *Miami Herald,* January 25, 1968; *Wall Street Journal,* January 25, 1968.

16. *Wall Street Journal,* March 30, 1968; Hepner interview; *Miami Herald,* January 25, 1968.

17. "Loan Company Joins Conglomerates," *Business Week,* September 6, 1969, 88.

18. Ibid.

19. Ibid.

20. Ibid.

21. Ibid.

22. Ibid.

23. *Wall Street Journal,* January 15, 1968; Schwartz interview; Mack interview; Hepner interview.

24. *Wall Street Journal,* January 15, 1968; Mack interview.

25. *New York Times,* July 9, 1968; *Wall Street Journal,* July 18, 1968.

26. Rich interview; Hepner interview.

27. *Wall Street Journal,* July 10 and 18, 1968.

28. Ibid., July 18, 1968.

29. Ibid.; *Miami News,* February 21, 1968; *Miami Herald,* January 26, 1969. As of February 21, 1968, Leonard Rosen owned 2,731,964 Gulf American shares for 28.3 percent and Jack Rosen owned 2,726,870 shares for 28.2 percent. Calculations were based on GAC common stock at $58.00 per share and paying $.50 per share dividend on January 24, 1969.

30. *Miami Herald,* January 26, 1968; *Wall Street Journal,* January 27, 1969; Hepner interview.

31. *New York Times,* July 18, 1968; "Loan Company Joins Conglomerates," 88.

32. GAC, *Annual Report,* 1967, 3; *Wall Street Journal,* July 18, 1968; *New York Times,* July 18, 1968.

33. Hepner interview; Meyer interview; Schwartz interview; Paulson, *Great Land Hustle,* 24.

34. Maddlone interview; Hepner interview.

35. Maddlone interview; Hepner interview; *New York Times,* October 25, 1968.

36. *Wall Street Journal,* July 25 and 29, 1968; *New York Times,* July 27, 1968.

37. *Wall Street Journal,* September 3 and 9, 1968.

38. Ibid., October 25, 1968; *Miami Herald,* October 23, 1968.

39. Hepner interview.

40. *Fort Myers News-Press,* December 31, 1968; *Miami Herald,* May 25, 1969.

41. *Fort Myers News-Press,* December 31, 1968.

42. Ibid.; *Miami Herald,* May 25 and January 26, 1969.

43. *Miami Herald,* May 25, 1969; *Wall Street Journal,* January 2, 1969.

44. *Wall Street Journal,* January 27 and February 10 and 11, 1969.

45. Ibid., January 27, 1969; *Fort Myers News-Press,* August 29, 1967.

46. *Fort Myers News-Press,* January 14, 1966; *Cape Coral Breeze,* June 6, 1968.

47. *Cape Coral Breeze,* April 1978; *Fort Myers News-Press,* January 7, 1968.

48. Armour, "Sand in Their Shoes," 16.

49. *Fort Myers News-Press,* January 24, 1968.

50. Schwartz interview; Rich interview.

51. "Florida's Land Development Giants," 21, 24, 26.

52. Mack interview.

Chapter 11. GAC's Demise

1. Richard Crane, interoffice memo to Thomas J. Murphy, January 29, 1969, Division of Land Sales, Series 141, RG 324, Box 3, File 1, State Archives.

2. *New York Times,* July 2, 1969; *Wall Street Journal,* July 2, 1969.

3. "Loan Company Joins Conglomerates," 84; *Miami Herald,* July 8, 1969; *Miami News,* July 8, 1969.

4. "Loan Company Joins Conglomerates," 88.

5. Ibid.

6. Ibid.; *Wall Street Journal,* December 30, 1969.

7. *New York Times,* January 31, 1970; *Miami News,* December 24, 1969; *Miami Herald,* February 4, 1970.

8. Hepner interview; Maddlone interview.

9. Hepner interview; Paulson, *Great Land Hustle,* 25.

10. Hepner interview; Rich interview; *New York Times,* April 4, 1981.

11. *Miami Herald,* January 24, 1968; *Miami News,* February 6, 1968; *Cape Coral Breeze,* August 7, 1969.

12. Rich interview.

13. Maddlone interview.

14. Hepner interview.

15. Rich interview.

16. Ibid.; Hepner interview.

17. Hepner interview; *Miami News,* December 30, 1969.

18. Hepner interview.

19. Ibid.; *Miami Herald,* February 24, 1971.

20. *Miami Herald,* May 4, 1971.

21. *Miami News,* October 29 and November 3, 1971.

22. Hepner interview; Bernard, *Lies That Came True,* 228.

23. Paulson, *Great Land Hustle,* 28.

24. *Fort Myers News-Press,* January 2, 1972.

25. Paulson, *Great Land Hustle,* 29; *New York Times,* December 29, 1971.

26. *Fort Myers News-Press,* March 22, 1978; *New York Times,* January 5, 1971.

27. *New York Times,* January 5, 1971.

28. Ibid.

29. *Miami News,* October 29 and December 28, 1971.

30. Ibid., December 28, 1972; *Miami Herald,* October 11 and 17, 1972.

31. *New York Times,* January 5 and December 29, 1971; *Miami Herald,* November 13, 1972.

32. *Miami Herald,* October 3, 1970. State estimates later revised the amount of illegal dredging to 5,069,918 cubic yards.

33. *St. Petersburg Times,* May 24, 1969; *Fort Myers News-Press,* May 21, 1969; DeBoast interview.

34. *Miami Herald,* October 7, 1970.

35. *Collier County* (Naples) *Daily News,* January 10, 1968.

36. *St. Petersburg Times,* March 5, 1977; Leslie Allen, Beryl Kuder, and Sarah L. Oakes, *Promised Lands: Subdivision in Florida's Wetlands* (New York: INFORM, 1977), 117–31.

37. *St. Petersburg Times,* July 23, 1973.

38. Allen, Kuder, and Oakes, *Promised Lands,* 124.

39. *St. Petersburg Times,* July 23, 1973.

40. Ibid.

41. Paulson, *Great Land Hustle,* 24.

42. *Miami Herald,* May 2, 1971.

43. Ibid., May 14, 1971.

44. *Miami News,* January 26, 1972.

45. Paulson, *Great Land Hustle,* 29.

46. Ibid., 25.

47. Ibid., 25–29; *Miami Herald,* November 9, 1971.

48. Paulson, *Great Land Hustle,* 28–29; *Miami News,* December 23, 1971.

49. *Miami News,* July 24, 1973.

50. Ibid., July 24 and December 12, 1973; *Miami Herald,* January 3, 1974, April 22, 1973.

51. *Miami Herald,* December 13, 1973.

52. Ibid.; *Miami News,* March 28, 1974.

53. *Miami News,* March 26, 1974; *Miami Herald,* March 27, 1974.

54. *Miami News,* March 26, 1974; *Miami Herald,* March 27, 1974.

55. *Miami News,* March 26, 1974; *Miami Herald,* March 27, 1974.

56. *Miami News,* March 29 and September 3, 1974.

57. Ibid., June 27, 1973.

58. *Miami Herald,* November 14, 1971.

59. Ibid., November 17, 1971, November 20, 1975.

60. Ibid., January 1, 1972.

61. Ibid., February 6, 1972, March 3, 1976.

62. Ibid., August 8, 1974; *Miami News,* April 24, 1974.

63. *Miami Herald,* November 20, 1975.

64. *Miami News,* December 16, 1974.

65. Ibid., August 8, 1975.

66. Ibid., September 8 and October 15, 1975.

67. Ibid., November 14, 1975; *Miami Herald,* November 5, 1975.

68. *Miami News,* January 18, October 15, and November 14, 1975; *Miami Herald,* November 5, 1975.

69. *Miami News,* December 4 and 11, 1975, January 15, 1976.

70. Ibid., June 7, 1976; *Miami Herald,* July 25, 1976.

71. *Miami Herald,* July 25, 1976.

72. Ibid., July 25 and October 15, 1976; *Miami News,* October 15, 1976.

73. *Miami News,* August 9, 1976; *Miami Herald,* August 10, 1976.

74. *Miami Herald,* June 18, 1977.

75. Ibid., January 20, 1977; *Miami News,* August 31, 1977.

76. *Miami News,* August 3, 1977; *Miami Herald,* August 31, 1977.

77. *Miami Herald,* July 28, 1978.

78. Ibid., December 16, 1978; *Miami News,* December 15, 1978.

79. *Miami Herald,* June 30 and October 18, 1979, April 12, 1980.

80. *Orlando Sentinel,* September 2, 1979.

81. *Miami Herald,* April 12, 1980; *Miami News,* September 25, 1980.

82. Allen, Kuder, and Oakes, *Promised Lands,* 117–31; *Fort Myers News-Press,* February 17, 1971. *Promised Lands* outlines in detail GAC's environmental difficulties with the state and the U.S. Army Corps of Engineers.

83. Hepner interview; Rich interview.

84. Hepner interview.

85. Raso interview.

86. *Fort Myers News-Press,* August 17, 1987.

Chapter 12. After Gulf American

1. Sandler interview.
2. Hepner interview; *Cape Coral Breeze,* November 27, 1969.
3. *New York Times,* December 28, 1969.
4. Ibid., December 29, 1971; *Official Records of the Register of Wills Office,* estate no. 28122, Baltimore County Courthouse, Towson, Md., 216.
5. *Fort Myers News-Press,* May 25, 1986; David Pauly, "Super-Salesman Under Fire," *Newsweek,* February 18, 1980, 82.
6. *Fort Myers News-Press,* May 25, 1986; Pauly, "Super-Salesman," 82.
7. *Fort Myers News-Press,* May 25, 1986; Pauly, "Super-Salesman," 82.
8. *Fort Myers News-Press,* May 25, 1986; Pauly, "Super-Salesman," 82.
9. *Fort Myers News-Press,* May 25, 1986; Pauly, "Super-Salesman," 82.
10. *Fort Myers News-Press,* May 25, 1968.
11. Ibid., January 10, 1978, April 15, 1977.
12. *Cape Coral Breeze,* November 5, 1979.
13. *Fort Myers News-Press,* February 17, 1980; Standard and Poor's Corporation, *Standard Corporation Descriptions* (New York: Standard and Poor's, 1989), 9095, sec. 1.
14. *Fort Myers News-Press,* February 17, 1980.
15. Pauly, "Super-Salesman," 82.
16. *Fort Myers News-Press,* February 17, 1980; *Wall Street Journal,* June 28, 1979.
17. *Wall Street Journal,* January 28, 1981; Standard and Poor's, *Corporation Descriptions,* 9095, sec. 1.
18. Weber interview; Hepner interview.
19. Hepner interview.
20. Pauly, "Super-Salesman," 82.
21. *Fort Myers News-Press,* May 25, 1986.
22. Ibid.
23. Ibid.
24. Ibid.
25. Ibid., August 17, 1987; *Cape Coral Breeze,* August 17, 1987; Standard and Poor's, *Corporation Descriptions,* 4308.
26. Bowen interview.
27. *Cape Coral Breeze,* April 1978.
28. Bowen interview.
29. Ibid.
30. Ibid.; *Cape Coral Breeze,* April 1978; DeBoast interview.
31. *Cape Coral Breeze,* April 1978.
32. Ibid.; Bowen interview.
33. *Cape Coral Breeze,* April 1978; Bowen interview; DeBoast interview.
34. The plaque is located in front of the Cape Coral City Hall.
35. *Cape Coral Breeze,* November 5, 1979.
36. Ibid., April 1983.
37. Schwartz interview.

Bibliography

Books

Akin, Edward N. *Flagler: Rockefeller Partner and Florida Baron.* Kent, Ohio: Kent State University Press, 1988.

Allen, Leslie, Beryl Kuder, and Sarah L. Oakes. *Promised Lands: Subdivision in Florida's Wetlands.* New York: INFORM, 1977.

Bernard, Eileen. *Lies That Came True.* Ocoee, Fla.: Anna, 1983.

Board, Prudy Taylor, and Patricia Pope Bartlett. *Lee County: A Pictorial History.* Norfolk, Va.: Donning, 1985.

Boorstin, Daniel J., ed. *Abstract of the Tenth Census of the United States 1880.* New York: Arno Press, 1976.

————. *Abstract of the Thirteenth Census of the United States 1920.* New York: Arno Press, 1976.

————. *Abstract of the Twelfth Census of the United States 1900.* New York: Arno Press, 1976.

Clark, Ronald W. *Edison: The Man Who Made the Future.* New York: G. P. Putnam's, 1977.

Conboy, Vince. *Exposé: Florida's Billion Dollar Land Fraud.* Naples, Fla.: Vince Conboy, 1972.

Covington, James W. *The Story of Southwestern Florida.* New York: Lewis Historical, 1957.

Cray, William C. *Miles Laboratories: A Centennial History.* Englewood Cliffs, N.J.: Prentice-Hall, 1984.

Dacy, George H. *Four Centuries of Florida Ranching.* St. Louis: Britt, 1940.

Davis, William W. *The Civil War and Reconstruction in Florida.* New York: Doubleday Page, 1913.

de Toledano, Ralph, and Philip V. Brennan, Jr. *Claude Kirk: Man and Myth.* Moonachie, N.J.: Pyramid Publications, 1970.

Dovell, J. E. *Florida: Historic, Dramatic, Contemporary.* 4 vols. New York: Lewis Historical, 1952.

Editor and Publisher International Yearbook. New York: Editor and Publisher, 1988.

Firestone, Harvey S. *Men and Rubber: The Story of Business.* New York: Doubleday Page, 1926.

Florida Across the Threshold: The Administration of Governor LeRoy Collins, January 4, 1955–January 3, 1961. Tallahassee: State Printer, 1961.

Ford, Henry. *My Life and Work.* New York: Doubleday Page, 1922.

Fry, Joseph A. *Henry S. Sanford: Diplomacy and Business in Nineteenth-Century America.* Reno: University of Nevada Press, 1982.

Godown, Marion, and Alberta Rawchuck. *Yesterday's Fort Myers.* Miami: E. A. Seeman, 1975.

Gonzalez, Thomas A. *The Caloosahatchee.* 1925. Reprint. Fort Myers Beach: Island Press, 1982.

Grismer, Karl H. *The Story of Fort Myers.* 1949. Reprint. Fort Myers Beach: Island Press, 1982.

———. *Tampa.* St. Petersburg: St. Petersburg Printing, 1950.

Hanna, Alfred J., and Kathryn Abbey Hanna. *Lake Okeechobee.* New York: Bobbs-Merrill, 1948.

Kane, Joseph N. *Famous First Facts.* New York: H. W. Wilson, 1981.

McIver, Stuart B. *Fort Lauderdale and Broward County.* Woodland Hills, Calif.: Windsor Publications, 1983.

Mahon, John K. *History of the Second Seminole War 1835–1842.* Gainesville: University of Florida Press, 1967.

Mendell, Ronald L., and Timothy B. Phares. *Who's Who in Football.* New Rochelle, N.Y.: Arlington House, 1974.

Neft, David W., Roland T. Johnson, Richard M. Cohen, and Jordan A. Deutsch. *The Sports Encyclopedia: Pro Football.* New York: Grosset and Dunlap, 1974.

Paulson, Morton C. *The Great Land Hustle.* Chicago: Henry Regnery, 1972.

Porter, John Sherman, ed. *Moody's Bank and Finance Manual.* New York: D. F. Shea, 1961.

———. *Moody's Bank and Finance Manual.* New York: Robert H. Messner, 1962.

Proctor, Samuel. *Napoleon Bonaparte Broward: Florida's Fighting Democrat.* Gainesville: University of Florida Press, 1950.

Research Associates. *The Economic Impact of Gulf American Corporation on the State of Florida.* Miami: Research Associates, 1967.

Romans, Bernard. *A Concise Natural History of East and West Florida.* 1775. Reprint. Gainesville: University of Florida Press, 1964.

St. Clair, Frank J., ed. *Moody's Bank and Finance Manual.* New York: Robert H. Messner, 1963.

———. *Moody's Bank and Finance Manual.* New York: Robert H. Messner, 1965.

———. *Moody's Bank and Finance Manual.* New York: Robert H. Messner, 1967.

———. *Moody's Bank and Finance Manual.* New York: Robert H. Messner, 1968.

Standard and Poor's Corporation. *Standard Corporation Descriptions.* New York: Standard and Poor's, 1989.

Tebeau, Charlton W. *History of Florida*. Coral Gables: University of Miami Press, 1971.

Vanderbilt, Byron M. *Thomas Edison, Chemist*. Washington, D.C.: American Chemical Society, 1971.

Weidling, Philip, and August Burghard. *Checkered Sunshine: The Story of Fort Lauderdale 1793–1955*. Fort Lauderdale: Wake Brook, 1974.

Williams, John Lee. *The Territory of Florida*. 1837. Reprint. Gainesville: University of Florida Press, 1962.

Young, Virginia S. *Mangrove Roots of Fort Lauderdale*. Fort Lauderdale: Poinsetta Press, 1976.

Zeiss, Betsy. *The Other Side of the River: Historical Cape Coral*. Cape Coral, Fla.: Betsy Zeiss, 1986.

Articles

Adams, George R. "The Caloosahatchee Massacre: Its Significance in the Second Seminole War." *Florida Historical Quarterly* 48 (April 1970): 368–80.

Armbrister, Trevor. "Land Frauds." *Saturday Evening Post* 236 (April 27, 1963): 17–22.

Armour, Lawrence A. "Sand in Their Shoes." *Barron's,* June 13, 1966, 3–17.

"Arthur Rutenberg: Builder of the Year." *Professional Builder* 52 (January 1989): 380–85.

Boyd, Mark F. "Horatio S. Dexter." *Florida Anthropologist* 13 (September 1968): 90–98.

Cook, Fred J. "Governor Kirk's Private Eyes." *Nation,* May 15, 1967, 61–62.

Covington, James W. "Seminole Migration into Florida 1700–1820." *Florida Historical Quarterly* 46 (April 1968): 340–57.

Davis, T. Frederick. "The Disston Land Purchase." *Florida Historical Quarterly* 17 (January 1939): 200–210.

Dillon, Rodney E., Jr. "The Little Affair: The Southwest Florida Campaign 1863–1864." *Florida Historical Quarterly* 42 (January 1984): 314–31.

Dodson, Pat. "Hamilton Disston's St. Cloud Sugar Plantation 1887–1901." *Florida Historical Quarterly* 49 (April 1971): 356–69.

———, ed. "Cruise of the Minnehaha." *Florida Historical Quarterly* 50 (April 1972): 385–413.

"Florida's Land Boom Gets Down to Earth." *Business Week,* April 13, 1968, 136–42.

"Florida's Land Development Giants." *Florida Trend* 13 (August 1970): 16–30.

George, Paul S. "Brokers, Binders, and Builders: Greater Miami's Boom of the Mid-1920s." *Florida Historical Quarterly* 65 (July 1986): 27–51.

Gulf American Corporation. *Annual Reports*. 1967. Microfilm. University of South Florida Library.

Gulf American Land Corporation. *Annual Reports*. 1961–66. Microfilm. University of South Florida Library.

Hammond, E. A. "The Spanish Fisheries of Charlotte Harbor." *Florida Historical Quarterly* 51 (April 1973): 355–80.

————, ed. "Sanibel Island and Its Vicinity 1833: A Document." *Florida Historical Quarterly* 48 (April 1970): 392–411.

Hirshberg, Al. "Hard Sell in Boom Land." *Life,* November 13, 1964, 67–74.

"How Bob Pritzker Runs a Three Billion Dollar Empire." *Business Week,* March 7, 1983, 64–69.

Hunter, John. "Selling Land in Florida." *New Republic,* September 2, 1967, 21–23.

"Loan Company Joins Conglomerates." *Business Week,* September 6, 1969, 84–88.

"McCall's Certified House." *McCall's,* July 1965, 112.

McCaughan, Russell. "The Florida Condominium Act Applied." *University of Florida Law Review* 17 (Summer 1964): 1–4.

Mahon, Gigi. "The War of Fortunes: The Wealthy Phipps Clan Is Rent with Strife." *Barron's,* July 31, 1978, 4–5.

"Milestones." *Time,* May 22, 1972, 104.

"Obituaries." *Newsweek,* February 17, 1986, 43.

Otto, John S. "Florida's Cattle-Ranching Frontier: Manatee and Brevard Counties 1860." *Florida Historical Quarterly* 44 (July 1985): 48–61.

Pauly, David. "Super-Salesman Under Fire." *Newsweek,* February 18, 1980, 82.

Peeples, Vernon E. "Charlotte Harbor Division of the Florida Southern Railroad." *Florida Historical Quarterly* 43 (January 1980): 291–302.

Pew, Thomas W., Jr. "Peddling the Great West." *Saturday Review,* September 4, 1971, 48–51.

Rainard, R. Lyn. "Ready Cash on Easy Terms: Local Responses to the Depression in Lee County." *Florida Historical Quarterly* 64 (January 1986): 284–300.

Research Publishing Corporation. "Florida Business Letter." *Florida Business Letter,* April 15, 1965, 1.

Rochon, Edwin W., and K. D. Campbell. "Publicly Held Companies: A Sprinkle of Red Ink Dampens Housing's Quest for Capital." *House and Home* 29 (July 1966): 87–91.

Rolland, Louis J. "General Development's Plan." *Financial World,* November 2, 1960, 22–25.

Sherrill, Robert G. "The Power Game: George Smathers, the Golden Senator from Florida." *Nation,* December 7, 1964, 426–37.

Smith, Richard Austin. "Florida: O.K., If the Brakes Work." *Fortune* 61 (January 1960): 120–26.

"They Packaged a Town." *Sales Management,* December 15, 1961, 42–43.

"When a State Opens Its Own War on Crime. . . ." *U.S. News and World Report,* May 22, 1967, 61–62.

Newspapers

Apalachicola Times, 1968.

(Phoenix) *Arizona Republic,* 1967.

(Tucson) *Arizona Daily Star,* 1967.

Baltimore Sun, 1967.

Cape Coral Breeze, 1961–64, 1966, 1968–70, 1977–80, 1982–83, 1987–88.

Cape Coral Sun, 1959, 1962–63.

Christian Science Monitor, 1962.

Collier County (Naples) *News,* 1968.

Decatur (Illinois) *Review,* 1967.

(Jacksonville) *Florida Times-Union and Citizen,* 1897.

(Melbourne) *Florida Today,* 1967.

Fort Lauderdale News and Sun Sentinel, 1968.

Fort Myers News-Press, 1924, 1957, 1960–61, 1963, 1965–69, 1971–75, 1977–78, 1980, 1983–84, 1986–87.

Fort Myers Press, 1885, 1887.

Fort Myers Tropical News, 1929.

GAC Sun, 1970.

Key West Citizen, 1962.

Miami Herald, 1956–57, 1959–60, 1962, 1964–80.

Miami News, 1960-69, 1971–78, 1980.

New York Times, 1952, 1961–63, 1965, 1967–71, 1981.

Nogales (Arizona) *Herald,* 1967–68.

Orlando Sentinel, 1967, 1979.

St. Petersburg Times, 1967–70, 1973, 1977.

Tampa Tribune, 1954, 1967–68.

Wall Street Journal, 1961–69, 1979, 1981.

Washington Post, 1967.

Interviews and letters

Bass, Louise Miles. Interview with Fort Myers Historical Museum staff. Fort Myers, February 29, 1984. Fort Myers Historical Museum Archives, Fort Myers.

Bernard, Eileen. Taped interview with author. St. James City, Florida, January 26, 1988. University of Florida Oral History Archives (OHA), Gainesville.

Bowen, Millard. Taped interview with author. Cape Coral, December 14, 1987. OHA, Gainesville.

Cavanagh, Charles. Taped interview with author. Fort Myers, November 18, 1987. OHA, Gainesville.

Crawford, Richard G. Taped interview with author. Cape Coral, December 10, 1987. OHA, Gainesville.

DeBoast, Richard D. Taped interview with author. Fort Myers, May 23, 1988. OHA, Gainesville.

Finkernagel, Robert H., Jr. Taped interview with author. Cape Coral, December 11, 1987. OHA, Gainesville.

Finkernagel, Robert H., Jr., and Paul W. Sanborn. Taped interview with author. Cape Coral, September 28, 1987. OHA, Gainesville.

Florida Secretary of State, Division of Corporations. Letter to author. December 12, 1989. In possession of author.

Fortiner, James S. Taped interview with author. Fort Myers, March 28, 1988. OHA, Gainesville.

Freiberg, Bernice. Taped interview with author. Baltimore, January 31, 1988. OHA, Gainesville.

Hansen, Edward K. Taped interview with author. Fort Myers, May 3, 1989. OHA, Gainesville.

Harborn, Mary Anderson. Taped interview with author. Cape Coral, September 29, 1987. OHA, Gainesville.

Hepner, Charles K. Taped interview with author. Miami, January 3, 1988. OHA, Gainesville.

Horenbein, Barry. Taped interview with author. Tallahassee, January 24, 1990. OHA, Gainesville.

McGinn, Edward, and Gwen McGinn. Taped interview with author. Cape Coral, December 10, 1987. OHA, Gainesville.

Mack, Connie, Jr. Taped interview with author. Fort Myers, July 20, 1988. OHA, Gainesville.

McNeely, Carol. Taped interview with author. Cape Coral, October 30, 1988. OHA, Gainesville.

Maddlone, Joseph S. Taped interview with author. Royal Palm Beach, Florida, February 16, 1988. OHA, Gainesville.

Meyer, Raymond. Taped interview with author. Cape Coral, January 25, 1988. OHA, Gainesville.

Miller, Joseph, and Agnes Miller. Taped interview with author. Coral Springs, Florida, January 27, 1988. OHA, Gainesville.

Pacelli, Edward V. Taped interview with author. Fort Myers, December 14, 1987. OHA, Gainesville.

Przystawik, Gunter. Taped interview with author. Cape Coral, January 25, 1988. OHA, Gainesville.

Raso, Joseph. Taped interview with author. Cape Coral, March 7, 1988. OHA, Gainesville.

Reynolds, William H., Jr. Taped interview with author. Fort Myers, December 14, 1987. OHA, Gainesville.

Rich, Leonard. Taped interview with author. North Miami Beach, January 27, 1988. OHA, Gainesville.

Rutenberg, Arthur. Interview with author. Clearwater, Florida, May 14, 1988.

Sandler, Solomon S. Taped interview with author. Hollywood, Florida, February 16, 1988. OHA, Gainesville.

Sayers, Richard G. Taped interview with author. Charlotte Harbour, Florida, December 23, 1987. OHA, Gainesville.

Schwartz, Kenneth J. Taped interview with author. Hollywood, Florida, November 16, 1987. OHA, Gainesville.

Warren, John M. Taped interview with author. Fort Myers, December 10, 1987. OHA, Gainesville.

Weber, Thomas W. Taped interview with author. Avon Park, Florida, March 14, 1988. OHA, Gainesville.

Public Documents

Florida. House of Representatives. *Journal of the Florida House of Representatives,* Extraordinary session, 1955—56.

Florida. Installment Land Sales Board. *Minutes of the Florida Installment Land Sales Board.* Division of Land Sales, Tallahassee.

Florida. Land Sales Board. *Minutes of the Florida Land Sales Board.* Division of Land Sales, Tallahassee.

Florida. Lee County. *Official Records of Lee County.* Deed Books 243, 274—278, Mortgage Book 160, Official Record Books 33, 46, 142. Fort Myers.

Florida. Lee County Commission. *Official Minutes of the Lee County Commission.* Books 20—22, 28—29. Fort Myers.

Florida. State Legislature. *Acts and Resolutions of the Legislature of Florida, First Session 1887.* Tallahassee: State Printer, 1887.

Florida. Trustees of the Internal Improvement Fund. *Minutes of the Trustees of the Internal Improvement Trust Fund.* Vol. 37. Tallahassee: State Printer, 1971.

Maryland. Baltimore County Register of Wills Office. *Official Records of the Register of Wills Office.* Towson, Maryland.

U.S. Congress. *Interstate Land Sales Full Disclosure Act.* 82 stat. 590, sec. 1401, August 1, 1968.

U.S. Congress. Senate. Committee on Banking and Currency. *Interstate Land Sales Full Disclosure Act.* 88th Cong., 2d sess., June 21 and 22 and August 18, 1966.

U.S. Congress. Senate. Committee on Banking and Currency, Subcommittee on Securities. *Interstate Land Sales Full Disclosure Act of 1967.* 90th Cong., 1st sess., February 28 and March 1, 1967.

U.S. Congress. Senate. Special Committee on Aging. *Hearings before the Subcommittee on Frauds and Misrepresentations Affecting the Elderly.* Pt. 2, 88th Cong., 2d sess., May 18—20, 1964.

Pamphlets, Unpublished Papers, and Manuscripts

Cochran, Gifford A. "Mr. Lincoln's Many-Faceted Minister and Entrepreneur Extraordinary, Henry Shelton Sanford 1823—1891." Typescript. P. K. Yonge Library, Gainesville.

Collins, LeRoy. Papers. Florida State Archives. Tallahassee.

Division of Land Sales. Correspondence and Papers of Florida Installment Land Sales Board. Florida State Archives. Tallahassee.

Division of Land Sales. Correspondence and Papers of Florida Land Sales Board. Florida State Archives. Tallahassee.

Fort Myers Hotel brochure, 1898. P. K. Yonge Library, Gainesville.

General Development Corporation. Promotional brochure. General Development Corporation vertical file. Miami-Dade Public Library, Miami.

Gulf American Land Corporation. Promotional sales and tourism brochures. In possession of author.

Gulf Guaranty Land and Title Company. Promotional sales and tourism brochures. In possession of author.

Kirk, Claude. Papers. Florida State Archives. Tallahassee.

Myler, Charles E. "An Analysis of Promotional Practices of Selected Land Developers in the State of Florida." Ph.D. diss., University of Florida, 1970.

Standard and Poor's Corporation. "Standard Listed Stock Reports." February 11, 1963, 963k.

Weeks, Jerry. "Florida Gold: The Emergence of the Florida Citrus Industry 1865–1895." Ph.D. diss., University of North Carolina at Chapel Hill, 1977.

Index

Abrams, Sylvan, 33, 115
Adams, Tom, 120, 231–32
AIC Financing Corporation of Chicago, 94
Allen, Stewart D., 189, 192, 194, 197, 208, 210
Allen, William P., 194, 198
Allstate Development Corporation, 64–65
American Airlines, 130–31
American Cyanamid Corporation, 39, 280 (n. 53)
American Football League, 107–8
American Stock Exchange, 48, 97, 181–82, 188, 191
American Variety Store, 153
Anamax Mining Company, 240
Anderson, H. D. "Andy," 45, 111
Anderson, Thomas; 197, 208
Arthur Rutenberg Corporation, 44
Arthur Young and Company of Atlanta, 210
Arvida Corporation, 94, 200, 227
Askew, Reubin, 231
Assalone, John R., Jr., 235, 238
Atkinson Corporation, 95
Audubon Society, 231–32
Auerbach, Dory, 166
Avatar Holding, 245

B. T. Babbitt Company, 24, 28
Baca Float Ranch, 63–64, 183
Bader, Curtis, 211
Baker, Thomas H., 56
Baker, William F., 146
Ball, Edward, 218
Baltimore Investment Associates, 54, 271 (n. 20)

Bankers Life and Casualty Company, 64, 94
Bank of America Corporation, 230, 236
Barefoot Bay, 64–65, 235, 242
Barnes, James, 252
Baron, William, 77, 227
Bass, Donald, 28
Bass, Louise Miles, 28, 266 (n. 64)
Baumel, Milton J., 98
Berks, Robert, 118
Bernard, Eileen, 39–40, 121, 280 (n. 53)
Bernstein, George, 236
Berra, Yogi, 108
Berry, Chester, 142
Bertoch, Carl A., 170–71, 176, 181–82, 191, 193–95, 197–99, 207–9, 217
Bessemer Investment Company, 54
Bessemer Properties, 54
Beth Jacob (synagogue), 24
Bigelow, H. Freeman, 219
Bilbray, James, 255–56
Blackburn, Charles M., 191
Boca Raton National Bank, 94
Borglum, Gutzon, 118
Borglum, Lincoln, 118, 279
Bowen, Millard, 153, 204, 257–58
Bradford, Joseph, 110
Bradford Hotel, 33, 45
Bradshaw, Donald, 164–65
Brown, Pat, 168
Brown, Winsor W., 111
Browne, James M., 238
Bryan, Edward R., 173, 213
Bryan, Richard, 255
Bryant, C. Farris, 164, 168, 174
Buchanan, James, 88
Bunck, Everett P., 156

Burlingame, Carl, 253–54
Burns, Haydon, 120, 165, 173–75, 285 (n. 13)
Burton, Chandler, 259

California Department of Real Estate, 234
Callahan, Frank, 241–45
Calvada, 251, 253–55
Calvada Protective Association, 251
Cannova, Frank S., 167
Cape Coral, 242, 256; bridge, 138–45; churches, 156; condominium construction, 157; design of, 29–31; initial construction, 37–38, 41–42; incorporation as city, 256–59; library, 154–56; naming of, 31; population, 136–37; schools, 145
Cape Coral Bank, 146, 192
Cape Coral Baptist Church, 156
Cape Coral *Breeze* (newspaper), 40, 111, 142, 191, 258
Cape Coral Chamber of Commerce, 156, 192, 203, 211
Cape Coral Civic Association, 143, 147, 149, 153, 156, 257, 282 (n. 25)
Cape Coral Construction Company, 43, 85, 99, 147
Cape Coral Gardens, 118, 120–21, 196, 231. See also Cape Coral Rose Gardens
Cape Coral Historical Museum, 279 (n. 41)
Cape Coral Medical Clinic, 156
Cape Coral Realty, 87, 99
Cape Coral Roads and Bridge District, 142, 144
Cape Coral Rose Gardens, 114–20, 232. See also Cape Coral Gardens
Cape Coral *Sun* (newspaper), 39, 121–22
Cape Coral Taxpayers Association, 142
Cape Coral Waterway Committee, 219
Carmine, William H., Jr., 54, 62, 83–84, 151–52, 171, 282 (n. 17)
Carnegie Steel Corporation, 54
Carroll, Robert P., 69
Carson, Johnny, 108
Cassel, Thompson K., 11, 279 (n. 22)
Cavanagh, Charles, 79, 128–32, 229
Chapman, Joseph F., Jr., 175
Charles Antell Company, 7–21, 24, 28–29, 33, 39, 46, 70–71, 76

Charlotte County Land and Title Company, 169
Charlotte County Spa, 25
Chemical Bank of New York, 94
Chesler, Louis A., 27, 136, 268
Chiles, Lawton, 183
Christ Lutheran Church, 156
Church of Jesus Christ of Latter Day Saints, 218
Civil Aeronautics Board, 129–30, 239
Clarke, Russell B., 184
Cleaves, Bea, 71
Coel, Daniel L., 72
Colgerry Realty, 62, 99
Collier, Barron G., Jr., 57
Collier County Commission, 158
Collins, LeRoy, 102–3
Comet-Marks, 72
Conboy, Vince, 173
Congress Inns, 51, 58, 65
Congress International, 99
Connie Raymond Construction Company, 42
Cook and Cook, 54
Coral Ridge Properties, 182, 199–200, 221
Council of Better Business Bureaus, 235
Cramer, Geraldine, 90
Cramer, Ralph, 90
Crawford, Richard G., 49, 108–12, 122, 142–43, 258, 282 (n. 25)
Crawford, Sally, 111, 282 (n. 25)
Criser, Marshall M., 164, 166–68
Crumley, Charles, 210
Cypress Gardens, 74, 114

Dade County Metro Commission, 205
Dale, C. Shelby, 184–85
Dancing Waters, 115–16. See also Waltzing Waters
Daniels, Elmore, 55
Darling, Dallas, 156
David, Theodore, 110
Davis, Harold B., 118
Dawson, Wallace L., 110
DeBoast, Richard D., 146, 151–52, 154, 157, 231, 258
DeLozier, F. James, Jr., 150
Delray National Bank, 94
Deltona Corporation, 68, 79, 106, 136, 158, 165, 167, 195, 221
Dempsey, Harry, 1, 70

Department of Housing and Urban
Development (HUD), 236–38, 240
Deseret Farms of Florida, 218–19, 222,
224
deWeldon, Felix, 118
Dexter, Horatio S., 9
Dickert, Henry, 156
Disney World, 65, 174
Dow Jones, 198, 208, 217
Dowling, William H., 12
Dowling and Camp Lumber Company,
12
Downing, Wes, 158
Doyle, Robert, 166
Duffala, Clarence "Butch," 42, 45, 282
(n. 25)
Duffala Construction Company, 42, 146
Duke, Patty, 20

East Coast Railway, 4, 124
Edison, Thomas A., 12
Eisenhower, Dwight D., 48
Empire, Walter Vail, 214
Empire Ranch, 214, 240
Engle, Lester, 200
Epiphany Episcopal Church, 156
Equitable Savings and Loan Association
of Portland, Oregon, 213, 219, 230

Fagan, Harry, 92, 108, 142, 152, 192
Fahkahatchee Strand, 60, 232
Fails, Willis, and McCall, 169
Faircloth, Earl, 183, 208
Faith Presbyterian Church, 156
Federal Aviation Administration (FAA),
124, 131
Federal Home Loan Bank Board, 146
Federal Reserve Board, 236
Federal Trade Commission (FTC),
237–38, 241
Federal Trade Commission Bureau of
Consumer Protection, 237
Fenestra, 95–96, 99, 276 (n. 24)
Ferguson, Thomas, 186–87, 198, 208,
231, 233, 238–39
Fickinger, Paul, 257–59
Finkelstein, Charles, 17, 267 (n. 8)
Finkernagel, Robert H., Jr., 107–8,
111–12, 116, 122, 147, 165, 173,
175–76, 196, 224, 227–28
Fiori, H. M., 142

First America Development
Corporation, 167
First Baptist Church of Fort Myers, 156
First Federal Savings and Loan
Association of Fort Myers, 146, 152,
192, 220
First National Bank of Boston, 94
First National Bank of Fort Myers, 92,
142
First United Methodist Church, 156
Flagler, Henry M., 124, 133
Florida Bar Association, 157
Florida Consultants, 185
Florida Department of Environmental
Regulation, 242
Florida Development Commission, 184
Florida Installment Land Sales Board
(FILSB), 164–79, 181, 248
Florida Intercollegiate Golf
Championship, 112
Florida Intercollegiate Tennis
Tournament, 112
Florida Land Sales Board (FLSB), 65,
165, 174–75, 182–205, 207–11,
214–21, 223, 226, 234, 245, 248
Florida Public Attractions Association,
114
Florida Ranchettes, 167
Florida Real Estate Commission,
162–64
Florik, Frank, Jr., 193–95
Fly and Buy Program, 127, 261
Flynn, Roger D., 194, 208–9
Fogarty, Fred, 173
Fortiner, James S., 52–55
Fortiner-Miller Realty and Development
Company, 53
Fort Myers, 9, 11–12
Fort Myers Airways, 125
Fort Myers Construction Company, 64,
99, 191
Foss, Joseph F., 107
Freehling, Herbert S., 244
Freiberg, Bernice, 21, 24, 73, 77–78,
80, 112, 115–16, 133, 168
Fullerton-Kearney Plastics, 45

GAC Corporation, 51, 64–65, 103, 106,
120, 122, 132, 187, 203, 212–20,
222–48; bankruptcy of,
241–45; reasons for bankruptcy,
245–47

GAC Credit, 241
GAC Finance Corporation, 229–30, 236
GAC Properties, 203, 222, 224, 227–29, 234, 241
GAC Realty, 213
Gainesville Chamber of Commerce, 109
GALC (Illinois), 99
Garden of Patriots, 117–18
Garretson, Marguerite J., 154
General Acceptance Corporation, 212, 215
General Development Corporation, 6, 26–27, 68–70, 79, 132, 136, 165, 167, 221, 268
General Electric, 93
Geraci, P. A., 151, 203–4
Gesell, Gerhard, 244
Golden Gate Estates, 26, 56, 60, 158–59, 201, 208, 211, 222, 234, 237; advertising of, 77–78, 88; construction difficulties, 58; development philosophy, 57, 159–60; sales abuses, 171, 173, 178, 190, 237
Goldwater, Barry, 165
Goodbody and Associates, 144, 216
Gordon, Alex, 205
Gould, Gerald H., 25, 27, 164, 174–75, 179, 181–82
Grand Flamingo Corporation, 252–53
Granger, Robert J., 92–93, 99–100, 104
Green, E. G., 152–54
Green, Milton, 127
Greenwood, Warren L., 166–67
Grey, Richard, 156
Gross, Alexander, 205
Grossman, Murray, 124
Guild Life Insurance Company, 51, 100–101
Gulf American Corporation:
advertising, 76–77; art gallery, 106, 215; condominium construction, 157; dinner party program, 79–80; financing handled by Leonard, 91–92; *Florida Opportunity Digest*, 76, 78; four sales divisions, 71–75; headquarters building, 96–97, 106–7, 240; impact on Florida, 247–48; initial sales, 40–41; issuing bonds, 92–93; land acquisitions, 51–66; lot-switching, 172, 177–79, 188; mail order sales, 70–71; name changes, 99; oil exploration, 101; outside public consultants, 74; ownership of, 98; racial discrimination in sales, 85–86, 179; reasons for sales success, 69; sales abuses, 170–71, 176–78, 188, 248; sales volume, 68; suspension of sales, 190–91, 195–96; telephone soliciting, 80–81; time-sharing, 75; training of salespeople, 86–87; VIT program, 124. *See also* Gulf American Land Corporation; Gulf Guaranty Land and Title Company
Gulf American Galleries, 106
Gulf American Land Corporation, 28, 47–48, 51, 97, 161; administrative organization, 45–46, 69–70, 75–76; land acquisitions, 51–66. *See also* Gulf American Corporation; Gulf Guaranty Land and Title Company
Gulf American Land Corporation of Arizona, 62, 99
Gulf and Western Industries, 212
Gulf Communicators, 99
Gulf Guaranty Land and Title Company, 28, 31, 38, 47–48, 50–52, 55. *See also* Gulf American Corporation, Gulf American Land Corporation
Gulf Utilities Corporation, 147–49

H. F. Ahmanson and Company of California, 236
Hahn, Paul, 108
Harborn, Mary Anderson, 40, 71
Harbour Heights, 25, 53, 179
Hardin, Walter S., 163
Harney, William S., 9
Harris, Herman, 72
Harris, L. B., 25
Harris and Whitebrook Advertising Agency, 30
Hartung, Marvin R., 243–44
Haydon Burns and Associates, 175
Hebrew Academy of Miami, 205
Hebrew Day School (Baltimore), 24
Hendry, Francis A., 10
Henshaw, Robert, 55–56
Henson, William, 112
Hepner, Charles K., 1–2, 20, 23, 31, 45–46, 51, 57, 61, 69, 73–75, 77, 79, 85–87, 128, 138, 201–3, 212, 217, 224–28, 246, 254
Herbert J. Sims and Company, 143–44
Herzfeld, Bernard H., 46, 96, 98, 103,

171–72, 187, 189–90, 194, 209–10,
214, 216
Hewitt, William "Bill," 108
High, Robert King, 174, 202
Hinkle, Thomas G., 110
Hirsch, Howard R., 165, 175
Hirshberg, Al, 83
Hobson, T. Frank, 167
Hodo, Monte, 45
Hole, Stanley W., 151
Hollywood (Florida) City Commission,
224
Hope, Bob, 118, 205
Horenbein, Barry, 102, 183, 185–87,
202
Horne, Mallory, 183–85
Howard, W. Thomas, 146
Hudson, Julian L., 148, 150, 211
Hughes, David, 241–42
Hunt, Lamar, 107
Hurricane Donna, 48–49
Hyatt Hotels, 96
Hyman, Paul, 241–42, 244

Imperial Homes, 44
INFORM, 232
Inter-County Telephone and Telegraph
Company, 152
Internal Improvement Trust Fund, 120,
219, 231–32
Isaacs, David, 80

J. C. Turner Lumber Company, 57
J. Colon English School, 145
J. E. Greiner and Company, 143–44
Jackson, Andrew, 9
Jackson and Perkins Rose Company,
116
Jacobson, Arthur, 77
Johnson, Carl E., 151
Johnson, Charles W., Jr., 182, 199,
209–10
Johnson, John N., 152
Jones, Mack H., 141, 144, 151
Jupiter Properties, 54

Kansas City Chiefs, 107
Kasher, Charles D., 17–18
Kaufman Real Estate, Investment, and
Mortgage Company, 64
Keating, David, 225
Keller, Cathryn C., 28, 52–53
Keller, Granville W., 28, 52–53, 56

Kemmerer, Russell E., 243–44
Kennedy, Robert F., 166
Kessler, Milt, 115, 279 (n. 41)
Key Biscayne, 27
Kicco Ranch, 59
Kilgore, Merle, 114
King, Larry, 113
King, Ziba, 10
Kirk, Claude R., Jr., 161, 173, 182–88,
194–98, 202–3, 216, 218, 220,
231–32, 239
Kissimmee Boat-A-Cade, 109
Kissimmee Chamber of Commerce, 109
Klein, Joseph, 74
Klein, Monroe J., 79
Kolar, Tom, 196

Laxalt, Paul, 255
Layden, James R., 80, 104, 176, 213
Lee County Commission, 130, 140–42,
144, 147, 170, 203–4, 211, 256–57
Lee County Electric Cooperative, 36,
152, 219
Lee County Land and Title Company, 6.
See also Lehigh Acres Development
Corporation
Lee County School Board, 145
Lee Investment Company, 62
Lehigh Acres, 30–31, 62–63, 70, 179
Lehigh Acres Development Corporation,
164–65, 176–77, 221. See also Lehigh
Development Corporation
Lehigh Development Corporation, 6
Leonard, Jack E., 114
Leslie, Orren S., 95
Lieberbaum and Company, 92
London, George, 46, 98
Lord, Jay P., 197
Loveland, Kenneth, 147–49
Lucky Lee Cattle Ranch, 27
Luss, Peter, 73, 93

MacArthur, John D., 64–65, 94
McCaughan, Russell, 157
McGinn, Gwen, 38–39, 46, 49, 71
Mack, Connie (Cornelius McGillicuddy),
5, 35
Mack, Connie, Jr., 35, 38, 71, 79, 81,
83–84, 92, 107–9, 121, 138, 140,
148, 151–52, 154, 214, 221, 258
Mackle, Barbara Jane, 106

Mackle brothers, 70, 136, 158, 203, 221, 268 (n. 41)
Mackle Construction Company, 26
Mackle, Elliott J., 27, 68, 164–65, 174–76, 182, 192, 195, 197, 202–3
Mackle, Francis E., 26–27
Mackle, Frank, Jr., 27, 68
Mackle, Robert F., 27, 68, 106
McMillian, A. L., 149
McWhirter, John W., Jr., 163–64, 166–67
McWilliams, J. W., 12
Maddlone, Joseph S., 51, 56, 75, 93–95, 97, 101–4, 143, 171, 194, 202, 216, 224, 226
Mallatratt, Gordon W., 213–14, 227
Mantle, Mickey, 20
Marmon Group, 96
Matlacha Cattle Company, 12–13, 55
Matlacha Plantation, 13
Mego Corporation, 256
Mendelsohn, Milton M., 25–27, 30–31, 51, 53, 63–64, 169, 179–80, 273 (n. 59)
Merrick, George E., 124
Metropolitan Life Insurance Company, 100
Meyer, Raymond, 49, 84, 99–100, 102, 127–28, 130, 153
Miami Dolphins, 107
Miles, Franklin L., 11–12, 28, 52–53, 266 (n. 64)
Miller, Addison B., 53
Miller, Joseph, 114, 123
Miller, N. E. "Bill," 180
Mills, Lowell H., 145–46, 282 (n. 25)
Modern Air Transport, 51, 100, 129–30, 175, 238–40
Moore, Lyman, 259
Morris, Lester, 70, 78, 227
Morris Cohen and Company, 93
Moyle, Jon C., 182
Musa Isle, 114
Musket, Bernard, 78

Nahama, Sam, 45, 138–40
Nahama Sportswear, 45
National Airlines, 127
National Bank of Westchester (Florida), 94
National Broadcasting Corporation (NBC), 85, 107

National Hobby Center, 123–24
National Inboard Hydroplane Championship, 113
Nevada Pardons Board, 255
Nevada Real Estate Division (NRED), 252
New Jersey Real Estate Commission, 172, 196, 209
New Mexico American Land Corporation, 62, 99
New York City Patrolmen's Benevolent Association, 169
New York Stock Exchange, 96, 230, 240–41
New York World's Fair, 118
Nitzberg, Ronald D., 73, 227
North American Milk Company, 93
North American Rockwell Corporation, 225
Nutting, G. Ogden, 112

O'Bannon, F. F. "Fingers," 13, 55
Ogden Newspapers, 112
O'Han, John C., 138–40

Pacelli, Edward V., 40–41, 45, 47, 50–51, 57–58, 72, 74, 88, 140, 153–54, 178–79, 197
Page Field, 125, 131–32
Palmer, Arnold, 108
Pan American Airways, 225
Parkinson's Disease Association, 101
Parkway Mortgage Company, 99–100
Parmalee, Robert, 36, 41
Pate, J. Foster, 151
Paulson, Morton C., 165–67
Paul Venze Agency, 20, 106, 112
Pavese, Frank, 150
Pearl Lagoon, 114
Pennsylvania Real Estate Commission, 196
Petrie, Granville "Pete," 87, 125, 147–48, 201
Philadelphia Athletics, 108
Phipps, Henry, 54
Phipps, Lillian B., 54
Phipps, Ogden M., 13, 54–56, 266 (n. 71)
Piggins, Edward S., 96
Piggott, W. Wilson, 151
Plant, Henry B., 10–11, 133
Poinciana Park, 65, 237, 242
Port Charlotte (Florida), 3, 27, 31, 136

Posner, Samuel, 153, 192
Preferred American Realty Security
    Fund (Parfund), 250–51
Preferred Equities Corporation (PEC),
    251–56
Pritzker, Abraham N., 95
Pritzker, Donald, 95
Pritzker, Jack, 95
Pritzker, Jay, 95
Pritzker, Robert, 95
Prudential Insurance Company of
    America, 94, 100, 128
Przystawik, Gunter, 116, 119, 121
Przystawik, Otto, 115
Pulitzer, Herbert "Peter," Jr., 55
Pulitzer, Joseph, 55
Pulitzer, Lilly, 55

Rader, Earle M., 30
Rader and Associates, 30–31, 52, 138,
    143, 185, 254
Raso, Joseph, 246–47, 282 (n. 25)
Ratner, Lee, 6, 25, 27, 179
Raymond, Sandy, 256
Reagan, Ronald, 255
Reichardt, Delbert D., 212, 218, 223,
    225, 229
Reinsurance Investment Corporation,
    100
Reis, Seymour, 73–74
Remuda Ranch Grants, 60, 159, 179,
    234, 237, 245; plans to drain, 61, 201
Revlon, 24
Reynolds, William H., 56
Reynolds, William H., Jr., 28, 35,
    52–53, 55–56
Rheem Manufacturing Company, 213
Rhode Island Consumer Protection
    Council, 235, 238
Rhode Island Department of Business
    Regulation, 235
Rich, Leonard, 61–62, 75, 77, 79, 81,
    88–89, 129, 200–202, 214, 223,
    226–27
Rio Rico, 63, 108, 182, 214, 234–35,
    245
River Ranch Acres, 59, 63, 159, 208,
    234, 237, 245
Robbie, Joseph, 107
Roberts, Charles, 77
Roberts Realty, 225
Rocket City, 26, 65, 273 (n. 59)

Rockwell, Willard F., Jr., 225
Rogers, Walter, 94
Rogers, Will, Jr., 108
Rolnick, Morton, 227
Rosch, J. Thomas, 237
Rosen, Abraham, 15
Rosen, Dorothy, 16, 31, 106, 256, 267
    (n. 2), 268 (n. 29)
Rosen, Edith, 15, 267 (n. 2)
Rosen, Fannie, 15, 260, 267 (n. 2)
Rosen, Julius J. "Jack": advertising
    leadership, 214; after Gulf American,
    249; anti-Semitism against, 153–54;
    business strengths, 69–70; charities,
    101; early life, 15; education, 16;
    family, 106; health problems, 220–21,
    273 (n. 9); Jewish faith, 24; motives,
    13, 27–28; relationship with Leonard,
    21–22, 46–47, 51, 69–70, 221, 260,
    273 (n. 9); sales philosophy, 57–60,
    63, 69, 161, 221
Rosen, Larry, 119, 279 (n. 45)
Rosen, Leonard: after Gulf American,
    250; anti-Semitism against, 153–54;
    appointed to FILSB, 165, 171;
    arthritis, 25; attitude toward money,
    101–2; business strengths, 69–70;
    charities, 101, 205; early life, 15;
    education, 16; handled financing,
    90–91; health problems, 252, 255–56;
    Jewish faith, 24; motives, 13, 27–28,
    41, 90; philandering, 22; relationship
    with Jack, 21–22, 46–47, 51, 69–70,
    221, 260, 273 (n. 9); sales philosophy,
    16–17, 45, 57–60, 63, 67, 161
Rosen, Ronald, 253, 256
Rosen, Sylvia, 15, 267 (n. 2)
Rosen Home Equipment Company, 16
Rosen Investment Corporation, 101
Rosmoser, J. Norman, Jr., 182, 193
Russell, James, 218, 230
Rustin, Richard E., 86
Rutenberg, Arthur, 42–44, 85
Rutenberg, Charles, 44
Rutgers Graduate School of Banking,
    93

St. Andrew's Catholic Church, 125, 156,
    279 (n. 41)
Salcines, E. J., 191
Sanborn, Paul W., 109, 112, 229, 247
Sanders, George, 63

Sandler, Ronald S., 64, 128
Sandler, Solomon S., 24–25, 47, 98,
  130, 199, 249, 267 (n. 2)
Sandy Investment Company, 28, 54
Santa Cruz County Board of
  Supervisors, 64
Saunders, Dexter, 93
Sayers, Richard G., 114, 122–23
Scarpuzzi, Jack, 121
Schloss, Harry D., 209
Schooley, Harry, 150
Schwartz, Kenneth J., 1, 22–23, 26,
  33–35, 37–39, 49, 69, 71–72, 74,
  81–82, 88, 101, 109–10, 112, 121,
  137–38, 140, 151–53, 179, 199–200,
  203, 205–6, 213, 260, 282 (n. 170)
Scottish Inns of America, 253–54
Securities and Exchange Commission,
  97, 168, 171–72, 241–44, 254
Seminoles, 8; impact on settlement,
  9–10; massacre on Caloosahatchee, 9
Sherrill, Robert G., 168
Sibley, Marion E., 194
Sims, James, 143
Slepin, Steve, 120–21
Slocum, Kenneth G., 177, 192, 198, 205,
  208, 217
Smathers, George, 165, 168
Smith, E. A. "Frog," 266 (n. 68–69)
Southeast Airlines, 125
Steffins, Frank M., 227–28, 234–35
Steinman, Harold, 115
Sterling, Linda, 256
Stern, William "Bill," 20, 108
Steve, Lowell, 234
Stout, Gregory, 251
Street and Company, 92–93
Strobel, Benjamin, 8
Strothman, W. R., 212
Stuken, Paul R., 243–44
Stuyvesant Insurance, 236
Summerlin, Jacob, 10
Summerlin, Samuel, 10
Sutphin, A., 140

Tanfield, Peggy, 110, 122
Taravella, Joseph P., 182, 192
Tate, Robert R., 110, 278 (n. 19)
Taylor, Douglas, 150
Taylor, Matthew, 114
Temple Beth-El, 156

Three Islands, 224–25, 228–30,
  246–47
Tittle, Y. A., 108
Tohari, Edward, 147–49, 204
Travel Guild of America, 128–33, 193
Trippe, Juan T., 225
Trumbull, Stephen, 162–63
Turchin, Robert L., 223
Turner, Harmon, 158–59

United Artists, 268 (n. 41)
U.S. Army Corps of Engineers, 31, 145,
  242, 292 (n. 82)
United States Homes and Development
  Corporation, 44
Utah American Land Corporation, 99

Vacation Spa Resorts, 254
Venze, Paul, 16, 20, 77, 112, 193
VIT program, 124–25, 130, 196
Volpe, John A., 118

Wackenhut, George R., 184
Wackenhut Corporation, 184, 199
Waltzing Waters, 116–18, 121. See also
  Dancing Waters
Warner, Richard, 187, 232
Warner Brothers, 268 (n. 41)
Warren, Fuller, 167
Warren, John M., 40, 71, 82–84
Watson, Ruby E., 153
Webb, Del, 167
Webb Realty Company, 167
Weber, Thomas, 1, 23, 31, 37–38,
  41–42, 46, 51, 58, 64–65, 99, 131,
  136, 148, 153–54, 158, 178–80, 254
Weiner, Earl L., 98
Weir, John, 94
Welch, Homer T., Jr., 36–37, 108, 152
Werblin, Joseph F. "Sonny," 107
Wetstein, Mert, 122
Wharton, Browning, 45, 282 (n. 25)
Wharton School, University of
  Pennsylvania, 33
Whiteside, Warren, 191
Widmann, Ernest, 213
Wilbur Smith and Associates, 141, 143
William H. Reynolds Company, 55–56,
  72
Williams, Broward, 164–65
Williams, Hank, Jr., 114
Williams, Harrison A., Jr., 166, 172–73

Wills, Francis Reed, 212
Wills, S. Hayward, 187, 203, 212–13,
    215–17, 222–30, 233, 236, 238, 241,
    244, 246–48
Wilson, Edward F., 28, 125
Winnerman, Robert, 44
Winter, Harrison L., 98
Wisher, Lavon Pigot, 130
Wolf, James, 177, 198, 208
Woodmen of the World Life Insurance
    Company, 45, 47, 97

Woody Kepner and Associates, 113, 122
World Wide Realty Corporation, 75

Yoak, Madge, 154
Yoak, Robert, 154
Young, Loretta, 112

Zion Securities Corporation, 218–19